FREE MEN ALL

The Johns Hopkins University Press
BALTIMORE AND LONDON

THOMAS D. MORRIS, *1938–*

FREE MEN ALL

The Personal Liberty Laws of the North
1780–1861

This book has been brought to publication with the
generous assistance of the Andrew W. Mellon Foundation.

The Johns Hopkins University Press, Baltimore, Maryland 21218
The Johns Hopkins University Press Ltd., London

Library of Congress Catalog Card Number 73-8126
ISBN 0-8018-1505-3

Library of Congress Cataloging in Publication data
will be found on the last printed page of this book.

To My Mother and Father,
Alvira and William Morris

Contents

Preface

Many antislavery efforts, when examined at the national level, can be made to appear temporizing and halfhearted, such as the policy of containing slavery in the South. Indeed, the indirect attack upon slavery in the territories rather than a direct attack upon it wherever it existed, has been described as a "technique of evasion."[1] Doubtless such a roundabout tactic as containment was partly the result of concern over the social disruption that would result from an abrupt abolition of the "peculiar institution," and partly the result of a general abhorrence of radicalism. But it was also due to the American constitutional system itself which prevented any direct federal legislative attack such as occurred in the British West Indies when Parliament abolished slavery in 1833. As long as people worked within the existing system (with its division of jurisdictions and functions between state and federal governments), there was relatively little that could be done at the national level except by indirection. By 1861 this had driven some abolitionists to agree with Stephen Symonds Foster who declared that a person living in pre-Civil War America had no option but to choose between "slaveholding and revolution."[2]

Within the free states there was less constraint. In the states above the Mason-Dixon line those opposed to slavery first developed rather complete programs for the elimination of slavery and then experimented with ways to protect people in danger of being seized as slaves and removed to the South. People could affirm through law the presumption that all men are free until proven otherwise by orderly procedures. This was the idea that underlay all of the Personal Liberty Laws. To secure this personal freedom those opposed to human bondage used, sometimes quite inventively, some of the basic common-law guarantees of liberty, such as trial by jury and the writ of habeas corpus. There are many forms of this writ used to fulfill various purposes, such as the removal of a person from confinement in order to testify in court or the removal of a person to a jurisdiction where he is alleged to have committed a crime. From a civil liberties standpoint the most important is the *habeas corpus ad subjiciendum* which is used to examine the reasons for any restraint imposed on a person. It was

---

[1]Martin Duberman, "The Northern Response to Slavery," in Martin Duberman, ed., *The Antislavery Vanguard: New Essays on the Abolitionists* (Princeton, 1965), 395–413.

[2]Stephen S. Foster, "Revolution the Only Remedy for Slavery," in William H. Pease and Jane H. Pease, eds., *The Anti-slavery Argument* (Indianapolis, 1965), 476.

this form of the writ that those opposing slavery used, and their use of it was a frank avowal of their view that slavery was incompatible with the traditional definitions and guarantees of freedom. Because of the federal character of the American union, however, serious and complicated jurisdictional questions often arose over the application of this writ. Recent studies have made it clear that in pre-Civil War America there was no way to have a national court habeas corpus remedy on behalf of persons restrained by state authority.[3] Whether there could be a state remedy or not on behalf of persons held under federal authority was one of the most hotly debated problems of the years before the outbreak of war.

At the same time that antislavery reformers tried to use such legal processes to protect persons in danger of being seized as slaves, black people often faced severe legal as well as social discrimination in the North. Leon Litwack's *North of Slavery: The Negro in the Free States, 1790–1860* has made this amply clear.[4] It should always be borne in mind then that the Personal Liberty Laws are only one side of a very complex set of legal systems— systems which reflected both idealism and meanness.

The focus of this study is on the idealism. It is a study of the ways people translated into law the presumption that all persons are born free and cannot be deprived of that freedom except by due process of law, even though they might be slaves. Consequently, the Personal Liberty Laws represented an alternative to the slave codes of the South, and to the view that human freedom could be achieved in the United States in the nineteenth century only by a destruction of the regime of law itself.

These laws also form part of the backdrop to the great Civil War Amendments, particularly the Fourteenth Amendment. They reflected, along with that amendment, a broad societal commitment to fundamental fairness as measured by access to time-honored, Anglo-American guarantees of personal freedom. Jacobus ten Broek contributed the important insight that the Fourteenth Amendment owed a great deal to abolitionist constitutionalism, but in developing this argument the case was overstated. Ten Broek contended that the key phrases in Section 1 of the amendment derived their meaning and significance from a movement that was "moral, ethical, religious, revivalist rather than legal in character." It was a movement, moreover, that was little concerned with the "ancient usages of the law," and those in it viewed the Constitution as "dogmatic, even fanatical reformers."[5] The commitment to such concepts as "equal protection of the law" and "due process of law," however, involved a wider spectrum in American thought than abolitionism. As embodied in state laws this broad commitment, and

[3]See, for example, William Wiececk, "The Great Writ and Reconstruction: The Habeas Corpus Act of 1867," *Journal of Southern History*, 36 (Nov., 1970): 530–49.
[4]Leon F. Litwack, *North of Slavery: The Negro in the Free States, 1790–1860* (Chicago and London, 1965).
[5]Jacobus ten Broek, *Equal under Law* (New York, 1965), 116.

not just the abolitionist viewpoint of it, is an important part of the background to the national guarantee of civil liberty that is Section 1 of the Fourteenth Amendment.

Nearly all the states above the Mason-Dixon line experimented at one time or another with such laws (the only exceptions are Illinois and the far western states that came into the Union in the 1850s). Instead of examining the laws of all these states, I have tried to select a sufficiently broad number of important ones to study in order to see the patterns and variety, and the ideas they rested upon. Many of the states patterned their laws after those of another state so that a complete study of all of them would tend to be overly long and repetitious. For those who might wish to look at the laws of the states omitted from this study, an appendix listing them is included. None, however, differs in any striking way from those examined here.

I selected the following five states for study: Pennsylvania and New York from the Middle Atlantic region, Massachusetts from New England, and Ohio and Wisconsin from the Old Northwest. Among the criteria for this selection were these: either the state led the way in the passage of a certain type of law (such as Pennsylvania and New York in the 1820s, and Massachusetts in the 1840s); or because a truly significant case arose in the particular state (such as in New York and Pennsylvania in the 1830s, and in Wisconsin and Ohio in the 1850s); or, finally, because the pattern of laws presented a clear contrast to the patterns of the other states examined (this was one of the primary reasons for the selection of Ohio). I also tried to select states from different regions (thus Pennsylvania and Ohio were included in part because they bordered slave states and would be likely to show different responses from Massachusetts and Wisconsin which were further removed from slavery).

The most difficult selection to make was among those states that later became the strongholds of Copperheadism: Illinois, Indiana, and Ohio. All three had strong prosouthern and antiblack segments within their populations whose views were reflected in their laws, and in this sense stand in sharp contrast to the other states selected. I chose Ohio over Indiana primarily because it promised to show the greatest intellectual ferment since abolitionists were much more prominent, and because a significant case arose in the state courts in 1859 that showed very clearly the conflict between the state and federal governments by the eve of the war.

A special problem was presented by Illinois. Of all the states above the Mason-Dixon line, Illinois alone, in 1829, adopted a law against blacks that rested upon the presumption prevalent in slave-owning communities that all blacks are slaves. The law stipulated that any Negro without a certificate of freedom would be deemed a runaway. In 1833 it passed the only law to grace its statute books that even arguably could be styled a Personal Liberty Law. It provided sanctions against anyone who forcibly arrested anyone else to remove him from the state without having established a claim according to the laws of the United States. Illinois then did not present a very good case for examining the Personal Liberty Laws; it is an important exception, but the only one, to the idea that people in the North incorporated into law the presumption that all men are born free and should not be deprived of that freedom except by due process.

Preparation of this study was a pleasure because of the thoughtful guidance of Arthur Bestor, the continued interest and encouragement of Stanley N. Katz and Aida DiPace Donald, and the uniform kindness of librarians and their staffs at the following institutions: the Library of Congress, National Archives, Library Company of Philadelphia, Pennsylvania Historical Society, New-York Historical Society, Massachusetts State Library, Massachusetts Historical Society, Boston Public Library, Houghton Library, Ohio Historical Society, the Legislative Reference Service of the Ohio State Library, the State Historical Society of Wisconsin, and the Law Library of the University of Washington. The research at these institutions was made possible in part by a grant of a United States Steel Foundation Fellowship.

Quotations from the Adams Papers are from the microfilm edition, by permission of the Massachusetts Historical Society. For helpful criticisms I am under an especial debt to the members of the Americanist Seminar at Portland State University and to the anonymous reader of the manuscript, whose suggestions have improved this study immeasurably. Appreciation, additionally, is due to three diligent typists: Maud Alexander, Nancy Maurer, and Karen Waters. Finally, I would like to acknowledge my deep indebtedness to my wife, Marge, for the unselfish manner in which she endured it all.

FREE MEN ALL

Slavery and Emancipation: The Rise of Conflicting Legal Systems 1

"We assert," proclaimed South Carolina in its *Declaration of the Causes of Secession of 1860*, "that fourteen of the States have deliberately refused for years past to fulfill their constitutional obligations, and we refer to their own statutes for the proof."[1] The statutes referred to were known collectively as the Personal Liberty Laws, and, along with the issue of slavery in the territories, were cited as one of the primary reasons for the breakup of the Union. Earlier in the year Senator Robert Toombs of Georgia asserted in Congress that the rights of slave owners had been nullified by teachings about a "higher law," by acts passed under the pretense of preventing kidnapping, and by "new constructions" of the writ of habeas corpus.[2] Speaking on the other side in the same debate, Senator Benjamin Wade of Ohio raised the critical question as northerners viewed it: "Cannot a sovereign State of this Union prevent the kidnapping of her free citizens because you have a right to claim a slave fleeing from service?"[3]

This particular controversy arose (and could only arise) in a nation where two conflicting systems of law existed side by side in different sections of the country. In one, slavery was an established institution; in the other it either had been or was being abolished. To abolish slavery involved much more than merely freeing individual slaves; it meant altering the structure of the law, eliminating principles of law that were based on the idea that men could be treated as property, and extending to all men the legal rights applicable to free men.

Where slavery was recognized by the law, slaves, "chattels personal," were property. Whatever rights they might possess were subordinated, in the eyes of the law, to the rights of the persons who owned them.[4] They were denied what Sir William Blackstone called one of the "absolute rights of individuals," the natural right of personal liberty, which he defined as the right to move about, to change one's situation without restraint "unless by due course of law."[5] Or as the proslavery legalist Thomas R. R. Cobb put it:

[1] *Declaration of the Immediate Causes Which Induce and Justify the Secession of South Carolina from the Federal Union* (Charleston, S.C., 1860).

[2] *Cong. Globe*, 36th Cong, 1st sess., March 7, 1860, Appendix, 155.

[3] *Ibid.*, 152. Despite the similarity in page numbers Wade's speech is not in the Appendix.

[4] John Codman Hurd, *The Law of Freedom and Bondage in the United States* (2 vols.; Boston, 1858–62), 2:2–218, lists the laws securing slavery.

[5] Sir William Blackstone, *Commentaries on the Laws of England* (4 vols.; London, 1765–69), 1:134.

1

"The right of personal liberty in the slaves is utterly inconsistent with the idea of slavery."[6]

But slavery was more than the subordination of one man to another; it was also a "system of racial adjustment and social order," as Ulrich B. Phillips observed some years ago.[7] The existence of free blacks, however, presented a very real and important difficulty in Anglo-American law, and created serious strains within this "social order." Because of color it was difficult to distinguish between a free black and a slave. Whatever standards or rules that were adopted to help define the status of a man would be crucial in resolving peacefully the tension between the recognition of human rights, and the recognition of a property right in human beings.

Within the American South the resolution of this tension was weighted in favor of slaveholders by means of a presumption that would serve as a guide to a court in any hearing involving the status of a black. The presumption was that all blacks were slaves. This was justified, as the *African Observer* noted in 1827, upon the ground "that all the negroes imported into these states were slaves, and therefore, the probability is, that the person in question is a slave."[8] The "probability" that a black in a slaveholding community was a slave of course was high, but this was only one reason and in a legal, as well as social sense, it was not the most important one for presuming that blackness implied slavery. A presumption of freedom could undermine the "rights" of a master as against his property, and might endanger the system of "racial adjustment." The proslavery standard was buttressed by the evidentiary rule, established either by statute or custom, that black people could only be witnesses in cases involving other blacks.[9] This meant that an alleged slave could not testify against the claim of a putative master.

Precisely when the presumption of slavery became a basis for adjudications is not clear, but it was well established before the Revolution. As early as 1680 the Reverend Morgan Godwyn wrote that "these two words, *Negro* and *slave*" had "by custom grown Homogeneous and Convertible."[10] During the colonial period both South Carolina and Georgia provided by statute that the burden of legal proof was on free blacks to show that they were not slaves.[11] This view was summed up neatly in 1806 by Spencer Roane of the Virginia Court of Appeals: "In the case of a person visibly appearing to be a

[6]Thomas R. R. Cobb, *An Inquiry into the Law of Negro Slavery in the United States of America. To which is prefixed, An Historical Sketch of Slavery* (Philadelphia, Savannah, 1858), 105.

Ulrich B. Phillips, *The Course of the South to Secession*, ed. E. Merton Coulter (New York, 1939), 152.

[8]*The African Observer*, (Dec., 1827), 272.

[9]George M. Stroud, *A Sketch of the Laws Relating to Slavery in the Several States of the United States of America* (Philadelphia, 1856), 44.

[10]Quoted in Winthrop Jordan, *White over Black: American Attitudes Toward the Negro, 1550-1812* (Chapel Hill, N.C., 1968), 97.

[11]*Ibid.*, 124; John Belton O'Neall, *The Negro Law of South Carolina, Collected and Digested* (Columbia, S.C., 1848), 5.

negro, the presumption is, in this country, that he is a slave, and it is incumbent on him to make out his right to freedom, but in the case of a person visibly appearing to be a white man, or an Indian, the presumption is that he is free, and it is necessary for his adversary to show that he is a slave."[12]

In the South the "rights" of slave owners were further secured when the colonial assemblies adopted the principle of the Roman law that a child derives its status from its mother.[13] Since miscegenation usually involved white males and black female slaves, the Roman-law principle insured that the offspring of such alliances were automatically slaves. When the reverse was the case, when a white female and a black male were involved, a special status sometimes was created for the child. In Pennsylvania, for example, such a child would be a servant until the age of thirty-one, "in consequence of its base birth."[14]

Also important for the maintenance of slavery was the system provided for recapturing fugitive slaves. In areas of heavy black population, slave patrols often were established to guard against insurrections and to apprehend runaways. But organized patrols were not essential in a legal sense. Customary law recognized an individual's right to recapture and reclaim runaways. If a piece of property (such as a horse) strayed away and was found, a person could repossess it without formality, if no one resisted or objected. Blackstone gave this casual right legal recognition. Under the common law, he wrote, recourse was to be allowed, on occasion, to this "extrajudicial or eccentrical kind of remedy," called the "right of recaption or reprisal":

> This happens, when any one hath deprived another of his property in goods or chattels personal, or wrongfully detains one's wife, child, or servant: in which case the owner of the goods, and the husband, parent, or master, may lawfully claim and retake them, wherever he happens to find them; so it be not in a riotous manner, or attended with a breach of the peace . . . . If therefore he can so contrive it as to gain possession of his property again, without force or terror, the law favours and will justify his proceeding. But, as the public peace is a superior consideration to any one man's private property; and as, if individuals were once allowed to use private force as a remedy for private injuries, all social justice must cease, the strong would give law to the weak, and every man would revert to a state of nature; for these reasons it is provided, that this natural right of recaption shall never

[12]*Hudgins* v. *Wrights*, 1 Hening & Munford 133. Another statement of this view occurred in a South Carolina case in 1819; "the word 'negroes' has a fixed meaning (slaves)," Helen Tunnicliff Catterall, *Judicial Cases Concerning American Slavery and the Negro* (5 vols.; Washington, D.C., 1926–37), 2:311. See also *De Lacy* v. *Antoine*, 7 Leigh's Reports 448 (Virginia, 1836); *Field* v. *Walker*, 17 Alabama 82; *Thornton* v. *Demoss*, 13 Mississippi 609.

[13]New York was the only colony north of the Mason-Dixon line that adopted the Roman law principle. Arthur Zilversmit, *The First Emancipation: The Abolition of Slavery in the North* (Chicago, 1967), 13.

[14]For a discussion of this law see the opinion of Justice Jacob Rush in 1789, *Respublica* v. *Negro Betsey*, 1 Dallas 475.

be exerted, where such exertion must occasion strife and bodily contention, or endanger the peace of society.[15]

Certainly Blackstone was aware of the need to place limitations on this "natural right," as anything less could have led to dangerous incursions on the rights of persons, and the "public peace."

Slave owners, however, blew recaption up into a major right, and virtually ignored the limitations. The frequent use of this right can be seen in newspaper advertisements offering rewards for the capture and return of runaways by private parties.[16] In 1795 the Supreme Court of Pennsylvania took notice of the fact that recovering fugitives without a recourse to the courts was a widely accepted practice in slaveholding communities, a mode of recovery approved by the court.[17] The most forceful expression of the slave owners' interpretation of recaption was made by Senator James M. Mason of Virginia in 1850. A claimant, he said, "could use whatever force may be necessary to effect the capture, without committing thereby a breach of the peace; and if force be offered by the slave or others, he may resist it to any extent that may be necessary to secure the possession of his property."[18] Together with the doctrine that color raised a presumption of slavery this alleged right of recaption left blacks (free or slave) exposed to forcible deprivation of liberty by putative masters.

With the abolition of slavery in one part of the Union, and the consequent move to eliminate such principles from the state law, two conflicting legal systems emerged in the United States. This process began during the 1780s amid the enthusiasm for the improvement of man's condition growing out of the Revolution.[19] At the outset, emancipation was sought primarily at the state level. It was state law, after all, that established and protected the institution. South of the Mason-Dixon line, for example, Thomas Jefferson worked for the passage of a gradual abolition law during the 1780s. Because the public in that region was unprepared to accept abolition this effort failed.[20] A number of southern states, however, did ease their laws concerning voluntary manumissions.[21] The enthusiasm for an amelioration of the system waned by the late 1780s with the decline in revolutionary zeal, and these same states began to increase the restrictions in their codes. North Carolina, for example, began to discourage manumissions and even authorized the reenslavement of some of those who had been freed.[22] By 1820

[15]Blackstone, *Commentaries*, 3:4–5.

[16]See, for example, the listing in Lester J. Cappon and Stella F. Duff, *Virginia Gazette Index, 1736–1780* (2 vols.; Williamsburg, 1950), 2:1088–91.

[17]*Respublica* v. *Richards*, 2 Dallas 225–28.

[18]*Cong. Globe*, 31st Cong., 1st sess., January 28, 1850, 235.

[19]Zilversmit, *The First Emancipation*, chap. 5.

[20]Mary Stoughton Locke, *Anti-Slavery in America from the Introduction of African Slaves to the Prohibition of the Slave Trade (1619–1808)* (Boston, 1901), 76.

[21]*Ibid.*, 74.

[22]*Ibid.*, 122–23.

Jefferson had come to the conclusion that "we have the wolf by the ears, and we can neither hold him, nor safely let him go. Justice is in one scale, and self-preservation in the other."[23]

North of the Mason-Dixon line the emancipatory movement was far more successful. Slavery was excluded from the states above that line in one of three distinct ways. Abolition was either gradual, or immediate, or slavery was prohibited from the beginning of settlement. This study will not be concerned with all fourteen states mentioned by South Carolina in 1860, but with the ways in which five of them dealt with some of the problems growing out of the process of abolition. The five are Pennsylvania and New York (from the Middle Atlantic region), Massachusetts (the largest of the New England states), and, finally, Ohio and Wisconsin (from the Old Northwest).

Pennsylvania, the southernmost state to abolish slavery, was the first to act. Since "all are the work of an Almighty hand," as the preamble to the gradual abolition law of 1780 stated, Pennsylvania moved to "extend a portion of that freedom to others, which hath been extended to us." But only a "portion."

With Delaware and Maryland (both slave states down to the Civil War) only a short distance from Philadelphia, and the southern boundary of the state being the Mason-Dixon line, Pennsylvania moved cautiously toward total abolition. Moreover, central to the revolutionary conception of natural rights was a high regard for the institution of private property. The ownership of private property was one of the most important human rights; usually it was not placed in opposition to those rights.[24] What resulted from this combination of geography and ideology was a law designed to provide for a gradual elimination of slavery. It was an accommodation with slave owners that set a pattern followed in certain other northern states. Abolition was to be neither abrupt nor disruptive.

Because of the continued recognition of a property right in human beings implicit in gradual abolition, one of the first difficulties to be resolved was the persistent problem of differentiating a free black from a slave. To allow a peaceful resolution, a procedure was adopted that incorporated a feature of colonial property law used to settle disputes about land titles.[25] A title to landed property not registered was deemed void. This provided a publicly registered document in place of the mere interested testimony of contesting parties. Slave owners thus had to register their slaves within a stated period of time; those not so registered would be considered free.

[23]H. A. Washington, ed., *The Writings of Thomas Jefferson* (9 vols.; Philadelphia, 1871), 7:159. The Boyd collection goes only to 1790.

[24]Jordan, *White over Black*, 350–51.

[25]Payson Jackson Treat, "Origin of the National Land System under the Confederation," in Vernon Carstensen, ed., *The Public Lands: Studies in the History of the Public Domain* (Madison, Wis., 1963), 10; Marshall Harris, *Origin of the Land Tenure System in the United States* (Ames, Iowa, 1953), 333.

The effect of this was to establish a clear-cut and all-important presumption of freedom. Section 10 of the act of 1780 made this explicit: "no man or woman of any nation or colour, except the Negroes or Mulattoes who shall be registered as aforesaid, shall, at any time hereafter, be deemed, adjudged or holden, within the territories of this commonwealth, as slaves or servants for life, but as free men and free women." The few exceptions to this general statement included: slaves of delegates in Congress, and slaves of non-residents of Pennsylvania, who might travel through the state with their domestics. Color, however, was barred as a criterion in determining a man's status: the presumption in Pennsylvania, regardless of color, was of freedom.

At the same time, the gradual abolition act stipulated that no relief would be given to fugitive slaves from other states. Pennsylvania did not go so far as to declare that any black within the boundaries of the state was ipso facto free unless registered under the state law. Masters, in fact, were guaranteed all the rights to reclaim runaways they possessed before the passage of the act,[26] which indicates the willingness of Pennsylvania to meet what were considered the legitimate demands of slaveholders. This guarantee involved substantially the same principle incorporated in the fugitive slave clause in the Ordinance of 1787, from which the clause in the Constitution was taken.

Despite this important concession the fact remained that registration provided a clearly defined standard for establishing a man's status, and the state was committed to the ultimate eradication of the institution of slavery. Moreover, the legal principles applicable to free men had been adopted to guide the courts in any judicial inquiry into a black's status. The first case in which the state supreme court construed the act was one in which a master lost his slaves because of his failure to register them.[27]

Another test of the new presumption came in 1792 when a group of refugees from Santo Domingo were turned down when they petitioned the legislature for permission to keep their slaves as an exception to the abolition laws of the state. The committee considering their petition rejected it because slavery was "obviously contrary to the . . . Constitution of this state." For a time after that antislavery people tried to secure a declaratory statute stating simply that slavery was unconstitutional, but their hopes were disappointed. Frustrated at the political level, they turned to the state judiciary. They were no more successful in that forum: in 1802 the High Court of Errors and Appeals declared that "slavery *is* consistent with the Constitution."[28]

[26]Alexander James Dallas, *Laws of the Commonwealth of Pennsylvania* (2 vols.; Philadelphia, 1797), 1:833–43. Hereafter a short form of citation will be used for the laws of the various states, such as *Penn. Session Laws, 1780*, unless the law is taken from a special collection or compilation.

[27]*Respublica* v. *Negro Betsey*, 1 Dallas 469.

[28]Zilversmit, *The First Emancipation*, 202–8, has the fullest account of this development. For the particulars see the *Journal of the Seventeenth Session of the Pennsylvania House of Representatives* (Lancaster, 1792), 39, 42, 45, 55, 60, 195–96, 201, 205, 291; *Journal of the Seventeenth Session of the Pennsylvania Senate* (Lancaster, 1792), 150–51. Hereafter a short

Despite this continued recognition of a legal interest in human beings as property, Pennsylvania gradually eliminated slavery. By 1820 there were only 211 slaves listed in the census.[29] There had been an accommodation with slave owners, but at the same time there had been positive action to remove the internal legal principles built upon the assumption that a person could be considered a thing.

When New York acted in 1799 it patterned its law after that of Pennsylvania. By 1817 the final step was taken toward total abolition in New York. All slaves born before passage of the gradual abolition act of 1799 were given their freedom as of July 4, 1827.[30]

Although Middle Atlantic states like Pennsylvania and New York adopted a compromise pattern, involving acceptance of slavery on a diminishing scale for a limited period, in Massachusetts, the largest state in New England, slavery was eliminated in a different manner. There the judiciary, not the legislature, took the initiative. Beginning in 1781, a series of cases involving a Negro, Quok Walker, and his master, Nathaniel Jennison, led the way. Justice William Cushing remarked, in the particular case that began in 1783, that because of the declaration in the state constitution that all men were free, "slavery is . . . as effectively abolished as it can be by granting of rights and privileges wholly incompatible and repugnant to its existence." The Jennison cases did not directly abolish slavery in the state, but they encouraged blacks to sue for their freedom. Some blacks, in fact, believed that the courts would not return them to servitude, so they just walked off from their masters. Slavery in Massachusetts simply disintegrated; the state gave no legal recognition to the status of slavery as did Pennsylvania and New York. There was no compromise, and virtually no transition period.[31]

---

form of citation will be used for the journals of the state legislatures, such as *Penn. House Journal, 1792*, with the exception of some from Massachusetts, which are only available in manuscript form. The Massachusetts journals will be cited by the short form noted, but the location of the documents will be noted as well. For the court case see Edward R. Turner, "The Abolition of Slavery in Pennsylvania," *Pennsylvania Magazine of History and Biography*, 36 (1912): 138–39. The actual text of this case is not extant.

[29] *Negro Population 1790–1915* (Department of Commerce; Bureau of the Census; Washington, 1918), 57.

[30] Edgar J. McManus, "Antislavery Legislation in New York," *Journal of Negro History*, 46 (Oct. 1961): 208–9; *ibid., A History of Negro Slavery in New York* (Syracuse, 1966), chap. 9; Zilversmit, *The First Emancipation*, 146–52, 280 ff.; *Laws of the State of New York Passed at the Sessions of the Legislature Held in the Years 1777 (to 1801) Inclusive* (5 vols.; Albany, 1886–87), 4: 388–89; *New York Session Laws, 1804*, 145–46; *New York Session Laws, 1817*, 4: 136–44.

[31] Zilversmit, *The First Emancipation*, 122–25, contains one of the best accounts of the decay of slavery in Massachusetts. The following should also be consulted: William O'Brien, S. J., "Did the Jennison Case Outlaw Slavery in Massachusetts?" *William and Mary Quarterly*, 3d ser., 17 (1960): 219–41; John D. Cushing, "The Cushing Court and the Abolition of Slavery in Massachusetts: More Notes on the 'Quok Walker Case,'" *American Journal of Legal History*, 5 (1961): 118–44; "Letters and Documents Relating to Slavery in Massachusetts," *Collections of the Massachusetts Historical Society*, 5th ser., 3 (1877): 373–442.

Slavery had existed in Massachusetts down to the 1780s, while in the Old Northwest steps were taken to prohibit its introduction in advance of American settlement. By the terms of the Ordinance of 1787 slavery was prohibited from this region, which included the future states of Ohio and Wisconsin (examined in this study), as well as Indiana, Illinois, and Michigan. Ohio reaffirmed the prohibition in its 1802 constitution, and the prohibition was well settled by the time Wisconsin became a state in the late 1840s.

Whether slavery was abolished gradually, undermined by the judiciary, or prohibited outright, it meant the ultimate elimination of those legal principles based on the idea that men could be treated as property. And this altered significantly the relationship between the states north and south of the Mason-Dixon line. From the 1780s on, that relationship became increasingly tense. Certain legal processes used to secure the personal rights of one man as against another became one of the cutting edges in the controversy that developed. The most important of these were trial by jury, the writ of habeas corpus, and the less familiar writ *de homine replegiando*. In those states where slavery was abolished, or was in the course of abolition, all men were entitled to invoke such processes since all men were presumed to be free. In slaveholding states, however, slaves lacked any standing to invoke most legal procedures in a court.

Jury trial, a mechanism for taking the community sense of justice in a given case, was a potent weapon against abuses of power. It had a long history (going back at least to Magna Charta) as one of the principal guarantees of freedom in Anglo-American jurisprudence. Indeed, it was a political principle as well as a legal device. Colonial Americans had tried to use it to defeat British policy in the Stamp Act controversy, and it was involved in the struggle against the antirepublican common law of seditious libel.[32] Jury trial was believed so important that those who framed constitutions during the revolutionary years uniformly guaranteed it in the new documents.

Practice connected with the habeas corpus at any given point is more obscure. Milton Cantor aptly noted that practice was "derived from tradition, trial-and-error usage, and compromise arrangements rather than statutory mandates."[33] He might well have added that it also derived from legal obscurantism.

[32]See, for example, the "Instruction of the Town of Braintree, Massachusetts on the Stamp Act, October 14, 1765," in Henry Steele Commager, ed., *Documents of American History* (2 vols. in 1; 6th ed.; New York, 1958), 1: 56–57; Lenoard W. Levy, *Legacy of Suppression: Freedom of Speech and Press in Early American History* (Cambridge, Mass., 1960); Mark DeWolfe Howe, "Juries as Judges of Criminal Law," *Harvard Law Review*, 52 (Feb., 1939): 582–616.

[33]Milton Cantor, "The Writ of Habeas Corpus: Early American Origins and Development," in Harold M. Hyman and Leonard W. Levy, *Freedom and Reform: Essays in Honor of Henry Steel Commager* (New York, 1967), 55–78; Dallin H. Oaks, "Habeas Corpus in the States, 1776–1865," *University of Chicago Law Review*, 32 (1961–65): 243–88; Maxwell Cohen, "Habeas Corpus Cum Causa—The Emergence of the Modern Writ," *Canadian Bar Review*, 18 (1940): 10, 172.

Habeas corpus cum causa (have the body, together with the cause of detention) was the form used to examine the reasons for a restraint imposed on a person. Upon the presentation of a prima facie case for issuing the writ, it would be directed to the person detaining another, commanding him to bring the person detained before the judge and to state the reasons for depriving him of his freedom. If the reasons given in the return to the writ were not sufficient at law to justify the restraint, the person would be freed by the court.

Variant forms of the *cum causa* were developed to differentiate its use in criminal and civil cases, but at the hands of eighteenth-century commentators these variants (*ad subjiciendum* and *ad faciendum et recipiendum*) emerged as entirely separate writs. The *habeas corpus ad subjiciendum* (the significant phrase, *cum causa*, had been dropped) finally came out of this tangle as the so-called great writ.[34] Unless they specified otherwise, American jurists usually had this writ in mind when they used the phrase, habeas corpus.

Without doubt its most important function was to provide for an inquiry into the legality of a governmental restraint on personal liberty. It was designed for "crisis usage," as Milton Cantor has written. By the last half of the seventeenth century, however, it was being invoked in cases of restraint by private persons, as well as by public officers; and this usage was known in America by the time of the Revolution.[35] Even before this development in habeas corpus practice, a terribly important fusion of ideas had taken place. During the early seventeenth century habeas corpus became "indissolubly" linked in people's minds with the ancient guarantees of Magna Charta. Two powerful ideas had been tied together: "One was the idea of Magna Charta as the ultimate affirmation of the personal freedom of Englishmen; the other, the idea of *habeas corpus* as the ultimate weapon for defending this freedom."[36] Thereafter, the connection between a wide-ranging conception of human freedom and this ancient common-law writ persisted in Anglo-American thinking. According to Rollin Hurd, an antislavery author who wrote a massive treatise on habeas corpus in the United States on the eve of the Civil War, this writ had been "raised to the importance and clothed with the power of a political principle, so that while and because it is an invaluable and incomparable protection for personal liberty, it is also in turn protected by the highest power in the State, constitutional and legislative, as a cherished popular right and safeguard of civil liberty."[37]

[34]In a work in progress, *Habeas Corpus and Anglo-American Constitutionalism 1591-1867*, Arthur Bestor discusses the question of terminology.

[35]John E. Wilmot, *Notes of Opinions and Judgments* (London, 1802), 96. See also Sir Matthew Hale, *Historia Placitorum Coronae: The History of the Pleas of the Crown* (2 vols.; Philadelphia, 1847), 2: 148, n. 6. Footnotes are by the American editors, W. A. Stokes and E. Ingersoll.

[36]Bestor, *Habeas Corpus*, chap. 1.

[37]Rollin C. Hurd, *A Treatise on the Right of Personal Liberty, and on the Writ of Habeas Corpus and the Practice Connected with it: With a View of the Law of Extradition of Fugitives* (Albany, 1858), 146.

Despite this trend in thinking about habeas corpus, there were important limitations upon its use for libertarian purposes in pre-Civil War America. During the 1780s, when a number of the new states began to adopt statutes securing the writ, the practice surrounding it was unsettled. The most important uncertainty concerned the force of a return to the writ. Some jurists believed that they possessed the power to conduct an independent inquiry into the facts alleged to justify depriving a man of his personal freedom. Others contended that if the facts asserted legally justified the detention, a judge would be bound: he could only discharge a prisoner if those facts had been proved false in some additional proceeding, such as a jury trial.[38] A few of the states that adopted habeas corpus statutes in the 1780s (this included Pennsylvania) settled the issue by authorizing judges to go behind the facts alleged in the return. Others did not give statutory authority for some time (New York provided it in 1813, in a codification of the state law).[39] This trend in the growth of habeas corpus was not embodied into British statutes until 1816. In 1847 W. A. Stokes and E. Ingersoll, American editors of Sir Matthew Hale's *Historia Placitorum Coronae*, noted that the American states had engrafted upon habeas corpus the power to hear "the whole merits and facts of the case . . . deciding upon the guilt or rather upon the *innocence* of the prisoner and absolutely discharging him without the intervention of a jury where the court is of opinion that the *facts* do not sustain the criminal charge."[40] For those claimed as fugitives, this was important because it meant that courts possessed the power to conduct a complete hearing, admitting into evidence facts to prove the freedom of the person seized as well as those used to justify the detention. Throughout the nineteenth century this power was disputed by proslavery legalists precisely because it could be an important weapon in the hands of state jurists willing to use it for libertarian purposes.

A more important limitation upon the scope of habeas corpus in pre-Civil War America arose because of the federal nature of the Union. In 1789 (with the adoption of the Judiciary Act) a truly significant concession was made to state power. A federal habeas corpus could not be issued to test the validity of a restraint imposed under authority of a state. It was not until the Reconstruction years that this limitation upon the federal process was fully removed. The most difficult, and warmly debated, problem before 1861, however, concerned the use of a state habeas corpus in cases where a person was held under color of federal law. Some argued that the state writ could provide a remedy in such cases, while others contended that, if admitted, this

38 Matthew Bacon, *A New Abridgement of the Law* (7 vols.; Philadelphia, 1811), 3: 438.
39 *Laws of the Commonwealth of Pennsylvania* (4 vols.; 1700–1810; Philadelphia, 1810), 2: 279; *New York Session Laws, 1787,* 1: 77; James Kent, *Commentaries on American Law* (4 vols; 10th ed.; Boston, 1860) 1: 645; Joseph R. Swan, *Statutes of the State of Ohio, of a General Nature, In Force January 1st, 1854: With References to Prior Repealed Laws* (Cincinnati, 1854), 451.
40 Hale, *Historia Placitorum Coronae,* 149.

would lead to a dangerous jurisdictional collision between the state and federal governments.[41]

Still, antislavery people tried to give it real efficacy, and in doing so they contributed to the growth of the "great writ." Habeas corpus, of course, had not developed in response to the peculiar problems of black people, or any other caste within society, but later state legislatures sometimes adapted habeas corpus practice in striking ways to meet the special needs of persons in danger of being seized as slaves. Massachusetts pointed the direction when it tied an antikidnapping provision onto the habeas corpus statute of 1785. This law eliminated state recognition of the so-called right of recaption, a right that had been recognized by Pennsylvania in its gradual abolition act. The Massachusetts law provided that persons lawfully residing in the state (a judicial question) could not be removed unless "by due course of law, to answer for some criminal offence committed in some other of the United States of America."[42]

As important as habeas corpus was in people's minds as an instrument to secure personal freedom from illicit restraint, it was not the only remedy. Of considerable utility was the writ *de homine replegiando* (personal replevin). Although Blackstone considered it "almost antiquated" in England, it was by no means so in the United States.[43] Probably this form of the writ of replevin, a process for the recovery of property, survived in this country because of the continued recognition of a legitimate property interest in men.

Common-law practice on this writ was cumbersome and time-consuming.[44] The writ was directed to the sheriff who took the plaintiff out of custody of the defendant upon the plaintiff giving security that he would be forthcoming to answer any charge, or claim, against him. If the plaintiff had been removed from the sheriff's jurisdiction, the officer would return that the man had been eloigned, upon which a process would issue (*a capias in withernam*) to imprison the defendant until he produced the party. Numerous delays and exceptions were allowed in the proceedings, which led Blackstone to conclude that the writ was an ineffective remedy; it had one principal advantage for blacks, however, and that was that trial on the issues joined was by jury. It was thus one means of implementing the constitutional guarantee.

Most state courts derived their power to issue the writ of replevin from the common law. Massachusetts, however, adopted a declaratory statute in 1787 guaranteeing the writ "as of right" to every person in the state "who shall be

---

[41]Oaks, "Habeas Corpus in the States," *passim*; William M. Wiecek, "The Great Writ and Reconstruction: The Habeas Corpus Act of 1867," *Journal of Southern History*, 36 (Nov. 1970): 530–49; and chaps. 9–11 of this study.

[42] *The Perpetual Laws of the Commonwealth of Massachusetts, From the Commencement of the Constitution, in October 1780, to the Last Wednesday in May, 1789* (Boston, 1789), 143–52.

[43]Blackstone, *Commentaries*, 3: 129.

[44]Oaks, "Habeas Corpus in the States," 281, is one of the best brief descriptions of this writ.

imprisoned, confined, or held in duress."[45] The writ had been used earlier in that state to protect blacks claimed as slaves. In the case of *Margaret* v. *Muzzy* in 1763, a Negro woman was replevied, and the issue of her freedom or slavery went to the jury.[46] In *Oliver* v. *Sale*, the year before, counsel for two black boys sold as slaves noted that the defendant, by selling them, had left himself open to a *homine replegiando*.[47]

Although the other states did not adopt such laws their courts did utilize the writ. A notable case occurred in Pennsylvania in 1786. In *Pirate, alias Belt* v. *Dalby*, which had arisen on a habeas corpus, Chief Justice Thomas McKean recommended that the action be reformed into a *homine replegiando*, so that the issue (slavery or freedom) might be determined by a jury. McKean did not doubt his authority to examine the issues of fact under habeas corpus, but he was very reluctant to do that. The jury then found for the master.[48] Despite the outcome in this case, replevin could be an important legal mechanism for securing personal freedom, particularly in a community hostile to slavery. Its continued vitality was attested to in the first major treatise on replevin, published in 1849, which noted that it was the remedy frequently used for illegally holding a black person as a slave.[49]

As northern states restructured their legal codes to give all men the standing to invoke such time-honored procedures for the vindication of liberty, and raised the presumption of freedom for all as a guide to court or jury, southern communities awoke to the dangers in the two common-law writs. Prior to 1795 in Virginia, for example, both writs had been allowed to blacks who claimed to be free. But, as the Virginia Court of Appeals noted in 1836, "as these remedies proved vexatious and unsafe, a new proceeding was prescribed . . . the homine replegiando was repealed, and the habeas corpus, was considered as no longer appropriate."[50] Usually, after the turn of the century, southern courts refused to accept jurisdiction of claims to freedom arising on habeas corpus. "The presumption arising from color, coupled with the sworn return to the writ of habeas corpus by the party holding them in custody that they are held and claimed as slaves," according to the Alabama Supreme Court, "is sufficient to oust the court of its jurisdiction, since an issue is tendered which the judge upon this summary proceeding is incompetent to try."[51]

After the 1780s, then, two conflicting systems of law existed side by side in different sections of the country, making it necessary to define a new set

[45]*The Laws of the Commonwealth of Massachusetts, From November 28, 1780 . . . To February 28, 1807* (3 vols.; Boston, 1807), 1: 362.

[46]Case No. 40 in L. Kinvin Wroth and Hiller B. Zobel, eds., *Legal Papers of John Adams* (3 vols.; Cambridge, Mass., 1965), 2: 58–59.

[47]Josiah Quincy, Jr., *Reports of Cases Argued and Adjudged in the Superior Court of Judicature of the Province of Massachusetts Bay, Between 1761 and 1772* (Boston, 1865), 33.

[48]*Pirate, alias Belt* v. *Dalby*, 1 Dallas, 167–69.

[49]Phineas Pemberton Morris, *A Practical Treatise on the Law of Replevin in the United States* (2d ed.; Philadelphia, 1869), 236.

[50]*DeLacy* v. *Antoine*, 7 Leigh's Reports 443.

[51]*Field* v. *Walker*, 17 Alabama 82; Oaks, "Habeas Corpus in the States," 263.

of constitutional relationships among the states. Three principal difficulties arose. When a sojourning slaveholder left a free state, the question was to determine whether the black he was taking with him might not be free or entitled to ultimate freedom; when claims to blacks were made, based on the contention that they were fugitive slaves, the problem was due process in adjudicating such claims; and when free men were kidnapped and taken to slave states for sale. The basic legal problem was to decide whether mere residence on free soil made a man free, or whether those states were bound to give judicial recognition to the status created by the laws of the slave states. If the American states had been completely independent sovereigns, this question would have been governed wholly by principles derived from international law, or by treaty.

Comity, one of the most important of those principles, meant granting an extraterritorial effect to the laws of one state by the sovereign power of another. When this was done, according to Joseph Story, it was "from a sort of moral necessity to do justice, in order that justice may be done to us in return."[52] T. R. R. Cobb put it differently: it was the only way "to promote justice between individuals and to produce a friendly intercourse between the sovereignties to which they belong."[53] The question of recognizing the status of slavery in a free state, however, put a severe strain on comity.

The English were among the first to be concerned with this problem within a federal system. A benchmark in their experience was a case decided in 1772 involving the conflict of laws between different jursdictions within the British Empire. James Sommersett had been held as a slave in a British colony and then taken to England by his master. The case arose on a habeas corpus, and in the return to the writ, Sommersett's alleged master stated that "the slave departed and refused to serve; whereupon he was kept, to be sold abroad." At the conclusion of his opinion for the court Lord Mansfield declared that,

> So high an act of dominion must be recognized by the law of the country where it is used. The State of slavery is of such a nature, that it is incapable of being introduced on any reasons, moral or political, but only by positive law, which preserves its force long after the reasons, occasion, and time itself from whence it was created, is erased from memory. It is so odious, that nothing can be suffered to support it, but positive law. Whatever inconvenience, therefore, may follow from the decision, I cannot say this case is allowed or approved by the law of England; and therefore the black must be discharged.[54]

Mansfield's decision virtually put an end to legal slavery in England. English law, in his judgment, did not provide the means to secure the rights of a slaveholder: he could not control his property lawfully, regardless of the

---

[52]Joseph Story, *Commentaries on the Conflict of Laws* (Boston, 1846), 39–45.
[53]Cobb, *Law of Slavery*, 173.
[54]*The Case of James Sommersett, a Negro, on a Habeas Corpus*, 20 State Trials, 82.

way a slave reached that country, whether by flight or by consent of the owner. This did not mean that a slave who arrived in England thereafter would be a freeman everywhere, however, as some antislavery people argued.[55]

The conflict of law question was explored further in 1827 in another significant English case, *The Slave Grace*. In that case Lord Stowell affirmed the legitimacy of the status of slavery created by the customary laws of Antigua. A slave would not be free if he returned to that colony from England. Stowell also commented on Mansfield's somewhat murky remark about positive law. "Ancient custom," he noted, "is generally recognized as a just foundation of all law," and slavery could exist by "that custom which operates with the force of law," as in Antigua.[56]

The American experience with the conflict of laws drew upon the English and ran in similar channels. Lord Mansfield's remark that slavery could be supported only by positive law especially had a deep impact upon American lawyers and jurists. Quok Walker's attorney, for example, in the case that paved the way for abolition in Massachusetts, argued that slavery was contrary to natural law and illegal unless established by positive law. This view was so influential that some of the courts even of slave-owning communities accepted the doctrine. The Kentucky Court of Appeals declared in 1820 that the right to hold slaves was a "right existing by positive law of a municipal character, without foundation in the law of nature, or the unwritten and common law."[57] And Justice Porter of the Louisiana Supreme Court noted in 1827: "by the laws of this country, slavery is permitted, and the rights of the master can be enforced. Suppose the individual subject to it is carried to England or Massachusetts;-would their courts sustain the argument that this state or condition was fixed by the laws of his domicil of origin? We know, they would not."[58]

[55] Jerome Nadelhaft, "The Somerset Case and Slavery: Myth, Reality, and Repercussions," *Journal of Negro History*, 51 (July, 1966): 193–209, traces the use made of the case by abolitionists.

[56] *The Slave Grace*, 2 State Trials, 284–86, (N. S.). Lord Stowell, nevertheless, admitted that Mansfield's decision ended slavery in England, Stowell to Joseph Story, September, 1828, in Catterall, *Judicial Cases*, 1: 36. Story replied that "Upon the fullest consideration, which I have been able to give the subject, I entirely concur in your views. . . . It appears to me that the decision is impregnable." Story to Stowell, September, 1828, in *ibid.*, 37.

[57] *Rankin* v. *Lydia*, 2 A. K. Marshall 470.

[58] *Saul* v. *His Creditors*, 5 Martin (N.S.) 679. Samuel Livermore, who argued this case before Porter, published a work the following year expressing the view that states were under a perfect obligation to give effect to the laws of foreign states. Samuel Livermore, *Dissertations on the Questions which Arise from the Contrariety of the Positive Laws of Different States and Nations* (New Orleans, 1828). William R. Leslie, "The Fugitive Slave Clause, 1787–1842; A Study in American Constitutional History and in the History of the Conflict of Laws" (Ph.D. dissertation, University of Michigan, 1945), 288, noted that this view threw around a man's status the "protecting cloak of universality, at the expense of sovereignty." Leslie has a full and favorable discussion of the case for legal universalism. Scarcely sympathetic to slavery he pointed out that Livermore's doctrine cut both both ways: it also protected the personal status of free blacks.

Writing on the other side during the 1850s, T. R. R. Cobb sharply criticized Lord Mansfield for failing to consider the obligation of the English courts under comity to recognize the status of slavery. He contended that the personal laws of a free state should apply only if a master voluntarily took up a permanent residence in that state; otherwise, the legal principles of the slaveholding community should be respected by the courts of the free states.[59]

When the new American states first confronted this problem, they were bound together under the Articles of Confederation drafted at the beginning of the Revolution. Each state, read Article II, "retains its sovereignty, freedom and independence, and every Power, Jurisdiction and right, which is not by the confederation expressly delegated to the United States, in Congress assembled." In order to "secure and perpetuate mutual friendship" the states agreed to a statement of interstate comity: "Full faith and credit shall be given in each of these states to the records, acts and judicial proceedings of the courts and magistrates of every other state."[60] Since the central government under the articles possessed no coercive power, this clause required only a performance of good faith. As long as a respect for the property interests of slave owners overshadowed the abhorrence of slavery, or concern for peaceful relations was greater than repugnance of the "peculiar institution," interstate comity, of course, could have provided a viable solution to the problems created after 1780 by the abolition of slavery in the North. Pennsylvania, as already noted, made a number of concessions out of comity in its gradual abolition law of 1780. Their importance was made clear in the first case to reach the state supreme court arising under the antikidnapping law of 1788 (which will be discussed in chapter 2). By making these concessions, said the court, "the policy of our own system is reconciled with a due respect to the systems of other States and countries."[61] During the 1780s blacks who made their way to Massachusetts, however, were likely to be declared free on the basis of the doctrines laid down by Lord Mansfield in Sommersett's case.[62]

Under the first constitution of the new American nation, then, the sovereign states were free to reject or qualify any obligation resting on them to give judicial recognition to the laws of foreign states, if they were considered contrary to public policy. They could exclude sojourning slave owners carrying slaves with them, and they could regulate the entire process for the recovery of runaways on their soil, or even refuse to allow such recoveries. With regard to slave owners traveling out of the slave states with slaves, the power of the states above the Mason-Dixon line remained unimpaired down

[59]Cobb, *Law of Slavery*, 173.
[60]Commager, *Documents*, 1: 111.
[61]*Respublica* v. *Richards*, 2 Dallas 227.
[62]Warren Choate Shaw, "The Fugitive Slave Issue in Massachusetts Politics, 1780–1837," (Ph.D. dissertation, University of Illinois, 1938), 11–23.

to the Civil War.[63] After 1787, however, this did not apply in the case of runaways.

When the Constitutional Convention met in Philadelphia in 1787 to "form a more perfect union," fundamental alterations were made in the relationships of the states to one another, and to the central government. Numerous stumbling blocks stood in the way, of course, and not the least of these was the thorny problem of slavery within a federal union. As Pierce Butler of South Carolina remarked: "The security the Southn. States want is that their negroes may not be taken from them which some gentlemen within or without doors, have a very good mind to do."[64] An intricate set of concessions and compromises were effected to quiet the apprehensions of slaveholders. Staughton Lynd, in fact, has argued provocatively that this involved accommodations over the government of the Northwest Territory as well as such concessions as the allowance of increased political strength for slave owners through the three-fifths clause of the Constitution.[65] It also involved an important concession on the matter of the reclamation of fugitive slaves.

Fully two years earlier the free states had shown a willingness to make an accommodation to meet the demands of slave owners. In the spring of 1785 Rufus King revived Jefferson's antislavery clause introduced the year before in the scheme for the government of the western territory. King's antislavery resolution went to a committee made up solely of northerners, who reported back on April 6, 1785, to the Continental Congress. What the committee had done was to tack onto King's resolution a provision for the recovery of fugitive slaves. This compromise was incorporated into the Ordinance of 1787 "without opposition."[66] Slavery would be prohibited in the territories, but at the same time slave owners were guaranteed that "any person escaping into the same, from whom labor or service is lawfully claimed in any one of the original States, such fugitive may be lawfully reclaimed, and conveyed to the person claiming his or her labor or service as aforesaid." The wording used here strongly suggests that this was an affirmation of the so-called right of recaption, but because the states remained sovereign under the Articles of Confederation, it was a guarantee that could not be enforced upon them.

Under the new Constitution it was another matter altogether. Slightly modified, the clause in the Ordinance of 1787 was applied to the Union as a whole when the new Constitution was drafted. Pierce Butler and Charles Pinckney of South Carolina opened up the whole question of runaways in the

[63]Hurd, *Law of Freedom and Bondage*, 2: 219.
[64]Max Farrand, ed., *The Records of the Federal Convention of 1787* (4 vols.; rev. ed.; New Haven and London, 1966), 1: 605.
[65]Staughton Lynd, "The Compromise of 1787," in *Class Conflict, Slavery, and the United States Constitution* (Indianapolis, New York, 1967).
[66]*Journals of the Continental Congress* (34 vols.; Library of Congress ed.; Washington, 1933), 28: 164, 239; 32: 343; Edmund C. Burnett, *Letters of Members of the Continental Congress* (8 vols.; Washington, 1936), 8: 110, 622, 632.

constitutional convention on August 28 when they moved to "require fugitive slaves and servants to be delivered up like criminals." James Wilson of Pennsylvania and Roger Sherman of Connecticut were the only delegates who objected on the floor of the convention. Sherman "saw no more propriety in the public seizing and surrendering a slave or servant, than a horse." Wilson objected because it would "oblige the Executive of the State to do it, at the public expense." Neither man challenged the idea that a runaway slave would remain a slave even though he reached free soil. The states would be bound to give judicial recognition to the status of slavery to the extent that they could not divest owners of runaways of their legitimate titles. There would be, in other words, a federal guarantee of the right of a slave owner to recover his property on free soil. This was the minimum guarantee of the clause that was finally adopted.

The objections to the proposed grant of extraterritorial effect to the laws of the slave states were solely to the suggested method of removal. A reasonable inference to be drawn from Sherman's criticism is that the whole business should be left to the individual exertion of a master, much the same as with the seizure of a horse. The owner of a slave would have the same rights in relation to his slave as he would have to any other variety of personal property. He could exercise a general right of recaption. If there was a dispute about the legitimacy of a seizure, presumably the person seized in the free state would have standing to invoke the state's procedures for the protection of personal freedom. The matter would then be handled much as it was in Pennsylvania.

Wilson's remarks leave a similar impression. It was enough to adopt the same compromise approach followed in Pennsylvania, and later in the Ordinance of 1787, and to make it binding throughout the Union. Such a concession, as important as it was, could be accepted by men who both respected property rights and who thought that slavery as an institution would disappear shortly from the nation. Wilson, for example, later noted that the prohibition on the slave trade laid "the foundation for banishing slavery out of this country." This method would produce "the same kind, gradual change, which was pursued in Pennsylvania."[67] By taking such a pragmatic position they believed they were leaving the way open for a peaceful abolition of the institution, for change without anguish. At the same time, they would be creating a strong national state which they ardently desired.

At any event, the proposal, as first made, was dropped in the face of this opposition. On August 29, 1787, a different version was submitted to the Committee on Style. Some changes were made in the clause on the floor. The most important was the substitution of the words "under the laws thereof" for "legally," since some thought that the latter word might imply that slavery was legal even when not established by positive law. As adopted,

[67]Jonathan Elliott, ed., *The Debates in the Several State Conventions on the Adoption of the Federal Constitution* (5 vols.; Philadelphia, 1836–45), 2: 452.

without a dissenting vote, it read, "No person held to service or labour in one state, under the laws thereof, escaping into another, shall, in consequence of any law or regulation therein, be discharged from such service or labour, but shall be delivered up on claim of the party to whom such service or labour may be due."[68]

Clearly the free states no longer possessed absolute discretion on the matter of runaway blacks. They were prohibited from divesting owners of fugitives of their legitimate titles. But the vital question was left unanswered: who possessed the power and obligation to carry this guarantee into effect? Because the clause was phrased in the passive voice, considerable uncertainty resulted. Was the clause addressed to the federal government, or to the states, or both; or was it meant to be self-operative, merely securing the right of a master to go into the free states and recover his property by his own efforts? If it was the latter, the purpose of the clause would be fulfilled in cases of dispute by the judiciaries, and the judges of the free states, by force of the clause, would be bound to accept as valid the status of slavery created by state law. This view, later adopted by some antislavery people, is lent force by other portions of Article IV, where the fugitive slave clause appears.[69] The clause providing for the extradition of fugitives from justice, for example, stipulates the use of state executives; and Section 1, the full faith and credit clause, stipulates congressional implementation. Still, the guarantee was in the federal Constitution, and some argued later that it was, therefore, a federal responsibility to secure it. Speculations about the intention of the framers, however, are somewhat feckless since the records of the constitutional convention are lean on this matter, and the fugitive clause itself is silent. Perhaps the most that can be said is that a compromise was reached to include nothing precise about the manner of delivery and removal. The few comments available, however, do suggest that at least a general right of recaption was secured.

The debates in the ratification conventions, unfortunately, are no more revealing. Southern antifederalists, who attacked nearly every feature of the proposed Constitution, saw little to praise in the fugitive slave clause. Patrick Henry, for example, said that "it was no more than this—that a runaway negro could be taken up in Maryland or New York." This was no comfort to Henry who perceived so much danger in the taxing power of Congress that the fugitive clause provided little protection for slave owners.[70] James

---

[68]Farrand, *The Records of the Federal Convention of 1787*, 2: 443, 446, 454, 577, 602, 621, 628.

[69]Kempes Y. Schnell, "Court Cases Involving Slavery: A Study of the Application of Antislavery Thought to Judicial Argument," (Ph.D. dissertation, University of Michigan, 1955), 156–57, argued that the fugitive slave clause extended the common-law right of recaption to the free states because the delegates of those states did not want to "overburden" the executive with "routine business."

[70]Elliott, *Debates*, 3: 456. See also *ibid.*, 453.

Madison, on the other side, tried to put the best face possible on the provision. "Another clause," he noted, "secures us that property which we now possess. At present, if any slave elopes to any of those states where slaves are free, he becomes emancipated by their laws; for the laws of states are uncharitable to one another in this respect." The fugitive clause, he concluded, "was expressly inserted, to enable owners of slaves to reclaim them. This is a better security than any that now exists."[71]

Slave owners did not remain content with this uncertain arrangement for very long. What had begun as a problem of turning over to Pennsylvania three citizens of Virginia involved in the murder of four Delaware Indians quickly reached an impasse when the same men were indicted under the Pennsylvania antikidnapping act of 1788.[72] On the surface the question was whether or not Congress should enact a law implementing the fugitive criminal clause of the Constitution. James Innes, the attorney general of Virginia, noted that the delivery and removal requested could be effected only under the authority of the Constitution of the United States, which prescribed no means for such a delivery and removal. According to William R. Leslie, the impasse resulted because no "voluntary constitutional implementation" of the clause of the Constitution seemed likely by the states. Possibly men believed this to be the case, but it does not mean that the states uniformly would refuse to pass implementing legislation, if they considered it their duty, as later developments would show. In the 1790s, in any event, the problem was turned over to Congress, which responded in 1793 with the first federal Fugitive Slave Law.[73]

The original Senate bill (different in some vital particulars from the final law) was reported out of a special committee on December 20, 1792.[74] The members of the committee were Senators George Read of Delaware, George Cabot of Massachusetts, and Samuel Johnston of North Carolina. They reported a bill of three sections. The first two concerned fugitives from justice, and the third dealt with runaway slaves.

[71] *Ibid.*, 3: 453. See also *ibid.*, 458; 4: 176, 286.
[72] William R. Leslie, "A Study in the Origins of Interstate Rendition: The Big Beaver Creek Murders," *American Historical Review*, 57 (Oct., 1951): 68.
[73] *American State Papers* (38 vols.; Washington, D.C., 1832–61), 37: 38–42. This includes all the correspondence laid before Congress on the subject by President Washington on October 27, 1791; Leslie, "A Study in the Origins of Interstate Rendition," 72, takes issue with the position that southerners demanded the act because fugitive slaves were being protected in the North, a position represented by C. W. A. David, "The Fugitive Slave Law of 1793 and its Antecedents," *Journal of Negro History*, 9 (January, 1924): 18–25. Leslie played down the central position of the Negro in the erection of the impasse. He also objected to the idea that the law was designed to prevent the kidnapping of free blacks, an objection that has much more force. This view is represented by Homer Carey Hockett, *The Constitutional History of the United States, 1826–1876* (New York, 1939), 189–90.
[74] The first fugitive slave bill was reported out of a special House committee in November, 1791, but there appears to be no extant copy of this bill. The first Senate draft is in the Senate file, 2A-B1 (Senate Records), National Archives.

The first two sections provided for a regular extradition procedure using state executives. Under the third, a slave claimant would have to present "the depositions of one or more credible persons" (oral testimony would not be accepted) to a magistrate of a county, city, or town corporate. When such evidence was presented a warrant for the arrest of the fugitive would be directed to those persons who, by the laws of the state, were authorized to execute warrants in original prosecutions. Such officers would apprehend the fugitive, and turn him over to the claimant. The person seized would receive no hearing. This was much looser than the final version of the law, but stricter evidentiary requirements were imposed in this draft bill. The remainder of the section provided penalties for obstructing an arrest, harboring a fugitive, or neglecting a duty. Prosecutions would be in courts established under federal authority, while implementation of the procedures for claimants would be in state courts.

The following week this bill was debated, and in the end it was returned to the committee, which was enlarged to include Roger Sherman of Connecticut and John Taylor of Caroline County, Virginia.[75] On January 3, 1793, Johnston reported a substitute bill.[76]

Where the original stipulated that a claim had to be made in the first instance, the new bill provided that a claimant or his agent could seize an alleged fugitive and take him or her before a federal court, or a magistrate of a county, city, or town corporate. Instead of the "depositions of one or more credible persons," the new bill allowed "oral testimony or affidavit" certified by a magistrate of the state from which the slave fled. Upon showing proof of service to the satisfaction of the judge or magistrate, a certificate of removal would be given to the claimant. The active agency in the seizure of a fugitive was to be the claimant himself, given sanction under the federal law. Left open was the question of whether or not a claimant had the right to remove an alleged fugitive without the certificate. If a claimant had not been successful in making a seizure, or, indeed, chose not to exert the effort, he could still, under the new bill, resort to the procedures outlined in the original bill, although there would be a limit on the time between the arrest, and the recovery of his property. If he did not apply in time he would lose his property. The committee then, constructed a compromise on the question of who bore the responsibility for the seizure of runaways.

A vitally important "proviso" also reported by the committee showed that some people were sensitive to the prerogatives of the states, and were aware of the danger to free Negroes in the process of reclamation. It read as follows: "Provided, That if such fugitive from labour is a native of, or hath resided in the state or territory wherein he or she shall be so arrested for the term of——years immediately previous to such arrest, proof of which he or she may produce before such judge or magistrate, no certificate as aforesaid

75 *Annals of Congress*, 2d Cong., 1st sess., Dec. 28, 1793, 623.
76 *Ibid.*, Jan. 3, 1793, 626.

shall be given, but the parties shall be left to contest their rights under the laws of the state where such arrest shall be made." Even though the bill did not mention it, this meant that alleged fugitives, if seized in the free states, might obtain a judicial inquiry into the restraint upon their freedom through habeas corpus, or a jury trial through the writ *de homine replegiando*, since the parties were to contest their rights "under the laws of the state" where they were seized. It also meant that in cases of disputed title the man would be presumed free, until proven otherwise, and that blacks would be allowed to testify in their own behalf, which of course was not true in slave jurisdictions.

The records do not show who proposed the amendments to the committee's substitute, or when, but by January 17, 1793, the bill received a third reading in the Senate, and the following day it passed. On February 4, 1793, it was considered in the House, an amendment was adopted, and the bill was passed.[77] The significant amendments involved striking out the proviso, and the provision for assistance in case a slave owner chose not to make the seizure himself.[78]

Under the act of February 12, 1793, then, a slave owner or his agent was "empowered to seize or arrest such fugitive from labour," and take him before a federal judge within the state, or before "any magistrate of a county, city or town corporate" where the seizure was made. Upon "proof to the satisfaction" of such official "either by oral testimony or affidavit taken before and certified by a magistrate of any state or territory" to the effect that the person seized did owe service, the official had the duty "to give a certificate thereof to such claimant . . . which shall be sufficient warrant for removing the said fugitive from labour, to the state or territory from which he or she fled." Anyone who obstructed a claimant "knowingly and willingly," or concealed a runaway would be subject to a $500 penalty, to go to the claimant on an action of debt.[79] What was provided, in other words, was a summary ministerial hearing, similar to an extradition hearing. Judicial officials in the North had some discretion since the proof offered had to satisfy them that the person seized did owe service. They had no authority to conduct a full investigation if there was a competing claim to freedom, however, and they had no explicit authority to admit the testimony of the person seized, even though it was not excluded in precise terms. According to the Judiciary Act of 1789, the laws of the several states would be rules of decision in federal courts[80] so that a jurist in a free state could, if he chose, bring the fugitive act into harmony with the Judiciary Act by allowing the testimony of a Negro who claimed he was free. The

[77] *Ibid.*, 622–30, 850.
[78] Amendments in the Senate file, 2A-B1.
[79] Richard Peters, ed., *The Public Statutes at Large of the United States of America* (11 vols.; Boston, 1845), Feb. 12, 1793, 1: chap. 7, 303–5.
[80] *Statutes*, Sept. 24, 1789, 1: chap. 20, 73.

language used in the fugitive law, however, strongly suggests that it was the testimony of a claimant alone that was to be admitted into evidence, and it was this testimony that had to "satisfy" the judge. Despite the stipulation in the Judiciary Act, it is clear that in situations involving alleged runaways some laws (those of slave states) were considered more equal than others (those of free states).

Implementing the guarantee in the fugitive slave clause in this way scarcely resolved for long the conflict of legal systems in the new federal Union. Had the states remained completely sovereign they would have resolved conflicts among themselves by comity, or by force. But with the adoption of the Constitution of 1787, slave owners were granted the right to recover their property beyond the borders of their own states, and this guarantee was backed by federal power. The precise relationship between that guarantee and the legal systems of the North, however, was confused. In the 1790s the problem of defining that relationship had barely begun. All that was entirely clear when Congress acted in 1793 was that state officials could be used to hear claims after a seizure had been made by a slave owner or his agent. Free-state congressmen, in the interests of union, had accommodated themselves to proslavery demands by ignoring the potential conflict of claims, the one to slavery, the other to freedom. No separate or additional federal procedures were established to test the second claim. But the real conflict left unresolved by the passage of the 1793 act was between a recognized right of recaption and a passively phrased right of an owner to have his property delivered up, on one hand, and the power of northern states to protect their citizens and others within their jurisdictions from kidnapping and abuse, on the other.

Kidnapping and Fugitives:
Early State and Federal Responses

"The enslaving our fellow-men, and selling them into cruel bondage, is a national evil, and will, I believe, most assuredly draw down national judgments," wrote the Quaker John Parrish in 1806.[1] As early as 1790 antislavery reformers tried to prevent this catastrophe by using federal power to cleanse the nation of the sin of slavery. In that year the petition of the Pennsylvania Abolition Society, whose president was Benjamin Franklin, prayed that Congress would "countenance the restoration of liberty to these unhappy men, who alone, in this land of freedom are degraded into perpetual bondage." Besides a general emancipatory scheme the society asked that Congress "step to the very verge of the power vested in you for discouraging every species of traffic in the persons of our fellow-men."[2]

This petition touched off an explosive response from representatives William L. Smith and Thomas Tudor Tucker of South Carolina. According to Smith the southern states never would have joined the Union if the Constitution had not "provided against the effect" of any "disposition" toward "general emancipation." Tucker was even more impassioned as he berated the abolitionists and warned the North: "Do these men expect a general emancipation of slaves by law? This would never be submitted to by the Southern States without a civil war."[3] There was, however, no reason to fear that northern congressmen would act to endanger the set of compromises involving slavery worked out in 1787 in order to ensure stability to the new Union. Elbridge Gerry of Massachusetts, who went further than most in Congress in support of federal power, for example, still deferred to the sensibilities of slave-owning communities. Congress, he said, had the right "if they see proper, to make a proposal to the Southern States" to purchase all slaves (this was to be paid for out of the resources of the Western lands).[4] Indeed, no one in Congress seriously objected when the House proceeded to adopt a self-denying resolution: "That Congress have no authority to interfere in the emancipation of slaves, or in the treatment of them within any of

[1]John Parrish, *Remarks on the Slavery of the Black People: Addressed to the Citizens of the United States, Particularly to those who are in Legislative or Executive Stations in the General or State Governments; and also to such Individuals as Hold them in Bondage* (Philadelphia, 1806), 3.
[2]*Annals of Congress*, 1st Cong., 2d sess., February 12, 1790, 1239–40.
[3]*Ibid.*, 1240, 1244.
[4]*Ibid.*, 1247. Cf. Dwight Lowell Dumond, *Antislavery: The Crusade for Freedom in America* (New York, 1961), 55.

the States; it remaining with the several states alone to provide any regulations therein, which humanity and true policy may require."[5] A national emancipation law then was constitutionally impermissible. The states would be at liberty to define their own social institutions unrestrained by any significant national laws or policies.

This operated as a powerful constraint upon the efforts of the gradual abolitionists, many of whom (such as Alexander Hamilton and John Jay of the New York Manumission Society) had played a significant role in the formation of the new Union. When the federal government refused to assert a right to eliminate gradually the property interest in human beings, most antislavery people[6] in the free states saw little alternative but to try to separate sharply slavery and freedom at both the state and federal levels, and to assure that those who were free would not be deprived of their personal liberty. These efforts reflected a broad commitment to a pattern of civility measured by access to traditional legal guarantees of personal freedom, and by the prosecution of those who sought to deprive another person of that freedom illegitimately. But it was a commitment bounded not only by ardent unionism but by the imperatives and uncertainties of federalism, by a continued recognition of the lawful holding of persons as property, and by a sometimes shortsighted appraisal of social reality. Despite the genuine commitment to the advance of human freedom, there remained an air of unreality about these early efforts because they were usually pursued without examining the social disabilities faced by black people, such as their inability independently to employ legal counsel, and their frequent ignorance or apathy about the so-called rule of law. The presumption of freedom for all men of course was a vitally important gain, and existing state procedures, such as habeas corpus and *homine replegiando*, could be used to free a person from an unlawful detention. The Pennsylvania Abolition Society, for one, often employed the latter writ to secure freedom to those blacks lawfully entitled to it.[7] As important as this was, however, it was not

[5] *Annals*, 1st Cong., 2d sess., March 23, 1790, 1524.

[6] Granville Sharp, the English abolitionist, was one person who did challenge the Fugitive Slave Law. In a letter to Maryland abolitionists he called it a "corruption, null and void in itself." Since it violated the divine law, and was contrary to the law of reason, he concluded, it could impose no binding obligation upon anyone. *Letter from Granville Sharp of London to the Maryland Society for Promoting the Abolition of Slavery, and the Relief of Free Negroes and others, Unlawfully Held in Bondage* (Baltimore, 1793), 3. See also George Bourne, *The Book and Slavery Irreconcilable: With Animadversions upon Dr. Smith's Philosophy* (Philadelphia, 1816), 27; Lydia Maria Child, *Isaac T. Hopper: A True Life* (Boston, 1853), 33–35. Among the first expressions of discontent in the United States was the following: "A Bill has passed both houses . . . entit. An Act respecting Fugitives, which, . . . , there is reason to fear will be productive of mischievous consequences." "G. G." to Alexander Addison, February 2, 1793, Philadelphia, Manuscript Collection Belonging to the Pennsylvania Society for Promoting the Abolition of Slavery, Historical Society of Pennsylvania, 3: 285. "G. G." did not state his objection precisely.

[7] Pennsylvania Abolition Society, Acting Committee, Minutes 1 (1798–1810); Pennsylvania Abolition Society Papers, Legal Section & Miscellany-Runaway Slaves, Historical Society

enough to stop the practice of kidnapping as long as blacks had to rely upon the intervention of a benevolent white, and as long as they had to face such uncertainties as whether or not a judge would admit black testimony in cases arising under the federal law, or would use habeas corpus to conduct a full inquiry into competing claims. Until they faced these elemental problems, the efforts of the early abolitionists, who approached their task from a socially conservative standpoint, often seem abstract and circuitous.

Until shortly after the War of 1812, antislavery people concentrated on an effort to secure both state and federal laws to deter or punish kidnapping, but they had simultaneously to confront some serious constitutional problems. Could Congress, for example, even legislate such matters? Everyone admitted that the states possessed sufficient power to punish outright kidnapping, but even so difficult questions remained. What was the precise effect, for example, of the federally recognized right of recaption upon the state's right to protect those within its jurisdiction who claimed to be free from a forcible and private deprivation of liberty?

Both Pennsylvania and Massachusetts had adopted their basic antikidnap laws before the new federal government was established under the Constitution of 1787. But the problems, and the policies, of these two states were notably different. On one hand, Massachusetts, in which slavery had disintegrated, and which had little direct and continuous contact with well-established slave-owning communities (except by sea), displayed a marked legal hostility to the institution. Its antikidnap law, part of the 1785 habeas corpus statute, made no distinction between a free black and a slave. After 1788 the only limitation upon the state's policy was the federal guarantee to slaveholders that they could recover their property, but the exact manner in which this qualified the state law on kidnapping was unclear. Antislavery people in Massachusetts remained content with this cloudy legal situation until the rise of the immediatist movement in the 1830s provoked a reexamination of the state's policies. Pennsylvania, on the other hand, was in a different position because of its location, and because of the accommodations that had been made with slave owners in 1780. Because of the state's continued recognition of a legitimate property interest in men, and of a general right of recaption, antislavery people faced the continuous problem of protecting free men, or those entitled to ultimate freedom, from the assaults of slaveholders.

Within a year after the passage of the gradual abolition act of 1780, the assaults began when slave owners requested an extension of time in which to register their property. This effort was defeated by a vigorous protest at the clear injustice of returning to slavery blacks who had been freed by their

---

of Pennsylvania, *passim*; see also Minutes of the Proceedings of the New York Society for promoting the Manumission of Slaves, (January 16, 1798–December 12, 1814), New York Historical Society, *passim*, hereafter cited as N.Y. Manumission Soc. Minutes; and Catterall, *Judicial Cases*, 4: 243, 251, 256, 258, 262–63, 271, 273–75, 277–78, 280, 282, 285, 372, 385, 389, 391.

master's failure to register them.[8] Unscrupulous slaveholders, undeterred by this failure, devised methods for defeating the operation of the law. Some would sell young blacks out of the state; others would take pregnant slaves over the borders to deliver, and then return with the mother alone.

To prevent such abuses the legislature adopted in 1788 an act supplementing the law of 1780. Under the terms of this new act no one coming into the state with the intention of becoming a resident was allowed to bring slaves. Indentured servants or slaves could not be removed from the state, with the object of changing their domicile, without their consent, and the consent of parents in the case of children. And the penalty for kidnapping any black with the intention of selling him into slavery was fixed at six months hard labor, and a one-hundred pound fine. No distinction was made between a free black and a slave, but, at the same time, masters possessed a general right of recaption under the law of 1780.[9] This difficulty was faced by the state supreme court in 1795 when a case arose in which a slave owner was indicted under the state's basic antikidnapping law of 1788 for seizing one of his runaways and taking him out of the state. "We were unanimously of opinion," commented the jurists, "as soon as it was proved the negro was a slave, that . . . his master had a right to seize and carry him away."[10]

By the turn of the century antislavery people increasingly were becoming aware of the prevalence and forms of kidnapping. In 1794 a national organization, the American Convention of Abolition Societies, had been formed to function as a national forum and coordinator for the antislavery movement. In 1801 the convention alerted member societies to the fact that "the inhuman crime of kidnapping . . . in some parts of our country, has recently increased to an alarming degree."[11] Two years later the New York Manumission Society reported to the convention that kidnapping had taken a new form: false claims made under the Fugitive Slave Law. "We recommend you," the convention response read, "to urge every suitable means to procure such modifications of your laws as they may need to fit them for holding out efficient and prompt restraints against these wicked proceedings, and for bringing the offenders to exemplary punishment."[12]

During the years before the War of 1812 antislavery people in Pennsylvania, along with those in New York where a similar legal situation existed, were the most active in the movement to secure new state laws. Perhaps the most notable thing about their effort was its moderation: in no way did they

[8]Zilversmit, *The First Emancipation*, 133–36.

[9]Dallas, *Laws of the Commonwealth*, 2: 586–90. On the passage of the 1788 law see Zilversmit, *The First Emancipation*, 133–36.

[10]*Respublica* v. *Richards*, Dallas 227.

[11]*Minutes of the Proceedings of a Convention of Delegates from the Abolition Societies Established in different Parts of the United States, assembled at Philadelphia* (Philadelphia, 1801), 40. The annual reports of this body, known as the American Convention of Abolition Societies, will be cited hereafter as the *Minutes of the American Convention.*

[12]*Ibid.*, 1803, 7.

challenge the state recognition of a legitimate property interest in human beings. As long as it was law they would acquiesce.

There were several attempts, all unsuccessful, to obtain changes in the Pennsylvania law of 1788. In 1811, to take one example, the Pennsylvania Abolition Society praised the "humane Policy of Penn.," but pointed out that the crime of "Man stealing" had not been prevented. Its recommendation was an increased fine. The state took no action, however, until the 1820s despite the continued interest of the antislavery people.[13]

Abolitionists in New York during these years achieved some notable successes, but they also suffered some important setbacks. As early as November, 1800, the New York Manumission Society noted that a domestic slave trade was being carried on "in violation of the spirit and intent" of the recent gradual abolition law; serious defects enabled "unprincipled men" to seize indented and free blacks for sale as slaves. Although it would work to put an end to such practices, the society avowed that it would not seek to disturb the rights of citizens of other states who "with their domestics remove into this State, or remove therefrom to any other State in the Union."[14]

In April, 1801, New York's legislature responded with a law framed to fulfill primarily the narrow purpose of interdicting the interstate slave trade.[15] According to the new law no slave could be brought into the state unless the owner stated under oath that he intended to reside there permanently, which would bring him within the act of 1799. A sojourner clause, however, allowed citizens of other states to travel through New York with their property. Another provision of this law amounted to a serious misfortune for Negroes entitled to ultimate freedom. Owners who had lived in the state for a year or more would be allowed to take their slaves with them if they were leaving permanently, which was a concession to slave owners Pennsylvania had refused to make in 1788. Before an owner removed his property, however, satisfactory proof had to be offered that he held a legitimate title to the person. If the proof was accepted the owner would receive a license to remove the black. Any master of a vessel who accepted a slave on board for the purpose of transportation out of the state could be fined if the slave was not accompanied with such a license.

This law was designed as a compromise: it would help cut off the slave trade, provide a minimum guarantee that free blacks would not be removed as slaves, and yet give masters the right to leave the state permanently with their property. It seriously infringed upon the right to ultimate freedom of a slave who came within the terms of the 1799 gradual abolition law, and

[13]*Penn. House Journal, 1803,* 77, 376, 567, 593; *ibid., 1805,* 142; *ibid., 1806,* 26, 31, 264; Minutes of the Pennsylvania Society for Promoting the Abolition of Slavery, (1800–1824), Historical Society of Pennsylvania, 2: 159. Hereafter cited as Penn. Abolition Soc. Minutes. *Penn. Senate Journal, 1811,* 109, 186, 214–15.

[14]N.Y. Manumission Soc. Minutes, (January 16, 1798–December 12, 1814), 48, 50–51.

[15]*New York Session Laws, 1801,* 547–52.

showed clearly the very cautious approach adopted to securing human freedom in the face of a competing claim to labor and service.

Unsatisfied but still cautious, the manumission society in 1807 suggested that this new law be amended to require a person leaving the state with a slave to prove by two credible witnesses that he had resided in the state during the past year, and that the slave had been in his service during that time. Since kidnappers would have few scruples about swearing false oaths, it was suggested that all the pains and penalties attached to perjury be extended to anyone giving a false deposition or swearing a false oath.[16] These suggestions were not adopted, but the following year the legislature did adopt an important antikidnap law. The penalty for kidnapping a black was fixed at fourteen years of hard labor. A second offense carried with it the penalty of "imprisonment at hard labor, or in solitude, or both, in said prison, for and during his natural life." Perhaps of more importance was the fact that this law brought New York's position into harmony with Pennsylvania's. It specified that a person "not being a slave" could not be removed from the state without "due process of law."[17] This was framed carefully to leave intact a general right of recaption while, at the same time, it meant that in cases of disputed claims the status of the person seized would be determined in New York, just as it was in Pennsylvania.

In 1813 the laws of New York were revised, and the penalties in the law of 1808 were reduced. At the same time, however, the revisers expressed their disgust with kidnappers when they included in their marginalia a reference to Exodus 21:16: "Whoever steals a man, whether he sells him or is found in possession of him, shall be put to death."[18]

New York enacted its antikidnapping legislation later than Pennsylvania, and, under the increased awareness of the crime after the turn of the century, provided more rigorous punishments. But the New York law, like Pennsylvania's, was built around a continued recognition that a legitimate property interest in people might exist. Both states, moreover, recognized a right of recaption but acted to secure a hearing within their own jurisdictions whenever there was a competing claim to freedom.

Although Massachusetts had refused to give legal recognition to a right of recaption when it adopted its basic antikidnap law in 1785 (part of its habeas corpus statute), the state policy was qualified by the federal fugitive slave clause. The federal guarantee placed Massachusetts in a position similar to that of New York and Pennsylvania, although it was not directly and dramatically confronted for some years.

Ohio's position in the first two decades of the nineteenth century was somewhat different. In 1804 Ohio provided explicit state procedures for the aid of claimants seeking the recovery of their property. These procedures

[16]N.Y. Manumission Soc. Minutes, (January 16, 1798–December 12, 1814), 106.
[17]*New York Session Laws, 1809*, 800. The New York Manumission Society claimed credit for this law. See the *Minutes of the American Convention 1809*, 9.
[18]*New York Session Laws, 1813*, 210.

were favorable to claimants, but they were eliminated in 1807. If anyone availed himself of the aid of Ohio's proffered support, however, he had to follow through; if he did not, he could be prosecuted for the removal of a black by self-help alone. In other words, the spur to action apparently was a concern for orderly procedure and respect for state processes rather than any hostility to the "rights" of slave owners. The penalty imposed was comparatively light and did not include a prison sentence.[19]

Virtually no one argued for increased penalties in this border state until the conclusion of the War of 1812, when both New York and Ohio provided new and more stringent penalties.[20] At that time, 1819, Ohio moved in a new direction to ensure orderly removals. Anyone who removed a black (any black) from the state without following the procedures outlined in the federal law of 1793 would be deemed guilty of a high misdemeanor. This was the first explicit refusal to recognize a general right of recaption by self-help alone, among those states studied here, after the adoption of the fugitive slave clause of the Constitution. Sadly the records in no way reveal why Ohio, which had shown more solicitude for the rights of claimants than any of the other states examined, took this step to eliminate one of those rights, one apparently recognized by the Constitution itself. A strong possibility, in view of its regard for orderly procedures shown even in its antiblack law of 1804, was a concern to provide a stable and ordered method of removal in place of the personalized "justice" represented by the "natural" right of recaption. This can only be established inferentially, however, and must remain obscure. Ohio's action, nevertheless, pointed a new direction that certain other states would follow in the 1820s.

Through the first two decades of the nineteenth century, then, the free states acted to secure a hearing within their jurisdictions for those who claimed to be free in the face of a competing claim to slavery, and at the same time they continued to accept the fact that a general right of recaption existed. This latter was a right Pennsylvania had conceded to slave owners even before the adoption of the Constitution, and after that, the federal guarantee served to qualify the state policy of Massachusetts, New York, and Ohio. It tended to constrict the legal remedies that these states would adopt in ensuring freedom to those entitled to it and protecting those claimed as slaves from being abused on free soil. All these early antikidnap laws, of course, were constructed around the premise that the federal constitution had provided an extraterritorial security to owners of slave property in the form of the fugitive slave clause. They were very cautious and carefully framed statutes.

Nearly everyone admitted that the states possessed ample power to punish kidnappers, but the power of Congress was another matter entirely. During the last four years of the eighteenth century, anti- and

---

[19] *Ohio Session Laws, 1804,* 356.
[20] *New York Session Laws, 1819,* chap. 41, Sec. 2; *Acts of a General Nature, Enacted, revised and ordered to be printed* (Columbus, Ohio, 1823), 338.

proslavery people were engaged in a debate to define the power and obligation of the federal government to protect free blacks from being forcibly restrained of their liberty, either by outright kidnappers or under color of the federal Fugitive Slave Law.

The first time Congress faced the problem was in 1796 when the Committee of Commerce and Manufactures asked instructions to bring in a bill requiring a ship's master to have a certificate "of the number and situation of any negroes or mulattoes he may have on board."[21] Registration would provide a relatively disinterested standard for distinguishing free blacks from slaves, and to that degree it would discourage kidnapping. Speaking on the committee's report John Swanwick of Pennsylvania noted that people, regardless of color, "if free . . . ought to be protected in the enjoyment of their freedom, not by state Legislatures but by the General Government."[22]

Slave owners, led by William L. Smith of South Carolina, were opposed to giving such instructions. Smith, although a determined nationalist in this period of his career,[23] had led the opposition to the commitment of the abolitionist petition in 1790, and he continued to oppose any federal action that might adversely affect slavery. The subject before the House, he contended, was a matter for local, not national regulation: kidnapping was one of those subjects left to the states by the Constitution.[24]

Several others doubted the "propriety" of using congressional power. Joshua Coit of Connecticut admitted the problem of kidnapping existed, but he feared greater evils if Congress acted. Besides, he observed, the "laws in the several States were fully adequate to the subject without further provisions."[25] Edward Livingston, moreover, found it difficult to understand "how the laws of the General Government could operate over those of the several States."[26] Swanwick pointed out that the federal law would provide some protection for free men in a region not covered by state antikidnapping laws, the interstate waters.[27] On January 12, 1797, the commerce committee, instructed to report by bill or otherwise, submitted a brief statement: "It is not expedient for this House to interfere with any existing law of the States on this subject."[28]

Within two weeks Swanwick again brought Congress' attention to the problem when he presented a petition of four former slaves. The petitioners cited the case of a man manumitted in North Carolina who was confined in the Philadelphia jail under the federal fugitive law. By virtue of a North Carolina law he had been seized after his manumission and resold into

[21]*Annals*, 4th Cong., 1st sess., April 18, 1796, 1025; *ibid.* Dec. 29, 1796, 1730.
[22]*Ibid.* Dec. 29, 1796, 1733.
[23]George C. Rogers, Jr., *Evolution of a Federalist: William Loughton Smith of Charleston (1758-1812)* (Columbia, S.C., 1962), 193 ff.
[24]*Annals*, 4th Cong., 1st sess., Dec. 29, 1796, 1731, 1734.
[25]*Ibid.*, 1730.
[26]*Ibid.*, 1730-31.
[27]*Ibid.*, 1731.
[28]*Ibid.*, Jan. 18, 1797, 1895.

slavery. He had then escaped, arriving finally in Philadelphia. At the time of his seizure as a runaway he had lived in that city for several years with his wife and children. His claimant had advertised for him "offering a reward of ten silver dollars to any person that would bring him back, or five times that sum to any person that would make due proof of his being killed, and no questions asked by whom." The petitioners who described this case prayed that "that public justice and protection which is the great object of Government" be extended to their class.[29]

What followed was the first direct criticism of the Fugitive Slave Law in Congress. Joseph B. Varnum of Massachusetts objected particularly to the allowance of ex parte testimony, an objection that would swell to major proportions shortly after the War of 1812. The danger in this, in his view, was obvious: "the person may be a freeman, for it would not be easy to know whether the evidence was good, at a distance from the State; the poor man is then sent to his State in slavery."[30] Varnum's language suggests that he believed an alleged slave possessed no right to testify in his own behalf under the federal law on runaways, which stood as an exception to the Judiciary Act of 1789 that provided that the laws of the several states would be rules of decision in federal courts hearing cases in those states.

Thomas Blount of North Carolina, on the other side, asked simply "what evidence there was to prove these men free, and except that was proved, the House had no right to attend to the petition."[31] James Madison added that if the blacks were free by the laws of North Carolina "they ought to apply to those laws, and have their privilege established." If they were slaves, "the Constitution gives them no hopes of being heard here."[32] The slave state law then closed off a full-scale congressional debate at that time.

Because this petition concerned a man who was a slave under the laws of a southern state, proslavery congressmen were able to divert this prayer for "public justice." When a number of free blacks from Philadelphia submitted a petition to Congress two years later, however, the legislators were forced to adopt a different strategy.

The Philadelphia Negroes asked for a national plan of abolition, the prohibition of the slave trade, and changes in the Fugitive Slave Law. They prayed for "justice and equity to all classes." "As we are men, we should be admitted to partake of the liberties and unalienable rights therein [in the Bill of Rights] held forth." The fugitive law, they contended, bore hard on the free black.[33]

[29] *Ibid.* Jan. 30, 1797, 2015–18. This petition is reprinted in Herbert Aptheker, ed., *A Documentary History of the Negro People in the United States* (2 vols.; New York, 1968), 1: 40–44.

[30] *Annals*, 4th Cong., 1st sess., Jan. 30, 1797, 2023.

[31] *Ibid.*, 2019.

[32] *Ibid.*, 2020.

[33] The Petition of the People of Colour, free men, within the City and Suburbs of Philadelphia, December 30, 1799, 6A.G1.1 (House Records), National Archives. This petition was reprinted in full in Parrish, *Remarks on the Slavery of the Black People*, 49–51, and summarized in Aptheker, *A Documentary History*, 44.

Those who argued for commitment of this petition conceded that Congress had no power to deal with the "general principles involved." Robert Waln of Pennsylvania, who submitted the petition, granted that Congress could not adopt a general plan of emancipation: that much had been decided in 1790. But Congress did have the power "of legislating on the state of free blacks."[34]

Proslavery congressmen, their fears doubtless intensified by the recent slave insurrection on Santo Domingo in the Caribbean, focused on the plea for a national abolition law. Henry Lee of Virginia, the famous "Light Horse Harry" of the Revolution, for example, argued that "that property which the people of the Southern States possess consisted of slaves, and therefore Congress had no authority but to protect it, and not take measures to deprive citizens of it."[35]

Once he conceded that Congress could not abolish slavery, Waln introduced a motion to commit only that portion of the petition relating to the slave trade and the Fugitive Slave Law. This was agreed to, and the petition went to a special committee which had already been set up to consider the slave trade. Someone on this committee drafted an elaborate report, but it was never submitted to the House for reasons which remain unclear.[36]

Free blacks, according to its author, were being seized as runaway slaves and sent into the interstate and foreign slave trade. "There is reason to believe," he wrote, "that many Blacks & People of Colour entitled to their Freedom in the former States (Delaware and Maryland) are under color of the Fugitive Law entrapped, kidnapped & carried off to the latter States (Carolina & Georgia) & to the West Indies, where their color is sufficient Evidence to hold them in a State of Slavery." The laws of the states, he believed, were insufficient to check this traffic because there was "a Defect of Power in the State Legislatures to Regulate & prescribe the Formalities to prevent them [the abuses of state laws] when Persons described in the Fugitive Law are to be transported by water."

The report suggested that a bill should be adopted "supplementary to the Fugitive Law providing that no Person claimed under that Law shall be removed from the State where he or she may be found without an examination first had before two Justices of the county & an Adjudication thereupon that he or she comes within the Description of the said Law." Had such a bill been introduced and passed it would have altered completely the existing law. Federal judicial power could have been exercised by state judges who would determine conclusively that a person claimed was or was not a runaway who owed service or labor. State courts, of course, already exercised

---

[34] *Annals*, 6th Cong., 1st sess., Jan. 2, 1800, 230.

[35] *Ibid.*, 231.

[36] The handwritten report of the committee was filed with the Jones petition, with the notation on the outside that it was not submitted to the House. 6A.G1.1 (House Records), National Archives. Since it was never submitted for consideration it is a mystery how, or why, this report was ever filed. Neither the *Annals* nor the *House Journal* provides a clue.

federal judicial power, but only in a preliminary hearing. The proposed supplement provided for a full judicial ınquiry, which would include the admission of testimony by the alleged slave.

Despite the fact that the petition provoked nothing more concrete than an unsubmitted, unsigned report, both the petition and the report show that some people at the turn of the century were not satisfied with the federal law on runaway slaves. After the turn of the century the one feature of that law singled out as particularly dangerous was the section concerning affidavits.

Before such criticism became widespread, Congress finally legislated on one of the problems discussed in the earlier debates, by the abolition societies and by state legislatures: the interstate slave trade. Section 9 of the March, 1807, act on the African slave trade provided that before any black could be transported in the coastwise trade the captain and owner of the vessel had to swear an oath that the person about to be shipped was legitimately held to service or labor. This distinguished the prohibited foreign from the domestic slave trade and provided a minimal protection for free blacks who might be caught up in the interstate traffic.[37]

But, at best, this was only a marginal victory. This law did not lead to the same "kind" and "gradual" abolition of slavery occurring in Pennsylvania as some had hoped. By the War of 1812, antislavery people were anxiously and hopefully turning to the federal government to secure more significant action against kidnapping. In 1812, for the first time, one of the state abolition societies urged, in a report to the American Convention, that a "general law" on kidnapping should be passed by Congress whose "scope and provision shall be as comprehensive as the evil, and whose features shall have more uniformity [than state legislation]."[38]

By the conclusion of the war with Britain, a favorable climate of opinion seemingly existed in which to obtain some federal action on behalf of free blacks. A wide-ranging humanitarianism swept the United States after 1815, as the country critically turned inward on itself. Reformism found many outlets with the coming of peace, both here and abroad, and it was in this sensitized atmosphere that Jesse Torrey published in Philadelphia in 1817 the first extended account of the interstate slave trade. He showed that although some of the people sold had been kidnapped outright, others had been the victims of false claims made under the federal law.[39] "They have lately invented a method of attaining their objects," he wrote, "through the instrumentality of the laws;-Having selected a suitable free coloured person,

[37]*Statutes*, March 2, 1807, 2: chap. 22, 426.
[38]*Minutes of the American Convention 1812*, 10.
[39]Jesse Torrey, *American Slave Trade; or, An Account of the Manner in which the Slave Dealers take Free People from some of the United States of America, and sell them as Slaves in other of the States* . . . (London, 1822), 66. See also the *Minutes of the American Convention 1819*, 34, 39–40; *Niles' Weekly Register*, 13: 80, 377; 14: 223, 328; 15: 267, 268, 384.

to make a *pitch* upon, the *conjuring* kidnapper employs a confederate, to ascertain the distinguishing marks of his body and then claims and obtains him as a slave, before a magistrate, by describing those marks, and proving the truth of the assertions, by his well-instructed accomplice."[40] Torrey expressed the hopes of most antislavery people when he wrote that Congress should legislate to "confine the traffic *totally* to legal *slaves*."[41]

Since proslavery congressmen had frustrated every effort[42] to secure a federal antikidnap law by arguing that the punishment of the crime was solely a state matter, antislavery people now turned more and more to a demand for changes in the testimonial provision of the Fugitive Slave Law of 1793 to achieve the objective set out by Torrey. Writing in 1816, Richard Peters, Jr., later a reporter of the U.S. Supreme Court, contended that admitting ex parte testimony violated "one of the fundamental principles of the administration of justice" because it allowed a decision "against the liberty of a fellow man, upon allegations, which he had no opportunity to contradict, and the witness in support of which, he is not permitted to confront or interrogate." Admitting such testimony as evidence, the Pennsylvania Abolition Society noted, laid the "foundation for a decision, by which all rights are destroyed." The real animus of the antislavery criticism became clear when Peters pointed out that some jurists had accepted the view that the production of the certificate granted after the summary hearing "is a sufficient return to any writ of Habeas Corpus, which may be issued, at any place between that where the arrest was made and the state or territory to which he or she is to be conducted."[43] Or as the Pennsylvania abolitionists observed, the production of the certificate "is a full answer to any writ of habeas corpus, or other judicial process, issued to examine into the right of the persons holding it, to detain the individual it described."[44] In other words, the legal processes of the free states, particularly the habeas corpus, which could assure that only "legal *slaves*" might be returned were subordinated to the needs of slave owners.

[40]*Ibid.*, 89–90.

[41]*Ibid.*, 52.

[42]Some people sought to achieve the objective by means of improvements in the 1807 law on the slave trade. Memorial of the Yearly Meeting of the Society of Friends held at Baltimore, against the traffic in Slavery, November 8, 1817. Memorial of the Philanthropic Society of Easton, Maryland, January 1818, 15A.G12.2 (Senate Records), National Archives; see also the Memorial of the Subscribers, citizens of the said United States, (n.d.; went to Committee on January 14, 1817), 14A.G13.3 (Senate Records) National Archives; The Memorial of the Representatives of the religious Society of Friends in Pennsylvania, New Jersey, Delaware, and the Eastern Shore of Maryland, December 20, 1816, 14A.G1.1 (House Records), National Archives.

[43]Richard Peters, Jr., to William Wayne, Philadelphia, December 31, 1816, Manuscript Collection Belonging to the Pennsylvania Society for Promoting the Abolition of Slavery, Historical Society of Pennyslvania, 7: 291.

[44]The Petition of the Pennsylvania Society for promoting the Abolition of Slavery . . . , January 20, 1817, 14A.G13.3 (Senate Records), National Archives.

Some free state jurists adopted a narrow view of the scope of their power under the state habeas corpus when confronted with a detention under the federal fugitive law. This made cases involving alleged runaways an important exception to the trend in the development of state habeas corpus jurisdiction. During the War of 1812 the New York Supreme Court marked that growth in the writ's usage by freeing a person from the custody of United States Army officers. Although he dissented at that time Chancellor William Kent, in his massive commentary on American law, later approved the contention that state courts had jurisdiction to issue the writ for persons held under federal authority, and even free them if the facts warranted.[45] The reticence of some free state judges to employ the writ in this way, in cases involving alleged fugitives, deeply disturbed many northerners.

Southerners were equally dissatisfied with the situation existing under the federal fugitive law. According to proslavery people northern courts often favored claims to freedom,[46] and in some areas antislavery people continuously flouted the law by assisting runaways, and without penalty. As early as 1793 southern congressmen pointed out that people in the South considered "it a great injury to the owners of that species of property, that runaways were employed in the Middle and Northern States, and even assisted in procuring a living."[47] As for the legal processes of the free states, Judge Spencer Roane of Virginia forcefully stated the proslavery view in December, 1821, in *Lewis* v. *Fullerton*: the right to reclaim fugitive slaves would be "nearly a nullity" if the courts of the free states could confer liberty by the simple expedient of a habeas corpus.[48]

After the war, with the demand for federal security for the personal liberty of those entitled to freedom rising in volume, and with the proslavery dissatisfaction with the existing law also rising, a major confrontation in Congress finally occurred. It came in late 1817 when a special House committee began considering the question of more effectively providing for the recovery of fugitives. On December 29, 1817, this committee introduced a bill to amend the act of 1793.[49]

One of the most notable things about the bill was its complete one-sidedness. It was a clear and complete statement of the proslavery viewpoint. It made northern judicial officers little more than agents of the southern courts, and required free state executives actively to assist in the arrest of runaways (the fugitive slave clause itself, of course, had assumed the form it

[45]Kent, *Commentaries*, 1: 448.
[46]In many cases they did favor such claims. Schnell, "Court Cases Involving Slavery," 164. A specific example would be the 1805 case involving Pierce Butler, a member of Congress from South Carolina. *Butler* v. *Hopper*, 4 Fed. Cas. 904 (1 Wash. C. C. 498).
[47]The southern view is summarized in McDougall, *Fugitive Slaves*, 20; *Annals*, 4th Cong., 1st sess., Dec. 29, 1796; Jan. 2, 1797, 1740–41, 1767.
[48]*Lewis* v. *Fullerton*, 1 Randolph's Reports, 23.
[49]*Annals*, 15th Cong., 1st sess., Dec. 15, 1817; Dec. 29, 1817, 466, 447, 513. The bill is numbered "H. R. 18, 15th Cong., 1st sess." (House Records), National Archives.

did because of opposition to such involvement).[50] The bill provided that if a judge or magistrate of the slave state from which a man fled was presented with satisfactory proof that the person claimed did owe service and labor, a certificate would be granted. This certificate would then be presented to any judge of a federal or state court, or a justice of the peace, in the state to which the fugitive escaped. It would then be the duty of such official to issue a warrant for the arrest of the runaway. Once apprehended the black would be brought before the official issuing the warrant. At the hearing all that was necessary to authorize a removal was the testimony of one person by "affidavit or otherwise," identifying the person arrested as the one named in the certificate. Once this was done the judge or magistrate would turn the black over to a state official who would deliver him or her to the claimant, or his agent, for removal.

Another provision of the original bill arousing excitement in Congress concerned the effect on the laws of the free states of a certificate granted in the southern states. This section was a bold and aggressive attempt to undermine the legal systems of the northern states insofar as they protected the personal liberty of blacks who might be claimed as slaves. Anyone who had obtained a certificate would have been granted immunity from any action, suit, or process prosecuted by or in behalf of the fugitive named, and from any arrest, or imprisonment for any crime growing out of the seizure, except for mayhem or murder. No one with a certificate could be arrested "by reason of pretence of assaulting, beating, imprisoning or otherwise maltreating such fugitive." A claimant could not have had his goods or chattels distrained or attached, which happened if there was a failure to answer a writ *de homine replegiando*. Neither a habeas corpus, nor a writ *de homine replegiando* could be used to examine the validity of a seizure under federal law (although these writs were not mentioned by name in the bill). If any officer issued any process to test the legality of such a seizure he would have to forfeit a sum to be specified in an action of debt. The courts of the North, in other words, were to be made completely subordinate to those of the South.

Several northern congressmen responded boldly to this obvious effort to subordinate both federal law and the laws of the free states to the needs of slave-owning communities, but they did not adopt a uniform constitutional position. Clifton Clagett in the House, and David Morrill in the Senate (both from New Hampshire) charged that the use to be made of state judicial officers was unconstitutional because it involved an illegitimate delegation of federal power. "The Courts of the United States," said Clagett, "are the only proper tribunals to take cognizance of the subject; the magistrates of a State, as such, are not bound by your law." Granting a warrant authorizing the seizure of a man, said Morrill, was a "preparatory judicial" act which was

[50]Cf. McDougall, *Fugitive Slaves*, 21.

part of the federal power; as such it could be exercised only by federal instrumentalities. In their view, a complete separation existed between the national and state governments, each being sovereign within its own proper sphere. Although neither cited Joseph Story's opinion for the U.S. Supreme Court in *Martin* v. *Hunter's Lessee*, decided at the February term 1816, it is likely they had it in mind. "The whole judicial power of the United States," Story had written, "should be, at all times, vested either in an original or appellate form, in some courts created under its authority."[51] Since state officials derived no part of their authority from the federal government they could not be vested with any part of the federal judicial power, Clagett argued.[52]

Congress, James Pindall of Virginia replied to such arguments, had often passed laws depending on the state courts for execution. Although he did not elaborate the cases in which Congress had given federal duties to state judges, he was right in saying that it had. James Kent, in his monumental study of American law, for example, noted that under acts of 1806, 1808, and 1815, county courts in certain revenue districts were authorized to take cognizance of prosecutions arising under the revenue laws of the United States.[53] Despite the fact that Congress had delegated such authority, however, some jurists contended that it could not impose binding obligations on state officials. Story believed that Congress could permit state courts to exercise a concurrent jurisdiction, but that it could not make this binding.[54] Pindall, on the other side, thought that Congress possessed a broad power to impose duties on state courts regarding subjects "coextensive with the powers of legislation." It could require state courts to implement federal law. Even if that doctrine were disputed (as, of course, it was) he contended there were special cases: fugitive slaves were one of these. Congress had the power both to secure a federally guaranteed right, and to force the states to fulfill their obligation to return runaway blacks. "It follows," he concluded, "that Congress can make a law to regulate the conduct of those State officers in the performance of their duty."[55]

Those arguing against the bill did not deny that Congress could legislate to secure federally guaranteed rights. The fugitive clause, in fact, was "imperative," according to Clagett; it required that Congress legislate to carry out a "solemn compact between the several States in the Union." But it had already acted and no further legislation was necessary to protect the rights of slave owners. If the law was to be amended, he concluded, it should be in

[51] *Martin* v. *Hunter's Lessee*, 1 Wheaton 330.
[52] *Annals*, 15th Cong., 1st sess., Jan. 28, 1818, 825–37; see also *ibid.*, March 9, 1818, 242–55.
[53] Kent, *Commentaries*, 1: 342.
[54] Joseph Story, *Commentaries on the Constitution of the United States* (2 vols.; 2d ed.; Boston, 1851), 2: 505; *Houston* v. *Moore*, 5 Wheaton 27–28.
[55] *Annals*, 15th Cong., 1st sess., Jan. 28, 1818, 827–28.

order to protect the free citizens whose rights had been abused.[56] Such arguments were unavailing, for the portion of the original bill making free state judiciaries agents of the southern courts, and utilizing free state executives in the arrest process, passed the House unaltered.

That portion of the bill which dealt with the effect of a certificate was so outlandish that it was quickly modified when it reached the floor of the House. The new section still went far to undermine the legal systems that the free states had built up to secure personal liberty. No action, suit, or process could be moved or prosecuted on behalf of the person seized in the state where the seizure took place, as long as the fugitive was detained by virtue of the federal law, with one notable exception. Courts would be allowed to issue the writ of habeas corpus (nothing was said about the writ *de homine replegiando*). But a sufficient return to the writ would be that the person in question was held by virtue of this act. Probably the change was made to avoid any charge that the habeas corpus was suspended unconstitutionally by the bill. The new section also, as a concession to the free states, eliminated the criminal immunities: a man could be held to answer for maltreating, beating, assaulting, or imprisoning another.[57]

Antislavery people were hardly mollified. In the Senate a significant debate occurred on this matter between James Burrill, Jr., of Rhode Island (that state's chief justice in 1816) and William Smith of South Carolina, by now an old warrior in behalf of slave owners.

Burrill contended that there was an unconstitutional suspension of the privilege of habeas corpus because "a person of color taken under it [the federal law] cannot have the right to his freedom tried by the judge before whom the return of the writ of habeas corpus is made."[58] Burrill clearly believed that a habeas corpus could be used to examine the question at issue—the freedom or slavery of the man seized—precisely the thing that proslavery jurists like Roane feared. A judge could go behind the return, and if he decided the man restrained was free he would be discharged.

Smith of South Carolina gave the fullest exposition of the slave-owners' viewpoint on this problem. Habeas corpus was never intended to give a right to a trial of the issues. "It merely gives the right to the person confined," he declared, "to demand an inquiry whether he is held in custody upon a ground warranted by law; and if the judge before whom he is brought finds he is detained by legal authority and upon legal grounds, he cannot discharge him but is obliged to remand him." It made no difference, said Smith, "whether the cause is a just one or not." It was inconceivable that a judge should "take upon himself alone" to try a claim to

[56]*Ibid.*, 825–27.

[57]This, and all other amendments to the bill, unless otherwise noted, are filed with the original bill in the National Archives.

[58]*Annals*, 15th Cong., 1st sess., March 6, 1818, 231.

freedom after a claimant satisfactorily had made out his proofs and received his certificate, as prescribed by law. "The writ of *habeas corpus* was never intended to give any such right."[59] Southern representatives were seeking to protect their "peculiar institution" by striking a crippling blow at one of the mainstays in free state law for protecting the personal liberty of persons within their jurisdiction. They refused to acknowledge the growth of the "great writ" that was taking place at the state level in early nineteenth-century America, at least in cases involving claims to service. The conflict between the legal principles of the slaveholding South and the free North hardly ever was revealed so clearly.

Besides challenging the proslavery views of habeas corpus, and the nature of the federal judicial power, northern congressmen tried to change the bill in certain significant ways. The boldest effort was John Sergeant's proposal "to materially change the nature of the bill by making judges of the State in which apprentices, slaves, etc., are seized, the tribunal to decide the fact of slavery, instead of the judges of the States whence the fugitives have escaped."[60] Sergeant's proposal, it is worth noting, rested upon a different constitutional base from that constructed by Clagett. Constitutional thinking in the North, by and large, was based on the premise that congressional action to implement the fugitive clause might be legitimate, and that state instrumentalities might be used to carry out the federal law (even though jurists like Story and congressmen like Clagett were pointing a new direction). Sergeant was merely working within this framework to grant free state judges the power to act on behalf of freedom. In the Fifteenth Congress, however, there was very little chance of this. Sergeant's proposal was passed over without a discussion.

At the same time other members of the House moved to amend the bill to make it more balanced. Charles Rich, a Vermont Republican, tried to tack on an antikidnapping provision. It would be unlawful to seize, confine, drive, transport, or in any manner convey a free black "without first having obtained a certificate." This portion of the amendment was an attempt to make sure that any seizure, just or not, would at least be carried out under the forms of law.[61] There was little chance that proslavery congressmen would ever accept the Rich proposal; so Henry R. Storrs, a New York Federalist, moved a substitute. This was also an antikidnapping measure, but it did nothing more than provide penalties for anyone who "knowingly and wilfully" obtained a certificate "without colorable claim." This substitute was so innocuous that even Pindall supported it, and it passed the House by a large majority.[62]

[59] *Ibid.*, 232.
[60] *Ibid.*, Jan. 28, 1818, 825–27; Sergeant may have been speaking for effect, as there is no copy of any amendment in the records that does what he proposed.
[61] *Ibid.*, 825.
[62] *Ibid.*, 825.

The following day, January 29, 1818, Rich moved that the amended bill be sent to a special committee with the object of further changing it "to guard more effectually the rights of free persons of color." Pindall immediately objected that there was a "want of necessary connexion" between the two subjects. This admission slave owners later ignored when they challenged any state legislation designed to protect free blacks as being unconstitutional, since it might involve the subject of fugitive slaves. But, at that time, Pindall's argument was compelling: the motion for commitment failed, without a division.[63] Shortly after this the amended bill passed the House.

An unsuccessful attempt was made in the Senate to amend the section which authorized affidavits. This was to be stricken and in its place the following was to be inserted: "the oath of one or more credible witnesses who shall, upon their own knowledge swear to the identity of such fugitive (the owner or claimant being for this purpose deemed to be a competent witness) or by the voluntary confession of such a fugitive."[64]

After it accepted a few minor amendments, and a new section limiting the force of the act to four years, the Senate passed the amended bill. The House, however, on March 16, 1818, ordered it tabled. It was not taken up during the remainder of this session of Congress.

The first major confrontation on the subject of fugitive slaves and free blacks since the passage of the law of 1793 then had been met, without any new legislation. Although the conflicting interests were represented and vocal, no compromise could be agreed upon. On the whole northerners had shown themselves to be far more conciliatory than southerners. Fugitive slaves were a special problem according to most southern congressmen. No legal process, the writ of habeas corpus included, would be allowed to limit the rights of slave owners to their property acquired under state law. In the beginning, indeed, some had wanted an exemption from the criminal processes of the free states as well.[65] Several northern congressmen, at the same time, even were willing to support the subordination of their own state judiciaries to the interests of slave claimants. Antislavery congressmen, however, met the proslavery challenge directly. Some of them went as far as denying that Congress could impose duties upon state officials to aid in the recovery of fugitives. Others took the view that congressional action in imposing duties might be legitimate, but that this

[63]*Ibid.*, Jan. 29, 1818, 830.

[64]The copy of this proposal is headed "HR 18. In the Senate of the United States Feb. 2, 1818 Read and Passed to a Second reading." The copy of the bill as amended in the Senate and returned to the House is also in the Archives. It has the same title with everything scratched out except "HR 18," and written in hand is "March 16, 1818—advised to lie upon the table." This version does not contain the proposed amendment.

[65]The completely one-sided nature of the South's constitutional theory as it matured is fully explored in Arthur Bestor, "State Sovereignty and Slavery: A Reinterpretation of Proslavery Constitutional Doctrine, 1846–1860," *Journal of the Illinois State Historical Society*, 54 (Summer, 1961): 117–80.

power should be exercised in such a way as to leave discretion in the hands of the free state judiciaries.

Despite the failure to get favorable action on the bill during 1817–18, proslavery congressmen had come close. In the next few years they made several attempts to revive it, but in every case they fell far short.[66] One of the basic reasons was their refusal to make any notable concessions to northern sentiment, which had been aroused more than ever before by the Missouri debates beginning in 1819. In the final debate on the amended fugitive bill in 1822, Cadwallader Colden of New York (a one-time mayor of New York City, and scarcely a radical) avowed that he was not "one of those visionary philanthropists who would contend for immediate and universal emancipation." He would not fail to give effect to the Constitution which he considered "sacred." But the bill under consideration, he believed, was "inconsistent with the principles of liberty, and had a direct and efficient agency to promote the traffic which had been carried on to a great extent of seizing free blacks and selling them for slaves."[67]

The effort to reconcile the property interests of slave claimants, and the personal liberty of free blacks, of course, was a difficult problem at best. It was virtually impossible to resolve when slave owners refused to recognize the concern of men like Colden as legitimate or worthy of attention. As the North awoke to the dangers in the federal law, it became impossible for the South to remold the act of 1793 to meet proslavery demands. It came down to the fact that neither side had sufficient political power to alter the existing arrangement. Slaveholders still had the Fugitive Slave Law, even though it was not everything they desired, whereas free blacks could still be the victims of that law; their only protection, it was by now apparent, existed in the laws of the states, to which antislavery reformers now increasingly turned their attention.

---

[66]*Annals*, 15th Cong., 2d sess., Jan. 15–16, 1819, 546, 551; *ibid.*, 17th Cong., 1st sess., 553, 1415, 1414; the bills, in the National Archives, are "H.R. 280, 15th Cong., 2d sess. Reported January 16, 1819," and "H.R. 35, 17th Cong., 1st sess., January 14, 1822."

[67]*Ibid.*, 17th Cong., 1st sess., March 27, 1822, 1379.

State "Interposition" 1820-1830: Pennsylvania and New York

Chief Justice William Tilghman of the Pennsylvania Supreme Court in 1819, in *Wright* v. *Deacon*, appears to have been the first northern jurist to use the "historical-necessity thesis"[1] as the basis for a judgment. This view held that the fugitive slave clause had to be incorporated in the Constitution for the sake of union. "Our southern brethren," he declared from the bench, "would not have consented to become parties to a constitution . . . unless their property in slaves had been secured." In his view procedures used to secure the personal liberty of free blacks, such as the writ *de homine replegiando*, could render that property insecure by obstructing the recovery of fugitives. In any case involving a claim to a runaway, therefore, this writ could not issue, as it would be in violation of the Constitution. "It plainly appears from the whole scope and tenor of the constitution and act of Congress," said Tilghman, "that the fugitive was to be delivered up, on a summary proceeding, without the delay of a trial in a court of common law."[2] Seven years before, in *Ex parte Lawrence*, the Pennsylvania Supreme Court held that although there had been an unfavorable judgment on a habeas corpus, a black could still have his claim to freedom tested by a jury by suing out a writ *de homine replegiando*.[3] Tilghman's reversal of that decision significantly altered, in favor of property rights, the compromise Pennsylvania had made with slavery in the 1780s.

This decision also brought one of the knotty problems of American constitutionalism into clear focus for antislavery reformers: the effect of a judicial ruling about disputed constitutional points upon political leaders and other courts. John Marshall, speaking in the Virginia convention of 1788, asked: "to what quarter will you look for protection from an infringement of the Constitution, if you will not give the power to the judiciary?"[4] Some thirty years later Joseph Story, in a speech before the Suffolk County bar, contended that "the privilege of bringing every law to the test of the constitution belongs to the humblest citizen, who owes no obedience to any legislative act which transcends the constitutional limits."[5] The limits

---

[1]Donald M. Roper, "In Quest of Judicial Objectivity: The Marshall Court and the Legitimation of Slavery," *Stanford Law Review*, 21 (February, 1969): 538.

[2]*Wright alias Hall* v. *Deacon*, 5 Sergeant and Rawle 62.

[3]*Ex parte Lawrence*, 5 Binney 304.

[4]Quoted in Raoul Berger, *Congress v. The Supreme Court* (Cambridge, Mass., 1969), 194.

[5]William W. Story, ed., *The Miscellaneous Writings of Joseph Story* (Boston, 1852), 227.

of obedience owed to judicial rulings, however, remained hazy. Those inclined to view judicial power as one of the most potent checks against the abuses of majoritarianism, or "legislative despotism" as it was sometimes called, tended to argue that the judgment of the highest appropriate appeals court was final. As a rule people did accept the grounds of decision in cases out of respect for the courts, or in some cases, out of simple inertia. Furthermore, the rule of *stare decisis* lent a measure of finality to a ruling. Together these operated as powerful restraints against open or frequent defiance of a court. If Tilghman's decision then was binding, any effort to guarantee that the issue of freedom or slavery would be triable by a jury within Pennsylvania would be frustrated. Conservative northern jurists, moreover, mindful of the dangers to the Union presented by "infringements" upon the "rights" of slave owners, could follow Tilghman's reasoning and thwart all antislavery efforts to secure complete hearings within free state jurisdictions. The effect of a judicial ruling in the American system, however, is more complex. The rule of precedent is not an *idée fixe* in American constitutional thought, even though it is a significant concept; precedents can be and sometimes are overturned if the reasons are compelling. And to say that people usually accept the grounds of decision in cases as guides for the future is little more than a descriptive statement, for they do not always act this way. The judiciary in a republican society must rest heavily upon this kind of acceptance of its role, but it should be clear that the "finality" of a judicial ruling falls somewhat short of being absolute.

An important undercurrent in American thought about judicial review in the early nineteenth century also limited the potential force of a court ruling. Clearly more apprehensive about judicial than legislative "despotism" in a republican society, Thomas Jefferson wrote the following to Abigail Adams in 1804: "But the opinion which gives to the Judges the right to decide what laws are constitutional, and what not, not only for themselves in their own sphere of action, but for the Legislative and Executive also in their spheres, would make the Judiciary a despotic branch."[6] In Pennsylvania Chief Justice John Bannister Gibson, in an 1825 dissent, argued for the right of the legislature to decide upon the extent of its own authority. In theory, he observed, "all the organs of government are of equal capacity."[7] And, of course, Andrew Jackson, in the Bank War, acted upon the assumption that he was not bound by the judgment of the U.S. Supreme Court in the case of *McCulloch* v. *Maryland*.

How people responded to particular judgments then depended, in some measure, upon their conception of the nature of judicial power. The precise force of Tilghman's decision in other words remained to be seen, but un-

[6]Quoted in Charles Warren, *The Supreme Court in United States History* (2 vols.; Boston, 1926), 1: 265.
[7]*Eakin* v. *Raub*, 12 Sergeant and Rawle (Penn.), 330.

doubtedly it was an important obstacle to those antislavery people in Pennsylvania who had been working to increase the legal securities for personal freedom at the state as well as the federal level.[8] When Tilghman undercut the writ *de homine replegiando* at the same time that the compromise was failing at the federal level, the pressure mounted for some action by the state.[9] And this coincided with the beginning of the debate in the Sixteenth Congress over the explosive issue of slavery in Missouri. In 1820 the Pennsylvania legislature responded to the pressures with a new antikidnapping law.

On January 15, 1820, Representative William Wilkins scored the use of ex parte testimony sanctioned by the federal fugitive law—it being received, he noted, "as conclusive evidence of right." Wilkins, who was a prominent Pittsburgh business leader and later a U.S. district court judge,[10] unequivocally denounced the existing law. The federal statute gave power, he pointed out, to kidnappers "whose very livelihood depends upon this odious traffic." A free Negro could be seized, and "after a mockery of trial," hurried across the Delaware river, and sold into slavery. If anyone went after him with a writ of habeas corpus to test the legality of the restraint, what would be the result? "The certificate," Wilkins said, "the ill gotten certificate is produced; the judge disclaims any jurisdiction, and the slave is irredeemably gone." Wilkins had a remedy in view: the state of Pennsylvania should legislate to supplement the act of Congress, eliminating the procedural deficiencies and uncertainties in the act of 1793 insofar as Pennsylvania's officials were concerned.[11]

Many doubted, however, that Pennsylvania had such authority. Representatives William J. Duane and James Cochran submitted a resolution on January 20, 1820, expressing this view. There was no doubt, they observed, that a person should not be deprived of liberty by a summary procedure, or that the decision of one man based on ex parte testimony should never be conclusive of the rights involved. Furthermore, the summary proceedings in the law of 1793 did not constitute due process of law guaranteed by the Fifth Amendment. Unjust as that law might be, however, "the power to alter the case, in any of those objectionable points, is vested in congress alone." State officials who had sworn to uphold the Constitution could not interfere.

[8]Even before Tilghman's decision the Pennsylvania Abolition Society had appointed a committee to draft a bill, to be introduced in the state legislature, providing a remedy for the "outrage committed on free People of Colour under the fugitive law of the United States." Penn. Abolition Soc. Minutes (1800–1824) 2: 302.

[9]See, for example, the petition from "sundry inhabitants" of Philadelphia asking that the legislature require that magistrates should "receive no evidence, but what shall be according to the strict rules of law." *Penn. House Journal, 1819–20*, 302.

[10]*Biographical Directory of the American Congress 1774–1961*, 85th Cong., 2d sess., House Document No. 442, 1816. Hereafter cited as *BDAC*.

[11]*Poulson's American Daily Advertiser*, January 25, 1820.

Still, there was one remedy the state could offer. Pennsylvania could deprive its magistrates of any power to act under the law of Congress: a position supported inferentially by Story in *Martin* v. *Hunter's Lessee* and by Clagett and Morrill in the earlier congressional debate. "The power which can create or annihilate, which can reward or punish, a magistrate," they contended, "can alone prescribe the duties that he may perform."[12]

At the end of March, 1820, the legislature passed the new law within a week, apparently with little discussion,[13] and along the lines suggested by Duane and Cochran. The first section of the act increased the penalty for kidnapping to up to twenty-one years in prison at hard labor. This section applied to those who seized a man "by force or violence," or by fraud or false pretense seduced him away with the intention of holding or selling him as a slave.[14] Four years later the state supreme court in *Commonwealth* v. *Case* held that the act of 1780, guaranteeing slave claimants all the rights they had before passage of the act, preserved their general right of recaption.[15] It is noteworthy that the court did not rest this right upon the fugitive slave clause. Masters, then, still possessed the right of recovering their property by their own efforts, but they could not seize a free man. Justice Tilghman's decision in favor of property rights, however, had undermined one of the most important legal procedures used to test a claim to freedom, even though the presumption remained that all men are free until proven otherwise.

The most important part of the state's new law, however, was the third section. Since it was widely believed that the state did not have the power to require its officials to follow different procedures once jurisdiction was accepted under the federal law, there appeared to be only one recourse. The state could deny the right of the federal government to use certain state officials to carry out the obligation of the fugitive slave clause. This section of the 1820 law removed the jurisdiction of aldermen and justices of the peace over cases involving claims to runaways. If any such official accepted jurisdiction under the law of 1793, he would be deemed guilty of a misdemeanor in office. Those judicial officials not prohibited from acting under the federal law were required by the fourth section to make a record, including a description of the person claimed.

Southerners in Congress had tried to subordinate northern judiciaries to the status of agents of the southern courts in fugitive slave cases, but in Pennsylvania the number of free state officials hearing such cases was reduced. The primary purpose behind the state's new legislation was to ex-

---

[12] *Penn. House Journal, 1819–20*, 339–41.

[13] *Penn. House Journal, 1819–20*, 983, 987, 1069, 1081, 1088.

[14] *Penn. Session Laws, 1820*, 104–6. Section 2 provided penalties for those who sold or knowingly purchased a black "for the purpose of fraudulently removing, exporting, or carrying him or her out of the state."

[15] *Commonwealth* v. *Case. Niles' Register*, Third Series, no. 5, vol. 3, 1824.

tend the utmost protection to free men considered possible within the limits believed set by the Constitution. There was little concern to sustain the property rights of masters, which were supported by federal law and by state judicial rulings such as Tilghman's. At the same time, withdrawing state assistance in the execution of the federal law made the recovery of fugitives difficult.[16]

Maryland was the slave state most directly affected by Pennsylvania's action, and it soon tried to influence Pennsylvania to repeal the law of 1820 and enact a more satisfactory measure in its place. The act of 1826 that resulted from this pressure was an attempt to find a workable balance between slaveholders' claims and the protection of free blacks, and to work out satisfactory legal procedures to make the recovery process peaceable. People tried to provide, at the state level, the kind of balance Congress had been unable to provide at the federal.

Any compromise is likely to be interpreted differently, depending on which side an author believes ought to have prevailed, and therefore which sacrifices were of vital principles. John Bach McMaster, on one hand, believed that the law of 1826 met the wishes of slaveholders: it was a fundamental sacrifice of the principles of human freedom and was passed "despite the loud and indignant protests of the antislavery people."[17] William R. Leslie, on the other hand, was concerned with the wider impact of the constitutional ideas. As long as states could obstruct federally secured rights those rights would be insecure, and this could apply with equal force to the rights of free black citizens as well as those of slave claimants. Leslie, then, saw the law as a radical departure based on a rejection of Pennsylvania's obligation to support the Fugitive Slave Law and the Constitution of the United States. It was "a precursor of later interference by northern states." This law intentionally, he believed, made it virtually impossible to recover fugitives in Pennsylvania. It was the first of the Personal Liberty Laws, by which Leslie appears to mean laws framed to nullify the federal law: it was a measure based on an explicit rejection of the idea of voluntary cooperation.[18]

Statements of some of the participants, and particularly those of the house leader, William M. Meredith,[19] suggest a different view. Throughout

[16]Leslie, "The Fugitive Slave Clause, 1787–1842," 179–80, takes the view that the law was the embodiment of the antislavery objective of aiding and assisting fugitive slaves.

[17]John Bach McMaster, *A History of the People of the United States, from the Revolution to the Civil War* (8 vols.; New York, 1900), 5: 218.

[18]William R. Leslie, "The Pennsylvania Fugitive Slave Act of 1826," *Journal of Southern History*, 18 (November, 1952). Edward Channing, *A History of the United States* (New York, 1943), 141, contended that the law only appeared to make it easier for slave owners to seize fugitives. Under the guise of an antikidnapping law it actually made it more difficult.

[19]Meredith was from a substantial background. His family was among the leaders of Philadelphia society. When the Whig party was formed Meredith became a leading member, and an opponent of the anti-Masons led by Thaddeus Stevens. Under Harrison he became

the course of the debate in the house Meredith wrote, and received, numerous letters concerning the proposed law. They reveal a great deal about the nature of the opposition to the bill and about the views of those who supported its final passage.

At the beginning of February, 1826, a proslavery bill drafted by Ezekiel F. Chambers, Archibald Lee, and Robert H. Goldsborough, commissioners sent from Maryland, was introduced in the Pennsylvania house. It was entitled "An act to give effect to the Constitution of the United States, relative to fugitives from labour, for the protection of free persons of colour, and to prevent kidnapping."[20]

Reactions among antislavery people in Pennsylvania were decidedly hostile to the proposed law. George M. Stroud, who wrote one of the standard antislavery treatises on the law of slavery the following year,[21] wrote to Meredith in unmistakable terms: "Don't let that infamous Slave bill pass your House."[22]

Among the most objectionable features of the bill was Section 6, which provided stiff penalties for anyone who accosted a man making a seizure of an alleged fugitive. Roberts Vaux, a leading member of the Pennsylvania Abolition Society, wrote to Meredith that this section contained penalties "which will never be submitted to by the freemen of this commonwealth." He particularly was indignant at the prospect of facing the penitentiary "from detaining for a moment in the street, or on the road, *a Maryland Slave driver who may be lashing his victim.*" Despite his indignation Vaux did not suggest a very radical course. The law of 1820, he felt, was sufficient. Pennsylvania was not bound to legislate for the South "on this hateful matter." Still, nothing should be done to impede the operation of the law of Congress.[23]

Such pressure scarcely was necessary, as Meredith explained in a letter to his father. "No one here contemplates the passage of the Bill as it stands," he wrote, "the sixth section I shall certainly vote against,-& very important modifications will be made in other parts of the Bill." "I believe all of us," he continued, "have no intention of going one jot beyond the strict constitutional obligation which is imposed upon us, & it is a satisfac-

United States attorney for the eastern district of Pennsylvania, and the secretary of the treasury under Taylor. Allen Johnson and Dumas Malone, eds., *Dictionary of American Biography* (22 vols.; New York, 1928–44), 12: 548–49. Hereafter cited as *DAB.*

[20]*Penn. House Journal, 1825–26,* 323; *Pennsylvania Archives* (Ninth Series), 8: 6403; *Penn. Senate Journal, 1825–26,* 282–83.

[21]George M. Stroud, *A Sketch of the Laws Relating to Slavery in the Several States of the United States of America* (Philadelphia, 1827).

[22]George M. Stroud to William M. Meredith, February 10, 1826, Meredith Papers, Historical Society of Pennsylvania.

[23]Roberts Vaux to Stephen Duncan and William M. Meredith, February 9, 1826, Meredith Papers, *ibid.* See also Gerard Ralston to William M. Meredith, February 9, 1826, *ibid.*; *Poulson's American Daily Advertiser,* February 10, 1826.

tion, that in going so far, the cause of humanity will be subserved, & nothing be done, which will not have the effect of placing the negro on an infinitely better footing than he stands at present."[24]

Organized opposition to the bill outside the legislature began a few days after its introduction. A special meeting of the Pennsylvania Abolition Society was called for February 10 to consider the proposed measure. At that meeting a committee was appointed to draft a protest, and another to deliver it to Harrisburg, "and to endeavour whilst there to prevail with the legislature to reject the before mentioned bill."[25] The protest began with the assertion that the bill contemplated a "deep infringement upon those constitutional rights and legal privileges in the exercise of which our fellow citizens have frequently received the legislative sanction." Further, it noted, "the government of the U.S. have full authority to carry into effect the provisions of their own Constitution."[26]

Although the memorialists did not challenge the right of Congress to implement the fugitive slave clause, they asserted that the state also had certain rights. Among them was the right "of giving effect to the constitution of the United States." The question was one of policy and not of constitutional power. It would be inexpedient, they believed, to repeal the law of 1820 as requested by the Maryland commissioners. Pennsylvania would be forsaking those northern states working for the ultimate extinction of slavery and aligning with the slaveholding South. The memorialists pleaded that they were ready to "perform *all* the obligations enjoined upon us to our Sister States by the Bond of our Union," but they feared that "the rights of our own citizens" might be forgotten. They also objected to promoting "an active domestic slave trade," which would be encouraged by the proposed bill.[27]

On the same day the abolition society was holding its special meeting in Philadelphia, the fourth section of the bill (providing for the use of state officials) was already being considered in Harrisburg. Some members of

[24]William M. Meredith to D. W. Meredith, February 11, 1826, Meredith Papers, Historical Society of Pennsylvania.

[25]Penn. Abolition Soc. Minutes (1825–47), 3: 28–29.

[26]At the side of the original draft of the memorial is a notation incorporated into the version sent the legislature: "We remark in the 8th Section of that instrument [the U.S. Constitution] a power to make all laws necessary and proper for carrying into execution the powers therein delegated, and all other powers thereby vested in that Government." The original draft is in box 7a of the Pennsylvania Abolition Society Papers, Historical Society of Pennsylvania. The final draft is in the Penn. Abolition Soc. Minutes (1825–47), 3: 30.

[27]This memorial generally followed a line suggested by William Rawle. "I would, as much as possible," he wrote, "avoid going into details, avoid pointing out particular objections (altho' they abound) for we always find, in such cases, that the advocates of a measure, will adjust to particular alterations if they can preserve the general principle." The society should object to the principle, it should object "to a State legislating at all by way of enforcing & even extending the provisions of a law of the U.S. in favour of a subject so revolting to us." William Rawle to the Abolition Society, February 10, 1826, Manuscript Collection Belonging to the Pennsylvania Abolition Society, Historical Society of Pennsylvania, 9: 210.

the legislature, it was evident, were bolder than the abolitionists. Representatives Jacob F. Heston and James Clark proposed a substitute for the proslavery bill. It provided that the state official to whom application had been made should bind the alleged runaway to appear at the next court of quarter sessions in the proper county. If the man seized was not able to find sufficient security for his appearance the official would commit him to the common jail. State officials would play an active role, but this was not a one-sided proposal because it was provided additionally that before an alleged fugitive would be delivered up he would be "entitled to a full benefit of a trial by jury."[28] The antislavery position was ably, and strongly presented, but it was not urged successfully (the substitute failed to carry by one vote). One probable cause for its failure was that it aroused the fear of conservatives like Meredith (who voted against it) that juries might decide in favor of a black, regardless of the facts presented or the law, and thereby defeat the clear constitutional obligation to return runaways. Acting as an agency to dispense "justice," a jury in a community hostile to slavery might well decide against the legitimate property interests of slave owners. Also standing in the way was Justice Tilghman's decision of 1819, which people like Meredith accepted as binding.

A few days after the failure of the substitute an amendment was introduced that received the support of the conservatives. It provided that no judge, justice of the peace, or alderman could issue a warrant on the application of a claimant's agent unless the agent produced the affidavit of the claimant, in addition to his oath, certified by an official of the state in which the claimant resided. The affidavit had to state the claimant's right to the service of the alleged runaway, as well as his name, age, and description.[29] This amendment was adopted by an overwhelming vote.

The house then turned to the section of the proposed bill authorizing a sheriff or constable to scize alleged runaways. Some wanted this amended to provide that the duty would not be obligatory.[30] This motion failed, however, by a vote of fifty-seven to fifteen. Clearly, Pennsylvania's legislators would not deny that the free states possessed an obligation under the fugitive clause to assist in the process of reclaiming fugitives. Rather, they would fulfill that obligation voluntarily, but in so doing they would define the procedures to be followed by state officials.

When the lobbyists of the Pennsylvania Abolition Society recognized this they adopted a new strategy. They tried, along with the Quakers, to secure modifications in the bill. Thomas Shipley, one of the abolitionists at Harrisburg, wrote to Isaac Barton on February 15 that "we have become acquainted with the most prominent members of the House, and I have no

---

[28] *Penn. House Journal, 1825-26*, 358-59.
[29] *Ibid.*, 377.
[30] *Ibid.*, 377.

doubt but if we could get Meredith to advocate our amendments they might all be introduced into the Bill." The most important amendments, he noted, stipulated that no interested or ex parte testimony would be received in evidence and that it would not be obligatory for state officials to accept jurisdiction of claims to alleged runaways. As it stood Shipley found the bill "better than the law of 1820." In fact, Goldsborough, one of the Maryland commissioners, had been so disappointed in the changes, Shipley wrote, that he had said the title should be changed to indicate a bill to prevent the recovery of fugitives. The following day, February 16, Shipley added a note to this letter that the bill had just passed the house, and that its single anti-slavery amendment provided that no interested testimony should be received on trial. His opinion at that point was that the bill was "worse for the Slave holders than no Law at all or the present act of 1820."[31]

Despite this favorable comment there was still considerable disagreement between the abolitionists and the conservative leader in the house, Meredith, who played an important role in defining the final shape of the bill. The principal disagreement concerned jury trials for alleged fugitives. On February 13, before the bill passed the house, Meredith's father wrote him that the abolitionists strongly objected "to subjecting the liberty of a *citizen* to the decision of a single magistrate, while his property to the value of $5 cannot be taken from him without the *intervention of a Jury.*"[32] Later Meredith's father apprised him of abolitionist Caleb Carmalt's hope that "the Bill may return to the H. of Rep. with an amendment giving colored persons who claim to be free the right to a trial by jury. If it should return, it is our earnest wish that this undoubted right might be granted them."[33] A jury trial amendment, as already noted, went too far for the cautious Meredith. But the state could act, in his view, to extend some protection to Negroes.

On February 12 he pointed out to Roberts Vaux that by existing law, a claimant, his agent, or attorney could seize any black at will, without a warrant. This, Meredith argued, could be prevented. "In a government of *Laws*-in a *free* government especially,-no man should be arrested, but by the warrant of the officer of the Law." "Consider the rights of *free negroes,*" he added, "*Citizens of this State*, who are at present exposed to seizure without *warrant of any kind*. Why should they not be placed upon the same footing with our other Citizens!" Moreover, humanity required

---

[31]Thomas Shipley to Isaac Barton, February 15, 1826, Manuscript Collection Belonging to the Pennsylvania Abolition Society, Historical Society of Pennsylvania, 9: 216. See also, *Penn. House Journal, 1825-26*, 386.

[32]D. W. Meredith to William M. Meredith, February 13, 1826, Meredith Papers, Historical Society of Pennsylvania. The senior Meredith, in this same letter, expressed astonishment that the abolitionists displayed "absolute ignorance with respect to the provisions (of) the constitution,—and of the Act of Congress of 1793,—and the effect of the Act of Assembly of 1820 which renders the former practically inoperative."

[33]D. W. Meredith to William M. Meredith, March 1, 1826, Meredith Papers, *ibid.*

this for the fugitive as well as for the free black. It would be far better to substitute the "mild custody of the law, to the violent & perhaps barbarous seizure by the party himself."[34] Two days later Meredith wrote to his friend Henry J. Williams and summarized his view of the proposed law. This "obnoxious Bill," he wrote,

> 1. Does not go a jot beyond our Constitutional obligation.—2. Provides for the peace, honor & dignity of the Commonwealth, which are not provided for as the law stands—3. Secures the *rights* of the free negro, which have *never* been secured in this State before—&4. gives to the unfortunate fugitives themselves, whom we are *bound* to deliver up-all that we *can* give them—The principles of *humanity* require that we should substitute the mild & benign custody of Law & its officers, to the harsh & barbarous seizure of the Claimant &c—The Law is better for the *State*, for the *free negroes*, for the *fugitive slaves*.[35]

The state, Meredith noted in a major speech in the house on the thirteenth, was under an obligation to "deliver up" fugitives from slavery, but it should be done with proper safeguards. There should be no arrest, under a government of laws, he said, repeating what he had written the day before to Vaux, "but under the process and by an officer of the Law." To the free blacks the provisions of the bill were, in his view, all-important. "They tend to give them what, to our disgrace be it spoken, they have never yet had, equal protection with ourselves, in relation to personal liberty."[36]

The bill that finally passed the house reflected these views.[37] On March 22, 1826, the senate, with only minor tampering, passed the house bill by a vote of sixteen to twelve. The house, however, disagreed to all the proposed changes except a few minor ones. The senate then receded from its other proposed amendments, and on Saturday, March 25, 1826, the bill became law.[38]

The first two sections of the new law were substantially the same as those in the act of 1820 (those concerning kidnapping). Section 3 was very different. It authorized a claimant to apply to any judge, justice of the peace, or alderman for a warrant to arrest an alleged fugitive. This warrant would be directed to the sheriff or constable of the proper city or

[34]William M. Meredith to Roberts Vaux, February 12, 1825 [sic], Vaux Papers, Historical Society of Pennsylvania.

[35]William M. Meredith to Henry J. Williams, February 14, 1826, Pennsylvania (box)–Legislature, New York Public Library.

[36]*Poulson's Daily American Advertiser*, February 20, 1826.

[37]At the end of February Meredith sent the amended bill to his friend H. J. Williams and noted that "I moved the new sections & the amendments; except those to the first & last sections which I had moved by others." William M. Meredith to Henry J. Williams, February 23, 1826, Pennsylvania (box)–Legislature, New York Public Library. This boast was not entirely accurate. One significant amendment which provided that the oath of the owner, owners, or other interested persons could not be received in evidence was neither to the first nor last sections, but to the sixth, and it was not introduced by Meredith., *Penn. House Journal*, 1825–26, 386.

[38]*Penn. Senate Journal, 1825–26*, 339, 353–54, 466, 481, 494, 511, 516–17, 522.

county who would arrest the black named and bring him before a judge of the proper county. This section, along with Section 11, provided for the "mild custody of the law." The eleventh repealed that part of the law of 1780 under which a claimant was authorized to exercise a right of recaption. This marked an important departure in the reading of the guarantee in the fugitive slave clause of the U.S. Constitution: no longer was a general right of recaption by self-help alone part of that guarantee insofar as Pennsylvania was concerned.

Another section provided that no warrant could issue on the application of an agent or attorney unless he produced, in addition to his own oath or affirmation, the affidavit of the claimant. This affidavit had to state his title to the service of the fugitive, and the name, age, and description of the alleged runaway. It also had to be certified by an official authorized to administer oaths in the state or territory of the claimant.

Once the arrest had been made the judge before whom the alleged fugitive was brought would issue a certificate for his removal, if he was satisfied that he owed service in another state. The oath of the owner or other interested persons, however, would not be received in evidence. Time was also provided for an alleged slave to obtain evidence to refute the claim (which settled for Pennsylvania officials the evidentiary vagary in the way the federal law on fugitives had been framed). If proper security was not given for the alleged fugitives's appearance, the judge was allowed to have him committed to the common jail at the expense of the person making the claim. This commitment would be for a "reasonable and just" period, after which the black would be brought before the judge by a habeas corpus "for final hearing and adjudication." If the claimant sought an adjournment it would not be granted unless he gave security to appear and prosecute his claim.

These were the most important provisions of the law of 1826.[39] Since under the Fugitive Slave Law judges were to be "satisfied" of the legitimacy of a claim, Pennsylvania had now established standards for satisfaction in the state courts hearing such cases. Nothing, of course, was said about the standards to be applied in federal courts.

Reactions to the law were generally favorable. The committee of the Pennsylvania Abolition Society reported their satisfaction with the bill, which they considered "a manifest improvement upon the previously existing laws." They also claimed to have secured, in conjunction with the Quakers, important alterations in the bill.[40] Robert Goldsborough, one of the Maryland commissioners, was also satisfied, despite his unfavorable comments during the course of the bill. He wrote to Meredith on March 29: "I am highly gratified at the passage of this law because I think it may be eminently useful to effect the desired object, and because it is a pledge,

---

[39] *Penn. Session Laws, 1826*, 150–55.
[40] Penn. Abolition Soc. Minutes (1825–47), 3: 35–36.

that states will adhere to the original obligations of the confederacy."
State interposition in this case was not objectionable to some of the leaders
of the slaveholding communities. Rather, it represented a promise that free
states would meet their obligations voluntarily, which was much more
important than any delays that might be caused because of the procedural
requirements of the new law.[41]

Pennsylvania's act of 1826 then was intended, at least by the leading
spokesmen for the bill, as a compromise between what were considered the
demands of the fugitive slave clause, and the responsibility to protect the
personal liberty of free blacks. To effect the latter the state had to interpose
its power between individuals and the federal government. If a claimant
attempted to exercise his right under federal law to seize a man without a
warrant, he would be subjected to prosecution as a kidnapper. And, if a
claimant proceeded according to the law of Pennsylvania, his oath would
not be admitted in evidence. In providing these basic safeguards for the
personal liberty of blacks, this law necessarily became a serious deterrent
to slave claimants, but it was not intended to operate that way. It was a
use of the state's power to protect free men while living up to what were
believed to be the obligations of the Constitution.

New York's law of 1828 presents the same interpretive problems as the
Pennsylvania act of 1826, although it has not been examined in the same
depth.[42] As William R. Leslie briefly noted, it was passed to restore the
jury trial. Kempes Y. Schnell said that it stipulated the use of the writs of
habeas corpus and *homine replegiando* to take a black from the possession
of the alleged owner. The most prominent characteristic of the act, in his
view, was its attempt "to restrain the kidnapping of free Negroes."
Dwight Dumond, who mentioned it only in connection with the court case
that grew out of it (see chapter 4), described it as a law authorizing the
seizure and return of fugitives.[43]

Even though this law did not result from direct pressure applied by a
slave state, it still represented an effort to achieve the same balance and the
same compromise worked out in Pennsylvania between slaveholders'
claims and protection for free blacks. It did, however, go a step beyond the
1826 statute.

At the constitutional convention of 1821 a number of changes were
made in the institutional structure of the state of New York. As a result a
committee was appointed to revise the laws of the state to bring them into

[41]Robert H. Goldsborough to W. M. Meredith, March 29, 1826, Meredith Papers, Historical Society of Pennsylvania.

[42]A contemporary commentary begun by John C. Spencer, one of the revisers responsible
for the law, but completed by an anonymous Albany attorney, *Notes on the Revised Statutes
of New-York* (Albany, 1830), 201, said only that the details were too technical for an extended discussion.

[43]Leslie, "The Fugitive Slave Clause, 1787-1842," 340; Schnell, "Court Cases Involving
Slavery," 184; Dumond, *Antislavery*, 319.

line with the new Constitution. From this opening the law of 1828 emerged. The original intention was to provide for a revision similar to the work done in 1801 and 1813. The revisers could suggest occasional amendments, but, on the whole, the work would be merely a compilation of existing law.[44]

One of the revisors, Erastus Root, began work on his own on the laws relating to taxes and highways.[45] His approach was that originally contemplated, a compilation.

John Duer and Benjamin Franklin Butler (the other two assigned the task of revision), however, had imbibed the Benthamite ideas on legal reform wafting over from England. Jeremy Bentham, a leading opponent of judicial lawmaking, forcefully argued for the infusion of scientific principles into the province of law. His desire was a comprehensive act of creation to make the law what it ought to be: an internally consistent, logically ordered body of rules with the objective of securing the greatest happiness for the greatest number.[46] Influenced by such ideas Duer and Butler argued that "valuable improvements might be made . . . by adopting a new and more scientific method." To illustrate, Duer prepared a sample revision of the acts relative to the court for the trial of impeachments and the correction of errors, and of the acts concerning the court of chancery. These revisions were sent to the legislature, along with a letter explaining what the revisers had in mind, in order to get an express authorization for a sweeping reform of the New York statutes. One of the principal advantages of such a revision, Duer and Butler argued, would be to make the laws "so concise, simple, and perspicuous, as to be intelligible, not only to professional men, but to persons of every capacity." They wanted to apply to the law, "the noblest of *all* sciences, those principles of an enlarged philosophy, which now obtain in every other department of knowledge."[47]

On April 21, 1825, the legislators responded favorably to their request. Root was paid for his services and dropped. By the act of 1825 Duer, Butler, and Henry Wheaton, who was the United States Supreme Court reporter at that time, were appointed to begin the broad revision. They started by drawing "instruction and examples" from the reforms in England, and along the same line, from the work of Edward Livingston, who was in the process of preparing a comprehensive code for Louisiana.[48] In

---

[44] *The Revised Statutes of the State of New York* (3 vols.; 2d ed. Albany, 1836), 3: Appendix, 403.

[45] William Allen Butler, *The Revision of the Statutes of the State of New York, and the Revisers* (New York and Albany, 1889), 11–12.

[46] A fine, brief introduction to Bentham is William Holdsworth, *Some Makers of English Law: The Tagore Lectures 1937-38* (Cambridge, Eng., 1966), 248–56. On the importance attached to legislative lawmaking, as opposed to judicial, see Roscoe Pound, *The Formative Era of American Law* (Boston, 1938), 38–81; Maxwell Bloomfield, "William Sampson and the Codifiers: The Roots of American Legal Reform, 1820–1830," *American Journal of Legal History,* 11 (1967); 234.

[47] *Revised Statutes* (2d ed.), 3: 403, 405, 407–10.

[48] See the progress report of March 15, 1826 in *Revised Statutes* (2d ed.) 3: 414.

the spring of 1827 Wheaton was appointed chargé d'affaires to Denmark. To replace him Governor DeWitt Clinton chose John C. Spencer, a devoted Clintonian. Of the three men who completed the work on the *Revised Statutes* only one, John Duer, was a notable opponent of slavery. It was, by and large, an extremely capable group of men, men who had shown no inclination to pursue a very radical course of action—men, in fact, much like Meredith of Pennsylvania in their values, training, and commitments.[49] Benjamin F. Butler, like Meredith, was a member of the American Colonization Society.[50] The solution to the racial problem suggested by this body, of course, was separation and the shipment of black people out of the United States.[51]

The result of all the labor, the two-volume *Revised Statutes of New York*, was one of the most important revisions of the nineteenth century. It passed the legislature without significant opposition. Throughout, a nonpartisan spirit was maintained; indeed, such an opponent of the Democrats as Jabez Hammond voted for Butler so that Butler could work in the legislature for the passage of the various parts of the revision.[52] Beginning in September, 1827, the different parts of the *Revised Statutes* were passed at succeeding sessions of the legislature.

There were four different parts, and each part was in turn divided into chapters, titles, articles, and sections. Parts three and four, which contained provisions concerned with the personal liberty of blacks, were passed during two separate sessions of the legislature in 1828, apparently without significant opposition or debate.[53] The article entitled, "Of the Writ of Habeas Corpus, to bring up a Person to testify, or to answer in certain cases," marked a significant departure from the existing law of New York. This section of the *Revised Statutes* built upon the compromise

[49]Butler had been a partner in the law office of Martin Van Buren from 1817 to 1821 when he became District Attorney of Albany County. He was a member of the Regency and a staunch Democrat down to the time of the Kansas-Nebraska Act of 1854. In 1833 he became attorney general in Andrew Jackson's cabinet. *DAB.* 3: 356. Erastus Root was also a leader in the Bucktail faction of the New York Democracy. At one point in his career he was nominated for governor by the "Workey's." By 1830, however, he had become disillusioned with the Democracy. He bolted and became a Whig. *DAB.* 16: 145. John Duer began his legal career studying law in the office of Alexander Hamilton. Most of his life was spent with the law rather than in politics. By the 1850s he became Chief Justice of the Superior Court of the City of New York. *DAB.* 5: 485. Spencer served in the General Assembly of the state, and in Congress. Later he joined the Anti-Masonic party, and still later he was to serve as a Whig secretary of war in John Tyler's cabinet in 1841. *DAB.* 17: 449. Duer was a delegate to the American Convention in 1829. Alice Dana Adams, *The Neglected Period of Anti-Slavery in America (1808–1831)* (Boston, 1908), 255.

[50]Benjamin F. Butler first appears as an officer of the Albany Auxiliary of The Colonization Society in 1824, *The Seventh Annual Report of the American Society for Colonizing the Free People of Colour of the United States* (Washington, D.C., 1824), 170; Meredith was listed as a subscriber in 1820, *Third Annual Report*, 143.

[51]P. J. Standenraus, *The African Colonization Movement 1816-1865* (New York, 1961).

[52]Jabez D. Hammond, *The History of Political Parties in the State of New-York* (2 vols.; Albany, 1842), 2: 262–63.

[53]*The Revised Statues of the State of New York* (3 vols.; 1st ed.; Albany, 1829), 1: vi.

worked out in Pennsylvania two years before. Like the earlier law, this one represented an attempt voluntarily to provide procedures by which the state could meet its obligation to assist in the reclamation of fugitive slaves, and at the same time protect the personal liberty of blacks within the state.

It authorized the arrest and return of fugitives, as did the Pennsylvania law.[54] A claimant, or his agent, had to apply to a court of the state authorized to issue writs of habeas corpus. Upon presentation of acceptable proof of his title the writ would be issued directly to the sheriff of the county where the runaway was known to reside. Habeas corpus was used here, for the first time, as a process of recaption of slaves. The lawmakers in making this use of the writ were working in terms of logical relationships rather than historical ones, marking a Benthamite influence. Building on the analogy to child-custody cases, in which the habeas corpus could be used by a parent to regain the custody of his child, they allowed slave owners to use it to regain custody of their property.[55]

Once the writ had been issued in behalf of the claimant the sheriff would arrest the alleged fugitive and bring him before the court issuing the writ to answer to the claim. The putative owner, before the writ could issue, had to set forth very explicitly the grounds for his claim, the time of escape of the alleged fugitive, and his present location. All this had to be done by affidavit. Once the black was presented to the court, a hearing would be held on the "allegations and proofs of the parties." The presiding judge, or judges, on discretion could allow time to either party to obtain additional evidence. If the time was extended the defendant could be committed to the sheriff for safekeeping; or he could take a bond, with sufficient sureties, to appear and abide by the decision of the court. If the court found for the defendant, the claimant would have to forfeit $100 to him as well as pay costs and expenses. He also would be subject to a damage suit. If the claim was upheld a certificate would be given to the claimant describing the black by name, age, size, and personal appearance. This certificate would authorize the claimant to remove the alleged fugitive, without unnecessary delay.

Another significant section provided that no claimant, or his agent, could remove a fugitive, or even "do any act towards such removal," unless it was in accordance with the procedure outlined in the earlier sections. No claimant would be authorized by state law to exercise a right of recaption. There could be no seizure and removal by self-help alone.

This by no means meant a refusal to recognize, or accept the obligation imposed by the fugitive slave clause as the revisers conceived it. Their original note explaining this new state procedure makes their objective clear. "The provisions here offered," they wrote, "conform substantially to those

---

[54]*Ibid.*, 2: 560–61.
[55]Oakes, "Habeas Corpus in the States," 278.

of the act of congress referred to, but vary the details so as to afford the utmost opportunity to a fair investigation, and to check any abuse of such a claim."[56]

The hearing before the court or officer issuing the writ of habeas corpus, however, was not considered by the revisers a sufficient protection for a free black who might be claimed as a fugitive. They, therefore, urged a confirmation of the right of a man to the writ *de homine replegiando*. An alleged fugitive would have a right to this writ in spite of the fact that the writ of habeas corpus had been issued for his arrest. Once the *homine replegiando* had issued, all proceedings on the habeas corpus would be suspended until final judgment by the jury.[57] These sections were drawn, the revisers observed, "for the purpose of enabling any person claimed as a fugitive, to have such claim tried by a jury, in the ordinary course of judicial proceedings." And for this purpose the writ *de homine replegiando* was "well adapted to the case." The effect of these sections, they concluded, would be "that no person can be removed under the authority of a judge of the United States, or of this state, upon the summary inquiry and decision contemplated by the act of congress, if a demand of a trial by jury shall have been made." New York clearly had gone a step beyond Pennsylvania. The legislators in New York obviously did not feel that the reasoning in *Wright* v. *Deacon* was compelling.

The revised laws of New York,[58] like the Pennsylvania act of 1826, nevertheless, represent a voluntary effort to find a workable balance between a duty to protect free blacks and the obligation to uphold the legitimate claims of slave owners. Congress had failed to provide this balance in 1817–18, so the effort was made to secure it in the states.

Both New York and Pennsylvania provided new state procedures for the assistance of claimants. State officials would become involved more actively in the reclamation process, something slaveholders had been seeking since the 1790s. At the same time both states acted on the assumption that they possessed the constitutional power to provide some standards for those officials who might be called upon to administer the federal law, and both states adopted a new reading of the guarantee to slave owners in the fugitive slave clause which did not include recaption by self-help alone. In New York, moreover, a black could have a jury trial (by suing out a writ *de homine replegiando*) even though a claimant had appealed to the federal courts. In Pennsylvania, Tilghman's 1819 decision and the apprehensions of people like Meredith stood in the way of using this writ in any case involving a claim to a runaway.

---

[56] *Revised Statutes* (2d ed.), 3: 783.

[57] *Ibid.* (1st ed.), 2: 561–62.

[58] Another section of the *Revised Statutes* set the penalty for kidnapping a man with the intention of selling him into slavery at ten years in the state prison. This was part 4, chapter 1, title 2, article 2, "Of rape, maiming, kidnapping, and other offences against the person, not herein enumerated."

Despite these variations both states were seeking to balance competing claims, and to find a way to make recoveries peaceable. In the 1830s and 1840s, however, when sectional tensions increased, both proslavery and antislavery people began to see vital sacrifices of principles in these laws.

Assaults Upon the Personal Liberty Laws 4

In 1829 David Walker's pamphlet appeared in Boston exhorting blacks, if necessary, to resort to violence to obtain their freedom. This call for revolutionary action in the *Appeal to the Colored Citizens of the World* created a stir in the South, intensifying the fear of slave insurrections: it was looked on as a vicious, inflammatory call for social disruption and violence.[1] The publication of Walker's pamphlet was one of those events that intensified the uneasiness of many southerners about their system of racial control by the late 1820s and early 1830s. Throughout the 1820s the persistence of Jeffersonian ideas created considerable tension in the South.[2] Jefferson's famous remark, noted earlier, was but one of the more articulate expressions of this tension: "We have the wolf by the ears, and we can neither hold him nor safely let him go. Justice is in one scale, and self-preservation in the other." By the end of that decade Stephen D. Miller, the governor of South Carolina, contended that "slavery is not a national evil; on the contrary, it is a national benefit."[3] As early as the mid-1820s the idea that slavery was a positive good had found able exponents in South Carolina. As Edward Brown said, slavery was "the stepping ladder by which countries have passed from barbarism to civilization."[4]

Such a momentous change in southern thinking about the "peculiar institution" resulted from serious internal and external challenges after the War of 1812. One such assault on the South's system of racial adjustment came in the Missouri debates. Up to that time, as William S. Jenkins has noted, slaveholders had been relatively complacent, willing to rest for their security on the constitutional compromises. But now those very compromises were being vigorously challenged by men like Rufus King who declared that "no human law, compact, or compromise can establish or continue slavery."[5] Such views shook the complacency of many slave owners.

---

[1]Clement Eaton, "A Dangerous Pamphlet in the Old South," *Journal of Southern History*, 2 (1936): 1–12.

[2]Clement Eaton, *The Freedom-of-Thought Struggle in the Old South* (New York, 1964), chap. 1; Rollin G. Osterweis, *Romanticism and Nationalism in the Old South* (New Haven, 1949), 21. Charles Grier Sellers, Jr., "The Travail of Slavery," in Charles Grier Sellers, ed., *The Southerner as American* (Chapel Hill, N.C., 1960), has shown how this tension persisted throughout the antebellum period.

[3]Quoted in William S. Jenkins, *Pro-Slavery Thought in the Old South* (Chapel Hill, N.C., 1935), 76–77.

[4]Quoted in *ibid.*, 73.

[5]Quoted in *ibid.*, 68.

Internally the system was severely battered by the Denmark Vesey conspiracy in Charleston in 1822.[6] Vesey's conspiracy was betrayed, but the anxiety it caused among white Charlestonians could not be eliminated so easily. "Our NEGROES are truly the *Jacobins* of the country," wrote Edwin C. Holland after the event, "they are the anarchists and the *domestic enemy*; *the common enemy of civilized society*, and the barbarians who would, IF THEY COULD, become the DESTROYERS *of our race*."[7] To control such a dangerous social element South Carolina tightened up its black code[8] and adopted the controversial Negro Seaman's Act.[9] The fears of a slave revolution were quickened again in late 1825 when a series of fires swept Charleston, and apprehension spread to the countryside when a slave conspiracy was uncovered in Georgetown in 1829.[10]

Following the publication of Walker's pamphlet in 1829 the fear of slave insurrections spread further and began to get a grip over the whole region south of the Mason-Dixon line. Legislatures throughout the South began passing measures designed to secure further white control over the black population.[11] Slave owners were becoming increasingly sensitive to the strains within the social system under which they lived; they sought some resolution of the inner tensions, and in the process Jeffersonian liberalism was eroded in the South. Many slaveholders began to see radicalism in the most temperate positions. Many of them even came to see danger in the schemes of the American Colonization Society, which was, said the *Charleston Mercury*, "justly regarded as murderous in its principles, and as tending inevitably to the destruction of the public peace."[12]

All this occurred before the rise of the immediatist movement in the North, which was born in part of the frustrations of facing an uncompromising South.[13] At the same time the rise of that movement further polarized the sections and increased southern sensitivity toward the "peculiar institution." William Lloyd Garrison's searing words echoed all over the region below the Mason-Dixon line: "I will not equivocate—I will not excuse—I will not retreat a single inch—AND I WILL BE HEARD."

[6]The most detailed account of Denmark Vesey and the conspiracy is John Lofton, *Insurrection in South Carolina: The Turbulent World of Denmark Vesey* (Yellow Springs, Ohio, 1964).

[7]William W. Freehling, *Prelude to Civil War: The Nullification Controversy in South Carolina, 1816–1836* (New York, 1965), 57, 59.

[8]Lofton, *Insurrection*, 196–7.

[9]*Ibid.*, 111–18; Donald G. Morgan, *Justice William Johnson: The First Dissenter* (Columbia, 1954), 192–96. The act required that all black seamen be seized and jailed while their ships remained in Charleston harbor. Justice Johnson declared that the law violated a treaty the United States had signed with Great Britain. He heard the case while on circuit.

[10]Freehling, *Prelude to Civil War*, 61–62.

[11]Herbert Aptheker, *Nat Turner's Slave Rebellion* (New York, 1966), 28 ff, has as good a summary of this legislation as any other. It included quarantine laws and laws prohibiting the sale of firearms to blacks, for example.

[12]Quoted in Jenkins, *Pro-Slavery Thought*, 76.

[13]David Brion Davis, "The Emergence of Immediatism in British and American Antislavery Thought, "*Mississippi Valley Historical Review*, 49 (September, 1962): 226.

Eight months after Garrison published those words in the first issue of *The Liberator* (January 1, 1831) Nat Turner led some of the blacks of Southampton County, Virginia, in the bloodiest slave uprising before the Civil War. Turner's rebellion, if anything, increased the concern of slave owners throughout the South for security from their human property.

One result of all this was the spread of the proslavery argument that slavery was a positive good, and of the view that any plan of emancipation would lead inevitably to bloodshed. Such arguments were designed to quiet the fears of whites and to instill "right thinking" throughout the white population about the South's system of racial domination.[14]

Closing off the debate in the South provided some psychological release, but the slave-owning communities still had to face the challenge from outside the region. During the 1830s proslavery apologists erected their defenses against this external menace. One of the most potent was the constitutional doctrine of state sovereignty. That South Carolina's attempt to exercise its alleged sovereign powers to nullify the federal tariff in 1832–33 was as much a response to the growing fears about slavery as economic oppression is evident from the remarks of some of the participants. After the Turner rebellion, for example, James Hamilton, Jr. informed James Hammond that the blood spilled by Turner and his followers was nothing compared to what would happen "if we do not stand manfully at the Safety Valve of Nullification."[15]

State nullification raised the specter of disunion and civil war but because the other slave states refused to stand behind South Carolina's outright nullification of federal law, and President Jackson forcefully repudiated it, the crisis was passed. Nevertheless, the South was beginning to move toward some very aggressive constitutional ideas in order to secure the "rights" of slave owners. By 1837 John C. Calhoun had moved well beyond the doctrine of state interposition: it was no longer enough for a state to defend itself by making a federal law inapplicable within that state's jurisdiction. On December 27, 1837, he introduced a series of resolutions in the United States Senate, including the demand that the federal government so "exercise its powers as to give . . . increased stability and security to the domestic institutions of the States that compose the Union."[16] At the moment this was too advanced for some southerners like Senator William Preston who declared that the federal government "had no right to interfere, either to protect or to invade any institution."[17] It was not too much, however, to impose the now infamous gag rule in 1836: "all petitions, memorials, resolutions, propositions, or papers, relating in any way, or to any extent whatever, to the subject of slavery, or the abolition

---

[14]Ralph E. Morrow, "The Proslavery Argument Revisited," *Mississippi Valley Historical Review*, 47 (June, 1961): 79–93.

[15]Freehling, *Prelude to Civil War*, 251.

[16]*Cong. Globe*, 25th Cong., 2d sess., Dec. 27, 1837, 55.

[17]*Ibid.*, Jan. 1838, Appendix, 22.

of slavery, shall, without being either printed or referred, be laid upon the table, and . . . no further action whatever shall be had thereon."[18]

All of these efforts during the 1820s and 1830s to create a closed society insofar as the racial question was concerned had important ramifications and echoes in the North. Antiabolitionism, feeding on racial antipathies and apprehension over the fate of the Union, was at a peak during the 1830s. "The prejudice of race," wrote Alexis de Tocqueville after his tour of the United States in 1831, "appears to be stronger in the states that have abolished slavery than in those where it still exists; and nowhere is it so intolerant as in those states where servitude has never been known."[19] Throughout the 1830s racial violence seemed to be on the increase in the North as riots erupted in a number of cities. One of the worst occurred in Philadelphia in August, 1834, during which one black was killed, a Negro Presbyterian church was destroyed, homes were wrecked, and numerous blacks were subjected to indignities at the hands of the infuriated white mob.[20]

At the same time antiabolitionist riots erupted in several cities provoked, in part at least, by fears aroused by the rise of the organized immediatist movement. Antiabolitionism, although not necessarily the violence associated with it, also was endorsed by many Jacksonian Democratic leaders throughout the 1830s. The circulation of abolitionist literature President Jackson branded as "unconstitutional and wicked," and by 1836 his postmaster general, Amos Kendall, was authorizing southern justices of the peace to fine local postmasters who did not immedidately burn the "incendiary publications." James Burden, the Democratic president of the Pennsylvania senate, took the view that "modern abolitionism" was upsetting the spirit of compromise without which the Union never could have been formed. Governor William L. Marcy of New York, after having agreed to requests from several southern governors seeking the return of runaways, defended the rights of the South, and referred to the abolitionists as "fanatics." Even Robert Rantoul, Jr., who later became a leading Democratic opponent of slavery, declared that the abolitionists were out to detroy the Union.[21]

Antiabolitionism, although most pronounced in the Democratic party, was not limited to the Jacksonians. Apprehensive over the future of the Union, Edward Everett in 1837, while governor of Massachusetts, for example, insisted that abolition would divide the Union.[22] In August, 1835,

[18] *Register of Debates*, 24th Cong., 1st sess., May 26, 1836, 4051–52.

[19] Alexis de Tocqueville, *Democracy in America*, ed. Phillips Bradley (2 vols.; New York, 1959), 1: 373.

[20] Dumond, *Antislavery*, 219.

[21] Lorman Ratner, *Powder Keg: Northern Opposition to the Antislavery Movement, 1831–1840* (New York, 1968), 54, 55, 57; Edward Pessen, *Jacksonian America: Society, Personality, and Politics* (Homewood, Ill., 1969), 322–24; Leonard L. Richards, *"Gentlemen of Property and Standing": Anti-abolition Mobs in Jacksonian America* (New York, 1970).

[22] Ratner, *Powder Keg*, 54.

the leading capitalists of Boston held a public meeting at Faneuil Hall to pledge to "our countrymen of the South" their support for the perpetuation of slavery, and to express "the almost universal sentiment of regret and indignation at the conduct of the abolitionists."[23]

Most northerners (whether moved by racial fears, fear of violence, or concern for the Union) were in no mood to support the "chimerical" schemes of the abolitionists during the 1830s.[24] On the contrary, many of them were quite willing to concede the legitimacy of the demand for protection for southern "rights." And by the 1830s the compromises worked out in the free states during the 1820s were looked on in the South as invasions of those rights. No longer would southerners echo Goldsborough's satisfaction with the Pennsylvania law because it gave evidence of the willingness of the North to accept voluntarily the responsibility imposed by the Constitution to return runaways. As a result many northerners abandoned those compromises, and instead turned to a defense of southern claims. Thrown into the crucible of sectional antagonisms and fears, the laws designed to protect the personal liberty of free blacks were themselves no longer secure.

The first major assault on one of the compromise laws came in Pennsylvania. Following the massacre of whites in Southampton County many blacks from southern states made their way North, with many of them settling in Philadelphia. Their presence created a great deal of tension in the city, which had already been rocked by racial riots. Edward Bettle, an antislavery Philadelphian, wrote in 1832 in fact that "the public mind here is more aroused even among respectable persons than it has been for several years." He added that he feared one of the results of the uneasiness in the city would be the repeal of the Personal Liberty Law of 1826 which would then leave kidnappers "free scope for their nefarious labors."[25]

There was good reason for Bettle's apprehension. At the beginning of 1832 an effort was made to repeal the law. Resolutions were introduced in the house to repeal the acts of 1820 and 1826 and give "full effect to the Act of 1793." Another resolution called for a prohibition on the migration of free blacks into the state.[26]

Negroes from Philadelphia memorialized the legislature against any such action. Up to the passage of those laws recaption without any recourse to law had been allowed in the state. "Such, we earnestly pray, may it

[23]Lawrence Lader, *The Bold Brahmins, New England's War Against Slavery; 1831–1863* (New York, 1961), 16.

[24]Ratner, *Powder Keg*, has identified four principal sources for the antiabolitionist sentiments of the 1830s: (1) racism; (2) fear of violence; (3) the belief that antislavery activity was being directed from abroad; and (4) the view that slavery was secured by the Constitution, and that antislavery endangered the Union by infringing on the legitimate claims of slave owners.

[25]Quoted in DuBois, *The Philadelphia Negro*, 27.

[26]Similar efforts to exclude blacks were made in other states. The fullest account of this movement is Litwack, *North of Slavery*.

never be again. Pennsylvania has revolted from the flagrant injustice. She has taken one step in advance." Instead of the "retrograde step now proposed" the legislature should move forward: it should provide that "the *decision of a jury* should be required upon so high a question as the liberty of a man."[27]

The Pennsylvania Abolition Society also protested the resolutions and urged the legislature to leave the existing laws intact. The state should not abandon "her high moral standing." A special committee was appointed to confer with members of the senate and house to see that no law was placed on the books "denying to one class of men on account of a different shade in their skin,-those privileges which under the constitution are solemnly recognized as the common rights of all."[28]

Under such pressure the movement to repeal the state's Personal Liberty Laws was turned back for the moment. The compromise in Pennsylvania remained until the Supreme Court struck it down in 1842 in *Prigg* v. *Pennsylvania.*

Massachusetts, on the other hand, obliged the South in 1835 by eliminating the writ *de homine replegiando* from the statute books. In 1832 commissioners were appointed to prepare a revision of the statutes of the state. Their proposal concerning the writ *de homine replegiando* was drawn substantially from the *Revised Statutes* of New York. There were, however, some "few modifications." The notes of the revisers show clearly what they had in mind. Habeas corpus, they wrote, "furnishes so complete and effectual a remedy for all cases of unlawful imprisonment or restraint, that the writ *de homine replegiando* is very seldom used." This later writ, however, still could be of some value. Its primary use was to protect a person seized without legal warrant or process as a fugitive from labor or service.[29] The Massachusetts revisers, although they wanted to retain the writ *de homine replegiando*, did not conceive of using it to stay any legal proceedings, as was the case in New York. The writ's use would be confined to cases in which restraint was without any lawful writ or process. It could apply against outright kidnappers and masters exercising their alleged right of recaption.

The Massachusetts legislature, however, without a word of debate, rejected the argument of the revisers (or perhaps merely ignored it). Section 38 of Chapter 111 of the *Revised Statutes*, adopted in 1835, consisted of the one sentence: "The writ *de homine replegiando* is abolished."[30]

[27] *Memorial to the Senate and House of Representatives of the Commonwealth of Pennsylvania from the people of colour of the city of Philadelphia and its vicinity* (Philadelphia, 1832), 4–5.

[28] Penn. Abolition Soc. Minutes (1825–47), 3: 152, 158–61; *Penn. House Journal, 1832,* 283.

[29] *Report of the Commissioners Appointed to Revise the General Statutes of the Commonwealth* (Boston, 1834), part 3, 220.

[30] Theron Metcalf and Horace Mann, *The Revised Statutes of the Commonwealth of Massachusetts, passed November 4, 1835* (Boston, 1836), 660.

Since the object of the revision was to make the state law "more plain and easy,"[31] the abolition of this old, ponderous writ possibly was thought to be a progressive legal step; but it is surely more than a mere coincidence that this writ (the function of which was to protect free blacks from unlawful seizure) was abolished only a few months after the conservatives had held their mass meeting to apologize to the South for Boston abolitionism.

An even more important assault was made on the New York law of 1828 because in that state the issues were debated publicly, and not muted. "The pursuers are making a great effort to overthrow the law of this State, which grants to every fugitive the right of a jury trial," the American Anti-Slavery Society noted.[32]

On April 5, 1830, a black man named Jack made good his escape from his owner in New Orleans. Three years later his owner, Mary Martin, presented an affidavit to the Recorder of New York setting forth her claim. The recorder, in compliance with the state law of 1828, issued a writ of habeas corpus to the sheriff of the city requiring him to seize the alleged runaway. At the hearing the recorder found in favor of Mary Martin. But this was only the beginning. In the highly charged atmosphere of the mid-1830s this case became the vehicle for securing the "rights" of claimants and undermining the compromise of 1828.

Following the decision in her favor Mary Martin appointed the sheriff to receive the fugitive for the purpose of removal to New Orleans. At this point Jack's case was picked up by an agent for the newly formed American Anti-Slavery Society.[33] A writ *de homine replegiando* was sued out against Mary Martin in order to secure a jury trial for Jack. In the case before the city's superior court, however, Jack again lost. Mary Martin's return to the *homine replegiando* had stipulated that she was a resident of New Orleans; that she had claimed Jack according to New York state law; that he was held to service under the laws of Louisiana; and—finally—that she now held him by virtue of the certificate granted by the recorder. Jack's counsel argued that she was a resident of New York, and not New Orleans, and that, therefore, she could not lawfully claim Jack, or anyone else, as a slave. His counsel did admit that Jack had been a slave under Louisiana law while his owner resided in New Orleans; but he claimed that after March, 1833, Mary Martin had become a resident of New York, and this residence nullified the former relationship. Since the alleged change of domicile had not been proved satisfactorily, and Jack had admitted being a slave in Louisiana, Mary Martin's claim was sustained in the superior court trial.

[31] *Report of the Commissioners*, part 3, 220.

[32] *First Annual Report of the American Anti-Slavery Society* (New York, 1834), 57.

[33] Manumission Society, New York City, Standing Committee, Minutes (July 15, 1817–January 11, 1842); listed under May 23, 1834, New-York Historical Society. There are no page numbers in these minutes. The few early records of the American Anti-Slavery Society do not verify the early involvement of the society.

A writ of error was sued out from this decision in the superior court to the Supreme Court of New York. The case was heard there during the May term, 1834.

In the supreme court the judgment reached in the superior court trial was upheld. Significantly, the opinion in the appellate court held that the matter was *res judicata* under the Constitution and laws of the United States.[34] This meant that the state courts did not have competent jurisdiction to decide this dispute: they could not decide between Mary Martin's avowry and Jack's plea. If sufficient proofs were offered by the claimant, regardless of whether they were true or false, federal law required that a certificate of removal be issued.

This decision in the supreme court was delivered by Justice Samuel Nelson, who contended that the fugitive slave clause rested upon a doubt that the states would "regard the rights of the owner, or properly protect them by local legislation." In his view the state could not "amend, qualify, or in any manner alter" the act of Congress. "It is obvious," he added, "if Congress have not the power to prescribe the mode and manner of the 'delivering up,' and thereby provide the means of enforcing the execution of the rights secured by this provision, its solemn guaranty may be wholly disregarded, in defiance of the government." Where a federal right, such as the right to reclaim fugitives, was created or secured the means were available to the federal government to sustain that right. A certificate granted under the law of 1793, then, was a sufficient warrant for the removal of an alleged runaway, and the state was precluded from obstructing this removal by an inquiry under the writ *de homine replegiando*. The New York law, he concluded, was unconstitutional.[35]

This was not, however, the end of the case of *Jack* v. *Martin*. New York's supreme court was not the highest appellate court in the state; it was merely an intermediate court of appeals. The highest court was the Court for the Correction of Errors. This court provided Jack with his last opportunity for a favorable adjudication in the state system. He had already lost in three separate hearings.

Jack's case was taken up on a writ of error by his counsel. Doubtless they were more interested, in this final hearing, in securing a judgment favorable to state power than in the freedom of their immediate client, Jack, who had already unsuccessfully availed himself of the procedures outlined in the state code. In their arguments before the court Jack's attorneys went straight to the heart of Justice Nelson's opinion.

Congress, in their view, had no power under the Constitution to legislate on the subject of persons held to service or labor. Properly interpreted the fugitive slave clause would be self-executing. The common-law remedies in such matters, they noted, were a general right on the part of the claimant to recover his property, and the writ *de homine replegiando* for the party

[34]*Jack* v. *Martin*, 12 Wendell 327.
[35]*Ibid.*, 12 Wendell 320.

seized. The statutory remedies under the *Revised Statutes*, they contended, corresponded to these common law remedies. As long as the question of freedom remained open, they argued further, "it is competent for *the state where the seizure takes place* to apply the remedy—because, the gravamen, the subject matter of the claim, and the parties, are within its jurisdiction-because, the party seized being *de facto* a citizen of that state, owing it allegiance and service, is entitled to its protection, until the right to remove is established *in that state*."[36] Jack's counsel then concluded their argument with Dr. Johnson's notorious nonsequitur on the complaint of the American colonials that they were sent to England to be tried for treason in America. "If, said he, they do not wish to be tried for treason in England, let them not commit treason in America. This is the very question—slave or traitor to be tried by a jury *here*. A man sent away as a slave has no means of appealing to a jury of the country as a freeman."[37]

In his argument before the court Mary Martin's counsel relied heavily on Justice Nelson's opinion in the supreme court. The federal law, he said, provided only for a summary investigation. "A preliminary decision by a court without jury of a matter of fact, for the purpose of determining the proper venue, which is not final as to the fact itself, but leaves it open for examination on the trial, is not an infraction of the right of trial by jury."[38] Any free black taken South, he argued, could obtain a writ *de homine replegiando* in the circuit court of the United States, but the state could not provide such a remedy.

The constitutional and legal issues to be decided by the Court for the Correction of Errors thus were defined ably by counsel on both sides of the dispute. Directly at issue was the power of the states to protect the personal liberty of blacks claimed as runaways and to regulate recoveries.

Before a decision was rendered in the case of *Jack* v. *Martin* the New York law came before federal Supreme Court Justice Smith Thompson in the case of *In re Martin* (which was not connected with *Jack* v. *Martin*) in the Circuit Court for the Southern District of New York.[39] The case involved a motion to quash the writ *de homine replegiando* issued from the federal circuit court to take an alleged fugitive, Peter Martin, out of the hands of a state officer who had seized him by virtue of the state law.

Thompson dismissed the contention that the failure to provide for a jury trial in the federal law made it void, with the observation that the inquiry before the magistrate was only a preliminary hearing to authorize a removal. There were only two issues in such a hearing: the identity of the

[36] *Jack* v. *Martin*, 14 Wendell 512.
[37] *Ibid.*, 515.
[38] *Ibid.*, 520.
[39] *In re Martin*, 2 Paine 348. The reporter of this case did not date it. In his opinion Justice Thompson noted that the New York Supreme Court had declared New York's law unconstitutional, but that this question was then pending before the Court of Errors. The decision in this case then was sometime after Nelson's opinion in 1834, and before the Court of Error's opinion in late 1835. Hurd, *Law of Freedom and Bondage*, 2: 455, placed *In re Martin* in 1837, and therefore missed its relation to *Jack* v. *Martin*.

person seized, and the obligation of service. Whether or not the man claimed was legitimately held to service was not at issue. That question could be raised in the state from which he fled.

Thompson then sustained the motion to quash the writ. He declined to pass directly on the state law since a case was pending in the state courts, but he did note that the fugitive slave clause required implementing legislation and, he added, "it cannot be presumed that it was intended to leave this to state legislation."

When the Court of Errors approached the problem of deciding on the constitutionality of the law of Congress and the act of the state, there were then two recent opinions (one in a state and one in a federal court) which had to be taken into serious consideration. Both opinions sustained congressional action, and neither was favorable to the compromise worked out in the late 1820s.

Two opinions were delivered in the Court of Errors in the case of *Jack* v. *Martin*: one by Senator Isaac W. Bishop, and the other by Chancellor Reuben Hyde Walworth. Both opinions affirmed the ruling of the state supreme court that Jack was a slave who had to be returned to the South, but Chancellor Walworth's really amounted to a dissent from the reasoning of the lower court.

Even more than Justice Nelson, Senator Bishop reflected the anxieties of many northerners during the middle 1830s. He relied heavily on the arguments of Justices Nelson and Thompson, and upon Justice Isaac Parker's opinion in 1823 in the Massachusetts case of *Commonwealth* v. *Griffith*. All three jurists contended that Congress had the power to legislate in order to secure a federally guaranteed right, and that the legislation passed provided only for a summary ministerial hearing for the purpose of authorizing a removal to another judicial forum. If all the states in the Union, Bishop noted, were allowed to legislate on the subject it would "in the end lead indirectly to the abolition of slavery." "I regard this," he concluded, "as but the entering wedge to other doctrines which are designed to extirpate slavery; and we may find when it is too late, that the patience of the south, however well founded upon principles, from repeated aggression will become exhausted."

Chancellor Walworth, on the other side, wrote an extensive opinion sustaining the exercise of state power. He began by noting that in cases such as *In re Martin* where the identity of the black was not an open question, and the fact was clear that he was a fugitive who owed service and labor under the laws of another state, there could be no objection to returning him to the state from which he fled. *Jack* v. *Martin*, of course, was just such a case. But what if the identity of the man was not clear, or he claimed that he was a free, native-born citizen of the state where he was seized? Walworth could not believe that the framers of the Constitution could have intended to authorize the transportation of a person claimed after "a mere summary examination before an inferior state magistrate."

He particularly found it difficult to believe that this was to be done in a manner "so as to deprive him of the benefit of the writ of *habeas corpus* and the right of trial by jury in the state where he is found."[40]

Did Congress have the power to legislate on the subject at all? For Walworth this was the critical question, and in searching the Constitution he was unable to find any authorization for congressional action. Congress could only legislate where the power had been clearly delegated, and in the absence of such a delegation the states were left free to act. The fugitive slave clause, in his view, secured certain rights to individuals, imposed restrictions and duties on the states and on other individuals, in relation to such rights. It vested no power in Congress. It did, however, leave intact the judicial power "of declaring and enforcing the rights secured by the constitution."

Walworth placed a great deal of emphasis on the function of the judiciary since the fugitive clause was self-executing, in his judgment:

> The object of the framers of the constitution, therefore, was not to provide a new mode by which the master might be enabled to recover the services of his fugitive slave, but merely to restrain the exercise of a power, which the state legislatures respectively would otherwise have possessed, to deprive the master of such pre-existing right of recaption. Under this provision of the constitution, even without any legislation on the subject, the right of the master to reclaim the fugitive slave is fully secured, so as to give him a valid claim in damages against any one who interferes with the right.[41]

The slave owner then had a general right of recaption guaranteed by the Constitution. An alleged runaway, on the other hand, had the right to the opposing remedies, the *homine replegiando*, or "the more summary proceeding by *habeas corpus*."

State courts, in his view, would protect masters in the exercise of their constitutional rights against any improper state legislation, and the federal Supreme Court had ample power to reverse an erroneous state court decision. If any legislation was necessary, Walworth concluded, "the state legislatures are perfectly competent to pass the necessary laws to carry this provision of the constitution into full effect."[42]

Jack v. *Martin* seriously undermined the compromise law of 1828, but because of the contradictory opinions in the Court of Errors the precise status of the law remained unclear. Despite the severe buffeting in Pennsylvania, that state's compromise law stood for awhile longer; whereas in Massachusetts, one of the mainstays in the system to secure personal freedom had been struck down.

---

[40]*Jack* v. *Martin*, 14 Wendell 524–25.

[41]*Ibid.*, 527.

[42]Hurd, *Law of Freedom and Bondage*, 2: 451, contended that the main point of Walworth's opinion "was his assertion of concurrent State jurisdiction, and particularly of the validity of the State law under which the case had arisen."

The attack by proslavery people and antiabolitionists presented a serious challenge to the opponents of slavery, a challenge that was to reach a peak in 1842. Before that happened, however, antislavery people counterattacked. At the end of 1837 Sarah Grimké described the situation from the abolitionist's viewpoint: "In New York oppression reigns. The fugitive there as well as in Pennsylvania is hunted like a partridge on the mountain and denied the right of Jury trial."[43]

[43]Sarah Grimké to Sarah Douglass, November 23, 1837, in Gilbert H. Barnes and Dwight L. Dumond, eds., *Letters of Theodore Dwight Weld, Angelina Grimké Weld and Sarah Grimké 1822–1844* (2 vols.; New York, 1934), 1: 481.

The Antislavery 5
Counterattack

During the mid-1830s antislavery reformers throughout the North responded to proslavery claims and attacks by strongly demanding the states to provide for jury trials, but this demand took many different forms and meant different things. These differences arose out of dissimilar state legal traditions, and out of a significant debate within the antislavery movement over purposes and strategies that was provoked by the rise of a militant form of antislavery during the early 1830s.

The antislavery movement of the early nineteenth century broadened out in the 1830s into the more far-reaching reform demands of the immediate abolitionists. This more thoroughgoing abolitionism was created partly because of the frustration of confronting an unyielding proslavery South, and partly because of the disappointments the earlier antislavery people had faced in dealing with the complicated problems of race in the United States. By the late 1820s many of the older abolitionists were openly expressing their despair over the perplexing racial problem. The last report sent to the American Convention by the Pennsylvania Abolition Society lamented the difficulty of impressing the black man with the "utility of sending his children to receive instruction, since their subsequent employments are likely to resemble his own, yet we must do our duty in providing the means of instruction and leave the result to that providence which justly values the humblest efforts, founded on good intentions."[1] Many abolitionists continued to do their "duty," but it usually fell far short of an effective solution, so much so in fact that some came to accept, however briefly, the idea of colonization as the only viable answer. Among the colonizationists were several leading immediatists of later years, such as Elizur Wright, Arthur Tappan, and Gerrit Smith. John Duer, earlier a member of the New York Manumission Society, was another person to join the colonizationist cause. For most of these people it was a short-lived and frustrating association. When William Lloyd Garrison published the first edition of his hard-hitting immediatist newspaper, *The Liberator*, one of the particular targets he aimed at was colonization. In the next few years a heated battle raged between the colonizationists and the abolitionists which occasionally ended in riots indirectly provoked by a few

[1] *Minutes of the American Convention* (1829), 56.

71

of the "gentlemen of property and standing" who were at the head of the colonization society.[2]

The other main target of Garrison was gradualism. His newspaper marked the emergence of the doctrine of "immediatism,"[3] which had not had a very wide appeal among the earlier societies. By the end of the decade societies demanding the immediate abolition of slavery, without colonization, had almost completely eclipsed the older gradualist organizations. Some people from those older societies, in fact, became prominent in the new: Thomas Shipley of the Pennsylvania Abolition Society, for example, became one of the founders of the immediatist American Anti-Slavery Society in 1833. The Pennsylvania Abolition Society continued to work in the antislavery cause, but most of the earlier abolitionist organizations began to crumble by the late 1830s and early 1840s.

Despite the fierce language often employed by many immediatists, they began in the 1830s with a rather temperate strategy. In 1833 in the Declaration of Sentiments of the newly formed American Anti-Slavery Society "moral and political action, as prescribed in the Constitution of the United States," was urged.[4] By the 1840s, however, the continuing frustrations of dealing with the bewildering problems of slavery and race within the American federal Union split the abolitionists apart. By then the Garrisonians openly repudiated the Constitution as proslavery, rejected political action in any traditional sense, and called for a dissolution of the Union: "No union with Slaveholders" became their motto. Other emancipationists clung to the strategic statement in the 1833 Declaration of Sentiments, although they began to construct some new and imaginative views about the relationship of slavery to the Constitution. One of the first and most innovative efforts was that of Alvan Stewart who presented his ideas in 1837. Resting his case upon the Fifth Amendment he concluded that no slavery could exist in the Union unless it was proved that a person had been lawfully deprived of freedom by indictment, trial, and judgment in a court of law; anything less could not be called "due process of law." In the absence of such evidence, he contended, "any judge in the United States, who is clothed with sufficient authority, to grant a writ of *Habeas Corpus*" possessed the power to "discharge the slave and give him full liberty."

---

[2]Richards, "*Gentlemen of Property and Standing*," 131–55; David Grimsted, "Rioting in Its Jacksonian Setting," *The American Historical Review, 77* (April, 1972): 361–98, has argued persuasively that the action of such people sometimes supported mobs, but that it is doubtful that this was their intention.

[3]One of the fuller accounts of the spread of the militant antislavery movement is Louis Filler, *The Crusade against Slavery, 1830–1860* (New York, 1960); an excellent, brief account is the introduction in William H. Pease and Jane H. Pease, eds., *The Antislavery Argument* (Indianapolis, 1965); see also Dumond, *Antislavery*; an excellent new study is Aileen S. Kraditor, *Means and Ends in American Abolitionism; Garrison and his Critics on Strategy and Tactics, 1834–1850* (New York, 1969).

[4]*Proceedings of the Anti-Slavery Convention, Assembled at Philadelphia, December 4, 5, and 6, 1833* (New York, 1833), 15.

Congress moreover could abolish slavery throughout the Union by adopting a declaratory statute "carrying into effect the spirit and intention of the Fifth Amendment."[5]

This strategic split within the immediatist movement, however, did not come until the late 1830s. During their formative years the newer abolitionist societies were concerned with organizing and spreading the doctrine of immediatism upon which they all agreed. During these early years they paid little attention to the problem of obtaining greater security for free blacks from being removed to the South as slaves, or to the nature of the obligation imposed upon states and individuals by the fugitive slave clause of the Constitution.[6]

Among the first signs of concern among these immediate emancipationists was the publication of Elizur Wright's *Chronicles of Kidnapping* in the spring of 1834, in which he described the operation of the Fugitive Slave Law in New York City. At the time he wrote, eleven persons were confined in the city jail as slaves. All eleven, Wright noted, had filed their writs *de homine replegiando*. Because of the assault on the state law by the "owners of human flesh," however, this procedure for securing personal liberty was insecure. Wright sounded the tocsin before the final decision in *Jack* v. *Martin*: "Citizens of New York: shall this humane law be overthrown?"[7]

By the end of the decade some within the antislavery movement were prepared to go much further: they openly avowed their hope that such laws would be used to prevent the recovery of fugitives altogether as a step toward total abolition, as conservatives like William M. Meredith doubtless had feared all along. At the sixth annual meeting of the Executive Committee of the American Anti-Slavery Society, meeting in New York City in 1839, Henry B. Stanton offered the following resolution: "Resolved, that the political power of the free States is sufficient, if properly exercised, to ultimately exterminate slavery in the nation." Speaking on this resolution Stanton declared that abolitionists should "obtain a jury trial for such fugitives as are not *brought* but *come* from the South. . . . Give the panting fugitive this inestimable right in every northern State, and he is safe,—for, where can you find twelve impartial men among us who will decide on their oaths, that a man has not a better right to himself than another has to him . . . that the right to liberty is not inalienable?"[8]

Many supporters of the antislavery cause, however, continued to recognize the force of the constitutional obligation not to divest owners of

[5]Quoted in Jacobus ten Broek, *Equal under Law* (New York, 1965), 67–68.

[6]Occasionally blacks kept up the demand for jury trial as at the fifth annual meeting of a society of free Negroes held in Philadelphia in 1835: *Minutes of the Fifth Annual Convention for the Improvement of the Free People of Colour* (Philadelphia, 1835), 28.

[7]Quoted in the *American Anti-Slavery Reporter*, June, 1834.

[8]*Sixth Annual Report of the Executive Committee of the American Anti-Slavery Society* (New York, 1839), 15–16.

what were considered legitimate titles to human beings acquired under the laws of slave-owning communities. In a memorial presented to the state legislature in 1837 the Pennsylvania Abolition Society admitted that "as it is generally accepted," the Constitution made the return of fugitives "obligatory upon the authorities of the free states." The state, however, had the right to prescribe the mode of delivery of any runaway coming within its jurisdiction. It also had the right "to enact such laws, as shall protect her citizens of every complexion from the ruthless assaults of unprincipled men, and shall secure to those who may be seized as runaway slaves, that form of trial which alone is consistent with her just and liberal policy."[9]

At the founding convention of the Pennsylvania Anti-Slavery Society, an immediatist organization, in late January and early February, 1837, the tensions between these various views came out very clearly. Benjamin Lundy, the old warhorse of abolitionism, represented the older, more cautious antislavery position on the matter of runaways. He readily admitted that the Constitution required the states to give up fugitive slaves, but, he added, it had to be "upon sufficient proof that claims against them were strictly legal." Free men had been seized and sold into slavery for life, he concluded, "and perhaps no better plan can be devised, than to grant the trial by jury in all cases of claims to service, that the acknowledged rights, privileges, and immunities of our own citizens may be duly guarded and protected."[10]

The more radical on this issue urged a jury trial on the "broad ground of justice and expediency." The published proceedings do not reveal any discussion by them of the constitutional obligation, although a unanimously adopted resolution shows the strains between them and those who espoused Lundy's argument. This resolution was as follows:

> *Resolved*, That whatever difference of opinion may exist in respect to the degree and kind of obligation resting on the people of the free states, under the Federal Constitution, to return fugitive slaves to their masters, there is no obligation imposed on the sovereign states, to surrender the liberties of any persons without trial by jury.[11]

This accurately reflects the fact that a diversity of purposes and views existed among antislavery reformers, as well as the fact that whatever their intentions or hopes, they could join in the demand for a jury trial in cases involving claims to service.

A jury trial, of course, was still available in theory in some jurisdictions through the writ *de homine replegiando*, although it had been rendered insecure through such decisions as *Wright* v. *Deacon* and *Jack* v. *Martin*, and in Massachusetts it had been abolished. By the late 1830s, in any event, the

[9]Penn. Abolition Soc. Minutes (1825–47), 3: 277.

[10]*Proceedings of the Pennsylvania Convention, assembled to organize a State Anti-Slavery Society, at Harrisburg, on the 31st of January and 1st, 2d, 3d of February 1837* (Philadelphia, 1837), 13.

[11]*Ibid.*, 57.

antislavery demand for jury trial was not focused on this writ, except in Massachusetts. By that time the writ was criticized as inadequate as well as insecure. Even if an alleged fugitive was granted the right to bring his writ, wrote Joshua Leavitt in an 1838 editorial in *The Emancipator*, it would be "far from satisfying justice or her friends." The antiquated common law remedy was "burdened with technicalities, involving unnecessary expense and liable to failure for want of due formality." It was hardly, Leavitt believed, "a remedy fit for a *poor man*." Despite the concern for human freedom behind New York's law, there was something unreal and unduly abstract about it, because it was completely inoperative "without the intervention of extraordinary philanthropy." It was also inadequate because it was not obligatory in all cases. Some antislavery people, at least, had now settled on the demand to make it "IMPERATIVE that every question of personal freedom shall be settled by a JURY."[12]

Such pressures within the states, however, were deflected or qualified by the legal and social patterns and traditions peculiar to each state. The situation was different in each, as was the result.

I

Shortly before the pressure began to build in Massachusetts to secure jury trial, the state supreme court handed down a very significant judgment in a case involving the question of the status of a slave brought into a free state by a sojourning slave owner. This was in the fall of 1836 in *Commonwealth* v. *Aves*. Chief Justice Lemuel Shaw, for a unanimous court, gave a powerful antislavery opinion in this case. Following Lord Mansfield in the *Sommersett Case* Shaw declared that slavery was "contrary to natural right and to laws designed for the security of personal liberty."[13] If comity had been extended by Massachusetts, said Shaw, masters could have brought their slaves to the state and exercised over them all the rights and powers of ownership acquired in a "foreign" state "for any length of time short of acquiring a domicil."[14] But this was not true in Massachusetts; if a master brought his slave into the state he would become free, because no laws existed to support the institution of slavery, but there were laws to prohibit the "forcible detention or forcible removal" of blacks. The only exception to the rule that the states possessed enough power "to make all laws necessary for the regulation of slavery and the rights of the slave owners, whilst the slaves remain within their territorial limits" was the case of fugitive slaves.[15]

[12] *The Emancipator*, quoted in the *Pennsylvania Freeman*, November 8, 1838.
[13] *Commonwealth* v. *Aves*, 18 Pickering 211.
[14] *Ibid.*, 18 Pickering 218. A highly sympathetic account of this case and one of the fullest, is Leonard Levy, *The Law of the Commonwealth and Chief Justice Shaw* (Harper Torchbook, New York, 1967), 62–71; see also Julius Yanuck, "The Fugitive Slave Law and the Constitution," (Ph.D. dissertation, Columbia University, 1953), 103.
[15] *Commonwealth* v. *Aves*, 18 Pickering 221.

Even the right of slaveholders to recover their runaway property, however, was insecure in Massachusetts. Just before Shaw handed down his decision in *Commonwealth* v. *Aves*, an exciting rescue of two alleged fugitives had taken place in Boston. Two black women had been taken off the brig *Chickasaw* and brought before Shaw on a habeas corpus, but before the hearing could be completed a mob forcibly rescued them from the court.[16]

By 1837, moreover, numerous form petitions began to arrive at the state capitol building asking for "the passage of such laws as will secure to those claimed as slaves in this Commonwealth a trial by jury." On January 20, 1837, James C. Alvord, a young man of twenty-nine who has been described as "the most brilliant of the younger lawyers of the Commonwealth" at that time,[17] successfully moved that the house Committee on the Judiciary be instructed to inquire into the expediency of restoring the *homine replegiando*, or to provide by some other process a jury trial for those under personal restraint.[18]

Two men, whose legal philosophies were strikingly different, stand out in the movement to restore the writ *de homine replegiando*: Alvord, and Robert Rantoul, Jr. Alvord, the leading proponent of restoration, was deeply devoted to the common law. The movement for codification, growing out of Benthamite ideas on legal reform, and reflected in the New York code, aroused little enthusiasm in him.[19] Rantoul, the leader of the Van Buren Democrats in the house was one of the most important opponents of the common law, as his *Oration* at *Scituate* in 1833 demonstrates.[20] He had also been opposed to the "modern" form of abolitionists who posed a serious threat to the Union. At the same time Rantoul opposed slavery. If commitment to "inflammatory" abolitionism had been at issue, or if devotion to either the common law or codification had been uppermost, Rantoul and Alvord would have been opponents. But the issue, rather, was between slavery and freedom. As John Greenleaf Whittier wrote to Rantoul: "I feel assured that slavery, in any form, is odious to thy feelings. Why not, then, say so; carry out thy democratic principles."[21] When the time came he did, for the bill to restore the *homine replegiando* passed without opposition.[22]

---

[16]*The Liberator*, August 6, 1836. The best account of this episode is Levy, *Law of the Commonwealth*, 72–78.

[17]Charles Warren, *History of the Harvard Law School and of Early Legal Conditions in America* (3 vols.; New York, 1908), 1: 484–85; see also the eulogy by Wendell Phillips, "James C. Alvord," *The Liberty Bell* (Boston, Massachusetts Anti-Slavery Fair, 1841), 74–75.

[18]*Mass., House Journal 1837*, Mass. State Library, 59: 86.

[19]James C. Alvord to Charles Sumner, May 3, 1836. Cited in Warren, *History of Harvard Law School*, 1: 504.

[20]In Perry Miller, ed., *The Legal Mind in America: From Independence to the Civil War* (New York, 1962), 220–29.

[21]John Greenleaf Whittier to Robert Rantoul, Jr., Boston, March 13, 1837, in Whittier, *Life and Letters of John Greenleaf Whittier* (2 vols.; Boston, 1894), 1: 202.

[22]*Mass. House Journal, 1837*, 59: 462; *Mass. Senate Journal, 1837*, Mass. State Library, 58: 516. At the end of March 1837 Whittier claimed a good deal of credit for this unanimity.

The report from the Committee on the Judiciary, written by Alvord, and delivered to the house on March 27, 1837, however, was as important as the restoration of the writ (the bill restoring the writ was passed in April). This report became a significant weapon in the antislavery arsenal.

Over the course of thirty-two pages Alvord carefully built up an argument for restoring the *homine replegiando*, which he considered of greater value than the habeas corpus. Habeas corpus, wrote Alvord, "is unsuited in its forms to the trial of facts, and the decisions under it are always by the court, and generally by a single judge. It lacks the great principle . . . which seems to require a concurrent remedy, giving to the party a trial by jury at his election."[23] The *homine replegiando*, he noted, was the "only mode, ever known in this Commonwealth, by which the question of the right of personal freedom could be directly passed upon by a jury."[24]

Alvord's resolution had been quite general, calling for restoration of the *homine replegiando* for those under personal restraint, but the form petitions sent to the committee had asked specifically for jury trial for those claimed as fugitive slaves. Some petitions implied, Alvord noted, that the trial by jury for alleged runaways should be provided "not by any independent enactment, but by engrafting a provision, effecting this object, upon the proceedings under the law of the United States." Such a provision, he maintained, would be useless if the federal law was unconstitutional as some argued, whereas it would be beyond the power of the state to provide the jury trial if the federal law was valid. A state could not legislate, he contended, when Congress had passed a law intended to cover the whole subject, and "when, as in this case, the spirit and object of that law would be defeated by the proposed action of the State."[25] New York, he recognized, had assumed "the power to regulate the whole process and proceedings," but Alvord considered this constitutionally illegitimate.[26] In Massachusetts, the only law regulating the manner in which fugitives could be reclaimed was the act of Congress of 1793.

But significant questions remained: "Can the person, arrested as a fugitive slave, before or after the certificate prescribed by the law of Congress is given, try his right to liberty in this Commonwealth by a collateral process, as the writ of habeas corpus, (or if the bill recommended by the Committee should pass,) by the writ of personal replevin? Or, on the other hand, is the process under the act of Congress, exclusive in its character, and the certificate granted under it conclusive in its effect upon the rights of the parties?"[27]

"We have caucused in season and out of season, threatened and coaxed, plead and scolded, until we've got the day." Whittier, *Life and Letters*, 1: 199.

[23] *Mass. House Document No. 51, 1837*, 8.

[24] *Ibid.*, 6.

[25] *Ibid.*, 10.

[26] *Ibid.*, 20–21.

[27] *Ibid.*, 14–15.

Alvord's answer was grounded upon the contention that the law of 1793 was unconstitutional. Some had argued that the federal act was tainted by violation of the Fourth, Fifth, and Seventh Amendments to the Constitution. The argument was refuted by saying that the proceedings applied only to slaves, and not citizens. Alvord's response to this was devastating: "A person who is seized here is *prima facie* a freeman, and the very matter to be tried is, *whether* he is a slave; and can that be *assumed* in the outset, in order to give jurisdiction to the magistrate, and validity to his judgment?"[28] But the law was also invalid because Congress had no power to enact it. "The fugitive slave clause merely prohibits the States," Alvord contended, "from passing certain laws, and enjoins a duty upon their citizens. But neither involves or draws after it any further power in the national government whatever. The clause is perfect it itself, and works its own object."[29] If the free states passed laws divesting slaveholders of legitimate titles the remedy lay with the federal judiciary and not with Congress. Masters then had the right to reclaim their property, while those seized had the right to the writs of habeas corpus and *homine replegiando*. "Any special legislation upon the particular subject, would be wholly unnecessary."[30]

Reactions in Massachusetts to the bill and the report predictably were mixed. The *Boston Daily Advertiser* and the *Boston Evening Transcript*, two conservative newspapers, ignored both. The *American Jurist and Law Magazine*, edited by Charles Sumner, Luther S. Cushing, and George S. Hillard, on the other side, was quite sympathetic. The report was "entirely free from all sectional prejudice or local feeling, and we believe, perfectly sound in its reasonings and conclusions."[31] *The Liberator* printed extensive extracts from the report,[32] and privately William Lloyd Garrison wrote on April 3d that "the old Commonwealth of Massachusetts will do her duty in grand style, and pioneer the way for her sister States in the cause of emancipation. We shall secure this session, undoubtedly, the right of Trial by jury to runaway slaves."[33] It was somewhat ironic for Garrison to praise the revival in Massachusetts of a writ that had survived into nineteenth-century America because of a continued recognition of a legitimate property interest in human beings. It was, moreover, a writ believed by Garrison's fellow abolitionist Leavitt to be unfit for a poor man. This demonstrates the weight of legal tradition within a state in framing responses to current social problems, as well as the familiar development in legal history whereby people ascribe new meanings to old forms and new purposes to old remedies. Garrison, of course, was not conceding the legitimacy of

[28]*Ibid.*, 28.
[29]*Ibid.*, 16.
[30]*Ibid.*, 31.
[31]*American Jurist and Law Magazine* (Boston, April 1837), 37: 95.
[32]*The Liberator*, April 21, 1837.
[33]William Lloyd Garrison to George Benson, Boston, April 3, 1837, Garrison Papers, Boston Public Library.

slavery. He simplified an old, cumbersome common-law writ to mean simply "jury trial"; and, as Henry B. Stanton argued, to secure a jury trial for anyone claimed as a fugitive would be a telling blow struck at the institution of slavery. Personal replevin, of course, did not provide jury trial for anyone claimed but only for those persons who claimed to be free, as the Alvord report made clear. This crucial distinction, however, Garrison was unaware of, or chose to ignore, which points up still another commonplace in legal history—a given remedy can mean different things to different people.

Four years after the restoration of the writ *de homine replegiando* Wendell Phillips, a Garrisonian, remained so impressed with the Alvord report that he believed that "wherever, in any state, that right is to be battled for again, the weapons and the shield are provided for the champion."[34] Massachusetts's action did have some impact outside the state,[35] but because of dissimilar situations and legal traditions Alvord's arguments had less direct influence than Phillips's fulsome praise would lead one to expect.

II

Partly because of the case of *Jack* v. *Martin* antislavery thinking in New York followed a different bent. The attack by antiabolitionists and slaveholders on the New York law had resulted in clarifying only one issue: the *homine replegiando* could not be the effective legal instrument there that Alvord hoped it would be in Massachusetts. At the same time, in the view of abolitionists, the existing process "could not in common law secure the recovery of a dog."[36]

Early in 1837 the emancipationists began to apply pressure on the legislature. At the end of January a form petition was circulated in the state which asserted that the fugitive slave clause did not require the delivery of persons merely claimed, "until the claim is *sustained* by that trial by jury which is elsewhere provided for in the *same* Constitution."[37] Although masters had been guaranteed the right to reclaim their property this had to be balanced against the rights of persons also guaranteed; and if Congress failed to secure the latter, the states could remove the deficiencies in the federal law.

In July, 1837, Elizur Wright issued a call for petitions from all over the state and, at the beginning of 1838, they began to pour in. The heaviest flow came from upstate New York, from the counties around Utica, Roch-

[34]Phillips, "James C. Alvord," 70.

[35]The American Anti-Slavery Society held up Massachusetts as an example to be followed. *Fourth Annual Report of the American Anti-Slavery Society, With the Speeches Delivered at the Anniversary Meeting Held in the City of New York, on the 9th May 1837* (New York, 1837), 117.

[36]*The First Annual Report of the New York Committee of Vigilance, for the Year 1837. Together with Important Facts Relative to their Proceedings* (New York, 1837), 16.

[37]*The Friend of Man*, January 26, 1837; see also *Human Rights*, February 1837.

ester, and Syracuse,[38] the home grounds of Alvan Stewart, the president of the New York State Anti-Slavery Society. The senate Committee on the Judiciary summarily dismissed the request,[39] as did the majority of the house committee.[40] The minority report of the house committee completely ignored the request for jury trial, even though it was favorable to the abolitionist position on the interstate slave trade.[41]

Partly because the political institutions had proved so totally unresponsive to the demand for jury trial, abolitionists tried to alter the political climate in the state in the fall elections of 1838. William Jay and Gerrit Smith, acting for the state antislavery society, prepared a questionnaire for the prospective officeholders. Luther Bradish and William Henry Seward, the Whig candidates for lieutenant governor and governor, and William Marcy, the Democratic gubernatorial candidate, answered. The Democratic candidate for lieutenant governor, John Tracy, did not. The first question was "Are you in favor of a law granting to persons in this state, claimed as fugitive slaves, a trial by jury?"

Marcy, who earlier had described the abolitionists as "fanatics," contended they were operating under a misapprehension. The *Revised Statutes* contained a provision on jury trial, and it had not been repealed by the legislature. Of course, it had been declared unconstitutional by the supreme court of the state, but that did not end the matter. He concluded that "if the proper tribunals of the country shall sustain the law, I shall be in favor of retaining it in our statutory codes."[42] If the United States Supreme Court upheld the law so would Marcy.

Seward was extremely cagey. After consulting with Thurlow Weed, who advised him not to answer at all, he gave a rather evasive reply.[43] "To me it seems that the more humble or degraded the individual over whom arbitrary power is attempted to be exercised, the stronger is his claim to the protection of a trial by jury." He did not believe, however, that any further legislation was needed; the existing law gave ample provision. If it was set aside, he would support another law granting jury trial that would meet any constitutional objections.[44]

[38]*New York House Journal, 1838*, 134, 139–40, 143–44, 171, 184, 189, 201, 208, 228–29, 252–53, 261, 279, 292, 298, 305, 312–13, 317, 326, 342, 348, 370, 375, 382, 387, 392, 399, 405, 414, 430, 444, 451–52, 457, 469, 493, 503, 516–17, 526, 571, 584, 646–47, 672, 681, 699, 723, 807, 848, 904–905, 915, 971; *New York Senate Journal, 1838*, 139, 199, 392.

[39]*New York Senate Journal, 1838*, 375.

[40]*New York House Journal, 1838*, 1101.

[41]*New York House Document No. 359, 1838.*

[42]*The Emancipator*, quoted in *The Pennsylvania Freeman*, November 8, 1838.

[43]Dumond, *Antislavery*, 292; Glyndon G. Van Deusen, *William Henry Seward* (New York, 1967), 51.

[44]*The Emancipator*, quoted in *The Pennsylvania Freeman*, November 8, 1838. Seward erroneously said that the question was then pending in the Court of Errors. Joshua Leavitt corrected this, and added that the decision of the Supreme Court setting aside jury trial prevailed as the law of the state.

Luther Bradish disagreed with both Marcy and Seward. *Jack* v. *Martin*, he noted, virtually had eliminated the provisions on jury trial in the *Revised Statutes*. But that was, in his judgment, an unsatisfactory decision. The fugitive slave clause, he contended, imposed an obligation on the states to arrest an alleged fugitive, "and put him upon the trial of the fact whether he be the fugitive slave of the party claiming him." It is precisely on the trial of this fact that the jury was needed, he maintained.[45] This position was generally held by antislavery people in New York, and it differed notably from Alvord's view that the states could not legislate on the subject of fugitive slaves.

Although immediate abolitionists opposed the election of Seward in 1838 the Whig victory that year changed the disposition of New York's legislature on the matter of fugitive slaves. This time the house acted favorably on the request of petitioners for a jury trial law.[46] A bill was reported in April, 1839,[47] and quickly passed.[48] It was reported out of the senate Committee on the Judiciary, without amendments, on May 4, 1839, but it did not come out of the Committee of the Whole before adjournment.[49]

Proceeding under a power (and a responsibility) derived from the federal Constitution, New York would have regulated the entire reclamation process if this bill had become law, and without regard to the existing federal law.[50] A master would not have been able to reclaim his property under the terms of the federal law of 1793, nor by exercising his right of recaption, supposedly guaranteed in the Constitution. Only state officials, following the procedures outlined in the bill (heavily stacked against a claimant), could act to secure a slave owner his human property. It is unlikely that southerners would have been pleased with this "willingness" of New York to fulfill its obligation under the fugitive slave clause.

Within two months of the burial of this bill in the senate committee, Governor Seward became embroiled in a controversy with Virginia that increased the political volatility of the slavery issue and assured Seward's support for a jury trial law. In July, 1839, Virginia sought the surrender of three black seamen, citizens of New York, who had unsuccessfully attempted to help a slave escape. Because of the growing power of the antislavery movement in the state Seward believed it was time to present his

[45]*Ibid.* See also the complimentary piece, *An Examination of Mr. Bradish's Answer to the Interrogatories Presented to Him by a Committee of the State Anti-Slavery Society, October 1, 1838* (Albany, 1838), 16.

[46]For the petitions see *New York House Journal, 1839*, 42, 54, 62, 77, 85, 148, 150, 170, 203, 209, 234, 358, 389, 418, 669.

[47]*Ibid.*, 1150.

[48]*Ibid.*, 1219–20.

[49]*New York Senate Journal, 1839*, 497.

[50]There is a copy of this bill, Assembly Bill No. 487, in the New York State Library in Albany.

views on slavery to the public.[51] He refused to surrender the men because the right to demand "between sovereign and independent nations, as defined by the law of nations, includes only those cases in which the acts constituting the offence charged are recognized as crimes by the universal law of all civilized countries." Since men were not recognized as property by the "universal law" of civilized nations the three "stealers" of a slave had committed no crime.

Virginia threatened reprisals. In his message to the legislature the governor of Virginia concluded that if no relief could be had from Seward's construction "it might ultimately become the important and solemn duty of Virginia to appeal from the cancelled obligations of the national compact to original rights and the law of self-preservation."[52] In time Virginia responded by inspecting all ships under New York registry, and successfully obtained the cooperation of Georgia and South Carolina so that Seward found himself involved in similar difficulties with those states.[53]

Conservatives in New York opposed Seward's course in this imbroglio,[54] but with the governor's support the antislavery faction in the legislature had sufficient strength to secure passage of several important measures relating to slavery. A number of them met with the governor during the controversy to draft the various bills and resolutions. One resolution, presented in the legislature by Rufus King's son, John A. King, protested the denial of the right of petition by Congress. An important bill, presented by Horace Healey of Genesee, repealed the law allowing slaves brought into the state to be held for nine months. This in effect, placed New York in the same position as Massachusetts after Shaw's judgment in *Commonwealth* v. *Aves*. Still another bill authorized the governor to seek the recovery of free persons who had been seized and removed to foreign states.[55] Henry W. Taylor of Ontario presented the jury trial bill. Other measures were prepared, but they did not pass: one, for example, prohibited the officers of the state from acting in the recapture of alleged fugitives, and the use of the states' jails.[56]

The jury-trial law, first reported in February, 1840,[57] was closely patterned after the 1839 bill, but it differed from that measure in one vitally important particular. Under the 1839 bill New York would have regulated

[51]Van Deusen, *William Henry Seward*, 65.

[52]Charles Z. Lincoln, ed., *State of New York: Messages from the Governors* (11 vols.; Albany, 1909), 3: 778.

[53]Van Deusen, *William Henry Seward*, 66.

[54]*Ibid.*, 66.

[55]*New York Session Laws, 1840*, 319.

[56]William H. Seward, *An Autobiography from 1801 to 1834. With a Memoir of His Life, and Selections from His Letters, 1831-1846*, By Frederick W. Seward (New York, 1891), 464-65.

[57]For the course of the bill in the legislature, see *New York House Journal, 1840*, 283, 630-34, 648, 657, 665, 678, 693, 701, 724-28, 757, 759, 776, 781, 790, 803, 810-14, 826-28, 832, 852-53; *New York Senate Journal, 1840*, 880.

the entire process by which runaways were returned to their masters, whereas under the law of 1840 allowance was made for removals pursuant to the federal law of 1793.[58] State officials, however, were required to follow the procedures outlined in the New York law. Any claimant, moreover, who forcibly removed or tried to remove an alleged fugitive from the state "without the authority of law" would be deemed guilty of kidnapping. A master then could apply to one of the few federal judges in the state for a certificate of removal, or he could use the state procedures, but he could not exercise his right of recaption.[59]

The law of 1840 also differed from that of 1828. As a result of the antislavery critique of the 1828 law, several improvements and innovations were made that took into account the difficulties faced by black people, consequently making the claimant's task harder. If a claimant proceeded under the new law he could still use a habeas corpus as a means to seize an alleged runaway, but the hearing on the claim would no longer be before the court issuing the writ. Instead, the claim would be heard by a jury. Working within the legal traditions of the state, New York's legislators had melded two common-law writs in an unusual manner. Habeas corpus had become a process for securing a jury trial similar to the old writ *de homine replegiando*, but without the unwieldy procedures associated with the latter. At the same time, it continued to be a writ that initiated the recovery process.

As Leavitt had pointed out, the law of 1828 operated only when there was a claim to freedom, but under the law of 1840 this was no longer the case. If a claimant proceeded under the new law, an examination of his claim by a jury was mandatory and, moreover, an alleged fugitive would have the assistance of state attorneys. This law then was even more stacked against claimants than the earlier measure, and accordingly could serve as a sturdy barrier against the return of fugitive slaves.

Opinion in the New York legislature, however, was not so radical as to support an explicit repudiation of the binding nature of the Constitution's fugitive slave clause, as sought by some leading abolitionists. However difficult it might be, claimants were still authorized to reclaim their property in the state. And this could be done with the assistance of the state, or under federal law. Under the law of 1840, moreover, state procedures could not be used to suspend federal proceedings as under the law of 1828. Under the earlier law, if there was a claim to freedom a jury trial could be had (through the *homine replegiando*) even though other proceedings in the case had already begun. After 1840 a claimant could choose to proceed

[58] The house judiciary committee had originally amended the bill to exempt from punishment persons who had obtained a certificate of removal under the act of 1793. This amendment was agreed to by a vote of forty-seven to thirty-seven. It was, however, deleted in the senate, and the house accepted this deletion. The law of 1840 authorized the removal of persons under the authority of law without stipulating that it had to be the law of the state.

[59] *New York Session Laws, 1840*, 174–77.

either according to the procedures outlined in the state law, which carried an automatic jury trial whether there was a claim to freedom or not, or under the more summary federal law as administered by the few federal judges in the state. The two were kept quite separate, so that it could not be said that the state had directly interfered with the operation of the federal law: it had merely defined new procedures for its own courts.

The New York law of 1840, clearly, was based on different premises from the Massachusetts act of 1837, and the results in the two states were strikingly different. In Massachusetts no procedures, other than those provided in the federal law, existed for a claimant to follow in order to recover his property. The Massachusetts law was designed to protect free blacks by providing for an inquiry into claims to freedom; the New York law was designed to protect them by providing for an inquiry into all claims to service, except those before the federal courts.

III

The movement to secure jury trial in Pennsylvania, going back into the 1820s, picked up momentum by December of 1836 when petitions began to arrive in large numbers at the state legislature.[60] In response an unsuccessful effort was made during the 1836–37 session to pass a jury trial law.[61]

Within a few months of this failure antislavery reformers began to exert pressure on a special constitutional convention meeting in Harrisburg.[62] As developments over the franchise (one of the principal issues being discussed) indicated, however, the prospects for a constitutional amendment explicitly securing jury trial to alleged fugitives were not bright. The successful effort to disfranchise blacks[63] led the Pennsylvania Abolition Society to deplore "a fixed hostility to the coloured population & a humble subserviency to the Southern policy" evident in the convention.[64] A powerful Whig who feared the political involvement of blacks was the conservative William M. Meredith, the man who had played such a critical role in the passage of the law of 1826. "Do not let us, by any false notions of humanity," he said, "and because our ancestors went so far as

---

[60] Penn. House Journal, 1836–37, 108, 132, 168, 188, 194, 199, 247, 284, 316, 344, 371, 406, 437, 467, 648, 671, 800; Penn. Senate Journal, 1836–37, 110, 125, 137, 143, 150, 159, 171, 197, 206, 212, 224, 228, 244, 273, 279, 285, 300, 315, 372.

[61] Penn. House Journal, 1836–37, 81, 157, 201–2, 350; Penn. Senate Journal, 1836–37, 251, 447–48, 451, 461, 466, 469, 473.

[62] John Agg, reporter, Proceedings and Debates of the Convention of the Commonwealth of Pennsylvania, to Propose Amendments to the Constitution, Commenced at Harrisburg, May 2, 1837. (Harrisburg, 1838), 3: 95, 369, 521, 567, 701, 757, 778; 5: 49, 98, 270, 414; 6: 60, 131, 161, 203, 242, 297, 340, 371; 10: 29, 274; 11: 76, 211, 253, 280. See also Pennsylvania Friends Association for Advocating the Cause of the Slave, Minute Book (1837–41), November 1, 1837, Manuscript Division, Library of Congress; Penn. Abolition Soc. Minutes (1825–47), 3: 294–95.

[63] A good account of disfranchisement is Litwack, North of Slavery, 69, 77–78, 85–87.

[64] Penn. Abolition Soc. Minutes (1825–47), 3: 326.

to pass an act that the people of colour should be no longer kept as slaves, but restored to personal liberty, be induced to confer upon these people, political rights."[65]

The debate over jury trial began on February 2, 1838, when James C. Biddle of Philadelphia, one of the leaders of the Whig-Antimasonic coalition, moved to amend the constitution by adding that a jury trial "shall be granted to all persons who may be arrested as fugitives from labor, and who shall claim to be freemen." A constitutional amendment would serve as a norm for state jurists, and in effect reverse the state's policy by undermining Justice Tilghman's 1819 decision (although it was not mentioned in the debates). In this state, Biddle noted, nobody "presumed another to be a slave."[66]

Biddle conceded that the fugitive slave clause was obligatory on the states, but he demanded that "every word and letter of it may be strictly construed, and that its due force may be given to it." In his view (as well as in that of many conservatives who opposed the jury trial amendment)[67] the right of recaption as interpreted by slaveholders was not secured by the Constitution. It contained "no principle so monstrous as that an individual may invade a sovereign state, and carry a human being away, from under its protection, without process of law—without the consent of the sovereign power of that commonwealth."[68]

Pennsylvania's officials, Biddle hoped, would have to proceed according to the standards set down in the law of 1826 and in the proposed constitutional amendment. He never did suggest state interference with the operation of the federal law in the federal courts. Neither he, nor anyone else in the convention, suggested that the state had the power to regulate the entire process of reclamation, as had been suggested in New York. The power was concurrent.

The chance for favorable action on the amendment, however, appeared slim when some who favored the franchise for black people indicated that they did not support the Biddle proposal. James Merrill, an associate of Thaddeus Stevens, was one of these.[69] He conceded that the state could provide a jury trial, but, in his view, it was not expedient. "Slaveholders did accept the law of 1826," he said, "and it gave protection to negroes, but if this amendment was adopted they would cease to, and they would revert to acting under the harsher federal law."[70]

Most of those opposed to the amendment would not even concede the right of the state to adopt it, much less its expediency. The obligation to secure the rights guaranteed in the fugitive slave clause, according to

[65] Debates of the Convention, 10: 104.
[66] Ibid., 11: 252.
[67] See the remarks by Joseph Hopkinson, ibid., 326.
[68] Ibid., 300.
[69] James G. Wilson and John Fiske, eds., Appletons' Cyclopaedia of American Biography (7 vols.; New York, 1888–1901), 4: 306.
[70] Debates of the Convention, 11: 307.

George W. Woodward, a conservative state jurist and later an unsuccessful Polk nominee for the U.S. Supreme Court,[71] rested with the "superintending power of the Union." If left to a state the obligation might well be ignored "because the sentiment of that state might be . . . entirely opposed to the institution of slavery in all its forms and aspects, and to such an extent as to make them disregard all the constitutional provisions which were thrown out for the protection of the slave-holding interests, and deny to those interests that which absolutely belonged to them under the constitution."[72] The conservative's dread of jury trial could not be expressed more plainly.

Throughout these debates some of the opposition to the amendment was disingenuous and nearly servile in the regard shown for the rights of masters. Joseph Hopkinson, a conservative federal-district-court judge,[73] for example, stoutly denied that free men ever had been or ever could be dragged away under the Fugitive Slave Law. The remedies in the act of Congress, he said, could only be applied to actual fugitive slaves. Abuses could occur, of course, but, said Hopkinson, "the injustice is more likely to be committed against the rights of the master than the liberty of the slave."[74]

Some opponents of the Biddle amendment openly avowed their enmity toward black people. Charles Jared Ingersoll, one of the leading Jacksonian Democrats in the state,[75] abusively observed: "Trial by jury for fugitive slaves! for blacks by whites! What a solecism, an absurdity. From Magna Charta down, trial by jury has been a trial by peers, by equals; vassals, says Blackstone, by their fellow vassals, lords by their brother lords."[76] If he would have allowed a jury trial for free blacks claimed as fugitives, which of course is doubtful, this would have meant that only Negroes could sit in judgment on such cases.

Although outright antipathy toward black people, then, was a factor in the final defeat of the amendment, concern for the continued stability of the Union was of even greater importance, as James Merrill's position strongly implied. This issue was more clearly discussed by Woodward. Could it be supposed, he asked, that you could subject a claimant to "all the expense, trouble and delay incidental to a trial before a jury, in relation to a mere matter of claim of that which is his own—is it, I ask, to be supposed that you can subject a gentleman to all this, and that he will still adhere to his compact?"[77]

---

[71] *Appletons'*, 6: 607; *BDAC*, 1848.
[72] *Debates of the Convention*, 11: 270–71.
[73] *BDAC*, 1075–76.
[74] *Debates of the Convention*, 11: 325.
[75] *DAB*, 9: 465–67. Ingersoll had also been the United States District Attorney in Pennsylvania for fourteen years.
[76] *Debates of the Convention*, 11: 297.
[77] *Ibid.*, 279.

Early in February, 1838, the vote was taken on the Biddle amendment; it was defeated seventy-six to thirty-nine. The Democrats were
almost unanimous in their opposition. The Whig-Antimasonic coalition
split wide open on the amendment. Democratic hostility, and the fear of
disruption of the Union worked to defeat this effort to obtain a jury trial
for those who claimed they were free in Pennsylvania.[78]

The day after the Biddle amendment was defeated in the constitutional convention Senator Francis James reported a jury trial bill out of
the judiciary committee of the state senate.[79] Late in February a similar
measure was introduced in the house, but it was never taken up.[80] Opposition to the senate bill rested upon the same arguments presented in the
convention. It was objected to specifically because the proposed jury
trial measure "violates, and in effect annihilates the act of Congress."[81]

Speaking for the bill Senator James adopted the theory pressed in
New York that the state had the right to regulate the whole process.
According to him Congress had no power to act on the subject, and the
act it had adopted was "an infringement not only of the *spirit* but of the
letter of the constitution." He scored the federal law primarily because
it infringed on the Fourth Amendment. "Now, sir," he said, "gentlemen
must show, either that persons who, from the color of their skin, may become the object of this unceremonious *seizure* are not embraced within
the meaning of the word *people*, or they must prove that the *seizure* is
not an *unreasonable* seizure. . . ."[82] James's forceful challenge to the federal law, however, was unavailing for the jury-trial bill was defeated in late
March by a vote of seventeen to eleven.[83]

Petitions continued to go to the legislature after the defeat of the
James bill,[84] but after that no further action was taken, and no further debates were held there until the 1840s. The compromise law of 1826 remained on the statute books, even though both proslavery and anti-
slavery people were dissatisfied. The struggle for a change in Pennsylvania had resulted in a stalemate, and perhaps the critical factor had
been the reluctance of apprehensive unionists to support the demand for

[78]Biddle made one final effort in the convention. He moved to amend the jury trial
provision of the constitution by adding "Nor shall it be denied by any judical officer or
tribunal of this commonwealth to persons who may be claimed as fugitives from labor, but
who shall assert their right to freedom." This motion failed when the previous question was
called. *Ibid..* 329.

[79]Pressure for a jury trial law had continued. See *Penn. Senate Journal, 1837–38*, 73,
124, 129, 135, 414, 428, 477, 551, 560, 586, 605; *Penn. House Journal, 1837–38*, 45, 133, 157,
182, 217, 219, 234, 255, 264, 284, 381, 528, 582, 650, 809, 906.

[80]*Penn. House Journal, 1837–38*, 597.

[81]*Penn. Senate Journal, 1837–38*, 614.

[82]James's argument was reprinted in William Yates, *Rights of Colored Men to Suffrage,
Citizenship and Trial by Jury: Being a Book of Fact, Arguments and Authorities, Historical
Notices and Sketches of Debates—With Notes* (Philadelphia, 1838), 94–95.

[83]*Penn. Senate Journal, 1837–38*, 596–97.

[84]*Penn. House Journal, 1841*, 82, 100–101, 171, 188, 215, 237, 263, 295, 320, 343, 418,

a jury trial (even though limited to those who made a claim to freedom), and their rejection of the proslavery view of the masters' rights.

IV

Conservatives in Pennsylvania had reacted to the rise of the proslavery argument and immediate abolitionism by clinging to the constitutional and legal principles embodied in the compromise of 1826. Antislavery people in Massachusetts had rallied behind legal traditionalism (support of a common law remedy), whereas in New York an automatic jury trial was provided in cases involving claims to service. The developments in all three states occurred within patterns established earlier, and the same was true in Ohio. Controlled by the Democrats, Ohio, with its large southern population, was better known for its harsh Black Code, than for any law designed to secure the personal freedom of its Negro citizens. During the 1830s, however, large sections of the state had been rocked by abolitionist agitation, and although antislavery people had little political weight at the time the chances for a public confrontation on the issue of jury trial were good.

During its formative period (the middle 1830s) the Ohio immediatist movement was more concerned with eliminating the Black Code, however, than with securing legal protection for free blacks claimed as fugitives, or with obstructing the recovery of actual runaways.[85] The first attempt to obtain a jury-trial law was a single petition presented to the legislature at the beginning of 1837. Abolitionists, nonetheless, were sanguine. "When petitions shall have been multiplied, the attention of the legislature intently directed to the subject, and their eyes fully opened to the unconstitutionality . . . of the statute [the Fugitive Slave Act] . . . we have little doubt that the prayer of the petitioners will be satisfactorily answered."[86] Pleading for a jury trial law in 1838 Gamaliel Bailey, editor of the leading state antislavery newspaper, *The Philanthropist*, added that "constant dropping wears away stone; importunity will prevail, where a single effort would fail."[87]

Like many immediatists throughout the North, Ohio's abolitionists demanded a jury trial for everyone claimed as a runaway, not just for those who claimed they were free. "A privilege thus highly valued," wrote Bailey, "should not be partial in its application, in a state claiming to be among the most free. It should be extended to all alike, to the poor as well as to the rich, to the weak, as well as to the powerful."[88]

472, 561; *Penn. Senate Journal, 1841*, 136, 211, 545.

[85]See, for example, the *Proceedings of the Ohio Anti-Slavery Society, Held in Mount Pleasant, Jefferson County, Ohio, on the Twenty-Seventh of April, 1835* (n.p., n.d.), 9.

[86]*Report of the Second Anniversary of the Ohio Anti-Slavery Society, Held in Mount Pleasant, Jefferson County, Ohio, on the Twenty-Seventh of April, 1837* (Cincinnati, 1837), 37.

[87]*The Philanthropist*, February 13, 1838.

[88]*Ibid.*, January 27, 1837.

Closely associated with the movement in New York through the agency system[89] Ohio's abolitionists drew heavily on the rich antislavery discussion going on in the East.[90] One constitutional idea, however, was peculiar to Ohio. It was developed in an argument by Salmon Portland Chase in the spring of 1837 before the Court of Common Pleas of Hamilton County. The federal law under which the fugitive was claimed, Chase argued, was void not only because it conflicted with the Constitution, but also because it was repugnant to the Northwest Ordinance. That ordinance (which guaranteed the right to a jury trial and habeas corpus), he contended, had not been repealed or altered by the adoption of the Constitution. It was in fact a paramount law: laws passed under the authority of the Constitution could in no way violate the provisions of the ordinance. Because the ordinance was a compact between the citizens of Ohio and the original states, its provision authorizing the return of runaways only applied to those who fled from one of the original states. The federal law, however, applied to fugitives from new states as well (such as Kentucky, the slave state bordering Ohio), so that it violated the ordinance in this way as well as in its failure to secure habeas corpus and jury trial.[91] Chase's argument did not convince the court, but it did have a lasting influence on the debate in Ohio.

By 1838 pressure for a jury-trial law had built to the point that the state legislators felt compelled to respond, but the response muddied the issue. Although it is unclear why it was done, some of the antislavery petitions were sent to the senate Standing Committee on the Judiciary, and some to a select committee of the senate. At the end of January, 1838, the judiciary committee made an adverse report, but the select committee made a favorable one at the beginning of March.

Without the fugitive slave clause the Constitution could not have been adopted, according to the judiciary committee. Congress, the committee believed, had the duty, "by necessary implication," to legislate in order to fulfill the obligation imposed. A state legislative committee, the members said, had no right to pronounce a law of Congress unconstitutional in order to pass conflicting legislation. "Constitutionality" was a judicial question. The members admitted that habeas corpus had to be granted to a person in bondage as well as to a free man. But it could afford little protection even to a free man, for as Gamaliel Bailey observed:

[89]See, for example, Dumond, *Antislavery*, chap. 21, "Theodore Weld: The Agency System." Ohio was abolitionized to no small degree by agents sent out from New York.

[90]For example, *The Philanthropist*, January 27, 1837, reprinted an article from the *Friend of Man* on "Kidnapping in Utica," and a speech by Francis James in the issue of November 7, 1837.

[91]*Speech of Salmon P. Chase, in the Case of the Colored Woman, Matilda, Who was Brought Before the Court of Common Pleas of Hamilton County, Ohio, By Writ of Habeas Corpus; March 11, 1837* (Cincinnati, 1837). Chase had contended that Matilda was free because she had come to Ohio with her master's consent, but the court chose not to follow *Commonwealth* v. *Aves*.

"No state court, not even the highest can interfere by habeas corpus or
otherwise, to arrest the proceeding before a magistrate, if that proceeding be authorized by an act of Congress, which is itself warranted by the
constitution."[92] For antislavery Ohioans like Bailey the crux of the matter
was the constitutionality of the federal law, and the committee had
already made its judgment on that problem. The most the committee
would concede was that a state could prohibit its officers from accepting
jurisdiction under the law of 1793 (as Pennsylvania had in 1820), although it did not feel this was necessary.[93]

The report of the select committee, on the other side, closely followed
the arguments developed by Chase. "The important principle involved
in this law," read the report, "is not, whether slaves should, or should
not, be reclaimed; it is, whether freemen should be liable to be seized in
this lawless manner, and consigned to perpetual bondage." This committee (following the New York pattern) reported out a bill prescribing
the mode of proceedings in all cases arising under the fugitive slave
clause. Along with the bill the committee reported two resolutions. The
first declared that the federal and state guarantees of jury trial, habeas
corpus, and freedom from unreasonable seizures were applicable to
cases arising under the fugitive slave clause. The second proclaimed,
"in the administration of justice, and in the protection of their natural
and constitutional rights, the same rules and principles of law should be
extended to all persons, irrespective of color, rank or condition."[94] Neither
resolution was considered by the senate, and within two weeks discussion of the bill was postponed until the next legislature.[95]

Before the bill came up again a case involving an Ohio clergyman,
John B. Mahan, occurred that had a critical influence over the discussion
about fugitive slaves. Mahan had been charged with assisting a number
of slaves to make their way to Canada from Kentucky. His acquittal
aroused considerable apprehension in Kentucky about that state's relations with Ohio concerning slave property. As a result a bipartisan commission was sent to Ohio to work out some accommodation.[96]

Confronted by this proslavery pressure Ohio's Democratic legislature
responded in February, 1839, with a law favorable to slave claimants.

[92] *The Philanthropist*, March 6, 1838.

[93] "Report of the Standing Committee on the Judiciary, to which was referred sundry
petitions of citizens of Ohio, praying that the right of trial by jury may be extended to every
human being in the State." *Ohio Senate Journal, 1837-38*, 305-10.

[94] "Report of the select committee to which was referred the numerous petitions of the
citizens of this State, asking the repeal of certain laws, imposing restrictions and disabilities
upon persons of color, not found in the constitution, and which the petitioners aver to be
contrary to its principles, and also praying that the right of trial by jury, may be secured to
all persons within its jurisdiction." *Ibid.*, 572-86.

[95] *Ibid.*, 760.

[96] Francis P. Weisenburger, *The Passing of the Frontier 1825-1850*, vol. 3 of Carl Wittke,
ed., *The History of the State of Ohio (6 vols.;* Columbus, Ohio, *1941-44),* 382.

There was considerable truth in Gamaliel Bailey's scorching editorial written just before passage: ". . . their demand is a very modest one;—it is only that Ohio should enact laws to strengthen the grasp of Kentucky masters on men, who they have stripped of their liberty—it is only that Ohio should be the patient, well-drilled, well-skilled, indefatigable, sleepless, unscrupulous slave-catcher of Kentucky. . . . This is a demand they dare not resist—and would not, if they dared. It is the *slaveholder* who speaks,—his voice has authority."[97]

The bill, however, did not become law without a bitter fight in the state senate led by Benjamin Franklin Wade.[98] Wade, and a small coterie of Whigs, tried to amend the bill in several ways, and finally they attempted a filibuster through an all-night session. Among the amendments proposed were ones providing for jury trial, prohibiting the admission of a master's testimony, allowing for appeal from the judge's decision, and prohibiting certain state officials from exercising jurisdiction under the federal law.[99]

The law of 1839, the "Black Law" as abolitionists called it, gave masters what they had been demanding for years: an active state participation in the arrest process. A warrant would be issued to the sheriff to arrest the person claimed after an application had been made to an authorized state official, based on the owner's oath or affirmation. After the arrest the alleged slave would be brought before a judge of a court of record before whom the claimant had to prove "to the satisfaction of such officer" that the Negro did owe service. No standards were provided for such "satisfaction." An alleged slave, however, could not be removed from the state without "sufficient legal authority for so doing, according to the laws of this state or of the United States."[100] Ohio's Democrats would not go so far as to accept the proslavery view of the right of recaption.

Early in 1841 a serious effort was made in the lower house of the Ohio legislature to alter the state's fugitive slave law. Two conclusions were apparent to the house judiciary committee, which had the subject under consideration: "First, that there should be *a* law on the subject; and, Second, that the present law is not what it should be, but that it is much better to *amend* than to *repeal* it."

Since this position was similar to those worked out in Pennsylvania and New York the constitutional arguments presented were also quite similar. The law of 1793, the committee noted, could impose no duty on

[97] *The Philanthropist*, February 19, 1839.

[98] H. L. Trefousse, *Benjamin Franklin Wade: Radical Republican from Ohio* (New York, 1963), 34–37; A. G. Riddle, *The Life of Benjamin F. Wade* (Cleveland, Ohio, 1886), 136–37.

[99] For the various amendments proposed see the *Ohio Senate Journal, 1838–39*, 339, 371–74, 387, 388–90, 393; *Ohio House Journal, 1838–39*, 405, 409–10, 417–18, 422, 540–43.

[100] J. R. Swan, *Statutes of the State of Ohio, of a General Nature, in Force, December 7, 1840* (Columbus, 1841), 595–600.

state officials, but the state was under a constitutional obligation to act, nevertheless. On this subject, as on many others, there could be a concurrent jurisdiction between federal and state authorities.

The difficulty was to determine the exact nature of the obligation. "*Who* are we to deliver up?" "Those who are *in fact*," said the committee, "what they may be alleged to be, slaves, who have escaped. This is the *extent* of our obligation. We are to deliver up *fugitives* from service or labor, not those who are merely *claimed* as such." The fact of servitude, the members concluded, should be determined by a jury. "The legal presumption . . . is *always* in favor of liberty. If so, as far as the Judiciary throws its protection over the rights of the people, why should one color be the recipients of that protection and the other be cast beyond its pale?"[101]

In March, 1841, the bill reported out of the judiciary committee was postponed indefinitely. If it had been adopted the bill would have brought Ohio into line behind New York, although Ohio's legislature was still working in terms of the compromises worked out in the 1820s in the eastern states. "It *is* absolutely necessary," the committee had concluded, "that there be legislation on the subject, not only to protect the rights of the person alleged to be a slave, but to secure to the master the perfect enjoyment of the rights guaranteed him by the constitution." If nothing else the emphasis had changed in New York, where little was heard about the rights of slave owners.

V

By the late 1830s there was little agreement in the North about the precise nature of the obligation imposed on the free states by the fugitive slave clause of the Constitution, even among those in the immediatist abolition societies, as the resolution adopted at the founding convention of the Pennsylvania Anti-Slavery Society demonstrates. Conservatives and moderates (including moderates in the antislavery movement) conceded that the fugitive clause placed an important limitation on the sovereign powers of the state.

Agreement among those who did accept the authority of the fugitive slave clause stopped at the acceptance of the obligation not to free blacks who escaped North. According to James C. Alvord in Massachusetts no further obligation had been imposed, no legislation (either federal or state) was necessary to secure the rights of masters. In New York, Pennsylvania, and Ohio, on the other hand, the debate turned over the respective powers and duties of the federal and state governments to legislate on the subject. Some had urged the states to regulate entirely

[101]"Report of the Standing Committee on the Judiciary." *Ohio House Journal, 1840–41*, 212–33.

the process by which runaways were returned to their masters, but in the end these three states settled on prescribing the modes of procedure for their own officials. On this point they did not go beyond the compromises of the 1820s, although the spirit differed strikingly from state to state. Pennsylvania stood still, while New York made some notable advances, and Ohio, according to Gamaliel Bailey, was "retrograding."[102]

Those who supported the demand in the late 1830s that the states provide a jury trial then were divided among themselves. State representative Albert A. Bliss of Ohio, a Whig and later state treasurer,[103] noted in 1841, for example, that the states were required to return only those who were in fact fugitives. A jury, he believed, which would decide the facts of a case (whether a man claimed was or was not a fugitive), would be the best agency to assure that only actual runaways were returned, and not free men. The objective was to secure the personal liberty of free blacks and not to infringe upon the legitimate rights of claimants. Some abolitionists, however, plainly wanted to use the jury trial to strike a blow at the "peculiar institution." Since the state could provide a jury trial, said one of them, "we are bound to rescue all the slaves we fairly can, by that means."[104]

[102] *The Philanthropist*, February 19, 1839.
[103] G. Frederick Wright, ed., *A Standard History of Lorain County Ohio* (Chicago and New York), 218.
[104] "The Right of Trial by Jury," *The Anti-Slavery Record* (August, 1837), 163.

The Personal Liberty Laws in the Supreme Court: *Prigg* vs. *Pennsylvania* 6

During the 1830s the free-state laws protecting the personal freedom of blacks, and particularly the compromise laws of the 1820s, had come under heavy attack from proslavery people and antiabolitionists as being destructive of the rights of slave owners and dangerous to the continued harmony of the Union. When abolitionists countered with the demand that all persons claimed as runaways be granted a jury trial, uneasy southerners shifted the dispute to another forum, the Supreme Court of the United States, where they hoped to obtain a final adjudication that would eliminate the uncertainty and provide the security they sought. A case that began in Pennsylvania in 1837 provided the means.

At the beginning of 1837 Edward Prigg and others, as agents of Margaret Ashmore of Harford County, Maryland, had applied to a justice of the peace in York County, Pennsylvania, for a warrant authorizing the arrest of certain runaways. By virtue of this warrant Margaret Morgan and her children were seized and brought before the justice who, at that point, refused to consider the case. The defendants then, without further recourse to law (state or federal), carried the woman and her children back to Harford County. Two months later the grand jury returned an indictment against Prigg and the others for kidnapping.

The governor of Pennsylvania then made an application to the governor of Maryland for the extradition of the accused kidnappers. Maryland's governor, however, refused to honor the request: instead, he laid the whole matter before the legislature.[1]

On March 7, 1838, the Maryland legislators responded with a series of declaratory resolutions.[2] They claimed that a citizen of their state was not subject to the laws of another state merely for exercising his right of recaption.[3] Resting on the assertion that this right was federally guaranteed and could not be "abridged, restrained or embarrassed" by state legisla-

---

[1] *Niles' Register*, March 5, 1842; Theodore Dwight Weld to Angelina G. Weld, Washington, February 9, 1842 in Barnes and Dumond, eds., *Letters of Weld, Weld, and Grimké*, 2: 916.

[2] *Maryland Session Laws, 1838*, Resolution no. 79.

[3] *Niles' Register*, May 25, 1839, listed three questions that had to be adjudicated: "(1) The right of a citizen of a slaveholding state to pursue his fugitive slaves into a non-slaveholding state, and to bring them away without a resort to the judicial tribunals, (2) The right of a master to the produce of his fugitive slave, born of her in a non-slaveholding state, (3) The constitutionality of the laws of Pennsylvania on the subject of fugitive slaves."

tion, the resolutions called for a vindication of recaption by the "National Judiciary." A special commissioner was then sent to Pennsylvania to try to obtain a dismissal of the prosecutions, or, if that was not possible, to make whatever arrangements were necessary to have the case referred to the U.S. Supreme Court. He was also to try to obtain modifications in the law of 1826.

Pennsylvania's legislators, at that time considering a jury trial bill, showed no inclination to accept alterations in the state law. Because of the existing uncertainties and pressures, however, they were disposed to have the matter adjudicated by the federal tribunal. An act was passed to institute *pro forma* proceedings, in order to expedite the case into the federal courts.[4] It went up to the U.S. Supreme Court on a writ of error in the May term, 1840.[5]

Directly at issue in the case, from the proslavery view, were the right of a master to reclaim and remove his property from a free state without a recourse to the courts, and the constitutionality of the laws of the free states (particularly those of Pennsylvania) that infringed upon that right.[6] Abolitionists, on the other side, tended to see the issues as the validity of the act of Pennsylvania, and the right of the free states to grant a jury trial to those claimed as runaways.[7]

The significance of the case was clearly attested to by counsel on both sides in their arguments before the Court. Prigg's attorney contended that the whole problem was "of vital interest to the peace and perpetuity of the Union itself."[8] The attorneys for Pennsylvania were equally concerned:

> Deny the right of the states to legislate on this subject for the preservation of their own peace and the protection of their own soil from insult and aggression, arrogate exclusive power for the general government to order and direct how, and by whom alleged fugitive slaves are to be restored to their masters or hired pursuers, and you arouse a spirit of discord and resistance, that will neither shrink nor slumber till the obligation itself be cancelled, or the Union which creates it be dissolved.[9]

But it was precisely the right of the federal government to act for which Prigg's counsel argued, since the object of the fugitive slave clause, to "recognize and protect the existing institutions of the South," would be de-

[4] *Pennsylvania Archives* (Fourth Series), 6: 550–51; *Penn. Session Laws, 1839*, 218–20.

[5] *Prigg* v. *Pennsylvania*, 16 Peters 558; *Niles' Register*, March 5, 1842.

[6] *Supra*, n. 3.

[7] See, for example, Theodore Dwight Weld to Angelina G. Weld, Washington, February 9, 1842 in Barnes and Dumond, eds. *Letters of Weld, Weld, and Grimké*, 2: 916. That antislavery people believed this to be an important case is illustrated by Salmon P. Chase's ledger book entitled "Notes on Anti-Slavery," Manuscript Division, Library of Congress. One section is entitled "American Anti-Slavery Chronology." This chronology was very sparse for the 1830s, but under the date January, 1837, Chase listed "Prigg & Penn.[a] case originated in Penn.[a] See Cin. Gaz. May 28, '39."

[8] *Prigg* v. *Pennsylvania*, 16 Peters 559.

[9] *Ibid.*, 606.

feated if the right of legislation was left to the states.[10] "If one can arrest and carry away a free man without due process of law," the Pennsylvania counsel countered, "if their persons are not inviolate; your Constitution is a waxen tablet, a writing in the sand; and instead of being, as is supposed, the freest country on earth, this is the vilest despotism which can be imagined."[11] The ultimate problem, as they saw it, was the issue presented by the conflict of two different legal systems. "Now, in a slaveholding state," it was noted, "colour always raises a presumption of slavery, which is directly contrary to the presumption in a free or non-slaveholding state; for in the latter, prima facie, every man is a free man."[12]

On March 1, 1842,[13] within three weeks of the conclusion of the oral arguments in *Prigg* v. *Pennsylvania*, Joseph Story, speaking for himself and Justices John Catron and John McKinley,[14] delivered the "opinion of the court."

Story began with an examination of the question that had sharply divided "the judicial mind of America"[15] for years: under what circumstances was a state obligated to give judicial recognition to the status of slavery? "By the general law of nations," Story noted, "no nation is bound to recognize the state of slavery, as to foreign slaves found within its territorial dominions, when it is in opposition to its own policy and institutions, in favor of the subjects of other nations where slavery is recognized."[16]

If the American states had remained completely sovereign entities there could be no question of their right to establish the procedures by which claims to runaways would be adjudicated. But the fugitive slave clause of the Constitution, Story observed, had profoundly altered the relationship between those states. That clause became part of the municipal law of the United States. It extended "a new and positive right, independent of comity, confined to no territorial limits, and bounded by no State institutions or policy."[17]

But precisely what did the clause mean? Story's rule of constitutional interpretation was to read the words of the clause so that they would "fairly secure" the rights guaranteed, to read them "with all the lights and aids of contemporary history."[18] And his view of that history was framed by the "historical necessity thesis" adopted by Justice Tilghman in *Wright* v. *Deacon* (1819). Without security from divestment of their "rights" by

[10] *Ibid.*, 563–65.

[11] *Ibid.*, 577.

[12] *Ibid.*, 576.

[13] U.S. Supreme Court, Dockets, vol. E, p. 2330. National Archives, Microfilm Publication No. M-216, roll 2.

[14] Cf, however, Joseph C. Burke, "What Did the Prigg Decision Really Decide?" *The Pennsylvania Magazine of History and Biography*, 93 (January, 1969): 80–81.

[15] Cobb, *Law of Slavery*, 116.

[16] *Prigg* v. *Pennsylvania*, 16 Peters 611.

[17] *Ibid.*, 611.

[18] *Ibid.*, 610–11. Hurd, *Law of Freedom and Bondage*, 2: 461, suggested that this canon of constitutional interpretation was an innovation. "Remarkable for flexibility in application"

free-state law, slave owners never would have consented to join the Union. The fugitive slave clause in Story's view, was "of the last importance to the safety and security of the southern States, and could not have been surrendered by them without endangering their whole property in slaves."[19]

The clause then guaranteed an "absolute right" to the "immediate possession" of one's property. Any law that "interrupts, limits, delays, or postpones" the enjoyment of that right contravened the Constitution. Any state law or regulation that in any way delayed the immediate possession *pro tanto* effected a "discharge."[20]

The fugitive slave clause, in his judgment, had secured an extraterritorial effect to the laws of the South on slavery. The right to the service or labor of a runaway slave was put "upon the same ground and to the same extent in every other state as in the State from which the slave escaped."[21] This "right," said Story, necessarily included all the "incidents." One was recaption by self-help alone. "We all know," he observed, "that this right of seizure and recaption is universally acknowledged in all the slaveholding states." To show what that right was at common law, Story quoted Blackstone's definition of the "eccentrical remedy." But he did not quote it in full; he left out a critical part, as follows:

> But, as the public peace is a superior consideration to any one man's private property; and as, if individuals were once allowed to use private force as a remedy for private injuries, all social justice must cease, the strong would give law to the weak, and every man would revert to a state of nature; for these reasons it is provided, that this natural right of caption shall never be exerted, where such exertion must occasion strife and bodily contention, or endanger the peace of society.

Story then conceded that recaption was a basic constitutional right, as Alvord had done in 1837. Slave owners had the right to seize and remove a runaway from a free state by their own efforts. But Story also noted that it had to be done without a breach of the peace or "illegal violence." He did not address himself to the problem raised when the person seized was in fact free. He considered only the question involved with actual runaways, as he considered Margaret Morgan to be.[22]

Story had not included it in the first edition of his commentaries on the Constitution, but he did in the second.

[19] *Prigg* v. *Pennsylvania*, 16 Peters 612.

[20] *Ibid.*, 612.

[21] *Ibid.*, 613.

[22] Some authors have tended to emphasize this part of the Court's judgment, while others have emphasized other facets, or put the question in a slightly different perspective. Schnell, "Court Cases Involving Slavery," 186–87, for example, noted the importance of the holding on recaption. Joseph L. Nogee, "The Prigg Case and Fugitive Slavery, 1842–1850," *Journal of Negro History*, 39 (April, 1954): 188, on the other hand, listed what he considered the real issues in the case: (1) Did the Constitution and act of 1793 preclude a trial by jury for fugitives? (2) To what extent could state legislation supplement the federal law? (3) Did Congress have authority to legislate on the subject? Burke, "What did the Prigg Decision Really Decide?" concentrated primarily on these last two questions.

Slave owners then possessed the right of recaption, but the fugitive slave clause also spoke of the right to have property delivered up on claim. Did Congress have the power to implement this guarantee? "If, indeed," said Story, "the Constitution guaranties the right, and if it requires the delivery upon the claim of the owner (as cannot well be doubted) the natural inference certainly is, that the national government is clothed with the appropriate authority and functions to enforce it."[23]

But could it also be argued that the clause was addressed to the states, placing on them a concurrent obligation to legislate as Pennsylvania had done in 1826? In Story's judgment the clause created a distinct legal relationship between slave owners and the federal government. The federal government was the subject of the rule of action.[24] States, in fact, were not involved in the duties enjoined at all: the right created was "confined to no territorial limits, and bounded by no State institutions or policy." The rule of action was created by the national sovereign power completely independent of the states, which, for the purposes of the fugitive clause, were almost nonexistent. It was, therefore, illegitimate for a state to interfere "as it were, by way of complement to the legislation of Congress, to prescribe additional regulations, and what they may deem auxiliary provisions for the same purpose." Congressional silence was expressive of its intention that no further legislation should be adopted.[25]

The right under the act of 1793 to utilize state instrumentalities had occasioned heated debates after the War of 1812. Counsel for Pennsylvania had struck forcefully at this feature of the law. Story held, as he did in his commentaries on the Constitution, that the duty to act could not be imposed by the federal government. State officials, on the other hand, could exercise jurisdiction under the federal law if they chose, "unless prohibited by State legislation."[26]

Story, finally, did concede that the states, in the exercise of their police power, possessed the jurisdiction to arrest and restrain runaways to secure themselves against their depredations and "evil example." He recognized that, although designed for other purposes, this type of state legislation might incidentally aid claimants.[27]

Pennsylvania's act of 1826, however, was not of this type. In the "opinion of the court" that law was unconstitutional and void.[28] The compromise laws of the 1820s could not stand.

It was generally agreed among the justices that the Pennsylvania act of 1826 was unconstitutional (with one exception to be discussed later), and

[23] Prigg v. Pennsylvania, 16 Peters 615–16.

[24] Hurd, Law of Freedom and Bondage, 2: 492.

[25] Prigg v. Pennsylvania, 16 Peters, 618; cf, Burke, "What Did the Prigg Decision Really Decide?" 81–82.

[26] Prigg v. Pennsylvania, 615.

[27] Ibid., 625.

[28] Ibid., 625–26.

that Edward Prigg should be freed from the weight of the indictment. The members divided sharply over the reasoning in Story's opinion, however, particularly on the question of the powers and duties of the states.

Two concurring justices joined the "opinion of the court" in holding that the fugitive slave clause created a rule of action for the federal government alone. One, James M. Wayne of Georgia, was proslavery and nationalist in his views, and the other, John McLean of Ohio, was antislavery.

Justice Wayne, in his concurrence, emphasized that the fugitive clause was also "affirmative of an obligation upon the States." The states were obliged not to pass laws divesting owners of their title, whereas the federal government had to pass legislation implementing the guarantee to claimants that they could recover their property in the free states. States were enjoined from discharging runaways, thus they could not establish procedures to adjudicate claims because the time necessary to have a hearing would amount to a "qualified or temporary discharge to the injury of the owner."[29] Justice Wayne also emphasized the importance of the clause to the South. "The provision," he said, "was not intended only to secure the property of individuals, but that through their rights, that the institutions of the States should be preserved, so long as any one of the States chose to continue slavery as a part of its policy."[30]

Justice McLean concurred in the view that the power and the duty to secure the rights of the master were exclusively in the federal government: this was essential to the "uniform efficacy of this constitutional provision."[31] States could pass no laws in aid of the right of the master, nor, of course, to obstruct the assertion of his right. At the same time, McLean differed from the "opinion of the court" because he believed that Congress could legitimately impose an obligation on state officers. He disagreed with Story on this point but it actually amounted to little because he admitted that a state could resist, and that no means were available to coerce a fulfillment of duties. If a state refused to cooperate, said McLean, the federal government "may rely upon its own agency in giving effect to the laws."

Only one justice, Henry Baldwin of Pennsylvania, expressed doubt about the constitutionality of the law of 1793, although his grounds are unclear. The only report of his views was the following: "Concurred with the court in reversing the judgment of the Supreme Court of Pennsylvania on the ground that the act of the Legislature was unconstitutional; inasmuch as the slavery of the person was admitted, the removal could not be kidnapping. But he dissented from the principles laid down by the court as the grounds of their opinion."[32]

---

[29] *Ibid.*, 648.
[30] *Ibid.*, 644.
[31] *Ibid.*, 662.
[32] *Ibid.*, 636. Justice Wayne, in his opinion, mentioned that only Baldwin did not admit that the act of Congress was constitutional. Hurd, *Law of Freedom and Bondage*, 2: 490–91, took

Justice Smith Thompson of New York (who had already considered the Fugitive Slave Law in the case *In re Martin*) joined the "opinion of the court" in affirming the validity of congressional action, but he did not find, as Story had, that the power of Congress was exclusive. Congressional action was more appropriate than state action, he noted, because of the need to have "the regulation uniform throughout the United States." But if a state, voluntarily and in good faith, chose to adopt a law implementing the fugitive slave clause he could see nothing that made such a law "unfit." If it conflicted with the act of Congress, of course, it would be void (as was the case with the Pennsylvania law of 1826).[33]

Chief Justice Roger B. Taney of Maryland, in a concurrence, took the view proslavery people, by and large, had held for sometime. He agreed with Story that the clause guaranteed a claimant the right to recover and remove his property by self-help alone and that a duty was enjoined on the federal government to pass implementing legislation to assist claimants in recovering runaways. He dissented, however, from Story's argument that the power to legislate was exclusively in Congress.

Maryland, he pointed out, continually had passed laws requiring state officials to arrest fugitives and commit them to the public jail "in order to keep them safely until the master has an opportunity of reclaiming them." If the name of the master was not known the arrest and detention would be advertised. If Story was correct these laws would be unconstitutional and void. Story had allowed the states the right to pass legislation to protect themselves from the "evil example" of fugitives, but, in Taney's view, this was scarcely enough, since most runaways would be very circumspect in their behavior, hoping to avert attention. In any case, Maryland did not justify its laws on the "questionable powers of internal and local police." The laws stood on "surer and firmer grounds": Maryland's laws were passed "in the performance of a duty believed to be enjoined upon it by the Constitution of the United States." That duty, in Taney's view, was "equally binding upon the faith of every State in the Union, and . . . justly regarded as obligatory upon all."[34] Pennsylvania, of course, had acted on the assumption that it was fulfilling a duty imposed by the Constitution, but its law infringed upon the rights of slave owners.

Justice Peter Daniel of Virginia also thought the states should legislate in aid of the rights of claimants. Story's position was fraught with serious consequences, he believed. "By the inculcation of a belief that any cooperation with the master becomes a violation of law," wrote Daniel, "the most

---

the view that Baldwin was impressed with the idea that the fugitive slave clause operated *proprio vigore*. The act, however, could be challenged on the ground that it conflicted with the personal guarantees in other parts of the Constitution (such as the guarantee against unreasonable searches and seizures). A more carefully framed congressional act might be constitutional.

[33] *Prigg* v. *Pennsylvania*, 16 Peters 634–35.
[34] *Ibid.*, 633.

active and efficient auxiliary which he could possibly call to his aid is entirely neutralized."[35]

Another question relating to state power, one that had been ignored in the "opinion of the court," was discussed in two of the concurring opinions: how much power did the states have to protect free blacks from being carried into slavery by "any summary process." "Legislation," said Justice Wayne, "may be confined to that end, and be made effectual, without making such a remedy applicable to fugitive slaves."[36] The states could not establish the procedures to adjudicate claims as Pennsylvania had in 1826, but they could protect free men by antikidnapping laws.

A much fuller examination of this problem was given by Justice McLean, who perceived wholly different perils in the opinion of the majority from those seen by Taney and Daniel. McLean was disturbed particularly by Story's views on recaption. Both the Constitution and the act of 1793, McLean believed, required that a fugitive be delivered up on claim. Masters were authorized by the federal law to seize a black and take him before a magistrate, and there, he argued, the claim was to be made. If recaption and removal were allowed, if the master could seize and remove a black man without claim, "he can commit no breach of the peace by using all the force necessary to accomplish his object." Story had said that a master had the absolute right to the immediate possession of his property, but that the seizure and removal had to be accomplished without "illegal violence," or breach of the peace. "If the master may lawfully seize and remove the fugitive out of the State where he may be found, without an exhibition of his claim," countered McLean, "he may lawfully resist any force, physical or legal, which the State, or the citizens of the State, may interpose." To argue otherwise would be "to abandon the ground assumed." The master was engaged in the lawful prosecution of a constitutional right. Recaption, as McLean saw it, carried with it the danger of destroying social justice as well as the peace and good order of the state. Such was scarcely the intention of the framers of the Constitution.[37]

The fundamental problem raised by Prigg's actions, in McLean's view, was this: "shall the presumption of right set up by the master, unsustained by any proof, or the presumption which arises from the laws and institutions of the State, prevail."[38] The act of Pennsylvania before the Court, according to McLean, did not conflict with the Constitution "in its terms," despite the fact that it was passed to establish procedures for the adjudication of claims. Prima facie it did not include slaves, as every man within the state was presumed to be free. "In a State where slavery is allowed, every colored person is presumed to be a slave," he noted, "and on the same

35 *Ibid.*, 657.
36 *Ibid.*, 650.
37 *Ibid.*, 668–70.
38 *Ibid.*, 672.

principle, in a non-slaveholding State, every person is presumed to be free without regard to color. On this principle the States, both slaveholding and non-slaveholding legislate."[39]

He believed a power and duty resided in the state to protect the personal liberty of its citizenry, and this power Congress, and the Constitution, did not infringe upon by authorizing a forcible seizure and removal. Each government has its own rights and duties: states could not legislate in aid of the rights of slave owners, but they could legislate to protect free men; Congress, on the other hand, could provide for the return of runaways. "This view," concluded McLean, "respects the rights of the master and the rights of the State. It neither jeopards nor retards the reclamation of the slave. It removes all State action prejudicial to the rights of the master; and recognizes in the State a power to guard and protect its own jurisdiction, and the peace of its citizens."[40] The opinion of the majority, however, virtually destroyed the presumption of freedom arising from the laws and institutions of the states north of the Mason-Dixon line.

The majority of the Court, then, held that states lacked the power to establish procedures for the adjudication of claims to runaways—this was a power vested exclusively in Congress. But at the same time, it believed that state officials could exercise a jurisdiction under the federal law, "unless," as Story added, "prohibited by State legislation." State officials administering the federal law had to follow the summary ministerial procedures outlined in the act of 1793.

Although all the members of the Court, except perhaps Justice Baldwin, affirmed the right and the duty of Congress to pass implementing legislation, none carefully examined the terms of the Fugitive Slave Law. The case did not involve "the general question as to the constitutionality of the Act of 1793." All that was considered was the question of the locus of power. Whether or not the act conformed to other provisions of the Constitution, such as the requirement of a jury trial in the Sixth Amendment, was not faced. Justice Story, for one, considered that an "open" question.[41]

---

[39] *Ibid.*, 669.

[40] On McLean's opinion see Charles Grove Haines and Foster H. Sherwood, *The Role of the Supreme Court in American Government and Politics, 1835–1864* (Berkeley and Los Angeles, 1957), 127; Hurd, *Law of Freedom and Bondage*, 2: 485–88; Yanuck, "The Fugitive Slave Law," 24; Schnell, "Court Cases Involving Slavery," 200.

[41] William Wetmore Story, ed., *Life and Letters of Joseph Story* (2 vols.; Boston, 1851), 2: 396. Some antislavery people also believed that strong constitutional arguments had been overlooked in the case of *Prigg* v. *Pennsylvania*. Edwin W. Clarke of New York, for example, believed that the fugitive clause should be tested by the Preamble to the Constitution. "To establish justice" would provide the canon of constitutional interpretation. Miscellaneous Manuscripts, Slavery, New-York Historical Society, Box 1. This view is expressed in an undated, unsigned, handwritten memorandum on the case. There is no pagination. From an examination of other manuscripts it appears to be in the hand of Clarke, who was connected with the Liberty Party; see, for example, Edwin W. Clarke to T. X. Meacham, August 14, 1840, Miscellaneous Manuscripts, Slavery, Box 1.

Three justices in concurring held that the states did have the power to legislate in aid of the right of a master to recover his property, and two (one, proslavery and the other, antislavery) maintained that the states could legislate to protect free men from being taken into slavery. Of these last two, Justice Wayne's position left little scope for any action other than the prosecution of kidnappers, whereas Justice McLean's, based on the presumption of freedom, allowed the states room to conduct independent inquiries. Justice McLean, moreover, was the only one to deny that the Constitution secured to slave owners a right to seize and remove their property without a recourse to law.

William Wetmore Story, Justice Story's son, was later to comment that the question his father had decided was "purely legal, and not ethical." He added that "the function of the Supreme Court was to pronounce what the law was, and not what it ought to be; and their conclusions, whether right or wrong, are simply on the facts of the law."[42] During the late 1820s Justice Story was in correspondence with Lord Stowell on slave cases in which both men, avowed opponents of slavery, expressed such views of the judicial function.[43] "Judicial objectivity," to borrow Professor Roper's phrase, had marked the Marshall Court's decisions in slave cases,[44] and it continued to be the touchstone for Story.

In his view the results of the case amounted to a "triumph of freedom," as he "repeatedly and earnestly" said to his friends and family when he returned to Massachusetts from the Capitol.[45] It localized slavery, making it a municipal institution of the states, not recognized by international law and recognized by the Constitution only in the fugitive slave clause. He also viewed it as a "triumph" because of the widespread thinking that it would be impracticable to reclaim runaways without the aid of state legislation; and, finally, because "power was put in the hands of the whole people to remodel the law, and establish, through Congress, a legislation in favor of freedom." If the states possessed concurrent or exclusive power over the

---

[42]Story, *Life and Letters*, 2: 391.

[43]*Ibid.*, 1: 552-61.

[44]Roper, "The Marshall Court and Judicial Objectivity."

[45]Story, *Life and Letters*, 2: 392 ff.; see also Yanuck, "The Fugitive Slave Law," 27, 31, for example, who contended that it was the best "possible result which abolitionists could have expected." William R. Leslie, on the other hand, concluded that Story's "a-moral politico-legal theories" prepared the way for civil war, they created the necessity for the "violent removal of property in slaves in order to secure unalienable rights." Leslie, "The Fugitive Slave Clause, 1787-1842," 289, 296, 356. The biographers of other justices have tended to find that Story's reasoning opened the door to a conflict which could have been averted if only the power and duty of the states to implement the fugitive clause had been affirmed. See, for example, Charles W. Smith, Jr., *Roger B. Taney: Jacksonian Jurist* (Chapel Hill, N.C., 1936), 152-53; Walker Lewis, *Without Fear or Favor: A Biography of Chief Justice Roger Taney* (Boston, 1965), 367-68; Carl Brent Swisher, *Roger B. Taney* (Camden, Conn., 1961), 422-23; John P. Frank, *Justice Daniel Dissenting: A Biography of Peter V. Daniel, 1784-1860* (Cambridge, 1964), 178.

subject, the free states would have no voice in establishing a uniform rule, whereas a slave state could "authorize recaption, within its own boundaries, under the most odious circumstances, without any legal process, if it chose, and upon the mere *prima facie* evidence of slavery, growing out of color."[46] Since Justice Story had affirmed the constitutional right of a slave owner to recapture his property without legal process, even in free states, this perhaps was a belated recognition of the vagaries in his opinion on the "eccentrical remedy." He might also have thought that slave states could declare, within their boundaries, that any seizure of a black, however effected, did not constitute a breach of the peace, and that any violence necessary was not "illegal violence."

Undoubtedly, because of Story's localization of slavery, and his validation of state noncooperation in the rendition process, the opinion in *Prigg* v. *Pennsylvania* could be interpreted as a "triumph of freedom." But in another sense the opinion appeared to be precisely the opposite because it seemed to withdraw from free blacks north of the Mason-Dixon line the equal protection of the laws, and to deny them standing to invoke the procedures used to secure personal liberty. In Story's view any state law delaying the immediate possession of a runaway violated the Constitution, and he asserted that the right to reclaim one's property was not bounded by any state institutions or policy. He ignored the fact that the so-called incidental property right might be exercised against a free man, and because he did, his judgment appeared to deprive blacks claimed as fugitives of the right to a judicial inquiry by means of habeas corpus, as well as of a trial by jury. On the other hand, since his holding was limited to the right a master had against his slave, it did not logically preclude the states from exercising their power to protect free men.[47]

Prigg v. *Pennsylvania* simply did not resolve some of the basic constitutional and legal problems presented by the abolition of slavery north of the Mason-Dixon line. Rather it opened up certain possibilities, and closed off, or appeared to close off, others. The Court had invalidated the earlier state efforts to establish the procedures for adjudicating claims and had validated state noncooperation in the rendition process. At the same time by sustaining a right of recaption uninhibited by the presumption of freedom, the "opinion of the court" appeared to deprive free men of the equal protection of the laws.

By and large the initial public response to the decision in Prigg's case was calm. The *North American Review*, for example, commented that the judgment was "received by the public with the quiet submission which they usually manifest when ordinary judicial decisions are announced."[48]

---

[46]Story, *Life and Letters*, 2: 395.

[47]Northern judges, after *Prigg* v. *Pennsylvania*, "permitted the free use of the writ of habeas corpus" as a remedy for kidnapping, Schnell, "Court Cases Involving Slavery," 204.

[48]*North American Review* (Oct. 1843), vol. 57, quoted in Warren, *The Supreme Court*, 2: 86.

Some of the leading legal journals of the time paid no attention to the decision. It was not reported in the *Monthly Law Reporter*, or the *American Jurist and Law Magazine*. The *American Law Journal*, published in Philadelphia, listed it with Story's rule of interpretation as an introductory comment.[49] The case, moreover, was not probed by the *National Intelligencer*, nor even by *Niles' Register*. The *North American Review*, on the other hand, did acknowledge some "murmurs" had been heard over the case.

They were more than "murmurs," as Ellis Gray Loring noted in a letter to John Quincy Adams in March, 1842. The decision, he wrote, "*cannot* be carried into force in Massachusetts." Loring was very cautious about justifying a forcible resistance to the law: he would only "hint" in private that the guilt of such resistance might be extenuated in some cases. But he feared that some men were not so cautious as he, and that "blood would run down the streets of Boston before a slave could be carried off."[50]

The response among abolitionists was heated. For Garrison *Prigg* v. *Pennsylvania* was the proximate cause of his complete break with the existing system, although he did not call for blood as Loring might have feared. "This is the last turn of the screw before it breaks," wrote Garrison, "the additional ounce that breaks the camel's back! *The Rubicon is passed*, if the slaveholding power is permitted to roam without molestation through the Northern states, 'seeking whom it may devour,' and dragging into its den the victims of its lust." The judgment of the Court was not law, thundered Garrison: it was contrary to law "which finds its seat in the bosom of God." Garrison's higher-law frame of reference led him to conclude that the decision should be "spit upon, hooted at, trampled in the dust, resolutely and openly, at all hazards, by every one who claims to be a man."[51] It also led him to conclude that from the Court's decision "there is no appeal to any higher judicatory, except to the people on the ground of revolutionary necessity." He was not, however, advocating a violent revolutionary action: he wanted a peaceful dissolution of the Union.[52]

As bitter as any was Alvan Stewart, Garrison's antagonist in the abolitionist movement. "Nothing in the 19th century," he contended in soaring prose, "had transcended the decisions of the 17th, by Jeffreys, Scroggs, and Pollefexen in the bloody trials of Lord Russell and Algernon Sidney, until this master and terrific decision of judicial tyranny flung all the judicial Neros of England into the regions of forlorn and returnless insignificance."[53] The Personal Liberty Laws had been struck down, and all that re-

---

[49]*American Law Journal* (Philadelphia, 1842), 1: "Selected Cases from 16 Peters' Reports."

[50]Ellis Gray Loring to John Quincy Adams, Boston, March 7, 1842, Adams Papers, Massachusetts Historical Society.

[51]*The Liberator*, March 11, 1842.

[52]Wendell Phillips Garrison, Francis Jackson Garrison, *William Lloyd Garrison 1805–1879: The Story of His Life Told by His Children* (4 vols.; Boston and New York, 1894), 3: 60.

[53]Luther Lawson Marsh, *Writings and Speeches of Alvan Stewart, on Slavery* (New York,

mained was the act of 1793. Congress, wrote Stewart, should abolish that act, and by so doing "place Canada on Mason and Dixon's line."[54] If that was done slavery could not survive five years in the border states.[55]

Charles Sumner, a protégé and close personal friend of Justice Story's, was placed in an awkward position by the decision since he was also an ardent opponent of the "Slave Power," and close to the antislavery movement in Massachusetts. He explained his view in a letter to Charles Francis Adams: he regarded "the judgment in that case as legally, I may say, *scientifically* correct." The decision flowed naturally from previous decisions of the Court and established rules of construction. Story was correct in overturning the legislation of the states, even though it undercut habeas corpus and trial by jury. That merely showed the "injustice of the system." For Sumner the blame for the existing situation rested not with the Court, but with Congress which did not "abrogate the law [of 1793] immediately, or add to it provisions in harmony with the Spirit of the Constitution."[56] William Ellery Channing, in an anxious work written in March, 1842, *The Duty of the Free States*, felt the same way. All that was left after the Court's decision was a federal law that was "reprobated, not by the passions, but by the deliberate moral judgments of large portions of the Free States; and such being the case, it cannot be executed." Congress should modify the law.[57] "The grand principle to be laid down is, that it is infinitely more important to preserve a free citizen from being made a slave than to send back a fugitive slave to his chain."[58]

The problem with Channing's view, and for that matter with Story's justification of his opinion as a "triumph of freedom," was quickly pointed out by Charles Francis Adams, however. Assuming that Garrison's call for a dissolution of the Union was an untenable solution, could the demand for a modification of the federal law be any more viable? It "demanded control of the national government politically," but in the early 1840s that objective appeared a long way off. At the time he made this assessment (June, 1842), Adams placed his hopes on a possible reorganization of political parties and on a developing moral sense in the free states.[59] For him the solution seemed clear, and so did the problem: for blacks, he wrote, "the theory of our institutions is a mockery."[60]

1860), 382. This comes from an article entitled "The Act of 1793," dated January 3, 1843.

[54]*Ibid.*, 387.

[55]*Ibid.*, 389. This is from "Extracts from Reply to the Junius Tract of the Rev. Calvin Colton, 1843."

[56]Charles Sumner to Charles Francis Adams, March 1, 1843, Adams Family Papers, Massachusetts Historical Society.

[57]William E. Channing, *The Works of William E. Channing* (6 vols.; Boston, New York, 1848), 6: 293–94.

[58]*Ibid.*, 289.

[59]Martin Duberman, *Charles Francis Adams: 1807–1886* (Boston, 1961), 79.

[60]Charles Francis Adams, "The Duty of the Free States," *Quincy Patriot*, June 25, 1842, in Charles Francis Adams, Miscellany: Scrapbook of his Newspaper Articles, 1835–50, Adams Family Papers.

The Pursuit of
a Containment Policy, 1842-1850 7

Prigg v. *Pennsylvania* was a grave disappointment to many people, but it was not sufficient in itself to provoke the experiments in noncooperation in the free states or the southern demand for further congressional action that followed. Most people accepted the decision with that "quiet submission" noted by the *North American Review*. Events were occurring, however, raising the slavery issue to new heights, and when this happened the states above the Mason-Dixon line began to reassess their positions on the questions associated with the existence of slavery in a federal union.

In 1843 the divisive question of the expansion of slavery was reopened because of the Tyler administration's response to the alleged British efforts which encouraged Texas to abolish slavery. Speaking for the British government Lord Aberdeen explained that although Britain hoped to see the world-wide abolition of slavery, it had no intention of forcing its views in Texas. Calhoun, now the secretary of state, responded in April, 1844, in a letter to the British minister, Richard Pakenham. British interference in Texas, said Calhoun, had made American annexation of the area imperative as a matter of self-defense. He proceeded with a lengthy defense of slavery: it was necessary to the continued prosperity of the United States and should be protected in Texas.[1]

The secretary of state's proslavery justification for annexation aroused the indignation and the fears of antislavery men and women throughout the North. In April, 1844, for example, Joseph Story, scarcely a radical on the subject of slavery, wrote to Ezekiel Bacon that "In my judgment the admission of Texas into the Union would be a grossly unconstitutional act; and I should not be surprised if it should lead to a dissolution of the Union. It will forever give the South a most mischievous, if not a ruinous preponderance in the Union."[2] The Liberty Party, an organization of the political abolitionists in the early 1840s, took the view, in its 1844 platform, that the pledge made when the Constitution was adopted, "that slavery should never be extended beyond its then existing limits; but should be gradually, and, yet, at no distant day, wholly abolished by State authority," had been "shamefully violated." The violation had occurred because the states had

[1]Charles Wiltse, *John C. Calhoun: Sectionalist, 1840–1850* (Indianapolis, 1951), 169; see, however, Chauncey W. Boucher, "In Re That Aggressive Slavocracy," *The Mississippi Valley Historical Review*, 8: (June-Sept., 1921).

[2]Story, *Life and Letters*, 2: 481.

not acted, and because of "the extension of slavery far beyond its original limits, by acts of Congress, admitting new slave States into the Union."[3]

By the spring of 1844 presidential politics had become deeply embroiled with the issue of the Texas annexation.[4] In April both Henry Clay and Martin Van Buren, the probable contenders, issued public letters opposing immediate annexation, hoping they could remove the whole issue from the campaign. This stance cost both men dearly as Democrat James Knox Polk emerged the presidential victor as an avowed expansionist.

As the United States went to war with Mexico behind Polk and the cry of "Manifest Destiny," the misgivings and the anger of antiexpansionists, whether they were abolitionists or not, mounted. Senator Thomas Corwin of Ohio, a colonizationist, speaking on the floor of the Senate, condemned the war as a senseless search for room to expand, a search that would precipitate a sectional clash over slavery.[5]

As the war progressed people began to turn their attention to the problems of the peace. By August, 1846, a truly crucial issue was presented when David Wilmot of Pennsylvania moved an amendment to a pending appropriation bill that was to pay for territorial concessions made by Mexico in a future peace treaty. The amendment provided for the prohibition of slavery in the territories acquired.[6] The House adopted the Wilmot Proviso, but the Senate rejected it.

After 1846 the political parties, and the nation, began to break apart and polarize along sectional lines over the issue presented: free soilism versus the expansion of slavery. Many people in the North joined behind the Wilmot Proviso: some, because the proviso "expressed the northern determination to prevent the spread not only of slavery but of the despised Negro as well,"[7] whereas others, because they believed that containing slavery in the states where it already existed was the only constitutional way to attack it within the federal Union.[8]

Many proslavery and antislavery people, after 1846, increasingly came to believe that slavery could be fatally weakened by federal policies oper-

[3]Kirk H. Porter and Donald Bruce Johnson, compilers, *National Party Platforms, 1840–1960* (Urbana, Ill., 1961), 5.

[4]Charles Grier Sellers, *James Knox Polk, Continentalist, 1843–1846* (Princeton, 1966), is one of the finest accounts of the impact of the Texas issue on the 1844 campaign. See also James C. N. Paul, *Rift in the Democracy*, (Philadelphia, 1951).

[5]Cited in Frederick Merk, *Manifest Destiny and Mission in American History: A Reinterpretation* (New York, 1963), 93.

[6]*Cong. Globe,* 29th Cong, 1st sess., August, 1846, 1217.

[7]Chaplain Morrison, *Democratic Politics and Sectionalism: The Wilmot Proviso Controversy* (Chapel Hill, N.C., 1967), 73.

[8]This was the view of most of the Conscience Whigs. On these people the finest study is Kinley J. Brauer, *Cotton versus Conscience: Massachusetts Whig Politics and Southwestern Expansion, 1843–1848* (Lexington, Ky., 1967). Martin Duberman, "The Northern Response to Slavery," in Martin Duberman, ed., *The Antislavery Vanguard: New Essays on the Abolitionists* (Princeton, 1965), 402, has argued that containment proceeded on the assumption that the South would accept a dissolution of its "peculiar institution." If this was unlikely containment would be little more than a "technique of evasion."

ating outside the boundaries of the slave states. It was widely held that the institution could not survive if it could be kept out of the territories.[9] Scholars have long recognized the central importance of the territorial issue in the polarization of the sections that ended in war, but less often recognized is that the Personal Liberty Laws of the 1840s were also blows struck at slavery extraterritorially. They were part of the search for a containment policy worked out in response to the rising issue. By 1842 William Ellery Channing described the obligation of the free states to be to "confine all action in regard to slavery to the narrowest limits which will satisfy the Constitution." Those states moreover were duty bound "to the most earnest efforts to protect that portion of their citizens exposed to the peril of being carried into bondage."[10] Disagreements over such matters as the nature of the constitutional obligation, the meaning and force of the Prigg decision, and the expediency of acting in the face of a strong southern opposition, however, made it difficult to achieve this purpose everywhere. The existing legal patterns and traditions of a state in addition tended to channel the search for a containment policy in certain directions: the weight of inertia, state parochialism, and legal traditionalism clearly were felt. On top of this, of course, prounionist and antiblack sentiments were powerful deterrents to some states initiating any action on such an explosive issue as the return of runaways. The end result of this bewildering set of factors was that the years between the Prigg decision and the adoption of a new, federal fugitive-slave law were filled with variety and confusion, action and inaction. The only coherent trend of those years was the sometimes-faltering quest for a containment policy, but the strength and form of this trend varied from state to state.

I

The noncooperative Personal Liberty Law passed in Massachusetts in 1843 set the pattern other states attempted to follow. It was adopted in response to a significant fugitive slave case, and came just at the time that concern in the state over the Texas issue was rising.

About the middle of October, 1842, George Latimer was seized in Boston by James B. Gray of Norfolk, Virginia, and placed in the court house.[11] Because of a hostile crowd of blacks, he was taken to the city jail and placed in the custody of the jailor. Latimer's counsel then secured a habeas corpus from Chief Justice Shaw of the state supreme court. Shaw

---

[9]Eugene D. Genovese, *The Political Economy of Slavery: Studies in the Economy & Society of the Slave South* (New York, 1967), chap. 10; Arthur Bestor, "The American Civil War as a Constitutional Crisis," *American Historical Review*, 69: (Jan., 1964), 325–52.

[10]Channing, *The Works of Channing*, 6: 288–89.

[11]*The Liberator*, October 28, 1842. Levy, *Law of the Commonwealth*, 78–85, is the best secondary account of the arrest and trials of Latimer. On the details of the case, and Shaw's decision, he is complete and masterful. Another good account, but with far less concern for the legal and constitutional issues, is Lader, *The Bold Brahmins*, 113 ff.

held that the claim was sufficient authority to hold the man following the decision in *Prigg* v. *Pennsylvania*.[12] Two days after the hearing before Shaw, the attorney for the putative owner applied to Justice Joseph Story on circuit for a certificate of removal under the federal law. Story granted a two-week delay to allow the claimant time to obtain evidence from Virginia. "Thus is Boston," commented *The Liberator*, "made the slave-hunting ground of the South, and thus does the city consent to aid and abet the vilest of Kidnappers!"[13]

On Monday, October 24, Latimer's counsel sued out a writ of personal replevin under the Personal Liberty Law of 1837. It was served on the jailor who held Latimer at Gray's request. Story had not remanded the alleged fugitive to the custody of the jailor, but to the custody of the claimant, so that Latimer was held in the Boston jail solely at the request of the slave owner. Nathaniel Coolidge, the jailor, was commanded to bring Latimer before the Court of Common Pleas where the cause of his detention would be examined by a jury. Coolidge refused to honor the writ.

Shaw, at the request of Latimer's counsel, then issued another writ of habeas corpus. This one commanded the jailor to state why he had refused to honor the writ of personal replevin, but it also showed the limited utility of the writ as Shaw, at the hearing, did not even require an answer to the arguments of Latimer's attorneys. In his opinion the Personal Liberty Law of 1837 was unconstitutional insofar as it applied to fugitives. It was a case, he said, governed by the Constitution and the law of Congress. It was not a case in which "an appeal to natural rights and the paramount law of liberty" could be relevant.[14]

A further postponement occurred when Justice Story became ill and was not able to hear the case. It was brought before Judge Peleg Sprague of the federal district court who postponed it for two more weeks to allow Latimer time to obtain testimony from Virginia that he had been set free by the will of a former owner. It is worth noting that Judge Sprague, by allowing the admission into evidence of the alleged fugitive's testimony, construed the "satisfaction" requirement of the federal law more broadly than did Justice Story.

This respite, in any event, brought a call for increased agitation from *The Liberator*: "during these two weeks, the city, the county, the Commonwealth, should be convulsed with excitement."[15] At the beginning of November Henry I. Bowditch, William P. Channing, the son of William Ellery Channing, and Frederick S. Cabot formed themselves into the

[12] *The Liberator*, October 28, 1842.

[13] *Ibid.*

[14] This account of the hearing was put together from *The Liberator*, November 4, 1842, and November 25, 1842, and from Levy, *Law of the Commonwealth*, 80–82; see also the *Monthly Law Reporter*, 5: 483.

[15] *The Liberator*, November 11, 1842.

"Latimer Committee," and began to publish a newspaper, *The Latimer Journal, and North Star*. During that turbulent two weeks these men got up a petition demanding the removal of the sheriff of Suffolk County from office if he did not order the jailor to release Latimer. This strategy worked where all the legal maneuvers had failed. The sheriff gave the order, and Coolidge released Latimer to the custody of his claimant, who now held him without any assistance whatever. Fearing he could not hold him long by his own force, Gray agreed to sell his slave. The case of George Latimer was over.[16]

Latimer's case, nevertheless, had provoked a righteous anger in the ranks of the Garrisonians and had deeply disturbed less thoroughgoing opponents of slavery as well. "With us," commented Garrison after Shaw's second habeas corpus hearing, "the forms of law, legal precedents, and constitutional arrangements are nothing, in opposition to the claims of our common humanity, the instincts of eternal justice, and the commands of God."[17] In a sermon preached at the Hollis Street Church the Reverend John Pierpont announced his approbation. The fugitive slave clause was "immoral, unnatural, contrary to common law and to the divine law, and therefore null and void, and of no binding force whatever, either on the courts or the people."[18]

All the indignation meetings resounded with the cry for people to become civilly disobedient. Conscientious opposition to the federal law would form "a wall of adamant" for the security of blacks who might be chased down by a "human hyena."[19] In 1844 this view was endorsed in the national platform of the Liberty Party.[20]

Zachariah Chandler, in an issue of the *Monthly Law Reporter*, tried to answer such critics of the law and the courts. He agreed that a conflict between human and natural law raised a moral right of revolution, but the judiciary had no power to declare the human law void. "Does not this preacher know," he wrote addressing himself to Pierpont, "that a judge has nothing to do with the moral character of laws which society chooses to make, and which, when made, it places him upon the bench to apply to the facts before him?"[21] Courts, of course, had the power to declare a law unconstitutional, but all that meant was that "the supreme power of the state has delegated to the legislature no authority to make the particular law."[22]

[16]Levy, *Law of the Commonwealth*, 84; McDougall, *Fugitive Slaves*, 40; Filler, *The Crusade Against Slavery*, 171.
[17]*The Liberator*, November 4, 1842.
[18]A fuller summary of Pierpont's sermon can be found in the *Monthly Law Reporter*, 5: 493 ff; *The Liberator*, November 11, 1842.
[19]*The Liberator*, November 11, 1842.
[20]Porter and Johnson, *National Party Platforms*, 8.
[21]*Monthly Law Reporter*, 5: 494.
[22]*Ibid.*, 496.

Antislavery radicals hardly agreed. Wendell Phillips, for example, argued that Shaw should have decided the issues in Latimer's case independently of the "illogical and presumptuous dicta of the case of Prigg and Pennsylvania."[23] *The Latimer Journal, and North Star* added that the federal law should have been declared unconstitutional because Congress possessed no authority to enact it, as Alvord and Walworth, among others, had argued.[24] Implicit in these comments was a view of habeas corpus that would bear fruit later. As noted earlier, one of the most important additions to habeas corpus usage that had developed in the state courts, or through statutory grants, was the power to go behind the facts alleged in a return to the writ and to conduct a full inquiry into the facts presented on both sides. The emphasis upon an examination of the facts had led Alvord to suggest that the *homine replegiando* was a more viable remedy for someone claimed as a slave because a jury trial—rather than a hearing before a judge—was better adapted to examine the facts. What abolitionists were now suggesting, whether they were fully aware of it or not, was that the habeas corpus jurisdiction be extended to include an examination of the law by which a person was restrained of personal liberty, and not just of the facts that justified the holding under that law. Alvan Stewart, of course, had pointed the direction for a bold and imaginative use of habeas corpus as early as 1837, but it had remained a somewhat quixotic suggestion that had practically no chance at all of being endorsed by the jurists of the free states or the federal courts. Abolitionists, however, were not yet focusing upon habeas corpus as an aggressive weapon against the "peculiar institution."

For the radicals, in any event, the objective was clear even though the precise method to achieve it was not. At a Garrisonian protest meeting at Faneuil Hall it was resolved that "Massachusetts is, and of right ought to be, a free and independent State; that she cannot allow her soil to be polluted by the footprints of slavery without trampling on her Bill of Rights, and subjecting herself to infamy; that she is solemnly bound to give succor and protection to all who may escape from the prison of bondage, and flee to her for safety."[25]

The demand for an outright repudiation of the constitutional obligation, however, was not supported widely in the state. By the end of the year agitation for some alteration in the state's relationship to slavery centered on a suggestion made at that same Faneuil Hall meeting. This was the idea that claimants should be prohibited from using any state instrumentalities, or facilities, in carrying out their business. The Latimer Committee sent

---

23 *The Liberator*, November 18, 1842.
24 *The Latimer Journal, and North Star*, November 11, 1842. An excellent collection of materials on the case, and a file of this newspaper, are in the Massachusetts Historical Society under the title *The Latimer Case*.
25 *The Liberator*, November 4, 1842.

out thousands of copies of what was called the "Great Massachusetts Petition" to postmasters and known "friends of human liberty in every town in the State." By the time the petition reached the legislature it had over 60,000 signatures.[26] The petitioners asked for three things: a law forbidding all state officers from aiding in the arrest, or detention of anyone claimed as a fugitive; a law forbidding the use of the jails, or other public property of the state, for the detention of anyone claimed; and a proposal to amend the federal Constitution to separate the people of Massachusetts forever from slavery.

These developments occurred just at the time when concern over the expansion of slavery was rising in the state because of the Texas issue. In January, 1843, the legislature declared that annexation would be dangerous to the peace and prosperity of the United States.[27] John Quincy Adams was just joining with a small group of northern Whigs to expose to the country what they considered the Texas "scheme."[28]

Adams's son, Charles Francis, also was aroused by these developments. At a meeting at Faneuil Hall in February, 1843, he accepted the task of advocate for the "Great Massachusetts Petition" before the legislature, of which he was a member.[29] Samuel E. Sewall and Wendell Phillips, among others, appeared before a Joint Special Committee considering the petition to argue for "further enactments to protect our liberties."[30] A little over a week after their appearance the report of the committee, including a bill, was submitted to the house.[31]

The report of the committee, written by Charles Francis Adams, was far from radical or inflammatory. For Adams the "forms of law, legal precedents, and constitutional arrangements" were important. Because of his commitment to the existing institutions he would not deny the binding nature of the constitutional obligation to return runaways, and he would not challenge the jurisdiction of the Supreme Court. However adverse *Prigg* v. *Pennsylvania* was "to all the noblest principles at the foundation of a republican government . . . it was sufficient that the regularly constituted tribunal had declared such to be the law, to secure for it acquiescence."[32]

Adams admitted that Shaw's decision concerning the writ of personal replevin was correct, but he was disturbed deeply that *Prigg* v. *Pennsyl-*

[26]A copy of this petition is in the Adams Family Papers, Reel 525, Massachusetts Historical Society.

[27]Brauer, *Cotton versus Conscience*, 55.

[28]*Ibid.*, 56.

[29]Vincent Y. Bowditch, *Life and Correspondence of Henry Ingersoll Bowditch* (2 vols.; Boston and New York, 1902), 1: 134. Duberman, *Charles Francis Adams*, 81.

[30]William F. Channing to Charles Francis Adams, Boston, February 3, 1843, Adams Family Papers, Massachusetts Historical Society; *The Latimer Journal, and North Star*, May 10, 1843.

[31]*Mass. House Journal, 1843*, Mass. State Library, 65: 241.

[32]*Mass. House Document No. 41, 1843*, 4.

vania had destroyed the common-law right to challenge a seizure by the writ *de homine replegiando*. The Court's decision, said Adams, proclaimed the "startling truth, that the continuance of bondage to the slave is of more worth to the mind of Americans than the continuance of liberty to the freeman."[33]

Prigg v. *Pennsylvania*, no doubt, was a serious stumbling block for Adams. He would not support a law conflicting with the judgment of the Supreme Court, but he was also committed to making "our institutions" more than a mere "mockery" for blacks. He found a way out in Story's validation of state noncooperation. The state should not, Adams sarcastically noted, "permit the prostitution of the criminal process of the State, or of its property set apart for certain specific purposes, to the base uses of men engaged in the honorable business of enslaving their fellows."[34] He therefore introduced the bill, "An Act further to protect personal liberty."

The remaining portion of his report concerned a constitutional amendment. His proposal was to discard the three-fifths clause in the federal Constitution.[35] As long as there was a parity in the number of free and slave states, of course, this could never be achieved. But it would be different if slavery could be contained and new free states be admitted to the Union.

The speed and unanimity with which the bill and resolution passed the legislature demonstrated the degree to which men of various points of view could come together on the ground staked out by Adams. On March 23, 1843, the bill passed the house without debate, and with "only one or two voting in the negative."[36] In the senate the next day it was passed by a vote of twenty-five to three.[37] Governor Marcus Morton signed it into law on March 24, 1843.

This new law prohibited any judge of a court of record or justice of the peace from accepting jurisdiction in a case involving a claim under the act of 1793. It also prohibited any officer of the state from arresting or detaining, or aiding in the arrest or detention of, any person claimed as a fugitive, and from detaining him in any public building in the state. The final section provided sanctions for any violation of the act, although judges were excepted.[38]

Massachusetts' Personal Liberty Law of 1843 represented a new departure in the North. As early as 1787 people in the free states had ex-

[33]*Ibid.*, 10.

[34]*Ibid.*, 27.

[35]*Ibid.*, 33.

[36]*The Latimer Journal, and North Star*, May 10, 1843. The vote was not recorded in the house journal.

[37]*Ibid.*, May 10, 1843. There was no debate recorded in the journal, or in the newspapers. *Mass. Senate Journal, 1843*, Mass. State Library, 64: 427. See also pp. 421, 425, and 441 for other proceedings.

[38]The bill as passed was identical to the bill as it came out of committee. The original is on pp. 36 and 37 of Adams' report, and the final bill is found in *Mass. Session Laws, 1843*, 33.

pressed opposition to being involved actively in maintaining slavery. They did not, however, propose that the state be withdrawn entirely from the process of reclaiming runaways: the courts, exercising jurisdiction under the federal law, would be left open for the adjudication of claims (this was true even in Pennsylvania under the law of 1820). These were now closed to slave owners pursuing their property. The state would fulfill its constitutional obligation by not passing laws divesting claimants of their titles. It would confine itself, as Channing had hoped, to the "narrowest limits which will satisfy the Constitution."

Uneasy conservatives, understandably, were critical of the new state law. *The Boston Daily Advertiser*, spokesman for the Cotton Whigs, for example, commented that the Massachusetts legislature should have had the good sense to adopt a course similar to Virginia's on the Latimer case: the Virginia legislature had voted to lay the whole subject on the table.[39]

Garrisonians, on the other hand, were ecstatic about the act. *The Liberator* praised it as "an effectual stopper on slave-hunting in the old Bay State." It would, in fact, be "tantamount to an act of emancipation for all slaves who shall escape to us from the South."[40] Garrison believed that the whole affair would produce a "mighty sensation, not only 'from Berkshire to Cape Cod,' but from one extremity of the country to the other."[41] *The Latimer Journal, and North Star* prophesied that it would prevent the rendition of fugitives from Massachusetts altogether, and that its principles would "spread rapidly through all the free States, arousing them all to a similar course."[42]

Perhaps the most vividly expressive response was in John Greenleaf Whittier's poem "Massachusetts to Virginia:"

We wage no war, we lift no arm, we fling no torch within
The fire-damps of the quaking mine beneath your soil of sin;
We leave ye with your bondmen, to wrestle, while ye can,
With the strong upward tendencies and godlike soul of man!

But for us and for our children, the vow which we have given
For freedom and humanity is registered in heaven;
No slave-hunt in our borders,—no pirate on our strand!
No fetters in the Bay State,—no slave upon our land![43]

Despite the sanguine response of the radicals, fugitives could still be returned from Massachusetts, and free men could still be enslaved. As Charles Sumner observed, Adams' report, and the law, would "do much good in correcting & shaping public sentiment," but the federal law re-

[39] *Boston Daily Advertiser*, March 23, 1843.
[40] *The Liberator*, April 7, 1843.
[41] William L. Garrison to Henry Wright, Boston, March 1, 1843, Garrison Papers, Boston Public Library, vol. 3, no. 103.
[42] *The Latimer Journal, and North Star*, May 10, 1843.
[43] John Greenleaf Whittier, *The Poetical Works of John Greenleaf Whittier* (4 vols.; Boston and New York, 1892), 3: 86.

mained, and it could be modified only by Congress.[44] Congress, however, had shown no disposition to favor the position of Massachusetts. The resolution calling for an amendment was given very little attention. The House committee considering it reported that it should not be adopted, and the Senate refused to even have it printed.[45]

In the early fall of 1846 (a little over a month after the Wilmot Proviso was adopted by the U. S. House), another fugitive slave case momentarily rocked Boston. A runaway from Louisiana was discovered by the owners of the ship on which he had stowed away, and they determined to send him back. He escaped, but was captured in the city and hurried on board the ship and back to slavery "before the agents of the law would, or the friends of humanity could come to his rescue."[46]

In response to this rendition a protest meeting was held at Faneuil Hall chaired by the venerable John Quincy Adams. For him the issue presented by the case was "whether this commonwealth is to maintain its independence as a state or not. It is a question whether your and my native commonwealth is capable of protecting the men who are under its laws, or not."[47] At this meeting a series of resolutions were adopted, a vigilance committee was established, and an indignant address was drafted. The vigilance committee established was charged with the duty of seeing that "all needed measures to secure the protection of the laws to all persons who may hereafter be in danger of abduction from this Commonwealth" should be taken.

The only opposition to the course adopted at the meeting came from radicals like Wendell Phillips who condemned the resolutions for not going far enough since they only called for a vindication of those rights secured by law. "Sir," said Phillips, "I think this is the time for Faneuil Hall to say not that we will never permit the slave-hunter, or his myrmidons, or his agents, to take up without legal warrant his slave escaped from bondage, but to say that he shall not take him—warrant or no warrant."[48]

Most men, however, chose to work within the limitations they believed set by the Constitution (Phillips was hissed at the meeting). Those antislavery leaders like the Adamses, committed both to "our institutions" and to making them more than a mere "mockery" for blacks, carried the day. Massachusetts would disassociate itself from slavery as much as possible; and those seized could be assured that there were men who would seek to

[44]Charles Sumner to Charles Francis Adams, March 1, 1843, Adams Family Papers, Massachusetts Historical Society; see also, William H. Seward to Charles Francis Adams, April 20, 1843, Adams Family Papers, *ibid.*

[45]Duberman, *Charles Francis Adams*, 84.

[46]*Address of the Committee Appointed by a Public Meeting, Held at Faneuil Hall, September 24, 1846, for the Purpose of Considering the Recent Case of Kidnapping From Our Soil and of Taking Measures to Prevent the Recurrence of Similar Outrages* (Boston, 1846), 4.

[47]*Ibid.*, Appendix, 2.

[48]*Ibid.*, Appendix, 17.

secure them the equal protection of the laws and the fullest benefit possible from the presumption of freedom arising from the states' institutions and policy. At the same time they would strike an extraterritorial blow at slavery by a noncooperative policy.

II

Pennsylvania, on the border between slavery and freedom, and subject to a heavy influx of runaways, was deeply divided over racial questions and was slow to follow the example of Massachusetts. The decade of the 1840s was particularly grim for black people in the state. Anti-Negro riots and economic pressure in Philadelphia caused a decrease in the black population of that city during this decade.[49]

Facing intense divisions over racial questions, the legislature scarcely moved at all on the subject of fugitive slaves,[50] since a sense of urgency did not prevail. It was not until February, 1845, that the impact of Prigg's case was even considered in some depth. At that time the house judiciary committee was instructed to examine the statutory provisions on kidnapping, and to see what the impact of the U.S. Supreme Court decision was, and if any action was needed.[51] No action was taken at that time.

As the temper of the country rose over slavery in the mid-1840s the attitude in the Pennsylvania legislature changed, although during the 1846 session action was diverted by the outbreak of war with Mexico. The legislature, "friendly & favorable" toward action on a personal liberty bill, "was much excited with measures of great public interest."[52] Still, the signs for the future appeared bright. "We think," wrote the lobbyists of the Pennsylvania Abolition Society, "that the Friends of Freedom may confidently expect the legislation which they ask in this state if they will make an early & earnest effort at the next session. . . ."[53]

The success of this suggestion became apparent when more petitions were submitted to the legislature than at any time since the high point of 1837–38.[54] They came at a very propitious moment, since the national discussion of slavery, provoked by the Wilmot Proviso only a few months before, had increased the awareness and sensitivity of people to the whole problem of the relationship of the free states to the "peculiar institution."

[49]DuBois, The Philadelphia Negro, 32.
[50]Penn. House Journal, 1843, 250, 263, 268, 275, 307, 449, 567; Penn. Senate Journal, 1843, 297, 307, 337, 455–56, 501, 505, 697. During 1844 only one bill was introduced, Penn. Senate Journal, 1844, 92, 193. For some of the petitions see, Ibid., 93, 277, 506; Penn. House Journal, 1844, 107, 547.
[51]Penn. House Journal, 1845, 132, 179, 181, 242, 290.
[52]Penn. Abolition Soc. Minutes. (1825–47), 3: 520–22. Bills had been introduced in both the house and senate. Penn. House Journal, 1846, 164, 481; Penn. Senate Journal, 1846, 439.
[53]Penn. Abolition Soc. Minutes. (1825–47), 3: 520–22.
[54]Penn. House Journal, 1847, 47, 67, 68 (numerous petitions from nine different counties are reported on these last two pages); Penn. Senate Journal, 1847, 52, 63, 75, 117, 125, 138, 195, 241, 248, 261, 280, 291, 299.

At the beginning of the year, for example, resolutions were adopted against the extension of slavery into any new territory acquired from Mexico during the war.[55]

The legislature, virtually inactive on slavery issues since the Supreme Court decision five years before, suddenly became alive to the problem of protecting the personal liberty of blacks who might be claimed as fugitives. At the beginning of February the house Committee of the Whole reported, without amendment, a bill that had been introduced the year before. It was read a second time, and then, following a motion to suspend the house rules, was read a third time. It was passed immediately, and sent to the senate. All of this occurred on February 6, 1847. There had been a minimum of debate, and no division was recorded. At the end of the month this same steam-roller process was repeated in the senate, and the bill was returned to the house, without amendment. A little over a week later Governor Francis R. Shunk signed it into law.[56]

Pennsylvania's Personal Liberty Law of 1847, passed so rapidly, was based upon the lines laid out in the opinions of the justices in *Prigg* v. *Pennsylvania*. It was an experiment in the possibilities left open by the case, as well as an effort at containment.

First of all, it provided sanctions for purchasing or removing a free black with the intention of reducing him to slavery. According to Justices Wayne and McLean a state had the right to protect its free citizens from seizure and removal into slavery without the authority of law.

The law also withdrew state assistance following the Massachusetts pattern of 1843. State officials were prohibited from accepting jurisdiction of cases arising under the law of 1793, and from using any jail or prison for the detention of anyone claimed as a fugitive.

Although Justice Story had upheld the right of a claimant to seize his slave, he had added that it had to be done without "illegal violence." Pennsylvania seized on this in framing another section of its 1847 law. It provided penalties for any claimant who made a seizure in a "violent, tumultuous and unreasonable manner."

Section 5 pushed hard at the outer edges of the opinions in *Prigg* v. *Pennsylvania*. It provided that the state's judges had "the right, power and authority, at all times, on application made, to issue the writ of habeas corpus, and to inquire into the causes and legality of the arrest or imprisonment of any human being within this commonwealth."

The remaining sections of the law repealed earlier state laws. That part of the act of 1788 allowing owners of slaves to bring them into the state for six months, and the part preventing a slave from giving testimony were repealed. The act of 1826,[57] which had remained on the statute books, al-

[55] *Pennsylvania Freeman*, February 11, 1847.
[56] *Penn. House Journal, 1847*, 76, 207, 470; *Penn. Senate Journal, 1847*, 199, 217, 312.
[57] *Penn. Session Laws, 1847*, 206-8.

though unused[58] and declared unconstitutional by the U. S. Supreme Court, was also revoked.

Conservatives, moderates, and radicals, Democrats and Whigs, had all come together to support passage of this law of 1847. The *Pennsylvania Freeman* expressed surprise at this "sudden unanimity" in the legislature.[59] But the same paper also explained it as succinctly as possible: "Anti-slavery public sentiment will make anti-slavery laws."[60] But it was not necessarily abolitionist sentiment.

Generally speaking, newspapers in the state either held their peace, or lavished praise on the new law. According to the *North American* "Slavery in Pennsylvania has received its deathblow."[61] The *Pennsylvania Freeman* considered it "a much more important act" than the resolutions protesting the extension of slavery into the territories.[62] *The Friend*, a Quaker newspaper, believed it "may well be considered as matter of congratulation to every benevolent mind."[63] The conservative *Philadelphia Public Ledger*, on the other hand, merely printed the bill without comment.[64]

In Maryland, the slave state most affected by Pennsylvania's action, the reaction to the new law was understandably hostile. *Niles' Register*, for example, commented that the law "tends to destroy the force of the law of congress of 1793."[65]

"Plain Speaker" from New York probably summed up accurately the response of most people in the North who were aware of the act. He considered it "a sign of the times not to be mistaken" that a border state like Pennsylvania should enact such a law. It was his hope that the legislature of his own state would plant itself beside "the old Keystone, with a firm resolve that her territory shall no longer be a hunting-ground for the kidnapper."[66]

III

In New York, however, the political situation worked against any effective action. By 1844 the Democratic party in the state held a slight majority in the popular vote.[67] In the state house in 1843, where the battle over

---

[58] A case begun in June, 1842, by the Pennsylvania Abolition Society against a man for a misdemeanor in office under the law of 1826, for example, was "thought best to abandon." Pennsylvania Abolition Society, Acting Committee, Minutes (1822–42), Historical Society of Pennsylvania, June 28, 1842, and September 23, 1842. There is no pagination in these minutes.

[59] *Pennsylvania Freeman*, March 4, 1947.

[60] *Ibid.*, March 11, 1847.

[61] Quoted in *ibid.*, February 11, 1847.

[62] *Ibid.*

[63] *The Friend*, vol. 20, Fourth Month 3, 1847, 220.

[64] *Philadelphia Public Ledger*, February 8, 1847.

[65] *Niles' Register*, March 20, 1847.

[66] *Pennsylvania Freeman*, March 11, 1847.

[67] Lee Benson, *The Concept of Jacksonian Democracy: New York as a Test Case* (New York, 1964), 134.

the law began, the Democrats were much stronger, with almost a two-to-one majority. They also held the governorship. New York's Democratic party, during the early 1840s, was one of the mainstays of Jacksonian Democracy, and it continued to operate within the antiabolitionist-prounionist frame of reference that had been staked out earlier, until the rising territorial issue split it apart.

Governor William C. Bouck, in his first annual message to the legislature, paid considerable attention to the problems of slavery and union. "So long as we remain in, and reap the advantages of, the Union," he noted, "we are bound by every consideration of honor and good faith to yield to others what we demand for ourselves, an honest fulfillment of the compact by which for many purposes we are made one people." In Bouck's judgment the state's Personal Liberty Law was not an act of good faith, and after the U. S. Supreme Court decision it had no place on the books.[68]

Accordingly, a bill was introduced in the house to repeal the law of 1840. On February 4, 1843, the judiciary committee submitted a report favorable to repeal. In the view of this committee the law violated the fugitive slave clause and was inconsistent with the Fugitive Slave Act of 1793. A law "similar in principle" had already been declared unconstitutional by the Supreme Court of the United States.[69] Representative Enoch Strong, a Whig and on the other side, called for a bill authorizing the attorney general of the state to make arrangements to bring New York's law before the U. S. Supreme Court. The Court should have an opportunity to clarify its decision in *Prigg* v. *Pennsylvania.*[70] But, for the moment, both Strong's resolution and the committee report were ordered tabled.

A month later the judiciary committee submitted a second report. The repeal bill had not been introduced along with the first report, but it was now, with amendments. This bill went beyond the original, which provided only for the repeal of the law of 1840. As now drawn the bill revoked that part of the *Revised Statutes* extending the writ *de homine replegiando*, the law of 1834 relative to proceedings on that writ,[71] and the act of 1840. This second report argued that Congress had occupied the field, and any state legislation on the same subject was null and void.[72]

Whig representative, Willis Hall, unsuccessfully moved to recommit the bill to the committee with instructions to report a resolution declaring the inexpediency of repeal. The vote on the motion demonstrated clearly

---

[68]Lincoln, *State of New York* 4: 6–8.

[69]*New York House Document No. 49, 1843.* "Report of the Committee on the judiciary, on the matters of difference between the States of New-York and Virginia."

[70]*New York House Journal, 1843*, 234, 288, 407, 431, 462, 647, 703, 825. The remonstrance from Salina was printed as public document no. 60. "Remonstrance of Numerous Citizens of the village of Salina, in the county of Onondaga, against the repeal of 'The extension of the trial by jury law.' "

[71]The law of 1834 did not effect any important change in the law of 1828.

[72]*New York House Document No. 141, 1843*, 4.; *New York House Journal, 1843*, 586.

the partisan nature of the whole repeal effort; only one Whig voted against Hall's motion.[73]

A little over a week after the committee report was submitted and referred to the Committee of the Whole, E. F. Warren, a Whig, submitted a minority report,[74] which was a most thorough analysis of the Personal Liberty Laws of New York. He brought a great deal of learning to the task of proving that it was unnecessary to repeal the state's laws on jury trial.

Warren tried to establish three points. In the first place, he argued, the law of 1840 was passed to protect free men and not to throw obstacles in the way of a claimant. His second point was simply that if the law was null and void it was a dead letter, and a formal repeal of that law would be both "nugatory and unusual." His final point was purely political—it would be dangerous to yield to Virginia in the dispute that had been raging since the late 1830s. That state had assumed an attitude toward New York "so unfriendly and menacing" that New York could not back down "without humiliation."[75]

To establish his first point Warren relied heavily on James Alvord's 1837 report to the Massachusetts legislature. Like him Warren viewed the writ *de homine replegiando* as the "great writ of liberty." A habeas corpus was less effective because it was addressed to the claimant, whose return would be conclusive.

Jack v. *Martin*, in Warren's judgment, did not invalidate the 1828 state law. Since Jack had admitted he was a slave, any conflict between the state law and the Fugitive Slave Law was "mere matter of speculative opinion." He did admit, however, that the case had left the force of the law in some doubt. To settle the issue the act of 1840 had been passed.[76]

The law of 1840, Warren argued, was, in fact, more favorable to claimants. In place of the cumbersome proceedings on the old common-law writ the act provided for a quick trial by jury. Moreover, the law applied only to state officers. The provision in the *Revised Statutes*, on the other hand, was general in its terms.

Proponents of repeal had pointed out that *Prigg* v. *Pennsylvania* condemned state legislation on the subject of fugitive slaves. "The law of the United States, and the law of the State now under consideration," Warren countered, "are not on the *same subject*." The federal law was confined to actual runaways, and in both *Jack* v. *Martin* and *Prigg* v. *Pennsylvania*, the person seized was an admitted slave. The state law was aimed only at pro-

---

[73] *New York House Journal, 1843*, 588.

[74] *New York House Document No. 141, 1843*. "Report of the Minority of the committee on the judiciary, on the subject of repealing the law extending the right of trial by jury, passed May 6, 1840, and also on the subject of repealing all laws relating to the writ *de homine replegiando*."

[75] *Ibid.*, 5–6.

[76] *Ibid.*, 16–17.

tecting free men.[77] Although Justice Story had upheld the right of recaption, Warren noted, he had not discussed the fact that where recaption existed the "antagonist right of replevin also exists."[78]

Warren's effort to convince the legislators that repeal was both unnecessary and dangerous had no effect in the house. The Committee of the Whole, which had the bill under consideration, reported favorably on April 14, 1843, and attempts to have this modified were defeated by partisan votes. Repeal had been endorsed in the house, but before the senate could act the legislature adjourned *sine die*.[79]

Whigs, naturally enough, placed responsibility for the passage of the repeal measure in the house squarely on the "subservient" spirit of the New York Democracy, and the commands of Van Buren's lieutenant, Silas Wright. "Such is the Democracy of 1843," commented Horace Greeley's *New York Daily Tribune*, "such is its regard for Freedom and the Rights of Man!"[80] Greeley was in much lighter spirits when the legislature adjourned: "New-York can yet humbug—and Virginia will find she is yet doomed to be humbugged!!"[81]

As New Yorkers turned to the issues raised by the annexation of Texas and by the outbreak of war with Mexico, the subject of the Personal Liberty Laws receded from view. There was no action in the ensuing three legislatures. By the time the subject came up again, during 1847, the New York Democracy was badly split over the territorial question raised by the Wilmot Proviso: Van Buren's Barnburner faction was then on the verge of joining Conscience Whigs to form the Free Soil Party. The Democratic party scarcely would act as a unit, either for repeal, or for the adoption of a new Personal Liberty Law.

Early in 1847 a select committee was set up in the house to consider the subject of fugitive slaves. At the beginning of May, 1847 (two months after passage of Pennsylvania's law), the committee reported back. This report cautiously moved about within the U. S. Supreme Court's 1842 decision to find some room for state action. It was admitted that if a conflict between federal and state law existed even the "high claims of liberty and humanity" would not justify the state in acting.

Some state law, however, was clearly needed. Kidnapping had increased to an alarming extent in the wake of the Supreme Court decision because Story's judgment had invalidated the writs of habeas corpus and *de homine replegiando*, insofar as cases involved claims to service. The committee did not believe that Section 5 of the Pennsylvania act of 1847 was legitimate. States could not go that far, but they could punish "illegal violence," and they could and should withdraw all state support for claim-

[77]*Ibid.*, 34–37, 43.
[78]*Ibid.*, 11.
[79]*New York House Journal, 1843*, 736, 869, 899–901, 972–73.
[80]*New York Daily Tribune*, April 19, 1843.
[81]*Ibid.*, April 20, 1843.

ants.[82] Despite this support from the select committee for the policy of containment, no action whatever was taken on the matter during the remainder of the 1847 session.

The following year a noncooperative personal liberty bill to achieve the ends outlined in the committee report was introduced in the senate. In January, 1848, the judiciary committee reported unfavorably on the bill. States, this committee erroneously stated, had no jurisdiction over the matter of fugitive slaves before the adoption of the Constitution of 1787. And since Congress could not vest jurisdiction in state courts it was unnecessary to prohibit state officers from acting. All power to retake slaves was in the owner, assisted by United States marshals and judges; the state could have no part in the matter at all.[83] Following this report, which said nothing about the laws on the books, the bill died without further consideration.

By the end of the 1840s, then, New York's position was, at best, nebulous. The state was not placed alongside Massachusetts and Pennsylvania, as "Plain Speaker" had hoped, unless the judgment of the senate judiciary committee in 1848 could be construed as a guide to the state courts. At the same time, the existing laws were not repealed: some people in the state believed they were now little more than "blank paper," while others, such as E. F. Warren, still considered them good law.

IV

Ohio, which had gone so far as to pass legislation implementing the fugitive slave clause in a way favorable to the demands of slave owners, had to reverse the previous trend in state action before it could take steps to secure the personal freedom of blacks. Antislavery in Ohio had been a vigorous movement, but for years it had had to battle with intrenched prejudice. During the 1840s the balance was to be tipped moderately because of the rising concern over slavery in the national arena.

As elsewhere in the North in the early 1840s the Ohio legislature adopted a "wait and see" policy regarding the impact of *Prigg* v. *Pennsylvania*.[84] The whole subject was considered by a select committee of the house in March, 1842. This committee considered it the duty of the states to provide the means by which a fugitive would be delivered up (on this point the committee believed Justice Story was in error). But, if the state law of 1839 was amended at all it should be to provide a jury trial. "We . . . cannot offer any good reason why an inquiry involving such im-

[82]*New York House Document No. 168, 1847*, "Report of the select committee on the subject of fugitive slaves."

[83]*New York Senate Document No. 14, 1848*, "Report of the Judiciary Committee on the bill entitled 'An act for the protection of personal liberty.' "

[84]Antislavery activists, of course, were calling for action. Gamaliel Bailey, for example, asked the state to adopt a law "prohibiting" the state's officers from "all interference in the case" of runaways. He also wanted it made a felony for a private citizen to assist in a seizure. *Philanthropist*, March 30, 1842.

portant consequences as the personal liberty of a human being for life, next in value to life itself, should not . . . be determined by a jury."[85] The committee members were not in sympathy with the social position of blacks, however, as this might imply. Their real regret was that there was any mingling of the races at all, or, indeed, that they even occupied the same territory.[86] But as long as they did, no good reason existed why they should not have the equal protection of the laws. The present was not, in spite of this, a very propitious time to provide it since the public mind was too feverish. In the judgment of the committee no good would result from legislating when it could not be done "dispassionately."

By the beginning of 1843 abolitionists in Ohio increasingly focused their attention on the problem. The Ohio State Liberty Convention, for example, submitted a number of resolutions to the legislature including a condemnation of the Supreme Court decision and a request for legislation similar to that being pressed in Massachusetts.[87] This was ignored, but in the face of the clear conflict between the judgment in *Prigg* v. *Pennsylvania* and the Ohio law of 1839, the legislature repealed the state law on January 19, 1843, and reenacted part of the kidnapping law passed in 1831 in its place.[88]

The following year a bill was introduced in the house to prohibit any citizen, not just officials, from giving any assistance whatever to anyone attempting to reclaim a runaway, the only exception being a United States officer.[89] This effort to obtain total noncooperation went way beyond what the other states had done, and, doubtless it was because of its extreme nature that it was doomed to defeat.

Two sharply opposed reports were submitted concerning this bill, which revealed the antinomies within the legislature over runaway blacks. The majority report was decidedly prosouthern. In the judgment of the majority of the judiciary committee Ohio had no power to enact the bill in question. The slave owners right of recaption carried with it the right to the use "of the ordinary means necessary to the convenient exercise of the rights. theirs specifically granted." Included among these would be the right to buy food, lodging, and whatever else might be needed; the labor and services of individuals also were among those incidental rights.[90]

Robert F. Paine submitted a minority report for himself. He accepted fully Story's argument that the problem of fugitive slaves was solely a na-

[85] *Ohio House Journal, 1842*, "Report of the Select committee, to which was referred petitions and memorials relating to the disabilities of Persons of Color," Appendix, no. 19, 3.

[86] *Ibid.*, 6.

[87] *The Philanthropist*, January 11, 1843.

[88] William C. Cochran, "The Western Reserve and the Fugitive Slave Law: A Prelude to the Civil War," *Collections of the Western Reserve Historical Society*, Publication no. 101 (Cleveland, 1920), 77. Ohio's 1831 law, which replaced the antikidnap law of 1819, provided for a punishment of from three to seven years at hard labor in the penitentiary. *Ohio Session Laws, 1831*, 442.

[89] *Ohio House Journal, 1844*, 45, 104.

[90] *Ibid.*, 55.

tional one.[91] Ohio should have nothing to do with the whole problem: it should, in other words, adopt a policy of containment. "Color," said Paine, "gives no foundation for a new distinction between right and wrong. That word has no place in the category of human liberty."[92] He concluded by citing the laws of Massachusetts and Maine, and asking "Why not follow their examples?" Ohio, however, chose not to follow Paine in his quest of containment.

At the beginning of 1847, at the time of the growing national debate over the extension of slavery, the state legislature quietly and without fanfare made an important alteration in the state law concerning the writ of habeas corpus. The new section read:

> That upon the return of any writ of habeas corpus, issued as aforesaid, if it shall appear that the person detained or imprisoned is in custody under any warrant or commitment in pursuance of law, the return shall be considered as prima facie evidence of the cause of detention; but if the person so imprisoned or detained is restrained of liberty by any alleged private authority, the return of said writ shall be considered only as a plea of the facts therein set forth, and the party claiming the custody shall be held to make proof of such facts; and upon the final disposition of any case arising upon a writ of habeas corpus, the court or judge determining the same shall make such order as to costs as the case may require.[93]

Insofar as this applied to runaway blacks, Ohio had acted to avoid any conflict of jurisdiction between the federal and state courts by restricting the scope of the state habeas corpus. No longer could the state writ be used as a process to provide for a full evidentiary hearing if a person was claimed under federal law. Ohio thus reversed the trend in the growth of habeas corpus practice that was noted in this same year, 1847, by the American editors of Hale's *Historia Placitorum Coronae*. Ohio's development then, for the moment at least, was in an opposite direction from Pennsylvania's, the other state bordering upon a slave-owning community. At the same time, of course, Ohio had set down a stricter standard in the case of a person exercising a right of recaption without recourse to the law. This merely followed an established tradition in the state's legal history, but it remained, nevertheless, a significant exception to the restrictions imposed upon habeas corpus usage because it was not in accord with the reasoning of Justice Story in the Prigg decision.[94]

Within two years, after years of antislavery agitation and under the stress of the growing sectional crisis, Ohio finally began to move in another direction. In 1849 Ohio's legislature repealed the Black Code, which had regulated the conduct of free blacks in the state during most of the cen-

[91]*Ibid.*, 61.
[92]*Ibid.*, 63.
[93]Joseph R. Swan, *Statutes of the State of Ohio, 1854*, 454.
[94]It was Ohio's Justice McLean, among others, who frequently used a habeas corpus to inquire into seizures during the 1840s, Schnell, "Court Cases Involving Slavery," 204.

tury.[95] Ohio, like the other free states, was beginning to reevaluate some of the legal problems involving black people that it had grappled with for many years; but, of course, with mixed results as far as antislavery reformers were concerned. Unlike Massachusetts and Pennsylvania, Ohio did not follow the course of containment.

V

Wisconsin, generally far removed from the problem of fugitive slaves, did not become a state until May, 1848. A general kidnapping law had been passed in 1839, but the territory had no legislation specifically designed to protect free blacks or to aid in the recovery of fugitives. *Prigg* v. *Pennsylvania* consequently produced no stir there. When the territory became a state the laws were collated and revised; the act of 1839 was adopted, but no other legislation was even proposed.[96]

Antislavery sentiment in Wisconsin, however, was in evidence during the 1840s. One case involving a fugitive slave gave a taste of things to come in the next decade. A girl named Caroline had been under the protection of some antislavery radicals when it was pointed out to them that they were in violation of the federal law. The answer was that "a bad law is better broken than obeyed." Their intention was to obey the higher law, "to let the oppressed go free." Caroline was transported successfully to Canada.[97]

The antislavery effort in Wisconsin, for the most part, was focused on other issues during the 1840s. During the struggle for statehood, one of the focal points was the question of Negro suffrage. The constitution of the new state provided for white-manhood suffrage. This was denounced by the *American Freeman*, the antislavery paper published at Waukesha, as containing the "principle of contempt for the rights of man."[98]

By 1848 Free-Soilers held the balance of power in the state, and both Whigs and Democrats had come around to that position. Wisconsin's legislature of 1849, for example, in which the Democrats had a majority, passed a series of instructions for the state's congressmen in Washington to op-

---

[95]Still, the legal situation was murky. Joseph R. Swan, the collector of the laws in 1854, was uncertain about the validity of the state laws; at the bottom of the kidnapping statute he noted: "It seems to contravene the fugitive slave law; but if it does not, it is in force." *Statutes of the State of Ohio*, 276.

[96]*The Revised Statutes of the State of Wisconsin, Passed at the Second Session of the Legislature, Commencing January 10, 1849* (Southport, 1849), 687.

[97]Chauncey C. Olin, "A History of the early Anti-Slavery excitement in the state of Wisconsin from 1842 to 1860" (MS on microfilm at the State Historical Society of Wisconsin), 12–28. The pagination in this manuscript is odd. The material up to the Glover rescue case in the 1850s is numbered separately from the remainder.

[98]Milo M. Quaife, ed., *The Attainment of Statehood. Collections of the Wisconsin State Historical Society*, Constitutional Series, vol. 4, 91.

pose the admission of more slave states into the Union.[99] Although the state had not yet begun to experiment with Personal Liberty Laws, it was generally committed to an antislavery posture in the sectional struggle. By the middle of the next decade this would burgeon.

VI

The Constitution, as construed by the Court in *Prigg* v. *Pennsylvania*, had placed serious obstacles in the way of those seeking to use state power to protect the personal liberty of free men. Undoubtedly a satisfactory resolution required political control of the national government. During the 1840s the policy of containing slavery in the states where it already existed, while at the same time carving free states out of the territories, held out the promise of such control, but it was a distant prospect at best. As the national discussion of this policy raised the tempo of the slavery controversy, some free states began to experiment with the possibilities left in the wake of the Supreme Court decision. But, of course, this required political control in the state by those favorable to such action, and it was not always obtained.

In Massachusetts and Pennsylvania all state assistance for slave claimants was withdrawn. New York's senate judiciary committee took the view in 1848 that the states, even without legislation, could not aid those seeking to recover their property. New York failed to act, but its existing laws (including those securing a jury trial) remained on the books despite the Prigg decision, as did the Massachusetts law of 1837 restoring the writ *de homine replegiando*. Ohio repealed its law of 1839 in aid of alleged owners, but it did not follow these other states and prohibit its officials from accepting jurisdiction under the federal law. Moreover, Ohio severely restricted the scope of state habeas-corpus practice in the same year that Pennsylvania explicitly guaranteed the writ to everyone without limitation.

After the Prigg decision the states could no longer establish the procedures for adjudicating claims, but they could act to disassociate themselves from slavery and thereby confine all action to the narrowest limits that would satisfy the Constitution. With greater or lesser force this option was pursued in all of the states examined here, except of course in Wisconsin, which did not become a state until the end of the decade.

The failure to obtain a forceful repudiation of the Prigg decision together with the many disappointments in the quest for a containment policy, both with respect to the territories and the matter of fugitive slaves, left many abolitionists deeply frustrated by the developments of the 1840s. By the end of the decade they became involved in a heated debate

[99]Vroman Mason, "The Fugitive Slave Law in Wisconsin, With Reference to Nullification Sentiment," *Proceedings of the Wisconsin State Historical Society* (1895), 117–18. See also Theodore Clarke Smith, "The Free Soil Party in Wisconsin," *ibid.*, (1894).

among themselves over some basic questions raised by the encounters of those years. "The Constitution of the United States.—What is it? Who made it? For whom and what was it made?"[100] Thus did Frederick Douglass pose the problems.

Despite the failures suffered by the antislavery movement during the 1840s several abolitionists, such as Alvan Stewart, G. W. F. Mellen, and William Goodell,[101] continued to view the Constitution as an antislavery document. Perhaps the fullest exposition of this viewpoint was presented by Lysander Spooner in a work entitled *The Unconstitutionality of Slavery*. To show how the Constitution could be understood as an antislavery document, Spooner adopted two basic rules of interpretation: "1st, that no intention, in violation of natural justice and natural right, (like that to sanction slavery,) can be ascribed to the constitution, unless that intention be expressed in terms that are *legally competent* to express such an intention; and, 2nd, that no terms, except those that are plenary, express, explicit, distinct, unequivocal, *and to which no other meaning can be given, are legally competent* to authorize or sanction anything contrary to natural right."[102] It need hardly be said that he found no such terms or intentions in the Constitution.[103] Other immediate emancipationists, however, were thoroughly disillusioned. "Such an ugly matter-of-fact looking thing as the United States Constitution," could not be salvaged, according to Douglass. It was a mistake to think of it as an abstraction. It was rather, he wrote, a "living, breathing fact, exerting a mighty power over the nation of which it is the bond of Union." And this document was committed to the preservation of the institution of slavery. There could be but one solution, and that was not "containment"; it was the "complete overthrow" of the existing Constitution. Only in this way could major social change be effected in this country.[104] Wendell Phillips, moreover, challenged Spooner's conception of law. Law, said Phillips, was a "practical science" which did not reflect "absolute justice." Although legislators should attempt to make the laws "carry out the highest present idea of justice," their acts would still be law even if they fell far short of the objective. Law, in other words, provided little hope for those who sought major social alterations in the United States. Phillips had inferred in 1842 that state judges might act inde-

---

[100]"The Constitution and Slavery," *The North Star*, March 16, 1849 in Philip Foner, ed., *The Life and Writings of Frederick Douglass* (New York, 1955), 1: 362.

[101]G. W. F. Mellen, *Argument on the Unconstitutionality of Slavery* (Boston, 1841); William Goodell, *View of American Constitutional Law, in its Bearing upon American Slavery* (Utica, 1844). See also James G. Birney, "Can Congress, under the Constitution, Abolish Slavery in the States?" in Ten Broeck, *Equal under Law*, Appendix C.

[102]Lysander Spooner, *The Unconstitutionality of Slavery* (Boston, 1860), 58–59.

[103]He adopted, for example, the view that the fugitive slave clause referred to indentured servants and not to slaves. *Ibid.*, 67–72.

[104]Douglass, *Life and Writings*, 1: 363. See also Wendell Phillips, ed., *The Constitution a Pro-Slavery Compact: or Selections from the Madison Papers, & c.* (New York, 1844), 104, 106.

pendently of the "illogical and presumptuous dicta" of the Prigg case, but by the time he wrote his review of Spooner's work in 1848 he conceded that neither habeas corpus nor jury trial necessarily were destructive of slavery. In fact, habeas corpus only provided a test of unlawful restraints, regardless of the justice of the law.[105]

Few people, however, seriously considered the somewhat quixotic arguments of men like Spooner, or experienced the severe despair of Douglass which led him, along with the Garrisonians, to call for a dissolution of the Union. Nor did they minimize the importance of the time-tested guarantees of personal liberty, the writ of habeas corpus and jury trial. Most people recognized that the Constitution did in fact protect slavery, even extraterritorially. But that did not mean that all antislavery action was futile. As Charles Sumner noted in a speech before a crowd of Massachusetts Whigs in 1846, it provided an instrument of government with "a *progressive* character." The so-called compromises of the Constitution were not binding forever on the people. The Founding Fathers, in his view, "did not treat the country as a Chinese foot,—never to grow after its infancy,— but anticipated the changes incident to its advance." Whigs, he concluded, had the responsibility to elect men to office who were "thorough, uncompromising advocates of the repeal of slavery,—of its abolition under the laws and Constitution of the United States."[106] As a step in the direction of repeal many antislavery people had come to the conclusion that slavery could be attacked extraterritorially and forced to "retire within its own bounds." Noncooperation in the rendition process was part of this strategy, but in several cases it had misfired and was, at best, an incomplete solution because of the hindrances remaining: the federal law of 1793 and the guarantee that slave owners could recover their property on free soil.

[105]Wendell Phillips, "Constitutionality of Slavery" *The Massachusetts Quarterly Review* 2 (Sept., 1848): 463–509.

[106]Charles Sumner, *The Works of Charles Sumner* (15 vols.; Boston, 1870–83), 1: 310–11, 313–14.

The Fugitive Slave Law of 1850 8

Just as some abolitionists were talking of a dissolution of the Union by the close of the 1840s, so proslavery hotspurs were committed to the same end because of what they called the "repeated unconstitutional aggressions" by the North on the rights of slave owners. By 1848–49 these people particularly had in mind the "aggression" contained in the Wilmot Proviso. The crisis of the later 1840s was precipitated by the struggle to define the status of slavery in the territories, which had grown acute because of the pressing demand for some form of government for California. The crisis, of course, went much deeper, as was noted early in 1849 in the "Address of the Southern Delegates in Congress to their Constituents." The central problem facing the South, in the view of these congressmen, was to obtain a unity of purpose and action, and the one facing the Union was to secure the cornerstone of the whole structure of our government, the right of property in slaves.[1] Containment of slavery in the existing states would endanger that cornerstone. By the late 1840s it was also challenged by other efforts, such as the prohibition of slavery in the District of Columbia and the constriction of the boundaries of the slave state of Texas. But the one challenge that loomed largest, next to the effort to keep slavery out of the territories, was found in the Personal Liberty Laws, part of the general policy of containing slavery. Calhoun considered these laws "one of the most fatal blows ever received by the South and the Union." They had rendered the constitutional obligation to return runaways "of non-effect, and with so much success that it may be regarded now as practically expunged from the Constitution."[2]

By the fall of 1849 proslavery militants were ready to discard rhetoric for action. A Mississippi state convention issued a call for a southern convention to meet in Nashville, Tennessee, the following June "to devise and adopt some mode of resistance to [northern] . . . aggressions."[3] The shadow of Nashville and the fear of an impending disruption of the Union by the secession of the slave states was to hang very heavily over the early deliberations of the Thirty-first Congress, which had to deal with the sectional crisis.

[1] Richard K. Cralle, ed., *The Works of John C. Calhoun* (6 vols.; New York, 1870), 6: 295.
[2] *Ibid.*, 292.
[3] Avery Craven. *The Coming of the Civil War* (Chicago, 1966), 245; *idem, The Growth of Southern Nationalism, 1848–1861* (New Orleans, 1953), 63.

On the most pressing issue, the question of slavery in the territories, two irreconcilable positions had been taken by the end of the 1840s. At one extreme stood the proponents of containment and, at the other, the exponents of the proslavery interpretation of the doctrine of state sovereignty. Between these two poles Lewis Cass of Michigan and Stephen A. Douglas of Illinois erected the standard of popular sovereignty. The people in the territories should decide for themselves whether or not slavery would be allowed. This policy of local self-determination was to be the basis of the temporary settlement of 1850.

Much thoughtful work has been done on the crisis of the late 1840s and on the Compromise of 1850, by which it was temporarily resolved.[4] Less focus has been directed on the congressional debates over the specific parts of that compromise package, including the Fugitive Slave Law.[5] This chapter will be concerned exclusively with the latter. Even though the issue of fugitive slaves was only a part of a much larger whole, and was not at center stage, the debates over that issue laid bare the fundamental conflict between divergent legal systems within a federal union that had helped bring on this major sectional confrontation.

As early as the spring of 1848, just after some of the free states had passed or discussed new Personal Liberty Laws, Senator Arthur P. Butler of South Carolina introduced a bill in Congress to modify the Fugitive Slave Law of 1793. In a report he submitted with the bill Butler examined the existing situation, which he found perilous. It was a "fearful truth," he contended, that the nonslaveholding states would not enforce the law, or accept their obligation under the federal compact.[6] The jaundiced view southerners held of the free-state laws by the late 1840s was evident when Butler charged that from the time of the crisis over Missouri there had been "a systematic aim" in all such laws "to make war" on slavery.[7] Instead of living up to their obligations northerners had stripped slave claimants of almost all rights guaranteed by the Constitution, leaving only the right of recaption. "But how to be executed? Why, at the risk of the owner's life."[8]

Until the territorial crisis of the following two years brought the country to a dangerous impasse, however, Congress was not ready to respond to

---

[4]See, for example, Holman Hamilton, *Prologue to Conflict: The Crisis and Compromise of 1850* (Lexington, 1964); Allan Nevins, *Ordeal of the Union* (2 vols.; New York, 1947), 1: 219–45; Hermann von Holst, *The Constitutional and Political History of the United States* (8 vols.; Chicago, 1881), 3: 456–563; Bestor, "State Sovereignty and Slavery," and "The Civil War as a Constitutional Crisis." Harry Jaffa, *Crisis of the House Divided: An Interpretation of the Issues in the Lincoln-Douglas Debates* (New York, 1959), is a thoughtful study of the territorial question in its later phase.

[5]The most recent is Stanley W. Campbell, *The Slave Catchers: Enforcement of the Fugitive Slave Law, 1850–1860* (Chapel Hill, N.C., 1970), chap. 1. Among the examinations of the law that was finally passed are Allen Johnson, "The Constitutionality of the Fugitive Slave Law," *Yale Law Journal* (1921), 31: 161, and Yanuck, "The Fugitive Slave Law."

[6]*Senate Reports*, 30th Cong., 1st sess., 1847–48, report no. 143, 5.

[7]*Ibid.*, 10.

[8]*Ibid.*, 15.

Butler's plea. At the beginning of the Thirty-first Congress the time had arrived. In the event, enough northerners cared more for the Union than for making "our institutions" something other than a "mockery" for blacks. Security for the rights of claimants at the expense of the personal liberty of Negroes, even though they might be free, and the subordination of the laws of the free states to the needs of slave owners were to be among the costs of union worked into the Compromise of 1850.

On January 3, 1850, Senator James M. Mason of Virginia, the most important proslavery spokesman in the fight for a stronger fugitive slave law, announced his intention to introduce Senator Butler's bill once more.[9] The following day the measure went to the Senate judiciary committee. A little over a week later it was reported out.[10]

The first fugitive slave bill introduced since 1822 bore only slight resemblance to the complicated measure finally passed in the fall of 1850. The primary purpose of the bill was to increase the number of officials involved in adjudicating claims under the federal law by spreading the responsibility to nonjudicial officers, such as postmasters and collectors of customs. Despite the dubious extension of judicial functions to such officers, which was challenged by northerners, the bill was as important for what it left unresolved: it did not strike directly at the presumption of freedom arising from the laws of the free states.

A week after the bill was reported out of committee, Senator Mason moved two amendments. The first increased the penalties, while the second provided that "in no trial or hearing under this act shall the testimony of such fugitive be admitted in evidence."[11]

Senator Mason took the leading part for the South in the debate that began on January 28, 1850, and in an aggressive mood he set forth one of the most explicit proslavery statements of the right of recaption ever given. This extraterritorial right, secured by the Constitution, he said, meant that no one had "a right to interpose between the claimant and the fugitive, or to inquire whether the slave be his, or whether he is a slave at all, far less to molest or hinder him in the capture."

Recaption, however, was not enough. Passage of an effective fugitive slave law was, for the people of the South, "indispensable to the security of their property and the integrity of their institutions." Anticipating the famous Georgia Platform of December, 1850, Mason concluded that this was a test question to determine whether or not slave owners could rely on the Constitution for the protection they believed was due, or whether "we are to rely upon our own counsels and our own strength."[12] As Larry Gara has observed, this position involved a "paradox": here were the leading

[9]*Cong. Globe*, 31st Cong., 1st sess., Jan. 3, 1850, 99.
[10]*Ibid.*, Jan. 4, 1850, 103; *ibid.*, Jan. 16, 1850, 171; *ibid.*, Jan. 24, 1850, Appendix, 79.
[11]*Ibid.*, Jan. 22, 1850, 210.
[12]*Ibid.*, Jan. 23, 1850, 233–35.

proponents of state sovereignty arguing for an increase in federal power, and making a "dangerous admission of national supremacy."[13]

Southerners were demanding, of course, what antislavery people could never accept under any circumstance. Senator William H. Seward of New York responded to Mason's arguments with an antislavery amendment by way of a substitute. His proposal was a complicated measure designed to secure anyone seized the rights to jury trial and habeas corpus. He argued in support of his bill that it merely brought the federal law into conformity with other constitutional provisions. The measure, however, had no chance of adoption in a Senate in which southerners held half the seats. Senator Foote of Mississippi, in particular, was enraged by the bill: he charged that it showed "pettifogging *craft*" designed to "propitiate the lowest, and basest, and most malevolent fanaticism." Even the printing of the bill was opposed. It was never again taken up, and it was never seriously discussed.[14]

At this juncture in the Senate debates, Senator Henry Clay, as he had in the past, came forward as the champion of compromise. The day after Seward introduced his bill, Clay submitted his famous compromise resolutions to deal with the whole sectional crisis. On the question of fugitive slaves, however, there was to be no compromise. Clay's seventh resolution fully endorsed the demand for a "more effectual provision" for returning runaways.[15] A week later he clarified what he meant by an "effectual provision." He would, he said, "go with the furthest Senator from the South in this body to make penal laws, to impose the heaviest sanctions upon the recovery of fugitive slaves, and the restoration of them to their owners." He would vote for the "most stringent measures" that could be devised to secure the rights of slaveholders on this matter.[16] Like other southern senators, Clay considered the failure of the free states to live up to their clear obligation on the subject—the "most irritating and inflammatory to those who live in slave States"—one of the major sources of the crisis facing the Union.

Two days after Clay submitted his "compromise resolutions" Senator Mason introduced a proslavery measure that he claimed later in the year had been drafted by a northerner and given to him by Senator Lewis Cass of Michigan.[17] This bill was offered as an amendment by way of a substitute for the bill from the judiciary committee.

There was a token compromise in Mason's new bill. Instead of a direct extension of judicial power to lower-grade federal officers, the bill gave district court judges some control over the delegation of power. They

[13]Larry Gara, "The Fugitive Slave Law: A Double Paradox," *Civil War History*, 10: no. 3 (Sept. 1964), 229–40.
[14]*Cong. Globe*, 31st Cong., 1st sess., Jan. 23, 1850, 236.
[15]*Ibid.*, Jan. 29, 1850, 246.
[16]*Ibid.*, Feb. 6, 1850, Appendix, 122–24.
[17]*Ibid.*, Aug. 22, 1850, Appendix, 1612 ff.

would be required to appoint no more than three commissioners for each county from among those persons already holding a federal office, which could include postmasters and collectors of customs; but it was still a concession of sorts.

The substitute also authorized the commissioners to appoint persons from time to time to execute any warrant granted. Either the commissioner himself, or those appointed by him, moreover, were granted the power to call bystanders to their aid, i.e., the *posse comitatus*. People in the North now were to be involved actively in maintaining the institution of slavery, the one thing they had striven to avoid from the start, and no more notably than in the Personal Liberty Laws of the 1840s.

The bill further authorized the claimant to obtain an arrest warrant, or seize a runaway himself and take him before a federal officer. On the presentation of satisfactory proof the claimant would be given his certificate of removal. Satisfactory proof would be in the form of a deposition or affidavit, in writing, taken by the court or commissioner, or "other satisfactory testimony" taken before someone authorized to administer oaths in the state from which the escape occurred. Testimony of the black would not be admitted in evidence. Furthermore, the certificate would be "conclusive of the right of the person or persons in whose favor granted to remove such fugitive to the State or Territory from which he escaped." This meant that the certificate would operate to prevent "all molestation" by any court, judge, or magistrate. The certificate could not be challenged by any court in the United States by means of a habeas corpus, or any other process. The writ could issue, but the certificate would be a conclusive answer.

The remainder of the Mason substitute dealt with penalties[18] and fees. A claimant would pay all the fees involved in a case. If a commissioner found for a slave claimant he would receive ten dollars, and five dollars if he did not.[19]

Mason's bill, much more than the Butler bill from the judiciary committee, represented the radical proslavery position. People in the northern states should be charged with the positive duty of assisting in upholding slavery whenever called upon. Free-state judiciaries should have no power to inquire into the validity of the seizure of any black: procedures like habeas corpus that had been developed over the course of centuries to secure personal liberty would have no meaningful place in the seizure of an alleged fugitive. The presumption of freedom arising from the institutions and policies of the free states would not be applicable. Since the free states, moreover, had refused to live up to their clear constitutional respon-

---

[18]There would be a $500 fine, and a 6-month jail sentence for "obstruction." There could also be up to $1,000 in civil damages. The criminal sanctions imposed were less than in Mason's original amendment to the Butler bill.

[19]*Cong. Globe*, 31st Cong., 1st sess., Jan. 31, 1850, 270–71.

sibilities the federal government would have to supply the instrumentalities for securing slave property.

By the end of January, 1850, then, antislavery and proslavery senators had placed before the Senate irreconcilable positions on how to resolve the conflict of legal systems within the federal union and to fulfill the constitutional obligation. The resolutions of these problems in 1850 depended to some extent, it appeared, upon the "moderates." Southern compromisers, such as Clay, had already shown that on this subject there could be little or no compromise. A leading spokesman for northern moderates tried to break the impasse in a major speech on March 7, 1850.

The "God-like Daniel" of Marshfield, Daniel Webster, declared that the South had a just grievance. On the subject of fugitive slaves "the South is right, and the North is wrong." In Webster's judgment the bill before the Senate would resolve the problem. "My friend at the head of the Judiciary Committee has a bill on the subject," he said, "now before the Senate, with some amendments to it, which I propose to support, with all its provisions, to the fullest extent."[20] Webster then was supporting Butler's bill with Mason's amendments. His own amendments (which will be discussed later) were merely afterthoughts that followed the reaction in the free states to his speech.[21]

Webster spoke for the conservative merchants and businessmen of the North who had a considerable stake in union with the planting class.[22] For them union was far more important than securing the personal liberty of the few free blacks who might become the victims of slave catchers. For Webster, moreover, union had more than a pecuniary value. It was worshiped for itself. His primary motive on March 7, as Allan Nevins wrote, was "love of Union, fear for the Union, ambition to save the Union."[23] For that he would make almost any concession on fugitive slaves demanded by the South.

The reaction of free-state senators, however, was not as favorable as he could have wished. Antislavery senators were predictably infuriated. Four days after Webster's speech, Seward delivered his famous "Higher Law" speech in which he declared that there was a law higher than the Constitu-

[20]*Ibid.*, March 7, 1850, 481.

[21]Another view of this portion of Webster's speech may be found in Claude M. Fuess, *Daniel Webster* (2 vols.; Hamden, Conn., 1963), 2: 231; Nevins, *Ordeal of the Union*, 1: 289; and Hamilton, *Prologue to Conflict*, 77–78. When Webster, on March 7, said "with some amendments to it," he had reference to amendments he proposed to introduce at a later date. Webster's close friend George Ticknor Curtis, *Life of Daniel Webster* (2 vols.; New York, 1870), 2: 422, also said that Webster supported Mason's bill with the understanding that he would move to amend it later.

[22]Richard N. Current, *Daniel Webster and the Rise of National Conservatism* (Boston, 1955), 159.

[23]Nevins, *Ordeal of the Union*, 1: 291. Some have seen a great political ambition at work in the speech. Von Holst, *Constitutional History*, 3: 504, for example, said that it was "a candidate speech and . . . its chief object was to win the favor of the South."

tion. Of somewhat more importance was the fact that moderates like Roger S. Baldwin of Connecticut tended to agree[24] with the Free-Soiler from New Hampshire, John P. Hale, who noted, on March 20, that the bill before the Senate "proceeds on the assumption that the man who is seized in a free State is of course a slave . . . Where is the trial by jury? Where is the habeas corpus? Where is the protection which the Constitution guarantees to the meanest citizen living under the law?"[25]

Outside the Senate the reactions ranged from adulation to bitter denunciation.[26] There can be little doubt, of course, that Webster's speech was pleasing to the South, or that it encouraged southerners to press forward their demands, or, indeed, that it marked a significant turning point in the debates in Congress.

One of Webster's concerns on March 7 was to solidify the "planter-capitalist axis," which was, according to Richard Current, "a mainstay of the conservative cause."[27] Whigs throughout the North, and particularly in his home state of Massachusetts, however, did not all rally publicly to Webster's lead. The *Boston Atlas* conceded that only about six Whig papers outside of Boston supported Webster's views, whereas about seventy opposed them.[28] Conscience Whigs like Charles Francis Adams were roused to opposition at Webster's apostasy. Adams noted a "transition from quietude to passion" in the state as a result of the speech.[29] At an anti-Webster meeting at Faneuil Hall on March 22, a letter was read from Adams saying he could read the Constitution only with the idea that under it "slavery would gradually wear out and expire." To read it as Webster did was to justify tyranny and undermine the confidence of the people.[30]

Antislavery radicals in Massachusetts were outraged. Wendell Phillips, for example, sarcastically thanked Webster for his "plain, unvarnished villany." And the Garrisonians, as had become almost habit with them, called for revolutionary action if Webster's view prevailed. At a meeting at Upton on March 18, it was resolved that if this occurred "PERISH THE UNION, and let the rights of Humanity be respected, and the integrity of Christianity preserved!"[31]

[24]*Cong. Globe*, 31st Cong., 1st sess., March 14, 1850, 526.
[25]*Ibid.*, March 20, 1850, Appendix, 1063.
[26]Hamilton, *Prologue to Conflict*, 79. Senator Daniel S. Dickinson, a New York Democrat, also received a good deal of praise from the South for his speeches in behalf of the Constitution. Northern conservatives were pleased with Dickinson. In view of his opinion in *Jack* v. *Martin* the praise extended by Reuben H. Walworth is of some interest, John R. Dickinson, *Speeches, Correspondence, Etc., of the late Daniel S. Dickinson, of New York* (2 vols.; New York, 1867), 1: 440–41.
[27]Current, *Daniel Webster*, 161.
[28]*Boston Atlas*, quoted in the *Boston Advertiser*, March 12, 1850.
[29]Charles Francis Adams, Diary, April 8, 1850, Adams Family Papers, Reel 71, Massachusetts Historical Society.
[30]*The Liberator*, March 29, 1850.
[31]*Ibid.*

At the end of April Horace Mann, then a representative in Congress from Massachusetts, came home "very fully charged with a speech against Mr. Webster."[32] The cold blasts from Mann were to sting Webster into a reply. At the conclusion of his first assault Mann asserted "that the man who can read this bill without having his blood boil in his veins, has a power of refrigeration that would cool the tropics."[33] Webster, who had a warm emotional attachment to the Union, was goaded into a reply, which he delivered in his "Newburyport Letter."

He tried to soothe northern sensibilities by showing that the absence of a jury-trial provision was in keeping with the object of the fugitive slave clause. The cases of fugitives from justice and fugitives from labor were identical, or nearly so. In the first, the person was only to be remitted, after a preliminary and summary examination, to the state from which he fled for the purpose of trial. In the second, the person "is only to be remitted, for an inquiry into his rights and the proper adjudication of them."[34]

A jury trial for fugitive slaves was not imperiously demanded by the Constitution, "either in its letter or in its spirit." Webster had, he claimed, "considered the subject with a conscientious desire to provide for such jury trial," but he found an almost insurmountable obstacle in the way: it was not southern intransigence; it was the Personal Liberty Laws. "It is not too much to say," he argued, "that to these State laws is to be attributed the actual and practical denial of trial by jury in these cases."[35] These laws prohibited the use of "those aids and facilities without which a jury trial is impossible." After reading the "Newburyport Letter" Charles Francis Adams wrote that his opinion of Webster "does not admit of reduction or it would experience it."[36]

A full-scale refutation of Webster's views was undertaken by Mann in a letter to the editors of the *Boston Atlas*. His letter was one extended paean for jury trial, and an effort to prove that the Constitution did require it in the case of runaway blacks. A claim for a fugitive, according to Mann, came within the judicial power of the United States and was subject to the requirement in the Seventh Amendment for a jury trial. One of the original writs at common law was *homine replegiando*, which was used to inquire into the question of slavery or freedom raised in a "suit." The matter then did come under the rubric, a "suit at common law," and was subject to the jury-trial provision of the Seventh Amendment.[37] Mann also cited the

[32]Charles Francis Adams, Diary, April 22, 1850, Adams Family Papers, Reel 71, Massachusetts Historical Society.

[33]Horace Mann, *Slavery: Letters and Speeches* (Boston, 1851), 274.

[34]Daniel Webster, *The Writings and Speeches of Daniel Webster* (18 vols.; Boston, 1903), 12: 229.

[35]*Ibid.*, 231.

[36]Charles Francis Adams, Diary, May 30, 1850, Adams Family Papers, Reel 71, Massachusetts Historical Society.

[37]Mann, *Slavery*, 299–304.

guarantee of the Fifth Amendment that no man could be deprived of his liberty without "due process of law." This phrase meant a trial by jury.[38] He would also test the proposed bill by the Fourth Amendment: "What 'seizure' can be more 'unreasonable,' than one whose object is, not an ultimate trial, but bondage forever, without trial?"[39]

Mann quickly disposed of Webster's argument that the provisions for the rendition of fugitives from justice and those from labor were nearly identical. The word used with regard to the first was "charged," and for the second it was "held." It was not enough, as for fugitives from justice, that a man be merely "charged" with being "held" to service. He actually must be "held." For fugitive slaves there was to be a transfer of venue not for the purpose of trial, as Webster said, but for evading a trial.[40]

Conscience Whigs and antislavery radicals then denounced Webster's policy of appeasement and condemned his reading of the Constitution. Publicly many of the Cotton Whigs warmly endorsed Webster's course. Over 700 of the most prominent citizens of Massachusetts signed a letter expressing an "entire concurrence in the sentiments of your speech, and our heartfelt thanks for the inestimable aid it has afforded towards the preservation and perpetuation of this Union."[41]

Despite the public endorsement Webster was informed at a dinner on May 2, at which he admitted he had not even read Mason's proposals, that it would be "madness" for him to support the bill. Among those dining with him that evening were Rufus Choate, Benjamin R. Curtis, and George Ticknor Curtis.[42] Earlier Edward Everett wrote him that some of the provisions of the bill were "unnecessarily stringent and otherwise ill-advised."[43] When the conservatives of his own state began to abandon him on this issue Webster acted.

On June 3 he introduced a bill to amend the act of 1793. This measure was to be entirely separate from the bill before the Senate, with its amendments. His bill further clarifies Webster's position in his March 7 speech. If he was holding out for amendments to the Mason bill, as some have believed, his amendments presumably would be made to that bill. They were not. In a letter the day after he introduced his bill he claimed that it had been drawn up at the beginning of the year, and was in his desk the day he delivered his speech. It is hard to escape the conclusion, however, that the measure was drawn up in response to the furor generated in Massachusetts by his capitulation of March 7.[44]

[38] *Ibid.*, 307.
[39] *Ibid.*, 309.
[40] *Ibid.*, 310.
[41] *The Liberator*, April 12, 1850.
[42] P. R. Frothingham, *Edward Everett, Orator and Statesman* (Boston, 1925), 320.
[43] *Ibid.*, 319.
[44] Daniel Webster to Peter Harvey, June 4, 1850, *Writings and Speeches of Webster*, 4: 547.

Webster's bill consisted of two sections. The first would extend the force of the act of 1793 to the territories, thus cutting the ground from beneath Chase. It also authorized the appointment of one or more commissioners per county who would be charged with hearing proofs and adjudicating claims. If the decision was for the claimant a certificate, "conclusive" of the right of removal, would be granted. Then came the all-important proviso. If an alleged fugitive denied that he was held to service or labor, and would swear an oath to that effect, the judge or commissioner who was hearing the case would immediately call for a jury to decide the matter. The second section of Webster's bill dealt with fees, all of which would be paid by the claimant.[45] The congressional response to Webster's bill was a resounding silence. It was not debated at that time, or even commented on outside Congress.[46]

In any event, by that time the main hope for compromise of all the disturbing questions in the crisis facing the Union already had come to center on the Clay resolutions. A special Committee of Thirteen was set up to consider them, including the seventh dealing with fugitive slaves. This committee was stacked against the antislavery element in the Senate. Clay himself was chairman. The other members were Lewis Cass of Michigan, the man who allegedly handed Mason the bill introduced at the end of January; Daniel S. Dickinson, the conservative New York Democrat; Jesse E. Bright of Indiana, the intimate of James Buchanan; Daniel Webster, who had not at this point come out for jury trial; Samuel S. Phelps of Vermont; James Cooper of Pennsylvania; William R. King of Alabama; James M. Mason of Virginia; Solomon W. Downs of Louisiana; Willie P. Mangum of North Carolina; John Bell of Tennessee; and J. Macpherson Berrien of Georgia. The report of this special committee was submitted to the Senate on May 8, 1850.

It provided for California statehood, set up two territorial governments, and resolved the Texas boundary and debt questions. Together these measures made up what is called the Omnibus Bill. The issue of fugitive slaves, although discussed in the same report, was not directly linked with these other matters.

On the matter of runaways Clay had moderated his unqualified endorsement of the extreme southern position. For the most part, the bill pending before the Senate was satisfactory, but Clay said he did have some compromise amendments to suggest. One provision he reported was that a claimant, "when practicable," should carry with him a record, from

[45]*Cong. Globe*, 31st Cong., 1st sess., June 3, 1850, 1111. In introducing the measure Webster claimed it was drawn up in consultation with some of the finest legal minds available, and particularly with "a high judicial authority," generally thought to be Benjamin R. Curtis.

[46]The first mention of the bill in Congress came on June 12 when Senator William L. Dayton, a New Jersey Whig, endorsed it. *Cong. Globe*, 31st Cong., 1st sess., June 12, 1850, Appendix, 816–17.

a competent tribunal, "adjudicating the facts of elopement and slavery, with a general description of the fugitive." This record would be held "competent and sufficient evidence" of the facts, and there would be nothing to do but identify the fugitive in the northern state.

The most troubling question, in his view, was the demand for a jury trial. Northern Whigs had shown considerable concern over this issue (northern Democrats had not taken a prominent part in the debate), and he now believed it wise to make some concession. Clay could not bring himself to support a jury trial in the free state where a fugitive was apprehended, since that would amount to "a virtual denial of justice to the claimant." It would be "tantamount to a positive refusal to execute the provision of the Constitution." The same could not be said of a jury trial in the state from which the slave fled. There "full justice is administered, with entire fairness and impartiality, in cases of all actions for freedom." Clay's proposal, then, was to provide for a jury trial in the slave state.[47]

Opposition to the amendments suggested by the Committee of Thirteen came principally from southern members of Congress. Clay, speaking in defense of these proposals on May 13, pointed out that the jury-trial provision would amount to very little. When a slave was seized in a free state he might well assert he was a free man, but when he was returned to the state from which he fled, Clay argued, he would "disavow all claim to freedom." At the same time something had to be done to mitigate the bitterness over the subject of runaways, and he believed that the proposal for a jury trial in the slave state would allay much of the agitation.[48]

Southern radicals were completely unsatisfied with Clay's amendments, or explanation. Senator Pierre Soule of Louisiana said that the amendments would "embarrass and obstruct the exercise of her [the South's] acknowledged rights." Anyone would think, said Soule, that the problem to be resolved was the abuse of southerners claiming free men as slaves.[49]

Clay's token gesture had virtually no chance as a viable compromise. It was rejected by southern radicals and by most northerners. At the beginning of the summer, in fact, compromise on the issue of fugitive slaves seemed a long way off. Northern and southern leaders had set forth their respective positions, and the compromise proposals were either meaningless like Clay's, or ignored like Webster's.

During the two months after Webster introduced his bill the subject of fugitive slaves receded into the background as the Senate took up the various measures that had come from the Committee of Thirteen. On July 31, 1850, the Omnibus Bill was wrecked in the Senate.[50] Each of the measures then had to be passed separately. A fugitive slave bill, although

---

[47] *Cong. Globe*, May 8, 1850, 944–48.
[48] *Ibid.*, May 13, 1850, Appendix, 571–72.
[49] *Ibid.*, May 21, 1850, Appendix, 631.
[50] Hamilton, *Prologue to Conflict*, 111.

not part of the Omnibus, came up for consideration for the first time since the spring on Monday, August 19, 1850. During the remainder of that week nearly all of the alternatives presented earlier were raised and heatedly debated.

At the beginning of the debates Senator Mason moved to amend the bill from the judiciary committee by way of another substitute. This one consisted of several sections and was, according to him, a compound of his amendments of January 31, of the measure from the judiciary committee, with some modifications, and of one of the amendments, also modified, suggested by the Committee of Thirteen. The first five sections were substantially the same as his own earlier proposals.

The first proposal made by Clay was included in another section. Mason's modification consisted in adding a proviso that it would not be obligatory to produce a transcript of a record. Provision was also made to compensate a claimant if his slave was rescued after having been arrested. If a slaveholder's claim on the United States Treasury was upheld he would be paid out of the money not otherwise appropriated, and this would be filed in the Treasury "as evidence of so much money due from the State or Territory where such rescue was effected to the United States." Clay had suggested this when he submitted the report of the Committee of Thirteen, although he did not propose an amendment to that effect then.[51]

Senator William L. Dayton, a New Jersey Whig who figured prominently in the August debates, speedily moved to amend the Mason bill. His amendment was the same as the Webster bill of June 3, which he acknowledged in introducing it. This proposal, he contended, would meet the existing difficulties by adding personnel needed to administer the law and by extending some protection to free blacks. The provision for a jury trial was necessary to soothe northern feelings, while at the same time it would occasion "no serious procrastination."[52]

Southern senators had ignored the Webster bill when first introduced, but now that it was proposed as an amendment to a bill many of them supported, they had no choice but to discuss it. Senator Mason led the attack on the Dayton amendment. If adopted, he said, it would serve notice that the federal government refused "in good faith to execute the provisions of the Constitution of the United States." Not one man in twenty would bother to go into a free state after a slave if this provision was in the law. A jury trial "necessarily carries with it a trial of the whole right, and a trial of the right to service will be gone into." All that should be determined in the free state, in his view, was whether the person seized was the fugitive from slavery, and not whether he was rightfully held as a slave.[53]

[51]*Cong. Globe*, 31st Cong., 1st sess., May 8, 1850, 944.

[52]*Ibid.*, Aug. 19, 1850, Appendix, 1583.

[53]*Ibid.*, Appendix, 1583–84. See also the remarks of Senator Berrien of Georgia, *ibid.*, Appendix, 1584.

Senators Dayton and Robert C. Winthrop, the Massachusetts Whig who
replaced Webster when he went into the Fillmore cabinet, led the supporters of the amendment in the debate. Runaways, according to Dayton,
are "a pest and an annoyance to us." "Our people," he observed, "are
everywhere disposed to give them up according to law, but according to
law only."[54] Senator Winthrop pointed out that the Mason bill assumed
that the person seized was a slave. And that was the whole question:
whether "such a person be your slave, or whether he be our freeman."
The first question should be tried in the South, but the second should be
tried in the free state where the man was seized.[55] Jury trial, moveover,
would actually aid the recovery of fugitives "because all laws depend in
no small degree for their efficiency upon the public sentiment of the State
or the community in which they are to be executed."[56]

Winthrop's remark about the importance of public sentiment particularly offended Jefferson Davis of Mississippi. Davis spiritedly argued that
a jury would simply reflect the popular feeling and would decide in accordance with preconceived opinions (a fear long held by many northern conservatives). Winthrop replied that Davis had confounded two distinct
ideas, the one of conforming law to the sentiment of the community on
slavery, and the other of conforming the law to the opinion of the community on the justice and propriety of the law itself. A jury trial would
conform to the sentiments of the community on what was just.[57] But this
view slave owners could not, or would not, appreciate.

The thinking of many radicals in the North was represented in this
debate by Chase. The Dayton amendments were acceptable but not entirely satisfactory. In the first place they required an affidavit from the
party claiming freedom before he could obtain a jury trial. This should not
be required. In the second place the so-called right of recaption was left in
force, which, before the decision in *Prigg* v. *Pennsylvania*, the states had
legislated away, and with very little complaint from the South. The difficulties arose only after that, when the Court authorized private seizures.
These difficulties could not be erased by any congressional action as long
as the Supreme Court decision was regarded as furnishing a rule of right
and action.[58] But in these debates Chase's was "a voice crying in the
wilderness."

When he had finished, the vote was taken on the Dayton amendments,
which were soundly defeated. Support came largely from free state Whigs;
southerners, whether Whig or Democrat, were opposed.[59]

Following the defeat of the northern Whig proposal Chase made a
futile attempt to amend the bill by inserting a provision requiring a jury

[54]*Ibid.*, Appendix, 1584.
[55]*Ibid.*, Appendix, 1585.
[56]*Ibid.*, Appendix, 1585.
[57]*Ibid.*, Appendix, 1588.
[58]*Ibid.*, Appendix, 1588.
[59]*Ibid.*, Appendix, 1588.

trial on any return to a warrant issued by a commissioner or judge.[60] Chase's amendment was defeated without a division even being recorded.[61]

Clearly aware that favorable action was unlikely Senator Winthrop then introduced an amendment "simply for the purpose of having the sense of the Senate taken upon it." Everything after the third section was to be stricken, and in place of the deleted material, a proviso added stating that no certificate would be a conclusive answer to a writ of habeas corpus, issued either by a state or a United States court. A commissioner, in fact, would be required to inform the person claimed of his right to this writ. By the terms of the proviso "the forms, proceedings, and residence shall be according to the laws of the place, as in other cases where said writ is issued."

Winthrop's amendment opened up the first major debate in Congress on the functions of habeas corpus in relation to fugitive slaves since the debate in 1818. Senators Mason and Berrien carried the attack for the South. They admitted that any man, "white or black, who declares on oath that he is illegally held in custody, is entitled to a writ of *habeas corpus*." Congress had no power to suspend this writ, except in cases of invasion or rebellion, or where the public safety required it. The question, however, was the force of the writ. Mason argued that the certificate of removal should be a conclusive return. The courts, as Senator Smith of South Carolina had argued earlier, could not go behind the return. Senators Dayton and Winthrop contended, on the other side, that the judgments of "petty commissioners" on such an important question as freedom or slavery should be subject to review.[62] A certificate granted by a commissioner should not be conclusive, in Dayton's view, because these officials decided that service was actually due. The certificate of the commissioner would only be conclusive of the right of removal, the southerners answered, it would not be conclusive in any case brought in a southern state to test the freedom of the black.[63]

As a matter of law Mason and Berrien appeared to be on strong ground, but the realities behind this view, as revealed by Mason later in the week, raised some serious questions. Among the rights guaranteed to slaveholders by the Constitution, he said, was the right to dispose of the property when it became refractory. Anybody should have known that "when these people become insubordinate and abscond, it becomes a matter of necessity on the part of the owner, probably in nineteen cases out of twenty at least, when he is recaptured and taken home, to dispose of him." It would be too dangerous to place the slave among his former fellows. It

[60]*Ibid.*, Appendix, 1589.

[61]*Ibid.*, Appendix, 1589.

[62]Winthrop also proposed that blacks be allowed to testify, but this was something he was willing to do without. *Ibid.*, Appendix, 1589–90.

[63]*Ibid.*, Appendix, 1589–90.

was absolutely necessary for the owner "speedily to dispose of and send him away."[64]

The final action of this first, long day of debate was the rejection of the Winthrop amendment. The debates on August 19 clearly revealed the antinomies within the Senate. On the northern side moderate Whigs unsuccessfully contended that some provision be made to assure people that free men would not be forcibly seized and sold into slavery and, equally important, that the law itself should conform to the community sense of justice, the idea of equality before the law. Both objectives could be obtained by securing a jury trial in cases of claims to freedom, or else an inquiry by habeas corpus. Radical abolitionists such as Chase wanted to go one step beyond this and require a jury trial in all cases of claims to service. The northern Democrats did not take a prominent part in the debate on August 19, but the fact that none challenged Mason's statement that his bill had been drafted by a northerner and given to him by Senator Cass of Michigan, a Democratic leader, suggests they were willing to give slave owners their demands on the matter of runaways. Southerners, for their part, took the view that any inquiry would be a delay defeating the right to immediate possession, a right sustained by the U.S. Supreme Court. A certificate of removal, in their view, should be a conclusive answer to any habeas corpus.

The only deviation from these views came later in the week when Senator Underwood of Kentucky introduced Henry Clay's proposal from the Committee of Thirteen.[65] Mason was outraged. In his judgment the requirement for a jury trial in a slave state infringed on the rights of a master guaranteed by the Constitution. Among those was the right to dispose of unruly slaves "speedily." Since an owner's rights were absolute his right of disposal was absolute, and any delay would be a denial of the rights recognized.[66] When the Underwood bill came up for a vote on Friday it was defeated overwhelmingly.

Earlier in the week, with the acquiescence of northern Democrats, the southerners had been able to secure the adoption of the Mason substitute. This bill, amended in a few particulars during the remainder of the week, became the Fugitive Slave Law of 1850.

One major difficulty—one that divided southerners—remained in the way of final acceptance of the Mason bill: placing financial responsibility for slaves who were not recovered.[67] The guarantee in the fugitive slave clause, Mason noted, meant "either enforcing the obligation, or paying an indemnity if the duty is not enforced." Senator Butler, however, feared

[64] *Ibid.*, Aug. 22, 1850, Appendix, 1610.

[65] *Ibid.*, Appendix, 1610. Cf. Henry Thomas Shanks, ed., *The Papers of Willie Person Mangum. (1847–1894)*, (5 vols.; Raleigh, 1950–56), 5: 736.

[66] *Cong. Globe*, 31st Cong., 1st sess., Aug. 22, 1850, Appendix, 1612 ff.

[67] *Ibid.*, Aug. 20, 1850, Appendix, 1591. The discussion on this problem was first focused on an amendment of Senator Thomas Pratt of Maryland providing payment if a fugitive was not seized after a warrant had been obtained.

that this view would lead people to rely "upon this 'good milch cow,' the Federal Government."[68] Jefferson Davis of Mississippi was concerned about a greater danger: once it was granted that the government could interpose its financial power between the individual and his property, "where shall we find an end to the action which anti-slavery feeling will suggest?" Senator Hopkins L. Turney of Tennessee was even more explicit. The Mason bill was nothing less than a scheme of emancipation whereby slaveholders themselves would have to pay part of the money to effect the plan.[69]

In the face of such fears and objections Mason moved that the portion of the bill allowing an indemnity for a rescued slave be dropped, and the liability shifted to the marshals and deputy marshals. This imposed on them the same liability incurred by a sheriff at common law. The Senate accepted these changes.[70]

Two final efforts to have the bill amended failed by substantial majorities,[71] and on Friday, August 23, the Senate proceeded to vote on engrossment of the Mason bill, as amended. The bill passed this crucial test easily.[72]

In the House the bill was rushed through after a motion was adopted not to open it up for debate. The bill was voted on and returned to the Senate on September 12. The House vote was 109 ayes, 76 nays, and 36 abstentions. Thirty-one northerners voted for the fugitive slave bill while southern representatives stood united.

As adopted on September 18, 1850, the Fugitive Slave Law amended the federal act of 1793. It significantly increased the number of officials authorized to hear claims and grant certificates of removal. The circuit courts of the United States and the superior courts of the territories were to appoint commissioners and to enlarge the number from time to time. The commissioners, in turn, were authorized to appoint "suitable persons" to execute any warrant or process they might issue. Either the commissioners, or those appointed by them, were empowered to summon the aid of bystanders, a *posse comitatus.* "All good citizens," furthermore, were "commanded to aid and assist in the prompt and efficient execution of this law, whenever their services may be required."

---

[68]*Ibid.*, Appendix, 1594–99.
[69]*Ibid.*, Aug. 22, 1850, Appendix, 1612–18.
[70]*Ibid.*, Aug. 23, 1850, Appendix, 1624–25.
[71]One was an effort by Chase to have the prospective fugitive slave law restricted to the states because the right of reclamation did not exist in the territories (the fugitive slave clause did not apply to the territories). This was too much even for the free-state senators. His proposal was defeated by a vote of forty-two to one. *Ibid.*, Appendix, 1620. The other amendment, introduced by John Davis of Massachusetts, provided protection for free blacks imprisoned "without any alleged crime or offence against law." His reference was to the southern laws imprisoning black seamen. This amendment was defeated by a vote of thirteen to twenty-four. *Ibid.*, Appendix, 1629.
[72]*Ibid.*, Appendix, 1629.

Claimants were authorized to procure warrants of arrest or to seize runaways themselves and bring them before the court or commissioner. The judge or commissioner (who was paid ten dollars if he found for the claimant and five dollars if he found against him) was charged with hearing and determining the case "in a summary manner." Upon presenting satisfactory proof of the claim a slave owner, or his agent, would receive a certificate of removal. "Satisfactory proof" could be in the form of a deposition or affidavit, in writing, taken by the court or commissioner hearing the claim, or it could be "other satisfactory testimony" taken before someone authorized to administer oaths in the state from which the escape occurred. If it was the latter, it had to be accompanied with a certificate proving the authority of the official who took the evidence, together with the seal of the officer. This seal would "be sufficient to establish the competency of the proof." The testimony of the alleged runaway would not be admitted in evidence, and, finally, the certificate of removal would be "conclusive of the right" of the claimant to remove the black, and would "prevent all molestation . . . by any process issued by any court, judge, magistrate, or other person whomsoever." The presumption of freedom, and the laws of the free states designed to secure the personal liberty of free men would not be allowed to defeat a claim that a man was a slave.

Anyone who obstructed a claimant making a seizure, "either with or without" a process, or rescued a runaway, or harbored one, would be subject to a one-thousand-dollar fine and imprisonment for six months. He also would have to pay a one-thousand-dollar fine in civil damages to a slave owner for each runaway lost. If a claimant feared that his slave would be rescued before he could get him outside the state where he was seized the marshal making the seizure was required to retain the man in custody, employ as many people as needed to overcome the threatened rescue, and deliver the fugitive to the owner in the state from which he fled.[73] And marshals would be financially responsible for escapes from custody.

Thomas Hart Benton later noted that the Mason bill became law because "under the fear of danger to the Union on one hand, and the charms of pacification and compromise on the other, a few heated spirits got the control, and had things their own way."[74] There is some truth in this judgment, but it can be misleading. The Fugitive Slave Law of 1850 was scarcely a compromise. Every effort by northerners to include some security for free blacks, particularly the trial by jury and habeas corpus, was defeated by a coalition of southerners and some northern Democrats. Even the compromise measure proposed by the border-state delegation from Kentucky providing for a jury trial in the slave state was defeated.

[73]*Statutes*, Sept. 18, 1850, 9: chap. 10, 462.
[74]Thomas Hart Benton, *Thirty Years' View* (2 vols.; New York, 1854), 2: 730.

Every guarantee, every security in the new law was for the "rights" of slave owners.

The parting shot in Congress on the law was fired in the House on September 25, 1850, by George W. Julian. "A tissue of more heartless and cold-blooded enactments," he said, "never disgraced the legislation of a civilized people." The law would not even be executed. "*Repeal*," he contended, "must be the fixed resolve of the non-slaveholding States, and the people of the South should distinctly understand that there can be no harmony with slaveholders until that resolve is consummated."[75] At a convention held at Milledgeville, Georgia, on the other side, it was declared in the so-called Georgia Platform that "upon the faithful execution of the Fugitive Slave Bill by the proper authorities, depends the preservation of our much loved Union."[76] And the *North Carolina Standard* declared that if the new law was not respected "*we leave you!* Before God and man . . . if you fail in this simple act of justice, *the bonds will be dissolved!*"[77]

[75] *Cong. Globe*, 31st Cong., 1st sess., Sept. 25, 1850, Appendix, 1301–02.
[76] Commager, *Documents*, 1: 324.
[77] Quoted in Craven, *Coming of the Civil War*, 265.

Positive Law, Higher Law, and the *Via Media* 9

At the end of 1850 the alternative facing the people of the South was to accept the compromise or reject it *in toto*, which would mean secession and probable civil war. They could not go part way and nullify a portion of the settlement because they were not faced (as northerners were, and as southerners had been in 1832) with a repugnant law operative within their states.[1] The majority were unwilling to repudiate the work of the Thirty-first Congress when faced with the alternative. Predominant opinion south of the Mason-Dixon line was reflected in the Georgia Platform of late 1850. Or as one who signed himself "Georgia" wrote in the *American Whig Review* in December, 1850: "The question is, will the North remain content with the so-called Compromise Bills, or will her people persist in attempts to violate the Constitution? The issue must be fought north of the Potomac."[2]

Sentiment north of the Mason-Dixon line in the early 1850s was more diverse. Undoubtedly many people, anxious to turn away from the crisis and bitterness that had marked the period 1849–50, were willing to uphold the compromise despite the distasteful Fugitive Slave Law. As Horace Greeley later wrote sarcastically, many people wanted "peace and prosperity, and were nowise inclined to cut each other's throats and burn each other's houses in a general quarrel concerning (as they regarded it) only the *status* of negroes."[3] The issue, as seen by such people, was defined more openly by the *Democratic Review* than by "Georgia": "Shall the Constitution and the law be enforced, or shall we separate? It is a question of alternatives."[4] The answer of those "intent on business," to use Greeley's phrase, was unequivocal. Over the entrance to the Castle Garden Meeting Hall in New York City on the evening of October 30, 1850, were "emblazoned" the words "The Union: It must and shall be preserved." Above the stage hung a portrait of George Washington "surrounded by the 'Stars and Stripes' and surmounted" by the inscription "One Country—One Constitution—One Destiny."[5] This meeting had been called by merchants

[1]Nevins, *Ordeal of the Union*, 1: 352–54.
[2]*The American Whig Review*, new series, 6–12 (December, 1850): 559.
[3]Horace Greeley, *The American Conflict: A History* (2 vols.; Washington, D.C., 1902), 1: 210–11.
[4]*The United States Magazine, and Democratic Review*, new series, 28 (April 1851): 359.
[5]*New York Tribune*, October 31, 1850.

to bring together the propertied leaders of New York to express their wholehearted support for the compromise measures, the "Peace Measures" as they were called.[6] One staunch conservative, George Templeton Strong, described the meeting as one of "much howling and hurrahing and other demonstrations of patriotic furor, and large quantity of vapid spouting."[7] He added that he was prepared to "hurrah for the Castle Garden platform."

One of the main subjects of that platform was the Fugitive Slave Law. The resolution adopted declared it to be fully in accord with the Constitution. Those who subscribed to this resolution were willing to "sustain this law, and the execution of the same, by all lawful means."[8]

For the most part those who spoke at Castle Garden arrayed themselves against slavery as an "evil," but they would not go so far as to say that it warranted a surgeon's knife. After all, a hack might cut away vital organs in the process. Some, however, such as George Wood, the president of the meeting, argued that slavery was not inherently sinful: slaves were merely one kind of property (interestingly, Wood had been one of the counsel for the slave Jack in the 1830s in the case of *Jack* v. *Martin*).[9]

Much of the evening was spent by five members of the New York bar[10] trying to calm any misgivings the merchants might have over the Fugitive Slave Law.[11] The fullest exposition came from William M. Evarts, the youngest of the five attorneys. The writ of habeas corpus, for example, was not denied he believed. It would issue but the certificate would be a satisfactory answer.[12] The absence of a jury-trial provision, moreover, was not of fundamental importance. Jury trial was not a natural right. "It is a positive and artificial institution, the growth of English liberty." And it was never designed to be used at an introductory hearing. The whole premise of the Fugitive Slave Law was that a fugitive would be remanded to the state from which he escaped "there to abide the full determination of the right between" himself and his claimant.

There was more danger, in the opinion of Evarts, in the notion that "private conscience" was above the law than there was in the Fugitive Slave Act. "The supremacy, absolute and universal, of the law, is an essential notion of every organized community, and he who doubts this

[6]Philip S. Foner, *Business & Slavery: The New York Merchants & the Irrepressible Conflict* (Chapel Hill, N.C., 1941), 42; *New York Evening Post*, October 31, 1850.

[7]Allan Nevins and Milton Halsey Thomas, eds., *The Diary of George Templeton Strong: The Turbulent Fifties, 1850-1859* (New York, 1952), 24.

[8]*New York Evening Post*, October 31, 1850.

[9]*New York Tribune*, October 31, 1850. See also Nevins and Thomas, *Diary of Strong*, 24.

[10]They were George Wood, James W. Gerard, James T. Brady, Edward Sandford, and William M. Evarts.

[11]Foner, *Business & Slavery*, 46.

[12]The same point was frequently made. See, for example, *The United States Magazine, and Democratic Review*, new series, 28 (April 1851): 358.

supremacy strikes at the foundation of society." Anyone who resisted the law, according to Evarts, wounded its authority, and "as surely enfeebles its protection." The line was to be drawn, for him, "between the foes of public order, the laws and the Constitution," and those in whose breasts the "love of country shall reign predominant."[13] No longer was there much concern among conservatives with the problem of conforming the law to the community sense of justice.

Such sentiments were echoed a month later at a meeting at Faneuil Hall in Boston.[14] The same support was marshaled there as at Castle Garden. For several days the call had been posted in the "Merchant's Reading Room" in Boston, and when it came time for the affair several of the leading conservative lawyers of the state were in attendance.

Benjamin R. Curtis, speaking at the meeting, saw the most dire consequences in a violent resistance to the execution of the Fugitive Slave Law. "If there is a case for forcible resistance of law, for refusal to execute one article in the compact which constitutes the government, for vilifying this compact by names which I should be unwilling to repeat, for stirring up the angry passions of men, and arraying one part of the country against another part, it can be nothing less than a case for revolution, and in a revolution it must end, if its progress be not checked."[15]

Merchants, lawyers, and politicians were not the only ones who took up the cry for "public order, the laws and the Constitution." Many clergymen joined the fray. One was John C. Lord who delivered an important sermon on Thanksgiving day, 1850, at the Central Presbyterian Church in Buffalo, New York. He castigated in no uncertain terms those who denounced the law. "We take the ground, that the action of civil governments within their appropriate jurisdiction is final and conclusive upon the citizen. To plead a higher law to justify disobedience to a human law," he continued, "the subject matter of which is within the cognizance of the State, is to reject the authority of God himself; who has committed to governments the power and authority which they exercise in civil affairs." The "higher law" might be found in the "gospel of Jean Jacques Rousseau, and in the revelation of the Sceptics and Jacobins," but it could not be found in the gospel of Jesus Christ. If men believed that the law was unconstitutional, Lord advised, they should test it in the courts. If they were not willing to do that, or to submit, there was only one honest position for "fanaticism" to assume: "declare at once and openly for a dissolution of

13Sherman Evarts, ed., *Arguments and Speeches of William Maxwell Evarts* (New York, 1919), 2: 420–34. See also William M. Evarts to Richard H. Dana, Jr., New York, December 7, 1850, Dana Papers, Massachusetts Historical Society.

14A similar meeting in Philadelphia is discussed in the *Pennsylvania Freeman*, March 6, 1851.

15Benjamin R. Curtis, Jr., *A Memoir of Benjamin Robbins Curtis* (2 vols; Boston, 1879), 1: 126–27; see also Rufus Choate, *Addresses and Orations of Rufus Choate* (Boston, 1891), 418.

the Union, or the subjugation of the South, by force of arms, to the North."[16]

In his first annual message to Congress (December, 1850) Millard Fillmore added his voice, and the prestige of the presidency, to the movement to pledge that the compromise would be honored. The 1850 measures, he said, "are regarded by me as a settlement in principle and substance—a final settlement of the dangerous and exciting subjects which they embraced."[17] Both major parties, when they met in 1852 to select presidential nominees, moreover, came out in support of the Peace Measures.[18]

In Congress procompromise sentiment was strong enough to defeat any effort to repeal the new federal law. Charles Sumner, early in 1852, tried to amend a bill providing appropriations for civil and diplomatic expenses to forbid the allowance of expenses incurred in executing the law of 1850, which was to be repealed. Speaking for his proposed amendment Sumner declared that "no unanimity of politicians can uphold the baseless assumption, that a law, or any conglomerate of laws, under the name of Compromise, or howsoever called, is final." "According to the true spirit of the Constitution," he declared, "and the sentiments of the fathers, *slavery* and not freedom is *sectional*, while *freedom* and not slavery is national."[19] For the moment, Sumner's impassioned plea fell on deaf ears.

The first full-scale judicial examination of the new fugitive law occurred in Boston in the spring of 1851. At the beginning of April, 1851, Thomas Sims, an alleged fugitive from Savannah, Georgia arrived in Boston, where he was seized as a runaway. Fear of a rescue led to the patrolling of the area around the jail by members of the "Sims Brigade," a few companies of the Boston brigade. Chains were thrown across the doors of the court house and other precautionary measures were taken. Several legal expedients were tried to secure Sims's release; a writ of personal replevin was sought as were several writs of habeas corpus from several judges. The most desperate gambit was to try to have Sims taken out of the custody of the man holding him for the claimant by virtue of a criminal charge (it was thought better to have him serve a brief time in a Massachusetts prison than the rest of his life on a Georgia plantation). At the hearing before George T. Curtis, the fugitive-slave commissioner, the counsel for Sims, Robert Rantoul, Jr., presented a strong argument against the Fugitive Slave Law, but on every point Commissioner Curtis ruled against him.[20]

[16] John C. Lord, *"The Higher Law" in its Application to the Fugitive Slave Bill. A Sermon on the Duties Men Owe to God and to Governments* (Buffalo, 1851), 27.

[17] James D. Richardson, *Compilation of the Messages and Papers of the Presidents, 1789–1897* (10 vols.; Washington, 1907), 4: 2629.

[18] Porter and Johnson, *National Party Platforms*, 17, 21.

[19] *Cong. Globe*, 32d Cong., 1st sess., Appendix, 1102–3. See also, "The Memorial of the Pennsylvania Society for promoting the abolition of slavery, . . . etc." of May 12, 1854, National Archives, 33A.H21 (Senate Records).

[20] *Trial of Thomas Sims, on An Issue of Personal Liberty, on the claim of James Potter, of Georgia, Against Him, as an alleged Fugitive from Service* (Boston, 1851), Rantoul's argu-

Rantoul's effort to have an inquiry by the state supreme court failed
when Chief Justice Shaw ruled that he could not even grant a habeas
corpus because he would have to decide against the petitioner, since the
application for the writ showed a sufficient cause for the detention. This
problem dealt with by Shaw—the effect of the federal law on runaways
upon a state habeas corpus—was one of the most warmly debated legal and
constitutional problems of the decade. Outraged at Shaw's refusal to issue
the writ, one state senator declared that the great writ of liberty was now
prostrated beneath the Fugitive Slave Law.[21] An effort to secure a special
law to require the court to issue the writ in Sims's case, however, was unsuccessful, but within a few days Shaw had been persuaded by a number
of "gentlemen of high standing" to listen to arguments against the federal
law on an application for the writ. The court listened and then handed
down a decision refusing the writ on the grounds that the law under which
Sims was held was constitutional. In the spring of 1851 Justice Samuel
Nelson of the U.S. Supreme Court, in a charge to a grand jury while on
circuit, was even more emphatic: state courts, he said, could not issue the
writ to inquire into the legality of the detention under color of the fugitive
law on the grounds that the detention was unwarranted under that law, or
that the law was unconstitutional, since to do so "would be fatal to the
authority of the Constitution, laws, and treaties of the general government." Two years later Justice Grier of the same court declared that state
courts could not use the writ "to review or sit in error upon the judgment or
process of the judicial officers of the United States" because the law of
1850 had made the certificate of a commissioner or a judge of a United
States court "conclusive evidence."[22] All of these opinions of course were
entitled to considerable weight, but according to John Codman Hurd, a
leading authority on the law of slavery and freedom, Shaw's opinion for
the Massachusetts court was especially significant: it was considered
thereafter as "the highest authority—to the degree that in opinions of
judges in later cases who have maintained the action of commissioners in
like circumstances, it has been taken to preclude all further juristical
discussion."[23] Shaw's opinion was indeed significant, but Hurd overstated
its effect. It was not assented to universally by jurists, and, of course, it remained to be seen how far state legislators would feel bound by it. Rollin
C. Hurd (no relation to John Codman Hurd), an antislavery commentator
on the writ of habeas corpus, contended in the mid-1850s that "it may be

---

ment is also in Luther Hamilton, ed., *Memoirs, Speeches and Writings of Robert Rantoul
Jr.* (Boston, 1854), 49–66. See also Richard Henry Dana, Jr., *The Journal of Richard Henry
Dana, Jr.*, ed. Robert F. Lucid (3 vols; Cambridge, Mass., 1968), 2: 420 ff.

[21]Levy, *Law of the Commonwealth*, 95 ff.

[22]"Fugitive Slave Law. U. S. Circuit Court. Before the Hon. Samuel Nelson, Associate
Justice of the Supreme Court of the United States," *The New York Legal Observer*, 9 (June
1851): 161–73; Hurd, *The Law of Freedom and Bondage*, 1: 495–96, n. 7.

[23]Hurd, *The Law of Freedom and Bondage*, 2: 653.

settled that state courts may grant the writ in all cases of illegal confinement under the authority of the United States." And, he added, "the
weight of authority clearly is that they may decide as to the legality of the
imprisonment; and discharge the prisoner if his detention be illegal, though
the determination may involve questions of the constitutionality of acts of
Congress, or of the jurisdiction of a court of the United States."[24] Shaw, of
course, took a slightly different view. In 1854 Justice Fletcher of the Massachusetts supreme court revealed that Shaw had based his decision in
Sims's case "upon the weight of the precedents & not in principle," and
that, moreover, "the weight of authority, chiefly Prigg's case, was in favor
of the Constitutionality of the law, i.e. so far as it cd. be open on a question
of Hab. Corp."[25]

Although the "weight of authority" was important in subordinating the
state habeas corpus to the Fugitive Slave Law in Massachusetts in the early
1850s, the question of the impact of the federal law upon the state remedy
remained a subject of considerable dispute throughout the decade. The precise place habeas corpus occupied within the interstices of the federal
union had long been unclear, but because of the proslavery effort to emas-
culate it in cases involving claims to runaways, the issue had been
sharpened. It is vital to note that in the quest to define the proper role for
this state remedy, the practice associated with the writ in cases of fugitives
underwent an important reorientation which led many abolitionists to a renewed concern with this legal process. As mentioned before, habeas corpus
usage had expanded at the state level to the point where courts used it to
conduct independent examinations of the facts alleged to justify a detention. Now, however, it was being used to examine the validity of the law
itself. According to Justice Fletcher, Shaw had arrived at his conclusion
because he felt bound by the precedent of the Prigg decision. The fact re-
mains that he did conduct an examination into the constitutionality of the
law, and not just an evidentiary hearing into the facts alleged to sustain
the restraint of Sims. And according to Justices Nelson and Grier this
carried him beyond the legitimate bounds of his power under the state writ.
The lack of a uniform view about state habeas corpus usage, of course,
was no aid to Thomas Sims who was returned to slavery. The fact that
he was publicly whipped thirty-nine times on his return to his master in
Savannah did not do much to support the argument of those who claimed
the whole process of returning fugitives was for the purpose of adjudicating the dispute.[26] Despite the important vagaries in the views of jurists
about the exact relationship between the federal law and the state remedy,

[24]Hurd, *A Treatise on the Right of Personal Liberty, and on the Writ of Habeas Corpus*,
167.

[25]Dana, *Journal* 2: 653.

[26]The fullest account of the Sims case is Leonard Levy, "Sims' Case: The Fugitive Slave
Law in Boston in 1851," *Journal of Negro History*, 25 (Jan., 1950): 39–75.

differences that would mount in importance by the middle of the decade, the compromise was upheld in the early 1850s.

That northern acquiescence in the settlement of 1850 which was reflected in union meetings, judicial rulings like Shaw's, and numerous sermons was further manifested in Pennsylvania, where a vigorous effort was made to prove that the state was willing to "abide by the Constitution," and to make some concessions to southern demands. In 1849 the Democrats obtained control of the state government and, under the impact of the sectional crisis, they bent every effort to alter the course the state had been following.

On March 22, 1850, months before the passage of the Fugitive Slave Law, Governor William F. Johnston, an antislavery Whig, transmitted several resolutions to the legislature from Virginia and Georgia. These resolves dealt with the whole problem of slavery. On the matter of fugitives Johnston left little doubt where he stood. He conceded that there was a constitutional obligation to return runaway slaves, but he added that a law that did not require "strict proof of the right of the master" would never satisfy the citizens of his state.[27]

A majority of a select committee of the house on federal relations, however, did not agree with the governor. "Each State is bound to comply with, and fulfill in good faith, all the solemn stipulations" of the Constitution. "Any obstacles interposed, or laws enacted by any State, in derogation of any of the covenants contained in that Constitution, are revolutionary, and should be promptly repealed and removed." The majority recommended repeal of the law of 1847.[28]

The struggle over repeal of the Personal Liberty Law in Pennsylvania, lasting until 1852, was a partisan affair.[29] Abolitionists charged that the whole effort was being made by Buchanan men looking to the presidential election of 1852.[30] Buchanan surely had intense presidential ambitions, but he was also a man, like Webster, very much concerned with union. Whichever was uppermost in his mind in 1850 it is certain that his partisans were back of the movement to repeal the state law.

On March 8, even before Johnston submitted the resolutions from the southern states, a bill was reported out of the judiciary committee of the house to repeal certain sections of the law. A report with the bill left no doubt why repeal was being sought. Even though the state law "was a legal and constitutional exercise of State legislative power," repeal would be a

[27] *Message of the Governor of Pennsylvania, Transmitting Resolutions Relative to Slavery, Passed by the Legislatures of Virginia and Georgia* (Harrisburg, 1850), 8.

[28] *Reports of the Majority and Minority of the Select Committee of the House, in Relation to the Existing Federal Relations of the State, As a Member of the Union* (Harrisburg, 1850). The minority report did not deal with the subject of fugitive slaves.

[29] Henry R. Mueller, *The Whig Party in Pennsylvania* (New York, 1922), 169.

[30] *Thirteenth Annual Report, Presented to the Pennsylvania Anti-Slavery Society, By its Executive Committee, October 15, 1850* (Philadelphia, 1850), 9.

salutary move in the face of the excitement caused by "the ultra views advanced on each side." On April 8, 1850, the bill passed the house by a strictly partisan vote.[31] Failure in the senate, where most of the pressure against repeal was concentrated,[32] doomed the measure during that session.

At the beginning of 1851 the bill was introduced again, although this time in the senate. At the end of March the senate agreed to limit repeal to the section closing the state's jails to the use of claimants. In this form the bill easily passed the senate. By the middle of April it had passed the house without amendments.[33]

It did not pass, however, without a great deal of opposition from outside the legislature. The *Pennsylvania Freeman* called for "remonstrances" against repeal,[34] and damned Charles Gibbons, one of its proponents, for his apostasy to the law he himself had supported in 1847.[35]

Without political power in the state, however, those opposed to repeal were frustrated. For a brief moment in the spring of 1851 they had an opportunity to relax. Governor Johnston pocket-vetoed the bill. The jails of Pennsylvania had been closed to the use of claimants, and he believed they should remain closed. He warned, moreover, that the writ of habeas corpus "would run into these unconstitutional places of detention."[36]

In the spring of 1851 the Democrats nominated a Buchanan associate, William Bigler, to oppose Governor Johnston in the fall elections. A leading issue in that campaign was the question of repeal. Buchanan wrote to Bigler in April, 1851, that "the Fugitive Slave law must be sustained; because I believe it is right in principle & in sustaining it we sustain the Union."[37] In a letter sent to a Union celebration in Easton, Bigler declared that "the fundamental law of our land cannot be sustained in part and abandoned in part; the Constitution must be maintained as a whole."[38]

Bigler acted upon his beliefs in 1852 following his victory over Johnston. One of his first official recommendations was to call for a repeal of the act of 1847. His next was to pardon a notorious kidnapper convicted under that law.[39]

[31] Mueller, *The Whig Party in Pennsylvania*, 169.

[32] *Penn. Senate Journal, 1850*, 585, 608, 616, 636, 646, 657, 672, 679, 691, 707, 710, 721, 724, 768, 781, 794, 806, 833, 855, 858, 872, 909, 1081.

[33] *Penn. House Journal, 1851*, 900–901.

[34] *Pennsylvania Freeman*, January 16, 1851. See also *Penn. House Journal, 1851*, 25, 28, 34, 47, 64, 66, 114, 142, 169, 209, 240, 272, 305, 319, 349, 374, 381, 415, 423, 441, 501, 634.

[35] *Pennsylvania Freeman*, March 13, 1851.

[36] *Penn. Senate Journal, 1852*, 15–16.

[37] James Buchanan to Col. William Bigler, April 10, 1851, William Bigler Papers, Historical Society of Pennsylvania.

[38] *The Huntington Globe*, July 31, 1851. See also, Mss. of an undated, untitled, handwritten speech, William Bigler Papers, Historical Society of Pennsylvania.

[39] Mueller, *Whig Party in Pennsylvania*, 194. On this case see *A Review of the Trial, Conviction and Sentence, of George F. Alberti, for Kidnapping*. (n.d.) Historical Society of Pennsylvania.

Bills were introduced into both houses of the Pennsylvania legislature to repeal parts of the law. Democrats were solidly behind these measures, and they received support from the conservative Whigs representing commercial interests.[40] As it emerged from the legislature only the section of the law of 1847 closing the state's jails was repealed. Governor Bigler signed it into law on April 9, 1852,[41] with what must have been considerable satisfaction. This was an important victory for those who sought to reverse the trend of the preceding decade and give to the South once again some evidence of their willingness to meet southern demands.

I

Despite this victory, and the indications that many were willing to swallow the distasteful Peace Measures, there was considerable indignation in the North when the new law was put into operation. The first case to arise under that law occurred in New York City. James Hamlet, a black who had worked for three years as a porter in the city, was seized within eight days of the passage of the law, speedily tried before the United States commissioner, and hurried off to Baltimore, leaving a wife and two children behind. Businessmen in the city, however, collected a fund and purchased Hamlet's freedom.[42]

Within a few months (January, 1851) Fred Wilkins, or "Shadrach" as he preferred to be called, was seized at the Cornhill Coffee House in Boston, but subsequently was rescued from the courtroom where he was held. According to Richard Henry Dana, Jr., one of the most noteworthy and appropriate aspects of the rescue was that "the Sword of Justice, wh. Mr. Riley [Deputy Marshal] had displayed on his desk, was carried off by an old negro."[43] This whole episode cast a shadow over the city as far as the proponents of the "laws and the Constitution" were concerned. They were determined that such a breach of the pledge to the South to abide by the compromise would not happen again. Within three days of Shadrach's escape, moreover, President Fillmore ordered prosecutions begun against those involved in the rescue, but nothing came of this effort.[44] Following

[40] *Pennsylvania Freeman*, February 19, 1852.

[41] *Penn. Senate Journal, 1852*, 24, 109–10, 132–33, 277, 201–202, 311–12, 320–21, 366–67, 447, 459–60, 482–84, 695, 703, 719; *Penn. House Journal, 1852*, 34, 95, 188, 360, 509, 527, 587, 701–2, 721.

[42] The fullest account of this case is *The Fugitive Slave Bill: Its History and Unconstitutionality: with an account of the Seizure and Enslavement of James Hamlet, and his Subsequent Restoration to Liberty* (New York, 1850). For good brief accounts see Foner, *Business & Slavery*, 35–36; Nevins, *Ordeal of the Union*, 1: 385; McDougall, *Fugitive Slaves*, 43–44; and Henrietta Buckmaster, *Let My People Go: The Story of the Underground Railroad and the Growth of the Abolition Movement* (Boston, 1959), 180.

[43] Dana, *Journal*, 2: 412.

[44] Harold Schwartz, "Fugitive Slave Days in Boston," *The New England Quarterly*, 27 (June, 1954): 195–97; *Report of the Proceedings at the Examination of Charles Davis, Esq.* (Boston, 1851). Davis was one of the men unsuccessfully prosecuted.

the escape of Shadrach the procompromise faction in Boston was given an opportunity to show its mettle in the Sims case, discussed earlier.

But it was precisely cases such as these that deeply disturbed antislavery people who refused to accept the view that the Fugitive Slave Law was part of a final settlement, or a price worth paying for peace, prosperity, and union. For such people the most important question of the day was not that posed by the *Democratic Review*: union or separation. As Samuel Willard saw it the imperative question posed by the new law was this: "When human law comes, or appears to come, into direct and inevitable conflict with the Divine law, which is to control the conduct of good citizens? This, I think, is emphatically the question of our day and country . . . the main issue between the opponents and the abettors, or passive instruments, of slavery."[45]

Answers to this question were not slow in coming. In the wake of the seizure of James Hamlet, for example, a number of protest meetings were held in New York. One of the first was held at Syracuse on October 4, 1850. A vigilance committee was formed at the meeting to assure that no man was deprived of his liberty without "due process of law." But the real tone was set by a Baptist clergyman who put the question, "Shall a live man ever be taken out of our city by force of this law?" and received for a reply a resounding "No! No!"[46] An even more poignant statement came from a meeting of blacks at the Zion Chapel in New York City. The speaker was the presiding officer, William P. Powell. "You are told to submit peaceably to the laws; will you do so? (No, no.) You are told to kiss the manacles that bind you; will you do so? (No, no, no.) The law is made by the people. The people have told you that you must do so; will you obey them? (No.) . . . This covenant with death, and agreement with hell, must be trampled under foot, resisted, disobeyed, and violated at all hazards. (Cheers.)"[47]

Individual active resistance was one form of protest being urged, passive resistance was another. Publicly the American and Foreign Antislavery Society suggested this alternative. People were urged to sign a pledge declaring that "Whereas the late act of Congress makes a refusal to aid in the capture of a fugitive a penal offence the subscribers being restrained by conscientious motives from rendering any active obedience to the law, do solemnly pledge ourselves to each other, rather to submit to its penalties, than to obey its provisions."[48]

Justification for this position was given by Willard, who answered the charge that resistance to the law tended to the destruction of all government. Men could refuse obedience to a specific civil law, "and still submit

[45]Samuel Willard, *The Grand Issue: An Ethico-Political Tract* (Boston, 1851), 3.
[46]Wilson, *Rise and Fall of the Slave Power*, 2: 306.
[47]*The Fugitive Bill . . . Enslavement of Hamlet*, Appendix, 32.
[48]*Ibid.*, 21.

so quietly to the severest penalties of that law, as to leave the wheels of Government to roll on." Such action would be accompanied by a complete obedience to those laws that appeared to be in harmony "with the beneficient will of God." Such a course of action would tend to strengthen support for those laws entitled to it, and would exert a reforming influence "on those which are capable of reformation, without a resort to those violent and bloody commotions, which often aggravate, instead of correcting inveterate and deep-rooted abuses."[49] The true doctrine then was "non-obedience and non-resistance."

Civil disobedience, whether active or passive, was based on the "higher-law" concept. This law, which was equated with the immutable principles of "truth and justice" or with divine law, was placed beside the Fugitive Slave Law of 1850, and the latter was found wanting.

It is by now a truism, because of the work of Edward S. Corwin, that the American Constitution and the state constitutions embody higher law precepts. This aspect of the organic law was highlighted by those concerned more with effecting change within the constitutional structure than with an individual response to an iniquitous law. They sought some reconciliation between the higher law and positive law. Frederick Robinson, formerly the president of the Massachusetts senate, at a meeting of the Democratic voters of the second congressional district of Massachusetts urged on the audience "the necessity of recurring to those FUNDAMENTAL PRINCIPLES OF HUMAN RIGHTS on which our free institutions are established."[50] Among those principles and maxims were the right of a trial by jury in the vicinity where the alleged fugitive was found, protection against deprivation of liberty "without due process of law," and the idea that all presumptions "of law and fact, are, and ought to be, in favor of liberty."

Robert Rantoul, Jr., speaking at the same meeting declared that "I love the Union and the Constitution . . . for the great end for which they were created; to secure and perpetuate liberty, not the liberty of a class super-imposed upon the thraldom of groaning multitudes, not the liberty of a ruling race cemented by the tears and blood of subject races, but human liberty, perfect liberty, common to all for whom the Union and the Constitution were made, to the whole 'people of the United States,' and to their 'posterity.'"[51] Byron Paine, a Democratic Free-Soiler from Wis-

---

[49]Willard, *The Grand Issue*, 5. See also W. H. Furness, *A Discourse Occasioned by the Boston Fugitive Slave Case, Delivered in the First Congregational Unitarian Church, Philadelphia, April 13, 1851* (Philadelphia, 1851); idem, *Christian Duty, Three Discourses Delivered in the First Congregational Unitarian Church of Philadelphia May 20th, June 4th and June 11th, 1854; With Reference to the Recent Execution of the Fugitive Slave Law in Boston and New York* (Philadelphia, 1854).

[50]*The Fugitive Slave Law. Speech of Hon. Robert Rantoul, Jr., of Beverly, Mass., Delivered Before the Grand Mass Convention of the Democratic Voters of the Second Congressional District of Massachusetts, Holden at Lynn, Thursday, April 3, 1851* (Phonographic Report by Dr. James W. Stone), 1.

[51]*Ibid.*, 4.

consin, put this another way. The question was "whether liberty or slavery constituted the object to be cherished & executed by our government. The Slaveholders say it is slavery; we say it is liberty, and now which is right?"[52] For Paine the best answer rested in state interposition: "I hold that it should rather be regarded as a peculiarly happy feature of our institutions that there is such a medium ground, and that when the evil spirits of usurpation and oppression enter into and possess the Federal Power, the States may interpose with such powers as they have, to arrest the progress of the evil, and to avert, if possible, the necessity of the last resort to the terrible ordeal of revolution."[53] This was the *via media*, the way between submission and revolution during the 1850s. To the abolitionists it clearly meant the nullification of the federal law on runaways. They would translate their moral convictions into orderly procedures at the state level and use these procedures to secure an ordered scheme of liberty in the face of the completely proslavery federal act of 1850. But they could be joined on the middle ground by those whose concern was primarily with fundamental fairness and procedural regularity, by people who could still admit that they possessed an obligation to return actual fugitives, an admission most abolitionists no longer made.[54]

II

Efforts to follow this middle way between revolution and submission began quite early. In all the states, except Vermont (which secured jury trial), it was an unsuccessful movement before events in the mid-1850s changed the climate of opinion north of the Mason-Dixon line; and Vermont is the exception that proves the rule—in that state, far-removed from slavery, action was taken almost immediately upon passage of the Fugitive Slave Law,[55] and before procompromise people had solidified their position. In the other northern states, where action was begun later, procompromisers were sufficiently strong to defeat the effort. These attempts generally have been ignored, but they are in fact important indications of the state of public feeling.

Apart from Vermont, the state in which the effort to follow the *via media* was pursued most vigorously from 1850 to 1853 was Massachusetts. Shortly after the attempted rendition of Shadrach a Joint Special Committee of the General Court took the whole problem under consideration. This committee solicited the assistance of Richard Henry Dana, Jr., and

[52]Byron Paine Papers, State Historical Society of Wisconsin. This speech is untitled and undated, but internal evidence provides a clue. It appears to have been delivered at a Democratic Free-Soil meeting on the eve of the presidential election of 1852.

[53]*Unconstitutionality of the Fugitive Act. Argument of Byron Paine, Esq. and Opinion of Hon. A. D. Smith, Associate Justice of the Supreme Court of the State of Wisconsin* (n.d.), 3.

[54]Charles Stearns, *The "Fugitive Slave Law" of the United States, Shown to be Unconstitutional, Impolitic, Inhuman, and Diabolical* (Boston, 1851), 30.

[55]McDougall, *Fugitive Slaves*, 67, 69.

Charles Sumner in drafting bills "to meet the dangers & outrages of the Fugitive Slave Bill." During the middle of March, 1851, Dana and Sumner drafted laws to present to the legislature, and part of their work[56] was incorporated in a bill reported out of the committee at the end of March.[57]

This bill was a sweeping act in thirteen sections. One of its features was to extend the act of 1843 to the new federal fugitive law. The bill also placed severe prohibitions on any member of the volunteer militia who, in that capacity, acted under orders of the United States Marshal, or his deputy, as part of a *posse comitatus* in a fugitive case.

An alleged fugitive, furthermore, was guaranteed the right to a writ of habeas corpus, and if he or she was unsuccessful in the hearing on the return, that person could claim a jury trial and "appeal to final judgment." There was no restriction on this. It applied to anyone under federal custody, as well as to anyone in the custody of a claimant.[58] Another notable provision was the stipulation that anyone seized as a runaway was to be provided with advice by the commonwealth's district attorneys. The inspiration for this could well have been the 1850 Vermont law; Sumner included it, although Dana believed it would have "little practical effect."[59]

Joseph T. Buckingham was the man who introduced the bill into the state senate, which is a fact of some interest. Buckingham was the former editor of the Whig *Boston Courier*. During the late 1840s he had leaned toward support of the Conscience Whigs in their opposition to the expansion of slavery, but he had never been identified with abolitionism: in fact, he had supported the more conservative Winthrop against Charles Sumner in the election of 1846.[60] His background, then, would not lead one to expect him to assume the position of advocate for a bill that ran headlong up against the Fugitive Slave Law of 1850. That he did is an indication of the explosiveness of the new federal law, and of the fact that it helped sharpen the issue between slavery and freedom within the Union.

"All men owe absolute allegiance to the law of God," Buckingham said when he introduced the bill, "which is, in its nature, a universal rule of conduct for mankind. . . . It is . . . the *higher* law, and so the standard of all other laws."[61] "A secondary standard-measure of the laws made by the people" was the Constitution of the United States, which was a "particular rule of conduct." Insofar as a law was contrary to the law of God it was morally invalid, and not binding, and insofar as contrary to the Constitu-

[56]Dana, *Journal*, 2: 416.

[57]The bill is in Mass. *Senate Document No. 51, 1851*, 15–19; *Mass. Senate Journal, 1851*, Mass. State Library, 72: 315, 329.

[58]Provision was also made in the bill for punishing a false claim, whether intentionally made or not, by subjecting the guilty party to a $500 fine and 10 years in prison. Anyone making a claim, moreover, would be required "to establish the same by evidence."

[59]Dana, *Journal*, 2: 416.

[60]Brauer, *Cotton versus Conscience*, 196–97, 202.

[61]*Mass. Senate Document No. 51, 1851*, 8.

tion it was "constitutionally invalid and void." The Fugitive Slave Law was invalid on both counts.

Because the Constitution was normative it must be interpreted, and this was to be done by a reference to the preamble which included the object "to insure justice." On no account could the fugitive law be construed as insuring justice. That law, furthermore, was void because it conflicted with other express provisions of the organic law. It authorized "unreasonable searches and seizures," it took away the right to a trial by jury, and it authorized the appointment of commissioners to exercise the federal judicial power when they had no right to do so.

Buckingham had some difficulty with the fugitive slave clause which he admitted was "technically legal," although he believed it might not be morally binding. His answer to this problem had been developed by James Alvord in the late 1830s. The status of a fugitive could not be altered by free-state law, and if a claimant could gain control of his property he would have the right to remove the runaway. The free state, on the other hand, was not under an obligation to enact implementing legislation.

Along with this report Buckingham submitted a series of resolutions protesting the Fugitive Slave Law and slavery in general, and affirming the allegiance of the state to the Union. Any permanent union, however, had to be based on the "overthrow of slavery, so far as the same can be constitutionally done, everywhere within the jurisdiction of the national government." The free states, moreover, had to be relieved of all responsibility for the maintenance of the system.[62]

Consideration of the work of the Joint Special Committee was delayed for a time, and before it could be taken up the rendition of Thomas Sims occurred. In response to that rendition the state senate established a special committee to inquire into the whole affair, and this committee submitted a lengthy report, including testimony from participants, along with two bills on April 22, 1851. The members found that the cities' officers had acted in violation of the law of 1843, and the federal marshal, who had refused to honor the writ of personal replevin, they concluded had been ill-advised. "A desire to atone for the loss of Shadrach, seems to have outweighed all consideration for State rights, and State legislation."[63]

Because the mayor had called out the militia the committee felt that legislation should be passed to prohibit such actions in the future. One of the measures proposed would restrict the mayor's power to call on the militia to limited times.[64] The second bill extended the prohibition in the act of 1843 "to all persons holding any office created or existing under any statute of this Commonwealth."[65]

[62] *Ibid.*, 14.
[63] *Mass. Senate Document No. 89, 1851*, 6.
[64] *Ibid.*, 56.
[65] *Ibid.*, 57.

On April 26, 1851, Buckingham proposed to amend the bill he had earlier introduced from the Joint Special Committee; his substitute was substantially the second measure reported by the special senate committee dealing with the Sims affair. A new section went beyond the law of 1843: it prohibited any justice of the peace or state officer from acting as an agent or attorney for anyone making a claim to another human being.[66] His proposed amendments were adopted, but the amended bill then failed to receive a third reading.[67] The two bills reported by the special committee, which had been tabled,[68] were not taken up. The resolutions Buckingham had introduced, on the other hand, were amended and adopted. The most important amendment, however, emasculated them: Massachusetts claimed "no right, under the Federal Constitution, to nullify, disregard or forcibly resist the provisions of an act of Congress."[69]

Massachusetts's first encounters with the new federal law had thus produced three bills. The two reported by the special senate committee, on one hand, were in line with the act of 1843: they involved prohibitions on state officials only. Their object was to tighten the ring in the containment policy. Buckingham's original proposal, on the other hand, involved an attempt to nullify the federal law on the assumption that it violated the higher law of God and the positive mandates of the Constitution. His bill, even as amended (the amendments did not strike at the portion of the bill granting habeas corpus and jury trial), was a fair prelude of things to come by the middle of the decade. Many people in Massachusetts obviously did not feel bound by Shaw's judgment in the Sims case.

The next year a bill similar to the Vermont law of 1850 was passed by the senate.[70] Things did not go as smoothly in the house. On May 11, 1852, James W. Stone wrote to Charles Sumner explaining the situation in the Massachusetts lower chamber. Stone was pessimistic. He informed Sumner that some of the most prominent men believed the bill, which was up for consideration that day, would pass, but he did not. Of the eighteen who voted for the bill in the senate only one was a Whig. The Webster contingent of the party was not supporting the measure. "So that you see," Stone wrote, "it has but little chance."[71] His hopes might have raised a little later in the day because the bill, by a vote of 156 to 141, was ordered to a third reading. His prediction, however, had been correct. Four days later the house voted against engrossment.[72]

[66]*Mass. Senate Document No. 95, 1851*, 1.
[67]*Mass. Senate Journal, 1851*, Mass. State Library, 72: 618–19. The vote was thirteen to sixteen.
[68]*Ibid.*, 424.
[69]*Ibid.*, 502.
[70]*Mass. Senate Document No. 76, 1852*, 1; *Mass. Senate Journal, 1852*, Mass. State Library, 73: 635–36.
[71]James W. Stone to Charles Sumner, Boston, May 11, 1852, Sumner Papers, Houghton Library.
[72]*Mass. House Journal, 1852*, Mass. State Library, 74: 724, 750. The vote was 158 to 167.

The following year a struggle ensued in the state constitutional convention between procompromise and antislavery people over the issue of habeas corpus in fugitive cases. Richard Henry Dana, Jr. moved that the following proposition be submitted to the people as a part of the new constitution: "The writ of habeas corpus shall be granted as of right in all cases in which a discretion is not especially conferred upon the court by the Legislature; but the Legislature may prescribe forms of proceeding preliminary to the obtaining of the writ."[73] Dana argued that it was necessary to have this constitutional security because the courts had shown a disposition to assume the right of discretion in some cases. His proposal clearly was still another response to Shaw's refusal to grant the writ in Sims's case. According to Massachusetts law, Dana contended, the writ was to be issued to anyone restrained of his liberty: "Now, if that does take a slave out of the custody of his master, we cannot help it; it is the law, and it must be enforced when necessity arises."

Benjamin Hallett was the spokesman for the conservatives in this debate. According to him a judge had the right to decide, by existing law, whether he would issue the writ or not. His primary objection to Dana's proposal was that it would lead to a conflict between the federal and state authorities, in which the "whole state" would be arrayed on one hand against the "whole United States" on the other. Even though the state court could find the federal law valid, as Shaw had already done in the case of the fugitive law, the prospect of a conflict between the states and the national government on this issue appears to have persuaded a majority in this convention.[74] Dana's proposal was not adopted.

In the other states action also was being sought in response to the new federal law, but less forcefully than in Massachusetts.

In his message of January 15, 1852, to the legislature, Governor Leonard J. Farwell of Wisconsin urged the adoption of resolutions demanding a "radical modification" or an "entire repeal" of the law of 1850. Farwell did not demand nullification. He urged, in fact, an "obedience and subjection to this, as well as all other laws so long as they exist and are in force." Resistance to law, he believed, would tend to overthrow the government. Although not acted on by the legislature a select committee dealing with the governor's request reported a series of resolutions urging repeal, and while conceding the right of the slave states "to fully control, sustain, or abolish" the institution, it prayed that "the free states should, in no way, be made responsible for its existence and maintenance."[75]

---

[73]*Official Report of the Debates and Proceedings in the State Convention Assembled May 4th, 1853, to Revise and Amend the Constitution of the Commonwealth of Massachusetts* (3 vols.; Boston, 1853), 2: 751.

[74]For this debate see *ibid.*, 3: 474–82.

[75]"Report of the Select Committee to whom was referred so much of the Governor's Message as relates to the Fugitive Slave Act," *Wisc. Senate Journal, 1852*, Appendix, 314–17. The report criticized the fugitive law on the grounds that it denied jury trial and the writ of habeas corpus, created commissioners in the free states, and endangered free blacks.

The following year a select committee of the house reported a bill securing habeas corpus and jury trial to persons claimed as runaways. This was justified on the ground that the federal government had arrogated power to itself, making it necessary for the states to "rebuke" the central government. It was up to the states to be the sole judges of the manner of complying with the terms of the compact. Since the state constitution declared that all men were born free and equal the presumption in all such cases "must ever be in favor of the absolute liberty of every subject of the government." Wisconsin's constitution eliminated the right of recaption by guaranteeing all persons against unreasonable searches and seizures. It also provided that no man should be deprived of liberty without due process of law. Wisconsin, therefore, should pass the bill presented to "shield the inhabitants of our state from all inconvenience and injustice incident to the enforcement of the fugitive slave act."[76] There is little question that this bill was intended to nullify the federal law. It did not get beyond a second reading.[77] The *Milwaukee Sentinel* noted on April 4, 1853, that it was "up for a small fight in the House," but this did not materialize.[78] Following this aborted effort to obtain a Personal Liberty Law in Wisconsin the state slipped back into quiescence until the middle 1850s.

Antislavery people in New York were no more successful. At the beginning of 1851 Representative Edwin S. Coffin, a free soiler, introduced into that state's lower chamber a bill to prevent the arrest or removal of free citizens except for crimes. A free citizen was defined as anyone who lived openly in the state for more than one year. Anyone who seized such a person and attempted to remove him from the state would be subject to punishment, a punishment that could be avoided only if he could prove that the person seized did not have the right to come and reside in the state. No ex parte affidavit, certificate, or deposition would be accepted in evidence to prove the point. Trial on the issue would be by jury.[79] Coffin's bill was buried in the judiciary committee, but even if it had been passed there is no doubt that John Jay was right when he wrote that "notwithstanding the care exhibited by its framers, I think it will conflict" with the federal law.[80] After this effort failed, New York's legislature, like Wisconsin's, turned to other problems of more pressing moment.

In Ohio an important series of resolutions introduced by Milton Sutliff, then a state senator and later a state supreme-court judge, were adopted in the spring of 1851, but no new legislation was proposed. The resolutions declared the act of 1850 unconstitutional because Congress had no power

[76] *Wisc. House Journal, 1853*, 97, 719–22.
[77] *Ibid.*, 734.
[78] *Milwaukee Sentinel*, April 4, 1853.
[79] *New York Tribune*, January 1851. *New York House Journal, 1851*, 50, 58–59, 71.
[80] John Jay to Charles Sumner, New York, January 14, 1851, Charles Sumner Papers, Houghton Library.

to legislate on the subject, and because the act was "repugnant to the express provisions of the Constitution," particularly the due-process clause. His third resolution declared it to be the duty of the state courts to allow the writ of habeas corpus in cases involving runaways.[81] These resolutions would serve as guides to the state courts and, at least in Sutliff's view, reversed the restriction upon state habeas corpus practice that had been adopted in 1847; but, of course, they did not repeal the earlier state law which left the situation in Ohio somewhat murky. Still, they were a significant statement of the view of some of the state's legislators, if not its jurists. With the adoption of these resolutions came a hiatus (until the middle 1850s) in the discussion of the problem of fugitive slaves and free blacks in the Ohio legislature.

III

With the notable exceptions of the Vermont law and the resolutions of the Ohio legislature, the dominant legislative characteristic of the years from 1850 to 1853 was one of acceptance of the compromise measures. This was a powerful force in preventing any upset of the work of the Thirty-first Congress. The only significant action completed during this period in the states examined (with the exception of the Ohio resolutions) was the repeal of a portion of Pennsylvania's Personal Liberty Law. Efforts to enact more thoroughgoing laws were defeated in Massachusetts in 1851 and 1852, and in the constitutional convention of 1853 the attempt further to secure habeas corpus was also unsuccessful. Failure also marked the efforts in New York in 1851 and in Wisconsin in 1852–53. Nevertheless, these efforts are important indications that many people within the state legislatures were seriously agitated by the federal law of 1850. Together with all the turmoil that went on outside the halls of the state legislative bodies, they are strong evidence that the fugitive law of 1850 rested upon a fragile base of support in the North. Not everyone, as Ralph Waldo Emerson said in a May 1851 speech condemning the new law, was willing to accept the "railroad and telegraph" in lieu of "reason and charity."[82]

---

[81]*Speech of Mr. Sutliff of Trumbull, on the Resolutions Introduced by Him Relative to the Constitutional Powers of Congress, and the Fugitive Slave Bill* (Columbus, Ohio, 1851); William C. Cochran, "The Western Reserve and the Fugitive Slave Law," 107–8.

[82]Ralph Waldo Emerson, *The Complete Works of Ralph Waldo Emerson* (12 vols.; Boston, 1903–4), 11: 183.

Interposition, 10
1854–1858

On May 24, 1854, Anthony Burns, a runaway slave working in Boston, was seized by a deputy marshal and brought before his claimant. Richard Henry Dana, Jr., quickly arrived and prevented a speedy rendition by securing a delay from the United States commissioner, Edward G. Loring. In the days that followed Boston was rocked by violence (one man was killed in an unsuccessful assault on the courthouse where Burns was kept) as radical antislavery leaders incited the public with biting speeches condemning the seizure and the fugitive law. At the same time Dana worked vigorously to secure Burns's release on legal grounds—by the use of habeas corpus and replevin proceedings.[1]

Burns was remanded to slavery, but it was at an exorbitant price: the estimate has run as high as $100,000. He was, moreover, the last runaway taken out of Boston. The scene on the day Burns was returned in the custody of federal troops was sardonically described by Theodore Parker.

> The day was brilliant; there was not a cloud; all about Boston there was a ring of happy, summer loveliness; the green beauty of June; the grass, the trees, the heaven, the light; and Boston itself was the theatre of incipient civil war!
>
> What a day for Boston! Citizens applauding that a man was to be carried into bondage! Drunken soldiers, hardly able to stand in the street, sung their ribald song—"Oh! carry me back to old Virginia!"[2]

Radicals like Parker, of course, were enraged by the Burns case. "It is not *speeches* that we want," he declared, "but action; not rash, crazy action, but calm, deliberate, systematic action—organization for the defence of personal liberty and the State Rights of the North." He wanted moreover "new and stringent laws for the defence of personal liberty, for punishing all who invade it on our soil."[3]

Radical abolitionists, however, were not the only people in Massachusetts who deeply resented the seizure and rendition of Anthony Burns. Parker doubtless overestimated the extent to which the public supported the federal law in the spring of 1854. Sentiment in the state at that time

[1]Samuel Shapiro, "The Rendition of Anthony Burns," *The Journal of Negro History*, 44 (Jan., 1959): 34–51.

[2]Theodore Parker, *The New Crime Against Humanity. A Sermon Preached at the Music Hall, in Boston, on Sunday, June 4, 1854* (Boston, 1854), 60.

[3]*Ibid.*, 72.

was seen quite differently by the anonymous author of the *Observations on the Rev. Dr. Gannett's Sermon, entitled "Relation of the North to Slavery."* He observed mounting evidence that there now existed a "strong disposition here in Massachusetts, to treat the government of the United States, at least in regard to one of its functions, as if it were a foreign power, whose authority over us we may and ought to bring to the test of actual resistance." The author of these observations was frightened thoroughly by this disposition; his counsel was obedience to the law.[4] Submission of the majority to the law however was no longer very sure. Even before Burns was returned to slavery a petition calling for a repeal of the Fugitive Slave Law had been circulated around the Merchant's Exchange. This petition was signed by conservatives who had volunteered to assist in the return of Thomas Sims only three years before.[5]

The major reason for this about-face in Boston in 1854 (and elsewhere in the free states) was Stephen A. Douglas's Kansas-Nebraska bill, which reopened the slavery issue in an abrupt and inflammatory way. Douglas was aware that opening territory closed to slavery for thirty-four years (by repealing the Missouri Compromise) would "raise a hell of a storm."[6]

At the time the bill was being debated in the United States Senate, ten free-state legislatures were in session, and several passed resolutions condemning the Kansas-Nebraska bill. What must have startled Douglas even more was the fact that Democratic-controlled states like Pennsylvania maintained an icy silence. Only one free state passed resolutions endorsing the bill, Douglas's home state of Illinois.[7]

The bill was condemned almost universally in Boston. Many leading Whigs, such as Samuel Eliot and Robert C. Winthrop (one had voted for, and the other against, the Fugitive Slave Law), had accepted the Compromise of 1850, but they now retracted. Amos Lawrence, a staunch Cotton Whig, warned that if the territories were thrown open to slavery the fugitive law would become a dead letter in the North.[8] Lysander Spooner noted this change in sentiment when he wrote to George Bradburn in June, 1854: "there has been a great movement in hunkerdom in favor of liberty, caused by the Burns case and Nebraska—I think some of it will *last*."[9]

---

[4]*Observations on the Rev. Dr. Gannett's Sermon, entitled "Relation of the North to Slavery"* (Boston, 1854), 28. On the other side see James Freeman Clarke, *The Rendition of Anthony Burns. Its Causes and Consequences. A Discourse on Christian Politics, Delivered in Williams Hall, Boston, on Whitsunday, June 4, 1854* (Boston, 1854); and, William I. Bowditch, *The Rendition of Anthony Burns* (Boston, 1854).

[5]Shapiro, "The Rendition of Anthony Burns," 37.

[6]George Fort Milton, *The Eve of Conflict: Stephen A. Douglas and the Needless War* (Boston and New York, 1934), 114.

[7]Nevins, *Ordeal of the Union*, 2: 146.

[8]Shapiro, "The Rendition of Anthony Burns," 34–35.

[9]Lysander Spooner to George Bradburn, Boston, June 21, 1854, Lysander Spooner Papers, New-York Historical Society.

Some of it did last, for a time at least. And when it began to fade a sharp struggle ensued between conservatives and radicals on this issue in nearly all the free states. In the wake of the Burns case, and more particularly, the Kansas-Nebraska bill, three New England states besides Massachusetts (Connecticut, Rhode Island, and Maine), and one midwestern state (Michigan) adopted Personal Liberty Laws. Three years later the U.S. Supreme Court provoked a further wave of legislation when it endorsed the proslavery constitutional doctrine on the territorial question in the case of *Dred Scott* v. *Sandford*.[10] After this decision many of the same states noted above, as well as others such as Ohio, either adopted still further legislation, or considered it.

The various laws passed in these years usually secured alleged fugitives the right to a writ of habeas corpus and to jury trial. They often prescribed punishments for kidnapping and provided legal counsel for persons seized as runaways (the inability of blacks to employ counsel independently was now widely recognized). They usually contained prohibitions on state officials, moreover. Massachusetts, Wisconsin, and Ohio all adopted new Personal Liberty Laws in the years from 1854 to 1858. One was introduced unsuccessfully in New York, while Pennsylvania alone (under firm Democratic control) of all these states failed even to consider a bill in these years. What northern "acquiescence" there was in the Compromise of 1850 was waning fast after 1854.

I

The first of the states here studied to act in a dramatic way in response to the changes wrought after Douglas's Kansas-Nebraska bill was Massachusetts. At the beginning of January, 1855, Governor Henry Gardner, a member of the newly formed, nativist Know-Nothing party, commended to the legislature the question of whether or not additional legislation was needed to secure the writ of habeas corpus and trial by jury to the citizens of the state. He cautioned the legislators to "scrupulously avoid such action as asserts or looks to the maintenance of any rights not clearly and constitutionally ours." He then added, "But weave every safeguard you justly may round these primal birthrights, older than our national birthday, and dear as its continued existence."[11]

The moment was propitious, and most of the members of the Know-Nothing legislature needed little coaxing from the governor. As early as January 13, 1855, James W. Stone informed Sumner that "never did we have such an opportunity as this."[12]

---

[10]On this case see, in particular, Bestor, "State Sovereignty and Slavery," *passim*.

[11]*The Liberator*, January 12, 1855.

[12]James W. Stone to Charles Sumner, Boston, January 13, 1855, Charles Sumner Papers, Houghton Library.

Legislative hearings were held during February, and on April 25, 1855, the Joint Standing Committee on Federal Relations reported a bill to the senate. This committee "scrupulously" followed the governor's advice: it moved about within the interstices of the Prigg decision, which it accepted as binding, to draft a bill that did not transgress the legitimate bounds of state power. Justice McLean's opinion was cited to demonstrate that free blacks might be seized and that the state had the right and the duty to protect them. Justice Story, moreover, had admitted that the police power of the state extended over all subjects within the territorial limits of the states, and had never been conceded to the United States. The committee believed that this allowed state legislation to protect citizens (and all persons were presumptively citizens) against the "misconduct and depredations" of slaveholders. The members did not discuss Story's view that any delay in the recovery *pro tanto* operated as a discharge and was thus unconstitutional, but they got around this by a distinction that Story had blurred. The personal liberty bill in question was framed to protect free blacks and was not constructed in its terms to throw up obstructions to lawful claims.[13]

On May 14, 1855, the senate passed the bill by an overwhelming margin.[14] When it was passed by the house five days later,[15] the bill had undergone certain changes. The senate agreed to these various house amendments, and the bill was sent up to Governor Gardner for his signature.[16]

This act of 1855 consisted of twenty-three sections and was, without a doubt, the most involved Personal Liberty Law ever passed. It fully reflected the public's increasing awareness of the problems confronting black people in the face of the federal law. Among the most important prohibitions were those forbidding anyone from acting as counsel for a slave claimant, and any state officer from issuing a warrant or process under the fugitive law. At the same time special commissioners would be appointed to defend a person claimed as a fugitive. An antikidnapping section also was included that provided for a fine of up to five thousand dollars and imprisonment for up to five years for those guilty of seizing someone who did not owe service or labor to the party making the claim.

More affirmatively, every person restrained of liberty was guaranteed the right to the writ of habeas corpus. The writ could be issued by any number of officials and was to be returnable to the Supreme Judicial Court, or any one of its justices. The court or justice, on application of either party, would order a jury trial if it appeared on the return that the person was restrained on a claim that he was a runaway slave. At the trial the jury had the right to give a general verdict on a plea of not guilty, "and

[13] *Mass. Senate Document No. 162, 1855.*
[14] *Mass. Senate Journal, 1855,* Mass. State Library, 76: 801.
[15] *Mass. House Journal, 1855,* Mass. State Library, 77: 1710.
[16] The bill as introduced in the senate is in *Mass. Senate Document No. 162, 1855,* 13–21. For the law as passed see *Mass. Session Laws, 1855,* 295–99.

the finding of a verdict of not guilty shall be final and conclusive." As in New York, a state habeas corpus was now a means to obtain a jury trial, although it was not, as in that state, a process to aid claimants to recover their property. The "community sense of justice," moreover, as taken in the jury trial, could not be diluted because the verdict was nonreviewable.

The sixth section of the new law, concerning the evidence to be admitted at the trial, marked a significant advance over the earlier Personal Liberty Laws. A claimant was required to state in writing the facts "on which he relies, with precision and certainty; and neither the claimant of the alleged fugitive, nor any person interested in his alleged obligation to service or labor, nor the alleged fugitive, shall be permitted to testify at the trial of the issue." The claimant, furthermore, bore the burden of proof upon every question of fact, and he had to substantiate his "facts" by the testimony of "at least two credible witnesses." No ex parte depositions or affidavits would be admissible as evidence on behalf of the claimant (the same restriction did not apply to the person claimed).

For the first time, moreover, a state faced directly a problem that doubtless had always been a serious one for blacks claimed as fugitives: self-incrimination. Not even the thoroughgoing abolitionist reformers had ever paid much attention to this problem, but the Massachusetts legislature now did: "no confessions, admissions or declarations of the alleged fugitive against himself shall be given in evidence." This was an important recognition that the traditional privilege against self-incrimination, like the right to counsel, required special action in the case of persons who might be claimed as slaves, persons who might confess to anything in the dismaying and terrifying atmosphere of a jail cell or a courtroom.

No cases arose under the Massachusetts law of 1855, and it is not difficult to understand why. It was a self-operative measure. The stringency of the sixth section alone would preclude all but the most hardy slave owner from bothering to prosecute his claim in the face of a competing claim to freedom.[17] Still, at law, the possibility of a fugitive being returned existed, even though it would be difficult to accomplish. The state was clearly obstructing the operation of the federal law of 1850, but it did not openly repudiate the constitutional obligation not to divest owners of their legitimate titles to their property.

On May 21, 1855, Governor Gardner gave his veto message to the legislature. He had submitted the bill to the justices of the Supreme Judicial Court, and to John H. Clifford, the state's attorney-general, for their opinions. All concurred that the law was unconstitutional because, in the American system, neither the state nor the federal government could rightfully defeat a lawful custody of a person when the other government had acquired a "priority of jurisdiction." When someone was held under fed-

[17] Mass. Session Laws, 1855, 295-99.

eral process the state could not interpose its power to arrest the procedure. The same would not be true necessarily if someone was merely in the custody of a claimant, but the Massachusetts law was not limited in its terms to such situations. Citing this advisory opinion Gardner argued that the proposed law would lead the state "into a position hostile to the harmony of the confederacy," and might even lead "to an armed conflict between our state and national systems of government."[18]

Massachusetts' Know-Nothing legislators, however, were of a different mind. The two-thirds necessary to override the governor's veto were found in both houses, and the "Act to protect the Rights and Liberties of the People of the Commonwealth of Massachusetts" became law on May 21, 1855.

Although they helped create an atmosphere conducive to its passage, conservatives now drew back in horror. "Never before was this State so deeply disgraced. Shame on Treason! Shame on the traitors to American liberty!" This was the editorial comment in the *Boston Post*.[19]

Two of the Cotton Whig papers were particularly indignant. The *Boston Atlas* placed the blame on Gardner for encouraging such a movement in the first place. "The legislature, composed of members of his party, elected under his banner, and in part through his influence and vote, has rushed into what he considers to be wild and reckless fanaticism, if not flat, unmitigated treason."[20] The *Boston Daily Advertiser* considered the law completely invalid since it conflicted with a law passed in pursuance of the Constitution of the United States, and the latter was the supreme law of the land. The pertinacity of the legislators in passing such a bill was an "idle piece of folly."[21]

Reactions among conservative circles outside Massachusetts were generally similar to that of the *New York Journal of Commerce*. It declared the state had taken a step that would lead to a disruption of the Union and, this paper added, without South Carolina's justification, since that state had attempted to nullify something "that was unconstitutional."[22]

A qualified praise came from *The Liberator*. "The Legislature passed a Personal Liberty Bill, in entire accordance with the principles of justice and humanity," Garrison commented, "as far as it goes." The law, he believed, should have gone further to forbid "the slave-hunter to seize and remove his prey" altogether.[23] He was dissatisfied with the law because it did not represent completely the thoroughgoing abolitionist position: it was, rather, an effort to embed the ethical judgments of the legislators in a

[18] *The Liberator*, May 25, 1855.
[19] *Boston Post*, quoted in *The Liberator*, June 1, 1855.
[20] *Boston Atlas*, May 22, 1855.
[21] *Boston Daily Advertiser*, May 22, 1855.
[22] *New York Journal of Commerce*, quoted in *The Liberator*, June 1, 1855.
[23] *The Liberator*, June 1, 1855.

law that met the clear injunction of the Constitution not to divest owners of their titles to runaways.

During the next two years this law became the object of attack by those who feared that it might seriously endanger the Union. At the beginning of the 1856 session of the General Court, Governor Gardner reiterated his objections to the measure and urged the legislature to reconsider the act. On January 18, 1856, Representative H. F. Thomas introduced the first of many bills calling for an entire repeal of the 1855 law.[24] Moderates countered with a proposal to repeal only certain sections. In April Representative Henry Shaw Briggs,[25] the son of the former Whig governor of the state George N. Briggs, reported a bill out of a joint special committee that provided for the repeal of the sections containing prohibitions on action by state functionaries: included were those prohibiting anyone from acting as counsel for a slave claimant, and any state officer from issuing a warrant or process under the fugitive law.

The Briggs bill, however, did not go far enough for some members of the house. Representative Elias Merwin of Boston, for example, declared that "if we are to resist the aggressions of the slave power successfully; if we are to make Kanzas [sic] free; we must have something better to work with than the rotten and flimsy material of State nullification."[26] Perhaps spurred on by such sentiments the house agreed to repeal the law of 1855 completely.[27] Before the final vote on engrossment, however, those who wished to save something of the law succeeded in replacing the repeal measure with the Briggs bill, with amendments.[28] This proposal, however, was indefinitely postponed in the state senate.[29]

Additional skirmishing occurred in the following legislative session,[30] but it was during the meeting of 1858 that the fight over the 1855 law broke out in earnest. The struggle was also manifested in that session when the antislavery legislators moved against Edward G. Loring, the state judge who had served as United States commissioner in the Burns case. By an almost two-to-one margin in both upper and lower chambers Loring was removed from the Suffolk County bench for his part in the affair.[31]

[24] *Debates and Proceedings in the Massachusetts Legislature, At the Session which was begun at the State House in Boston, on Wednesday the second day of January, and was prorogued on Friday, the sixth day of June, 1856* (Boston, 1856), 20–21.

[25] *Appleton's,* 1: 375; Izra J. Warner, *Generals in Blue: Lives of the Union Commanders* (Baton Rouge, 1964), 44.

[26] *Debates and Proceedings,* 320.

[27] *Ibid.,* 318–19.

[28] *Ibid.,* 336–38.

[29] *Ibid.,* 343.

[30] *Mass. House Journal, 1857,* 70, 514–15, 543, 780, 811, 814; *Mass. Senate Journal, 1857,* Mass. State Library, 77: 78, 539, 549, 749.

[31] Lader, *The Bold Brahmins,* 216; Allan Nevins, *The Emergence of Lincoln* (2 vols.; New York, 1951), 2: 30: Claude M. Fuess, *The Life of Caleb Cushing* (2 vols.; Hamden, Conn., 1965), 2: 211 ff.

Despite this victory the law of 1855 was not kept intact. Conservative, prosouthern forces in the legislature, led by Caleb Cushing who had returned to the Massachusetts house after his tenure as attorney general of the United States under Pierce, demanded an entire repeal of the "unconstitutional" Personal Liberty Law.[32] They were only able, however, to obtain 34 votes for repeal, as opposed to 122 against it.[33] On the other side, those anxious to reconcile the law of the state and their constitutional scruples, or mindful that some provisions of the law were "ungracious," were willing to support modification. This position was strong enough to secure passage of a bill repealing certain portions of the 1855 law, substantially the same ones covered by the Briggs bill two years before.[34] Left intact were the significant portions securing personal freedom: those guaranteeing habeas corpus, jury trial, and state counsel for persons seized as slaves.

Growing out of the furor raised over the Kansas-Nebraska bill and the spectacular Burns rendition, then, Massachusetts had adopted one of the most complete Personal Liberty Laws ever to appear on the statute books of the free states. Some of the provisions, of course, were of arguable constitutionality. And when the "movement in hunkerdom in favor of liberty" began to recede, this law became a focal point in the struggle to define the posture of the state in relation to slavery. Prosouthern conservatives, such as Caleb Cushing, struck back in an effort to obtain a total repeal, whereas moderates were willing to eliminate a few sections of the law, but not at the expense of the core of the measure which secured orderly procedures for testing claims to freedom. In 1858 the view of the moderates prevailed.

II

In March, 1854, shortly before the capture and return of Anthony Burns in Boston, a runaway named Joshua Glover was seized in a cabin on the outskirts of Racine, Wisconsin, where he had been playing cards with two black companions.[35] Glover, who had been clubbed, was taken to Milwaukee by his claimant and a United States deputy marshal, where he was placed in the county jail. Chauncey C. Olin, an associate of Sherman M.

---

[32]Fuess, *Cushing*, 2: 214–215.

[33]*Mass. House Journal, 1858*, Mass. State Library, 80: 521. For other proceedings on the Personal Liberty Law see *ibid.*, 80: 56, 66, 130, 270, 383–84, 403, 455, 494, 518, 528, 535–53; *Mass. Senate Journal, 1858*, Mass. State Library, 79: 506, 527, 545–46, 583. See also, *Mass. Senate Document No. 86, 1858*.

[34]*Mass. Session Laws, 1858*, 151.

[35]There are numerous accounts of this case. See, for example, Joseph Schafer, "Stormy Days in Court—The Booth Case," *Wisconsin Magazine of History* (1936), 20: 89–110; V. Mason, "The Fugitive Slave Law in Wisconsin," 117–44; A. M. Thomson, *A Political History of Wisconsin* (Milwaukee, 1902), 96–109; Haines and Sherwood, *The Role of the Supreme Court, 1835–1864*; 224–42; Bestor, "State Sovereignty and Slavery," 138–42. An account by a contemporary is Olin, "A History of the early Anti-Slavery excitement."

Booth, the antislavery editor who became involved, related that when the latter heard the fugitive was in custody "all bruised and bloody and had marks of the most inhuman and brutal treatment," he rode furiously about the streets yelling "to the rescue" at the top of his voice.[36] Because he was the most conspicuous member of the movement to free Glover, Booth was arrested by United States Marshal Stephan V. R. Ableman for a violation of the federal statute. The United States commissioner found sufficient evidence to have Booth held for trial and had him placed in a local jail.

At the end of May, 1854, before the trial, Booth applied to Associate Justice A. D. Smith of the Wisconsin Supreme Court for a writ of habeas corpus. The petition for the writ charged, among other things, that the Fugitive Slave Law, under which the arrest warrant had been issued, was unconstitutional and void. Justice Smith, unlike Justice Shaw of Massachusetts, did not hesitate to issue the writ.

On the return of the writ Booth was represented by Byron Paine. In an argument that won the plaudits of antislavery people such as Charles Sumner and Wendell Phillips,[37] Paine mercilessly dissected the decisions of previous courts, particularly the Supreme Court's judgment in *Prigg* v. *Pennsylvania*. No power over fugitives was given to the central government, he argued. Anyone who contended for such a right had to "pretend" that the phrase "shall be delivered up" was addressed to the national government.[38] It was a matter solely within the purview of the states. He concluded his extensive argument, based in large measure on Robert Rantoul, Jr.'s in the case of Thomas Sims, with a fiery exhortation to the court:

> The freemen of the North who have long reposed in conscious strength, with a generous forbearance towards the wrongs and insults of their deadly foe, have at last become aroused by provocations that could not be borne. They are marshaling their hosts for the coming conflict, between the two great antagonistical elements, liberty and slavery, that is to settle which shall finally fall before the other.—The trampling of the gathering hosts is already heard,—the murmuring of the rising storm is wafted upon every gale. The North is snapping asunder the bands that have bound it in subjection to the slave power, as Sampson broke the withs of tow! The last link that binds it, is the judicial sanction that power has received! Let that be broken, and the people are free! . . . Can we not have one decision in all this land, that shall vindicate liberty and law?[39]

On May 22, 1854, Justice Smith freed Booth on the ground that the federal law was unconstitutional. His principal basis for this judgment was that

[36]Olin, "A History of the early Anti-Slavery excitement," 4.

[37]Charles Sumner to Byron Paine, Washington, August 8, 1854, Byron Paine Papers, State Historical Society of Wisconsin; Wendell Phillips to Byron Paine, November 29 (no year given), *ibid.*

[38]*Argument of Byron Paine*, 15.

[39]*Ibid.*, 23.

the law provided for the trial of "a constitutional issue by officers having no recognized authority to do so." The federal law, moreover, violated the due process provisions of the U.S. Constitution.[40] An unconstitutional law, being void, could confer no authority to imprison a man for its violation, he concluded.

Smith's decision on the habeas corpus has been sharply criticized by many later commentators.[41] It bears repeating, however, that in the 1850s the question of the powers conferred on state courts by habeas corpus jurisdiction in relation to federal power was unsettled and very controversial. Rollin C. Hurd's judgment, it will be recalled, was that a state court could discharge a person if his detention was illegal, even though that determination could involve "questions of the constitutionality of acts of Congress, or of the jurisdiction of a court of the United States." Because of the complete proslavery victory in 1850 this question was being thrust onto center stage in the controversy over the rights and powers of the states in relation to blacks within their jurisdictions who might be claimed as runaways.

At the request of the federal marshal the proceedings before Justice Smith were examined by the full membership of the state supreme court, and Smith's decision was affirmed on July 19, 1854.[42] From this judgment the marshal appealed to the U.S. Supreme Court. Booth was rearrested (January, 1855) and tried in the United States district court while this appeal was pending. Again Booth appealed to the Wisconsin Supreme Court for a habeas corpus to obtain his release from imprisonment by virtue of an unconstitutional law. While the appeal from the first judgment was pending in the U.S. Supreme Court, the Wisconsin Supreme Court again released Booth. On February 3, 1855, Justice Crawford of the state court declared that a state was empowered to free its citizens from illegal confinement, for without this power "the state would be stripped of one of the most essential attributes of sovereignty, and would present the spectacle of a state claiming the allegiance of its citizens, without the power to protect them in the enjoyment of their personal liberty upon its own soil."[43] This second case was also appealed to the U.S. Supreme Court.

Caleb Cushing, at that time the U.S. attorney general, applied for a writ of error before the U.S. Supreme Court in April, 1855. It was granted, and made returnable in December of that year. Before the disposition of

[40] *In re Sherman Booth*, 3 Wisconsin 1.

[41] Warren, *The Supreme Court*, 2: 533 said, for example, that Smith's decision was "an extraordinary interference of a State judge with a federal marshal's custody." Horace H. Hagan, "Ableman vs. Booth," *American Bar Association Journal* (January, 1931), 20, was the most caustic: "How chaos was to be prevented under such a system, one state expanding, another restricting the powers of the Federal Government the learned jurist did not pause to point out."

[42] *In re Sherman M. Booth*, 3 Wisconsin 67.

[43] *In re Booth and Rycraft*, 3 Wisconsin 144.176.

the writ by the Wisconsin court was known antislavery people moved to have all the questions at issue receive a full hearing in Washington. At the beginning of 1855 Sherman Booth wrote to Charles Sumner asking him to join in arguing the case "in behalf of liberty." Booth's friends suggested that Sumner, and perhaps Salmon P. Chase, could present a powerful argument. "It were well," Sumner later wrote Byron Paine, Booth's attorney, "that the self-defensive power of the States should be recognized."[44] This effort however was cut off when the Wisconsin court during May, 1855, began to throw up barriers to the jurisdiction of the U.S. Supreme Court. The state court directed its clerk to make no return to the writ of error. He had, however, already given a certified copy of the record to the district attorney. On March 6, 1857, the federal court granted the motion of the U.S. attorney general to file the copy of the record received from the clerk, despite the order of the state court.[45]

At the same time that Booth was working to prepare a defense of liberty before the Supreme Court, antislavery legislators were moving in the state assembly to "divest ourselves from responsibility or accountability, for the evils or curses of an institution, abhorrent to every moral sense."[46] Since the state supreme court had declared the fugitive law unconstitutional, the majority of the judiciary committee could see no reason for allowing the use of the state jails to imprison a man convicted under that law. Accordingly, they introduced a personal liberty bill to prohibit the use of the state jails. The bill easily passed the house, but was defeated in the senate.[47]

Two years later, the Wisconsin legislature successfully moved to affirm the position taken by the state court. On February 6, 1857, a personal liberty bill was introduced in the senate.[48] The purpose behind this bill, and its relationship to the Booth cases, was clear from the start. An amendment offered in the senate stipulating that state judges would be bound by the federal acts of 1793 and 1850 "notwithstanding the provisions of this act" was voted down by a two-to-one margin.[49] By the same vote the bill was promptly adopted. An amendment was accepted in the lower house, in addition, which allowed that the state would pay all costs incurred by anyone prosecuted under the Fugitive Slave Act.[50] One Republican "urged immediate action, inasmuch as there was a case existing to which it was desirable to have the bill apply."[51] The senate, however, refused to accept this amendment.[52]

[44]Sherman M. Booth to Charles Sumner, Milwaukee, February 21, 1855, Miscellaneous Manuscripts, State Historical Society of Wisconsin; Charles Sumner to Byron Paine, January 18, 1856, Byron Paine Papers, State Historical Society of Wisconsin.

[45]*Ableman* v. *Booth*, 62 U.S. 172.

[46]*Wisc. House Journal, 1855*, 755. This is from the report of the house judiciary committee.

[47]*Ibid.*, 831–33, 845–46, 1034.

[48]*Wisc. Senate Journal, 1857*, 165–66.

[49]*Ibid.*, 241–42.

[50]*Wisc. House Journal, 1857*, 456.

[51]*Milwaukee Sentinel*, February 19, 1857.

[52]*Wisc. Senate Journal, 1857*, 296.

One final effort was made in the assembly to defeat the bill. A motion was made that everything after the enacting clause be stricken and one section added. The addition declared that the fugitive act of 1850 was "a constitutional and valid public act." This was amended with the words: "and the decision and judgment of the Supreme Court of this State upon the said Fugitive Slave Law is hereby repealed." This extraordinary effort of the Democrats to "repeal" a judicial ruling was soundly crushed.[53] On February 19, 1857, the bill was signed into law by the governor. Four days later Moses Strong made a futile effort to amend a bill to vacate streets in Milwaukee by a substitute declaring the repeal of the new Personal Liberty Law.[54]

As passed the bill was entitled "Of the Writ of Habeas Corpus Relative to Fugitive Slaves." It was substantially the same as the Massachusetts law of 1855 in that it provided counsel for anyone claimed as a runaway, guaranteed the right to the writ of habeas corpus and to a jury trial, and punished kidnapping. The final section of this act, however, was peculiar to Wisconsin and was in effect a variation on the amendment rejected by the senate. That amendment had directed the state to pay all costs involved in prosecutions under the Fugitive Slave Law. The final section of the bill prohibited the sale of any real estate or personal property in the state to enforce a judgment obtained under the federal law. The defendant in such a case was authorized to prosecute an action in order to secure possession of his property.[55]

The *Milwaukee Sentinel*, a Republican sheet, noted that the new law "holds up the shield of State Sovereignty to protect citizens of Wisconsin from the aggressions of the Slave Power."[56] The *Daily Wisconsin* viewed the bill primarily as an aid to Booth: "We shall now have an opportunity to see what effect the new act of the Legislature will produce on the U.S. officers. It is a clear conflict of jurisdiction."[57] Toward the end of the month the *Daily Argus and Democrat*, without editorial comment, printed the remarks of F. W. Horn, a Democrat in the assembly. Horn thought the most charitable interpretation of the action of the Republicans was to view the bill as an attempt to protect free blacks. He believed, however, "in my inmost soul that this law is passed to keep every run away nigger in this State away from his lawful owner."[58]

It was just over a week later that the U.S. Supreme Court granted the attorney general's motion to file a copy of the record submitted by the clerk

[53] *Wisc. House Journal, 1857*, 459.

[54] *Ibid.*, 561.

[55] *The Revised Statutes of the State of Wisconsin* (Madison, 1858), 912-14. Two copies of the bill are in the state archives. One is marked enrolled, and the other engrossed. A separate sheet of paper is attached to the latter, with this final clause written on it in pencil. State Historical Society of Wisconsin. Archives Division. The journals do not reveal when this amendment was introduced, or passed.

[56] *Milwaukee Sentinel*, February 21, 1857.

[57] *Daily Wisconsin*, February 21, 1857.

[58] *Daily Argus and Democrat*, February 26, 1857.

of the Wisconsin Supreme Court. On the same day it handed down its epochal decision in *Dred Scott* v. *Sandford*. In the aftermath of that decision, and before judgment was rendered in the case of *Ableman* v. *Booth*, the territorial crisis in Kansas reached a climax in the struggle in Congress over the proslavery Lecompton constitution, which produced a definitive split in the Democratic party when Douglas broke with Buchanan in February, 1858.[59] The future of Kansas was resolved by delaying its admission into the Union until its population had grown enough to entitle it to one representative, but the split within the Democracy could not be mended so easily. It was, in fact, widened during the Lincoln-Douglas debates (August–October, 1858), when constitutional issues were given a sharp formulation in the public mind, and Douglas clearly committed himself to a position on the territories unacceptable to the southern wing of the party.

These issues were fresh in the public mind when Jeremiah S. Black of Pennsylvania, attorney general of the United States, presented the argument for the federal government in the case of *Ableman* v. *Booth* in the Supreme Court on January 19, 1859. Black sought to establish six points: (1) judges of a state court were bound to make some return to a writ of error, and if they refused they could be punished "as for a contempt"; (2) the federal law of 1850 was constitutional; (3) the judgment of a federal court "conclusively settles and determines" all "questions of constitutional law or statutory construction and of pleading" in cases involving offenders against a law of the United States; (4) no state court could free a man on habeas corpus when he was held by a federal court of exclusive jurisdiction; (5) federal officers were bound to disregard the attempt of a state court to "take a criminal out of the hands of a federal court which has jurisdiction"; (6) if a state court "lawlessly" obstructed the administration of criminal justice in a federal court that court was bound to protect its officers.[60] No one appeared for the state of Wisconsin or for Sherman M. Booth.

The brief, unanimous decision of the Court was handed down on March 7, 1859, almost two years to the day from its judgment in the Dred Scott case. Speaking for the Court, Chief Justice Taney began with a loose formulation of the position of Wisconsin's court. He rejected what he called the asserted "supremacy of the state courts over the courts of the United States."[61] What the state supreme court had actually said was that the state must have the power to protect its citizens on its soil from imprisonment by virtue of an unconstitutional law. It did not claim a general supervisory power over all cases arising under the federal Constitution even when no issue of personal liberty was involved. The supremacy "conferred" on the federal government, Taney proceeded, "could not peacefully be

[59]Milton, *Eve of Conflict*, chap. 17.
[60]*Ableman* v. *Booth*, 62 U.S., 170.
[61]*Ibid.*, 173.

maintained unless it was clothed with judicial power equally paramount in authority to carry it into execution; for if left to the courts of justice of the several States, conflicting decisions would unavoidably take place, and the local tribunals could hardly be expected to be always free from local influences."

He did not deny that the state courts could use habeas corpus to inquire into any imprisonment, however. But once apprised of the fact that the person in question was held by federal authority, neither habeas corpus "nor any other process issued under state authority, can pass over the line of division between the two sovereignties." Although it was unnecessary to examine the question of the constitutionality of the federal law, Taney declared that it was "in all of its provisions, fully authorized by the Constitution of the United States."[62]

As Charles Warren saw it Taney's opinion was "the most powerful of all his notable opinions." It was a decision upholding national supremacy without regard for the effect it might have on the slavery issue.[63] Arthur Bestor, on the other hand, has contended that the case did not uphold federal supremacy in an inclusive sense, only the federal judicial supremacy. At that time this meant the reverse of the "supremacy of national policy over local or sectional policy."[64] Taney had said that the federal courts had the responsibility to declare congressional acts unconstitutional if they were in violation of the clear provisions of the Constitution. This meant, as *Dred Scott* v. *Sandford* had shown, that the federal judiciary would "give effect, extraterritorially, to the legal principles developed by slave states in connection with the peculiar kind of property they alone possessed and were competent to legislate about." Federal judicial supremacy meant "enforcing the extraterritorial principles deduced from state sovereignty."

Taney's judgment, at any rate, had vitiated one of the most potent state procedures for the protection of personal liberty. The Personal Liberty Laws received a staggering blow when the Court found that states did not have the power to conduct an inquiry into confinements under federal authority. The Court had rejected the contention that the states could free federal prisoners by habeas corpus even though it would involve an examination into the constitutionality of the federal law. *Ableman* v. *Booth* all but completed the process begun in *Prigg* v. *Pennsylvania* of undermining state security for personal freedom. A year after the decision in the Booth case Senator Benjamin Wade of Ohio posed the question cited at the beginning of this study: "Cannot a sovereign State of this Union prevent the kidnapping of her free citizens because you have a right to claim a slave fleeing from Service?"[65] The decision in the case of Sherman M. Booth had already provided the answer: a sovereign state was severely restricted

[62]*Ibid.*, 177.
[63]Warren, *The Supreme Court*, 2: 336–37; Lewis, *Without Fear or Favor*, 439.
[64]Bestor, "State Sovereignty and Slavery," 25 ff.
[65]*Cong. Globe*, 36th Cong., 1st sess., March 7, 1860, Appendix, 152.

in what it could do to protect its citizens precisely because slave owners had the right to reclaim runaways.

Following the Court's decision the Wisconsin legislature lashed back in a set of bold resolutions. They declared the assumption of jurisdiction by the Court was "an arbitrary act of power, unauthorized by the Constitution, and virtually superceding the benefit of the writ of habeas corpus, and prostrating the rights and liberties of the people, at the foot of unlimited power." They concluded that "the several states which formed that instrument being sovereign and independent, have the unquestionable right to judge of its infraction, and that a *positive defiance* by those sovereignties of all unauthorized acts done, or attempted to be done, under color of that instrument is the right remedy."[66] Here Wisconsin's legislators borrowed the exact words of the Kentucky Resolutions of 1799,[67] except they substituted the phrase "positive defiance" for "nullification." At the same time the people of the state elected Byron Paine, Booth's counsel, as a member of the supreme court. Charles Sumner, in congratulating Paine, wrote an exultant letter on May 12, 1859, in which he declared that a "new order of things in our country" would be forthcoming. "Trial by Jury, *habeas corpus*, and the other safeguards of the rights of all—struck down by the preposterous and tyrannical pretensions of slavery under the National Constitution,—will again become realities."[68]

III

The response of Ohio to the mounting sectional crisis, for the moment, was conditioned by its longstanding policy of accommodation and conciliation on the matter of runaways, as well as by the fear of an explosive conflict between state and federal jurisdictions. The state did, however, adopt new laws in the wake of the decision in Dred Scott's case, and it did consider new measures even before that. In 1854 a bill was introduced in response to the Kansas-Nebraska Act and the excitement it engendered, but it was buried in the judiciary committee of the state senate.[69]

At the beginning of 1856 a spectacular, bloody attempt to recover a runaway led to a flurry of activity in the legislature. A black woman and her four children were seized in Cincinnati, but before the claimant could get the woman and her children under complete control she had killed her youngest child and had tried to kill the others "to save those children from

[66]*Wisc. House Journal, 1859*, 864. An earlier set of resolutions declared that the state would appeal to the people. The resolutions calling for positive defiance replaced this. *ibid.*, 777. Resolutions supporting the judgment of the U.S. Supreme Court were rejected. *ibid.*, 778.

[67]Commager, *Documents*, 1: 184.

[68]Charles Sumner to Byron Paine, May 12, 1859, Byron Paine Papers, State Historical Society of Wisconsin.

[69]*Ohio Senate Journal, 1854*, 205, 208, 215.

a life, every moment of which was to be infinitely worse than death," in the opinion of state senator Oliver P. Brown, a strong antislavery Republican.[70] On February 1, 1856, in response to this case, the senate judiciary committee was instructed to examine the problem of whether or not the state could act to secure a jury trial for alleged fugitives without infringing upon federal law or the Constitution.[71] By the middle of March, 1856, Senator Brown was ready to introduce a series of bills concerning fugitives. Among them were bills to punish citizens of the state voluntarily assisting in slave-catching, to prevent the use of Ohio jails for detaining "so called fugitives from slavery," and to punish certain state officials aiding in the capture of runaways.[72] None of these measures, which were patterned generally after the containment policies of other states, came out of the Committee of the Whole.[73] There was, moreover, no full-scale discussion of the possibility of securing a jury trial: doubtless, the belief was that to grant this right would bring the state into conflict with the federal government.

The senate, on the other hand, passed an antikidnapping bill in March,[74] and in April adopted a resolution urging the repeal of the federal fugitive law as "repugnant to the plainest principles of justice and humanity," and "inconsistent and unwarranted by the constitution."[75] The house agreed to the resolution, but the antikidnapping bill was buried in the house judiciary committee.[76] The resolution adopted, it is worth pointing out, was more symbolic than substantial, and actually was no advance over the Sutliff resolutions of 1851 (in fact, it did not go as far because it did not reaffirm the right of those restrained of personal freedom to a habeas corpus remedy).

The following year a temporary antislavery majority in the Ohio legislature succeeded in adopting three mild laws concerning free blacks and fugitive slaves. On April 16, 1857, the first was passed (a little over a month after the decision in the Dred Scott case): it prohibited the confinement of "certain persons" in the jails of Ohio.[77]

At the beginning of April the Senate Committee on Federal Relations, which had under consideration a resolution condemning the Dred Scott decision, reported a bill "To prevent slaveholding and kidnapping in Ohio."[78]

---

[70] *Ohio Senate Journal, 1856*, 119; on Senator Brown see *History of Portage County, Ohio* (Chicago, 1885), 341.

[71] *Ohio Senate Journal, 1856*, 125.

[72] *Ibid.*, 274.

[73] *Ibid.*, 323, 332, 357.

[74] *Ibid.*, 153, 158, 231, 271, 273, 316, 325.

[75] *Ibid.*, 421.

[76] *Ohio House Journal, 1856*, 189, 420, 432, 537, 538, 539, 556.

[77] *Ibid., 1857*, 246, 433: For the text of the law see *Acts of a General Nature and Local Laws and Joint Resolutions, Passed by the Fifty Second General Assembly, of the State of Ohio LIV* (Columbus, Ohio, 1857), 170.

[78] *Ohio House Journal, 1857*, 329.

This bill, which became law on April 17,[79] provided for the punishment of anyone who attempted to hold or control a person as a slave, to seize or arrest a person, or to use force for controlling a person upon the pretense that person was a fugitive, or to try to take a person out of the state into some other jurisdiction to be held as a slave. A final section stipulated that the act would not apply to those proceeding under authority of the Constitution of the United States, or any federal law made in pursuance of it.

On the same day the third bill—"An Act to prevent kidnapping"—became law. This measure, carefully framed, repealed the existing kidnapping law.[80] It provided for the punishment of anyone who removed or attempted to remove a free black or mulatto unless such person had first been taken before a proper federal official. The state would not obstruct renditions made under the federal law, but at the same time it would act to protect free blacks from outright kidnapping.

All three bills had become law in the wake of the U.S. Supreme Court's validation of the proslavery position on the territories: they were, in other words, moderate responses to a distasteful federal court decision. Every effort of antislavery reformers to obtain more thoroughgoing legislation was quickly defeated, and it is highly probable that these bills would not have become law without the intervention of the Dred Scott case.

In the fall elections of 1857 "Administration Democrats" secured control of the state legislature because of the apathy following the presidential election of 1856, in the view of one scholar.[81] In any event, the new Democratic legislature promptly repealed the act closing Ohio's jails to slave claimants and the one to prevent slaveholding and kidnapping in Ohio.[82] They left on the books "An Act to prevent kidnapping," which was limited in its terms to free men.

Prior to the decision in *Ableman* v. *Booth*, then, Ohio continued to follow a very moderate course on the matter of the state's right and responsibility to act in protecting the personal freedom of those in danger of being removed to the South as slaves. Established legal patterns, the strength of prosouthern Democrats, and the fear of a direct conflict between the state and federal governments account for the cautious approach of this border state.

IV

Of the two Middle Atlantic states examined in this study only New York was stirred during the middle 1850s. At the beginning of March, 1855, a

[79]*Acts and Resolutions*, 54: 186.
[80]*Ohio Session Laws, 1857*, 221–22.
[81]Cochran, "The Western Reserve and the Fugitive Slave Law," 118.
[82]*Ohio Session Laws, 1858*, 10, 19. For the proceedings on these repeal measures see the *Ohio Senate Journal, 1858*, 15, 20, 34, 38, 52, 67, 72–73, 75–76, 78–79, 89–90, 211, 216.

bill was introduced into the state assembly to secure a jury trial for alleged fugitives. Four days later the Ohio abolitionist Joshua R. Giddings, who was in New York at the time, wrote a sanguine letter in which he declared that "the legislature of New York appears to be doing well in their efforts to break down the infamous fugitive law."[83] His hopes, however, were dashed as the bill never emerged from a select committee to which it had been sent.[84]

Two years later, following the Dred Scott decision, New York's legislature again considered the problem of free blacks and runaways, but this time within a slightly different framework. A joint, special committee was set up to consider the full impact of Chief Justice Taney's decision, and to report the effect it might have on the citizens of the state and what action the state might take. On April 10, 1857, this committee reported a series of resolutions and a bill. One of the resolutions declared that "This State will not allow slavery within her borders, in any form, or under any pretense, or for any time, however short, let the consequences be what they may." This position was justified on the grounds laid down in the Virginia Resolution of 1798.[85]

The bill attached to this report included an affirmation of the right of blacks to be citizens of the state with all the rights and privileges of other citizens. It also provided that "Every slave who shall come, or be brought, or be, in this State, with the consent of his or her master or mistress, or who shall come or be brought or be involuntarily in this State, shall be free."

In the opinion of the special correspondent of the *New York Tribune* the bill was timid: "The report and resolutions are very well, but the proposed law, it seems to me, fetches up the rear rather limpingly, and does not by any means imply that the leaders of the Republican party are quite prepared to throw the tea overboard." In his judgment a bill should have been introduced declaring "all men treading the soil of New-York, unaccused of crime, shall be free and entitled to the protection of their freedom, regardless of the manner in which they reached the State." He was practical enough to recognize that the legislature would not go that far and suggested as an alternative that the state pass a law like the Massachusetts act of 1855.[86]

The editor of the moderate *New York Times*, on the other hand, found more in the bill than in the report or resolutions. The bill, after all, was the "most practical result of the labors of the Committee," and it deserved "the unqualified support of the citizens of New York. Such a bill it is their

[83] Joshua R. Giddings to Grotius R. Giddings, Rome, New York, March 6, 1855, Joshua R. Giddings Papers, Ohio Historical Society.
[84] *New York House Journal, 1855*, 525, 527.
[85] The bill, report, and resolutions are all in the *New York Tribune*, April 10, 1857.
[86] *New York Tribune*, April 11, 1857.

duty to pass at a time when the high prerogatives and inherent sovereignty of the great State which they represent have been threatened with invasion."[87] The *New York Herald* contended that it would be a hardship for a slaveholder if he must face both the prospect of losing his slave and of going to prison whenever he crossed the borders into New York. The *Tribune* replied that the bill was just like the existing law against kidnapping, "and is intended as a further security to our free colored residents against acts of violence and coercion, which kidnappers might feel themselves encouraged to attempt by the extraordinary slaveholding dicta put forth as law by the five slaveholders in the Dred Scott case."[88]

In the legislature a motion was made, on April 16, 1857, to amend the bill by adding a provision that it would not be deemed to discharge anyone from service or labor who should escape into the state.[89] This was voted down by a two-to-one margin.[90]

Representative John H. Wooster, a Republican, then moved a substitute which provided that "Every person who shall come, or be brought into, or be in this State, shall be free."[91] Wooster claimed no conflict existed between his new section and the federal Constitution. "If a negro is 'property,' and such a one should escape hither," he explained, "the person claiming him can recover him as other 'property' is recovered."[92] This was too much for the conservatives, one of whom said that "it would press the Republican party into abolitionism."[93] Wooster's substitute was voted down, but the support it received showed that New York might be fertile ground for more sweeping action in the future. One representative, for example, said he was in favor of a law guaranteeing that "no fugitive from service should ever be taken back into slavery from her borders."[94]

On April 17, 1857, the original bill passed the assembly,[95] but in the senate it failed to receive sufficient votes to send it to the Committee of the Whole.[96] The next day the legislature adjourned.

The only comment in the newspapers on the failure of the bill came from the special correspondent of the *Tribune*. The people had a right to expect a Personal Liberty Law. "A sort of Personal Liberty bill," he noted, had passed the assembly, but was not acted on in the senate. If it had been, he doubted it would have passed.[97] Some New York legislators, nevertheless, had come close to a total repudiation of the constitutional obligation,

[87]*New York Times*, April 11, 1857.
[88]*New York Herald*, cited in the *New York Tribune*, April 13, 1857.
[89]*New York Tribune*, April 18, 1857.
[90]*New York House Journal, 1857*, 1485.
[91]*Ibid.*, 1494.
[92]*New York Tribune*, April 18, 1857 .
[93]*Ibid.*
[94]*Ibid.*
[95]*New York House Journal, 1857*, 1494.
[96]*New York Senate Journal, 1857*, 1029, 1032–33.
[97]*New York Tribune*, April 20, 1857.

which demonstrated the growing exasperation of those opposing the successes of proslavery constitutionalism.

V

After 1854 the states north of the Mason-Dixon line would no longer accept the finality of the settlement reached in 1850: many people in those states no longer believed in the sanctity or priority of the federal law. The proslavery victory in the Kansas-Nebraska Act had thus reopened the slavery controversy and, often coupled with spectacular renditions, had provoked a reevaluation of the relationship of the free states to slavery and of the responsibility of those states to their citizens. Free states began vigorously to pursue the *via media*; they began to experiment in the range of possible ways to protect free citizens and obstruct the federal law, without divesting claimants of legitimate titles by state law in violation of the constitutional obligation. This effort spread after the proslavery constitutional decision of the Taney court in *Dred Scott* v. *Sandford* closed off any possibility of a compromise on the territorial question.

Even though Massachusetts and Wisconsin had gone beyond the free states farther south, all of the states examined in this study were, by 1858, on record as being in favor of the view that the states had the power and the obligation to protect the rights of persons within their jurisdictions by orderly procedures. Massachusetts and Wisconsin had guaranteed the right to a judicial inquiry in 1855 and 1857, respectively. Pennsylvania's law of 1847 and the New York law of 1840 also secured this right. Ohio's law of 1847 guaranteed a full inquiry whenever someone was in private custody, and the resolutions introduced by Milton Sutliff and adopted in 1851 broadened this guarantee, as a matter of legislative policy at least, to include all restraints on personal liberty. In 1859 in the Booth cases, however, the U.S. Supreme Court reviewed this commitment, and the victory in that decision for national judicial power set the stage for the final phase of the story of the Personal Liberty Laws in the context of pre-Civil War constitutionalism.

Habeas Corpus and Total Repudiation 1859-1860 11

Frustrated by the judgment of the U.S. Supreme Court in the Wisconsin case, and living under the increasing strain of the sectional crisis which was fast moving toward a violent conclusion (John Brown's raid on Harper's Ferry came in October, 1859), abolitionists began a movement to obtain a frank repudiation by the states of any obligation under the fugitive slave clause of the Constitution. This movement was uniformly unsuccessful, but it does indicate the increased radicalization of antislavery opinion in the free states in the last two years before the outbreak of the Civil War. As far back as 1844 the Liberty party took the view that "we owe it to the Sovereign Ruler of the Universe" to treat the fugitive clause, whenever applied to a runaway black, "as utterly null and void, and consequently as forming no part of the Constitution of the United States, whenever we are called upon, or sworn, to support it."[1] In 1859-60 many abolitionists more vigorously than ever before sought to have the states endorse this view and act as if they were completely sovereign with respect to the fugitive rendition problem.

The Personal Liberty Laws passed down to 1858 (and, for the most part, those that had been urged) had been framed carefully to leave intact the constitutional right of a slave owner to recover his property on free soil. But now many agreed with the opinion of Samuel J. May that "By the infamous decision and opinion [in *Ableman* v. *Booth*], the door is thrown wide open for any amount of injustice to be done to the entire colored population, whether *slave* or *free*." May felt it had been understood at the time the fugitive clause had been adopted that slavery was soon to disappear from this country altogether. But that promise had not been kept. When a party to an agreement "refuses to discharge the duty wh. it stipulated to discharge, the other party is exonerated, absolved, *free*, in law and equity, from any obligation under the instrument."[2]

Wisconsin's legislative resolutions of 1859, adopted in this spirit, had called for a "positive defiance," but as long as the federal officials did not move against Sherman Booth and the state supreme court seemed prepared to keep up to the mark, there appeared little need for direct action

[1] Porter and Johnson, *National Party Platforms*, 8.
[2] "Notes on Arguments for and against [a] Personal Liberty Law," Samuel J. May Papers, Boston Public Library, 13: 40.

186

by the state legislature. Federal authorities, facing a delicate situation, chose not to move against Booth until the spring of 1860 when he was re-arrested.[3] Booth considered himself a martyr to the cause and refused to pay his fine.[4] When it became clear that the state courts would not free him this time, despite Paine, antislavery zealots began to call for "violent remedies."[5] The final chapter in the Booth cases, however, was written in June, 1861, after war had broken out, when the state supreme court, with new justices sitting, upheld a judgment against his printing press.[6]

The closest parallel to the position assumed by Wisconsin in these years was in Ohio where a political upheaval had elevated Salmon P. Chase to the governorship. That state's supreme court in 1859 did act in defiance of the federal court's judgment in *Ableman* v. *Booth*, and by the spring of that year northern Ohio was in turmoil over the Fugitive Slave Law. In the fall of 1858 two slave hunters seized a boy near Oberlin, Ohio. What followed has been described as the "indignant uprising of a whole town."[7] The citizens of Oberlin pursued the slave catchers to Wellington where they effected a peaceful rescue. Several of these rescuers were then arraigned before the United States District Court at Cleveland. Of the thirty seven persons indicted, however, only two were convicted, and they received comparatively light sentences.[8]

At a meeting held in Cleveland in support of the two convicted men (Simeon Bushnell and Charles H. Langston) in May, 1859, the abolitionist governor Chase declared that "If the process for the release of any prisoner should issue from the Courts of the State, he was free to say that so long as Ohio was a Sovereign State, that process should be executed."[9] This, of course, was after the decision in *Ableman* v. *Booth*. Benjamin Wade was even more blunt: "If the Supreme Court of Ohio does not grant the habeas corpus, the people of the Western Reserve must Grant it—sword in hand if need be."[10]

Abolitionists were somewhat mollified when the Ohio Supreme Court did issue writs of habeas corpus to inquire into the validity of the convictions of Bushnell and Langston. Despite what the federal court had said the state judges proceeded to examine for themselves the question of the

[3]Swisher, *Roger B. Taney*, 531.

[4]Sherman M. Booth to Charles Durkee, *In Prison*, Milwaukee, March 16, 1860, Miscellaneous Manuscripts, State Historical Society of Wisconsin.

[5]J. C. Sholes to John Fox Potter, April 2, 1860, John Fox Potter Papers, State Historical Society of Wisconsin.

[6]*Arnold* v. *Booth*, 14 Wisconsin 180.

[7]McDougall, *Fugitive Slaves*, 49; Cochran, "The Western Reserve and the Fugitive Slave Law," 159.

[8]A good brief account is Wilbur H. Siebert, *The Underground Railroad from Slavery to Freedom* (New York, 1898), 279, 335-37. The fullest contemporary account of this case is J. R. Shipherd, *History of Oberlin-Wellington Rescue* (Boston, 1859).

[9]Quoted in Cochran, "The Western Reserve and the Fugitive Slave Law," 186.

[10]Quoted in *ibid.*, 192.

constitutionality of the federal law. The majority held that it was a valid enactment. Only Milton Sutliff, who had introduced the 1851 resolutions upholding the power of the state courts to issue a habeas corpus, and denouncing the federal law, declared it unconstitutional.[11] If the state court had followed Sutliff it was believed widely at the time that Governor Chase was prepared to use state troops to uphold the decision against the federal government.[12] That it did not averted a major crisis. The court, nevertheless, had defied the federal Supreme Court merely by examining the federal law under which Bushnell and Langston were imprisoned.

Ohio's legislature, on the other hand, was not so bold as the governor and the court. At the time the Republicans were in control of the state government, but the Republican party in Ohio, as elsewhere, was made up of moderates as well as radicals, and the moderates helped keep the state legislature from pursuing an extreme course in 1859–60.

During the 1859 session a house committee reported that the prayer for a law against all slave-hunting in Ohio could not be granted, and recommended that petitions asking for such a law be laid on the table without comment in the future. Passage of such a law, it was reported, would be a "palpable violation" of the Constitution, a repudiation of a "solemn obligation." Instead of introducing such a law the committee reported a resolution which was adopted declaring that "the people of Ohio, are forever opposed to sectional and unconstitutional legislation and deprecate in future all memorials praying for such enactments."[13]

At the beginning of 1860 an unsuccessful effort was made to reenact the Personal Liberty Laws of 1857, but there was no attempt to repudiate the constitutional obligation to allow slave owners the right to recover their property within the state.[14] Despite the dangerous situation in the state, and the strength of abolitionist sentiment, no new Personal Liberty Law was adopted. As in other states the fears of moderates combined with the opposition of the conservatives prevented action.

I

In Massachusetts a different situation prevailed. The state supreme court, under Chief Justice Shaw, scarcely would follow the courts of Ohio and Wisconsin. Without hope of support from the judiciary the radicals began a spirited movement to secure an outright repudiation of the constitutional obligation by the state legislature. No longer would they be content with a demand for a jury trial. Even before the judgment in *Ableman* v.

[11] *United States* v. *Simeon Bushnell, United States* v. *Langston,* and *Ex parte Bushnell,* 9 Ohio State, 77–325.

[12] Warren, *The Supreme Court,* 2: 345.

[13] See the discussion in the *Annual Report of the American Anti-Slavery Society, By the Executive Committee, For the Year Ending May 1, 1859* (New York, 1860), 109.

[14] *Ohio Senate Journal, 1860,* 20, 35, 41, 223, 227–28; *Ohio House Journal, 1860,* 292, 299.

Booth was known a petition had been circulated about the state by abolitionists: "The undersigned, citizens of Massachusetts, respectfully ask you to enact that no person, who has been held as a slave, shall be delivered up, by any officer or court, State or Federal, within this Commonwealth, to any one claiming him on the ground that he 'owes service or labor' to such claimant, by the laws of one of the slave States of this Union." This petition went to the Committee on Federal Relations of the lower chamber of the General Court, which held public hearings on the matter in February, 1859.

Speaking before this committee, Wendell Phillips developed at length a radical antislavery position. Law, in his view, was a fluid concept. To be valid, law must "represent public opinion," it must meet immediate social needs. No government, even one having widespread public support, however, could violate the laws of justice and of God. If any "parchment contract" existed that violated these standards, and the fugitive slave clause was one, "it is void for immorality, and from incapacity of the contracting parties to make such a compact."

All Phillips asked was "that you shall organize the public sentiment of Massachusetts into a statute." This could be done by providing that anyone seized as a fugitive would be immediately freed by a habeas corpus issued from the state supreme court. If such a law could not be made "effectual through the Supreme Court," the people would "make it effectual over that Court; for the humanity of the people will be represented by the institutions of Massachusetts, in some form or other."[15]

Caleb Cushing, the leader of the Democratic party in the Massachusetts legislature, was reported to be "scandalized" by these proceedings.[16] This was not true of the Republican majority on the Committee on Federal Relations. On March 11, 1859, four days after the decision in *Ableman* v. *Booth*, they reported a bill, consisting of only two sections. Section 1 of the bill declared that "No person now in this Commonwealth, or who may hereafter come into it or be brought into it, shall be considered as property or treated as such." The second section provided that "Whoever shall arrest, imprison, or carry out of this Commonwealth, or shall attempt to arrest, imprison, or carry out of this Commonwealth, any person, for the alleged reason that such person owes service or labor as a slave, to the party claiming him, shall be punished by imprisonment in the state prison not exceeding five years."[17] An amendment was then introduced that

[15]*No Slave-Hunting in the Old Bay State. Speech of Wendell Phillips, Esq., before the Committee on Federal Relations, In support of the Petitions asking for a law to prevent the Recapture of Fugitive Slaves, in the Hall of the House of Representatives, Thursday, February 17, 1859* (Boston, 1859).

[16]Samuel May to Richard Davis Webb, Boston, February 8, 1859, Samuel May Papers, Boston Public Library, vol. 7, no. 29.

[17]*Mass. House Document No. 173, 1859*, 2.

struck directly at the federal Supreme Court decision in *Ableman* v. *Booth*. It stated that anyone seized could be liberated by a habeas corpus.[18]

A minority report, seething with indignation, was submitted by Martin Griffin and Daniel Lovell. Having taken an oath to support the Constitution, which was a political instrument and not a code of morals, they shrank from an act that was a "virtual declaration of disunion and of civil war." Even though they might abhor the obligation imposed in the Constitution they felt themselves at the abyss looking into a dark and bloody future, and they could not take the step toward a violent upheaval.[19]

Although this effort to prohibit slave-hunting in Massachusetts was a failure in 1859—to the delight of conservatives like Caleb Cushing and the chagrin of radicals like Samuel May[20]—it was not abandoned. Petitions poured into the next session of the legislature.[21] By that time the sectional crisis had reached a critical point. John Brown's raid in October, 1859, had succeeded in polarizing the radicals, North and South, more than ever before. Moderate Republicans, facing a presidential contest in the fall, however, were reluctant to endorse an obvious violation of the Constitution. As in Ohio their caution combined with conservative opposition condemned the radical effort to another failure.

A bill was introduced in 1860 (the same one introduced by the Committee on Federal Relations the year before),[22] but it was not considered. Instead of action on this bill the special senate committee, considering the anti-slave-hunting petitions, asked, and received, "leave to withdraw,"[23] which meant, Garrison bitterly remarked, "let slave-hunters have leave still to pursue their prey on the soil of Massachusetts!"[24] This ended the story of the Personal Liberty Laws in Massachusetts before Lincoln's election precipitated the crisis that ended in civil war.

II

At the beginning of January, 1859, the *National Anti-Slavery Standard* urged abolitionists in New York to follow the example of Massachusetts radicals and flood the new Republican legislature with petitions praying for a law to prohibit slave-hunting.[25] A great deal of pressure was put on

[18]*Ibid.*, 2–3.

[19]*Ibid.*, 4–7. See also *Mass. House Document No. 256, 1859; Mass. House Document No. 220, 1859.*

[20]Samuel J. May to Caroline Weston, Florence, Italy, May 10, 1859, Weston Papers, Boston Public Library, vol. 29, no. 64.

[21]See, for example, *Mass. House Journal, 1860*, Mass. State Library, 83: 58, 65, 77, 85–86, 90, 92, 98, 101, 113, 121, 128, 139, 155, 162, 168, 187, 196, 206, 209, 215, 221, 231–32, 241–42, 246, 251–52, 261, 263, 269, 290, 330, 353, 355, 372.

[22]*Mass. Senate Journal, 1860*, Mass. State Library, 81: 545; *Mass. Senate Document No. 126, 1860.*

[23]*Mass. Senate Journal, 1860*, Mass., State Library, 81: 514–15, 528, 556.

[24]William Lloyd Garrison to W. P. Garrison, Boston, March 22, 1860, Garrison Papers, Boston Public Library, vol. 5, no. 105.

[25]*National Anti-Slavery Standard*, January 8, 1859.

the legislature,[26] which responded on February 2, 1859, when a select committee reported a bill of fourteen sections, many of which were patterned after the Massachusetts act of 1855.[27] But Section 6, the vital one in the committee's bill, was not. It declared that "Every person who may have been held as a slave, who shall come or be brought or be in this state with the consent of his or her alleged master or mistress, or who shall come or be brought or be in this state, shall be free."

On March 7 (the day *Ableman* v. *Booth* was decided) the house began consideration of the bill in the Committee of the Whole. Charles S. Spencer, from the select committee, was the spokesman for the measure. The combative nature of this new type of Personal Liberty Law was made amply clear. "The tendency of laws like that now under consideration," said Spencer, "is to check the Slave power in its aggressive march, to roll back the black and threatening wave of Southern oppression, to teach the Slave power that it will have absolute need of its utmost efforts to preserve its existence within its present boundaries, without grasping by robbery or bribery the territories of other governments in order to aggrandize and perpetuate slavery."[28] He tried to show that the sixth section, the "*heart* of this law," was constitutional, even though it was a clear repudiation of the obligation imposed in the Constitution. By no due process of law recognized in the state of New York could a man be deprived of his "ownership of himself or of his liberty, except for crime or fraudulent indebtedness."[29] Spencer used Alvan Stewart's argument of the late 1830s to show that slavery itself was unconstitutional, at least insofar as New York was concerned. A month later the bill passed the assembly by an overwhelming vote,[30] but it was not considered in the senate.

At the end of March, while the debate was going on in the assembly, a separate bill was introduced in the senate. It was virtually identical to the bill as amended that had been introduced in the Massachusetts house two weeks before.[31] Conservatives had another opportunity to denounce the radicals for what amounted to treason, in the view of A. S. Diven, a Republican, speaking for the majority of the New York Senate Judiciary Committee. Defying laws while they are in force "can only be characterized as rebellion." Even if it was granted, as many people contended, that the

[26]See, for example, the *New York House Journal, 1859*, 243, 262, 265, 284, 301, 335, 346, 366, 408, 419, 429, 451, 475, 495, 513, 523, 539–41, 564, 593, 619, 662, 705, 717, 724, 810, 811, 873, 1014, 1057, 1156.
[27]As originally reported this bill is in Charles S. Spencer, *An Appeal for Freedom, Made in the Assembly of the State of New York, March 7th, 1859* (Albany, 1859), 3–5.
[28]*Ibid.*, 21.
[29]*Ibid.*, 13. Another speech in favor of the bill was Arthur Holmes, *The Constitution and Personal Liberty. Speech of Hon. Arthur Holmes, of Cortland. In Assembly March 9, 1859* (Albany, 1859). Holmes did not deal in a clear manner with the inconsistency between Section 6 and the fugitive slave clause.
[30]*New York House Journal, 1859*, 1182.
[31]*New York Senate Document No. 117, 1859*, 1.

Fugitive Slave Law was unconstitutional it would not justify the state in repudiating the constitutional provision itself. By the compact forming the federal Union, Diven noted, "we expressly agreed not to pass such laws."[32]

After the legislature adjourned a special antislavery lobby was formed to direct the effort in New York aimed at the next legislature.[33] It used all its influence on the favorably inclined members to persuade them to make speeches in behalf of forceful action.[34]

On February 11, 1860, Shotwell Powell, for the majority of a select house committee, reported two separate bills.[35] The majority report dealt primarily with the second bill, which was "similar" to the bill that passed the assembly the year before. Most of the opposition during the debates, on the other hand, was concentrated on the first bill, the first section of which was the most important. It declared that "Every person who shall come or be brought into this State shall be free."[36] Essentially the same statement was made in the second bill as well.

The Republican majority supported this radical statement with biblical and constitutional arguments. Their first was "because God has explicitly forbidden the rendition of fugitive servants to their masters." The Declaration of Independence, moreover, declared that all men were created equal and had an inalienable right to liberty, and it is, they noted, the first duty of civil government to protect the personal liberty "of all human beings within its jurisdiction." They rejected the argument that state action would alienate "our brethren of the south." About four million of these "brethren" were slaves, and of the remainder only a small percentage were slaveholders. The other southern whites would have no desire to have fugitives sent back "to compete with and degrade their free labor."[37]

Even though the "higher law" gave ample justification for the state to act, the majority felt a "fair and liberal construction" of the federal Constitution also provided sufficient authority. Their reading of the fugitive slave clause was derived from those radicals of the 1830s and 1840s like Gerrit Smith and Alvan Stewart who argued that the clause did not refer to fugitive slaves, but to apprentices from whom labor was "due."[38]

The bloodstained hands of John Brown appeared larger than life in the report of the minority. They abhorred the thought that the radicals would

[32]*Ibid.*, 3, 7, 10. See also *New York Senate Document No. 120, 1859; New York Senate Document No. 122, 1859.*

[33]*National Anti-Slavery Standard,* April 28, 1860; *Report of the Select Committee on the Petitions to Prevent Slave Hunting in the State of New York* (Albany, 1860), 1. This report was published separately; *New York House Journal, 1860,* 49–50, 58, 70–71, 80–81, 88, 100, 117, 120, 122, 141, 148, 164, 171, 202, 273, 280, 312, 339, 353, 395, 406, 429, 445, 482, 678.

[34]*National Anti-Slavery Standard,* April 28, 1860.

[35]*New York House Journal, 1860,* 356–57.

[36]This bill is given in *Speech of Hon. Theophilus C. Callicot of Kings, Against the Personal Liberty Bill. In Assembly, March 14, 1860* (Albany, 1860), 1. The other bill is characterized in the *Report of the Select Committee,* 6.

[37]*Report of the Select Committee,* 4.

[38]*Ibid.*, 6.

succeed in placing the state in direct opposition to the Constitution. This policy was framed, they felt, in the "hot-beds of abolitionism and treason, by a class of fanatics who endorse the deeds of treason, murder, and bloodshed, lately perpetrated in the quiet and peaceful villages of our sister State, and setting at defiance the power and authority of our federal government."[39]

This debate over the proper construction of the Constitution continued in the Committee of the Whole on March 14. Theophilus C. Callicot took his standard of interpretation from the judiciary which overwhelmingly declared the Fugitive Slave Law constitutional. The obligation imposed in the fugitive slave clause was clear beyond all cavil, and to act as the radicals urged could be little else but treason. States had certain powers, but among them was not the power to change the status of a fugitive slave.[40]

According to B. R. Johnson, on the other side, the federal government had no power to subjugate or oppress men. The Fugitive Slave Law could have no binding force in New York because the state had never "surrendered our rights in this direction." The "rights" he referred to were those of an independent and sovereign state to secure to everyone the benefits of due process of law and trial by jury.[41]

Both bills, despite the pressure of the antislavery lobby, were buried in the Committee of the Whole.[42] As in Massachusetts the moderate Republicans held the key, and in the face of the intense crisis facing the country in a presidential election year they were very reluctant to take such an aggressive step. Despite all the agitation in New York no new Personal Liberty Law was passed during the decade after the enactment of the Fugitive Slave Law.

III

As early as the fall of 1858 radicals in Pennsylvania began a move to secure a law like those sought in New York and Massachusetts in 1859-60. At the twenty-first annual meeting of the Pennsylvania Anti-Slavery Society it was resolved that one of the State's principal objectives should be to "put an end to all slavehunting."[43] On February 14, 1859, a bill was introduced in the house that went part of the way to meet their request.[44]

[39] *New York House Document No. 100, 1860.*
[40] *Speech of Hon. Theophilus C. Callicot* (Albany, 1860).
[41] *Speech of Hon. B. R. Johnson, on the Personal Liberty Bill. In Assembly, March 14, 1860* (Albany, 1860).
[42] For the proceedings on these bills see *New York House Journal, 1860,* 531, 544, 647, 651, 748–49, 769, 815.
[43] *Twenty-First Annual Report Presented to the Pennsylvania Anti-Slavery Society, By its Executive Committee, October 6th, 1858, with the Resolutions of the Annual Meeting, Constitution of the Society and Declaration of Sentiments* (Philadelphia, 1858), 19; Pennsylvania Anti-Slavery Society, Executive Committee, Minutes (1856–70) Historical Society of Pennsylvania, Book no. 4, p. 27.
[44] *Penn. House Journal, 1859,* 311.

This bill was intended to reinforce the state law of 1847 and clarify its provions on habeas corpus. It was substantially the same as the Massachusetts law of 1855, except that it did not provide for state-appointed attorneys. Clearly, it was intended to obstruct the Fugitive Slave Law, but it did not repudiate the constitutional injunction as was being done in the personal liberty bills introduced in Massachusetts and New York at this time.[45]

The principal spokesman for the bill was Representative Elias H. Irish. On March 14 Irish answered the Democrats who noted that the U.S. Supreme Court had settled the question by declaring the act of 1850 constitutional. "Neither an act of Congress nor a decision of the supreme court," he said, "nor both together, can alter or amend the Constitution." In his judgment, the congressional act of 1850 clearly violated the guarantee of a jury trial. He then pointed out the difficulty of resolving the conflict between the rights of property and the right to liberty; "it will not do to say that all are so entitled [to jury trial], except fugitive slaves, for how shall the State know which of them are fugitives, and which are not, except by a verdict of a jury."[46] It was time, he concluded, that Pennsylvania stand up against slavery, the "monarch of the time," which "rides like death on the pale horse over the nation."

Even though the Democratic party was badly divided in Pennsylvania, despite the fact that one of its sons sat in the White House, it still controlled the state assembly.[47] There was very little chance that the personal liberty bill would even receive a full hearing. Until the beginning of April, 1859, it languished in the house without much consideration. On Saturday morning, April 2, a black man was seized in Harrisburg under a warrant issued by a United States commissioner. For a brief moment this event stirred up the assembly,[48] but the bill was never brought to a vote.

Antislavery radicals continued to work for a strong Personal Liberty Law in Pennsylvania, but they were momentarily diverted by the excitement growing out of John Brown's raid.[49] They did circulate petitions which were sent to the legislature throughout its 1860 session.[50] With a Democratic party looking toward the up-and-coming convention at Charleston, however, there was even less chance that a bill would be considered than the year before. No bill, in point of fact, was even introduced. Ardent unionists were clearly on top in this border state. Even before the

---

[45] *Legislative Record. Proceedings of the General Assembly of the Commonwealth of Pennsylvania, for the Session Commencing January 4, 1859* (Harrisburg, 1859), 385–88. This is a special edition of the legislative debates.

[46] *Ibid.*, 387.

[47] Nichols, *The Disruption of American Democracy*, 206, 208–9, is a very good description of the struggles within the Democratic party in Pennsylvania.

[48] *Public Ledger*, April 4, 1859; *Penn. House Journal, 1859*, 940–41.

[49] Pennsylvania Anti-Slavery Society, Executive Committee, Minutes (1856–70), Historical Society of Pennsylvania, Book no. 4, pp. 37, 39.

[50] *Penn. Senate Journal, 1860*, 96, 121, 132, 137, 199, 222, 259, 260, 306; *Penn. House Journal, 1860*, 123, 169, 179, 237, 280, 325, 338, 374–75, 437–38.

1860 session they had held a Union meeting in Philadelphia at which they condemned any effort to frustrate the law of Congress.[51]

IV

On the eve of the Civil War, then, the last stage in the development of the effort to secure personal freedom by state action, a frank repudiation of the constitutional obligation, was turned back, completing the story of the Personal Liberty Laws in the context of pre-Civil War constitutionalism. This stage had been ushered in by the decision of the U.S. Supreme Court in *Ableman* v. *Booth* which sharply restricted the range of possible alternatives left to the states. Despite that decision all of the states examined in this study retained measures upon their books in 1860 which testified to their commitment to the idea of liberty under law. They clearly avowed their belief that slavery was incompatible with the traditional definitions and guarantees of freedom and, in fact, identified the crusade against slavery with the centuries-long struggle for freedom by deliberately using the legal instruments forged in that crucible.

Some state laws doubtless were of arguable constitutionality, whereas others were far less controversial. Constitutionality is a normative concept, but it is not an absolute. The answer to the question, "Which of these laws are, or were, constitutional?" would depend upon what is chosen as the incontrovertible measure of constitutionality. If the decisions of the Supreme Court in *Prigg* v. *Pennsylvania* and *Ableman* v. *Booth* are adopted, then many of the vital provisions of these laws could be adjudged invalid, although even this could be debated. On the other hand, if one chose a present-day, or an antislavery, interpretation of the due process clause, or a strict construction of the fugitive slave clause, or perhaps a broad interpretation of the habeas corpus or jury-trial provisions of the federal Constitution as the standard, then *Prigg* v. *Pennsylvania* and parts of *Ableman* v. *Booth* (for example, the statement that the law of 1850 was valid) could be considered erroneous, and the Personal Liberty Laws, even the most extreme, defensible on constitutional grounds.

Some Personal Liberty Laws, of course, could stand up to any of these tests. Almost all would fall before proslavery constitutionalism. If these laws are ranged from least to most controversial, they can be broken down as follows: those providing punishment for persons convicted of kidnapping; ones providing counsel for persons claimed as slaves; those denying the use of state jails to house alleged runaways; those punishing state officials for performing duties under the federal fugitive slave laws; ones requiring state procedures in addition to, or as an alternative to, federal procedures for the rendition of runaways; those requiring, or authorizing, a

---

[51]*Great Union Meeting. Philadelphia. December 7, 1859* (Philadelphia, 1859), 10.

jury trial before an alleged fugitive could be removed; and those making state habeas corpus available to anyone claimed as a fugitive.

Of these the least dubious perhaps would be the antikidnapping laws. Several of the states adopted such measures as far back as the 1780s. Justices Wayne and McLean had suggested in *Prigg* v. *Pennsylvania* that they were or could be proper. The way they were sometimes framed in the free states before 1842, however, made them controversial. Before the decision in *Prigg* v. *Pennsylvania* the antikidnapping laws were used to substitute the "mild custody of the law" for the "brutal seizure" by the master himself. They were part of the free-state answer to the proslavery interpretation of the so-called right of recaption. Because of this they did not discriminate between the seizure of a free black and an actual fugitive. After the Supreme Court decision upholding the proslavery view of recaption the free states generally recast their antikidnapping laws to specify that the person seized had to be a free man. In 1860 all states studied here had antikidnapping laws on their books, and only one had been passed before *Prigg* v. *Pennsylvania*—New York's law of 1840. That law provided for a penalty against anyone who forcibly removed or attempted to remove "without the authority of law" any fugitive or person claimed as a fugitive. All of the others stipulated that the man seized must be free. Of the antikidnapping laws on the books in 1860 then only New York's was of dubious constitutionality because it was not limited in its terms to free men. Many of the others, however, were challenged because they were part of Personal Liberty Laws that had other sections which were more controversial.

Charging state officials (whether specially appointed commissioners, or district attorneys) with the responsibility to provide legal assistance to those claimed as fugitives was equally free from attack on constitutional grounds. Even conservatives in the North opposed to the Personal Liberty Laws admitted that this was not unconstitutional, although it might be inexpedient and offensive. In Massachusetts, for example, it was challenged only on the ground that the special officers were charged with carrying out a law that was unconstitutional in some of its other provisions.[52] In 1860 three of the five states examined here had laws providing legal assistance: Massachusetts, Wisconsin, and New York.

Those laws prohibiting the use of state jails to house alleged runaways, however offensive they might be to the South, were clearly in line with Story's judgment in *Prigg* v. *Pennsylvania*. The only challenge against these measures could be on the ground that the states had a positive duty to legislate in aid of a claimant, the position maintained by Chief Justice Taney and proslavery constitutionalists in general. In any event, by 1860 only the jails of Massachusetts were still closed. Pennsylvania, which had closed its prisons in 1847, opened them again in 1852, and Ohio closed its

[52]*Boston Daily Advertiser*, May 29, 1855.

jails only for one year. This form of noncooperation with slave claimants, endorsed by the Supreme Court, was restricted to the period after 1842.

The laws punishing state officials performing duties under the federal law go back to Pennsylvania's act of 1820. In 1860 Pennsylvania, Massachusetts, and New York all had such provisions on the books. The earliest prohibitions were passed on the assumptions that a state which had created an official had the power to define his jurisdiction and the procedures he would operate under, and that the federal government had no power to impose duties on state officials. Prior to 1842 when Story endorsed Pennsylvania's view of the right of the federal government to impose duties, this was a heatedly debated constitutional problem. Story's arguments that the federal government could not impose duties on state officials, and that the fugitive slave clause created a duty for the federal government alone, opened the way for the free states to experiment with the noncooperative type of Personal Liberty Law during the 1840s and the 1850s.

The one type of Personal Liberty Law that was of no practical moment in 1860 required state procedures in addition to, or as an alternative to, federal procedures. These were found in the compromise measures of the 1820s which had been designed to balance the legitimate claims of ṣlave owners, and claims of freedom. They proceeded upon the assumption that the states were charged with a positive duty under the fugitive slave clause, and with the obligation to protect the personal freedom of those within their jurisdictions. This type of Personal Liberty Law was struck down in 1842. Speaking for the Court Story maintained that the states had neither the duty nor the right to pass legislation implementing the fugitive slave clause. Proslavery constitutionalists like Taney continued to argue that the free states were charged with the positive duty to pass legislation in aid of claimants. That legislation, however, could in no way obstruct a claimant, as in the operation of Pennsylvania's law of 1826. Abolitionists, on the other side, often contended that the fugitive slave clause was addressed to the states. Doubtless their hope was that the free states would legislate in such a way as to make it extremely difficult, if not impossible, for a claimant to recover his property. In any event, even though the argument raged after 1842, the free states no longer made any effort to pass laws framed as measures to fulfill the constitutional obligation to return runaway blacks. Only one such law remained on the books in 1860, and it had been passed after the compromising spirit of the 1820s faded; New York's law of 1840 provided an alternative method of procedure to the federal law.

The two remaining laws were without doubt the most controversial in 1860: those securing habeas corpus and jury trial to persons claimed as fugitives. Three of these states guaranteed a jury trial by law in 1860: New York's jury trial provision was part of its 1840 law; Wisconsin's was part of the law of 1857; whereas Massachusetts actually had two provisions securing jury trial (the one drawn from the 1837 law of personal replevin, and the one found in the 1855 statute). Jury trial, of course, had actually been provided from the beginning under the common-law writ *de homine replegiando*. This writ was available to anyone under restraint, and that included actual fugitives. Several state court decisions (the most notable was Tilghman's opinion in *Wright* v. *Deacon* in 1819), however, had undermined this writ when they declared it inappropriate in cases involving fugitive slaves. Jury-trial provisions, moreover, were very seriously weakened by Story's judgment that a master had the right to the immediate possession of his property, and that any delay constituted *pro tanto* a discharge, and thereby a violation of the Constitution.

On their face, however, the jury-trial provisions applied to free men only and not to actual fugitives. A man, in most cases, had to claim that he was a free person before he could receive the jury trial. Claimants, on the other hand, had been guaranteed the right (in *Prigg* v. *Pennsylvania*) to recover their property without hindrance from free-state law. According to the laws of the states above the Mason-Dixon line all men were presumed free, whereas according to those of the states below that line all blacks were presumed to be slaves. If the black seized on free soil was indeed a fugitive slave then, of course, no right would be ignored by denying him a jury trial, or a habeas corpus hearing. If, on the other hand, he was a free man, to deny him these would be to deny him basic constitutional and legal rights.

Habeas corpus provisions could be defended upon the same grounds as the jury-trial provisions: In their terms they applied only to free men and fulfilled the obligation of the state to protect those within its jurisdiction against an unlawful restraint.

The way habeas corpus powers were used, or could be used, by the judiciaries of the free states was challenged on two grounds: one purely legal, and the other constitutional. In the first place, proslavery legal theorists narrowly defined the power given to the courts exercising habeas corpus jurisdiction. They contended that this writ was never intended to be used to obtain a full and independent inquiry into a restraint, but only into whether or not a legal reason was stated for the holding. If a man was claimed as a fugitive slave, whether he was an actual fugitive or not, that would be a sufficient return according to this view. Some antislavery radicals, on the other side, suggested that habeas corpus might be used as a means to abolish slavery. Alvan Stewart had argued that the courts could use their habeas corpus power to declare slavery unconstitutional as a patent violation of due process. Such an argument, however, never became an important part of pre-Civil War constitutionalism as exemplified in the Personal Liberty Laws that had been adopted.

The constitutional challenge concerned the question of the powers of the state courts on habeas corpus to inquire into the constitutionality of a federal law. Both Wisconsin and Ohio asserted this right in major cases in the late 1850s. Wisconsin's declaration that a state must have the right to protect its citizens against imprisonment under an invalid law (even though it be a federal law) was incorporated in the major treatise on habeas corpus written before the Civil War, but this was controverted by the federal Supreme Court in 1859. Ohio's supreme court, however, proceeded on the same assumption even after the U.S. Supreme Court decision.

This is where the question stood on the eve of the Civil War. All of the states, of course, had general habeas corpus statutes going back in some cases to the 1780s which could be considered applicable to anyone deprived of his liberty, but in addition four of the five states studied here still had habeas corpus legislation on the books in 1860 designed quite specifically to aid anyone seized as a fugitive slave (Ohio, Pennsylvania, Massachusetts, and Wisconsin). Ohio and Pennsylvania adopted their legislation in 1847, while the other two adopted theirs in the middle 1850s. They differed considerably one from another. Ohio's law, for example, provided that anyone held in private custody was entitled to a full inquiry. Those held by state or federal officials were not guaranteed this right: in their case the return of the official would be taken to establish a prima facie case. Some considered this modified by the resolutions adopted by the legislature in 1851. Pennsylvania's law was merely a general declaration that the writ would be available to anyone in custody. Massachusetts and Wisconsin, on the other hand, inventively wove together the functions of habeas corpus and personal replevin. In those states, farther removed from slave-owning communities, habeas corpus could be used as a means of obtaining a jury trial. The same was true in New York, but there a form of the writ was also the first step in aiding a claimant to recover his property.

V

On January 24, 1860, Senator Robert Toombs of Georgia launched a vitriolic attack on the legislation of the free states and on the recent efforts to obtain laws preventing slave-hunting. On the floor of the United States Senate he taunted the "Black Republicans" who "mock at constitutional obligations, jeer at oaths."[53] In every state where they held power the Fugitive Slave Law was a dead letter. It had been nullified, he explained in a later speech, by "higher-law" teachings, acts passed under the fraudulent pretense of preventing kidnapping, and "new constructions" such as

[53] *Cong. Globe*, 36th Cong., 1st sess., Jan. 24, 1860, Appendix, 91.

with the writ of habeas corpus.[54] He was indignant particularly about the judgments of the Wisconsin Supreme Court, and the effort to obtain a new Personal Liberty Law in New York. Wisconsin, said Toombs, "who got rotten before she got ripe, comes to us even in the first few years of her admission, with her hands all smeared with the blood of a violated Constitution, all polluted with perjury."[55] The law introduced in New York exceeded those in other states "in iniquity, in plain, open, shameless, and profligate perfidy."[56]

Over the course of the next few months several senators from the free states assailed by Toombs attempted to answer him. The exchange between Senator J. R. Doolittle of Wisconsin and Toombs on February 24 best reveals the positions at which many people in both sections had arrived on this issue by 1860.

The very essence of the whole inquiry under habeas corpus, Doolittle noted, was to determine whether or not someone was confined with or without law. If a person was confined under the authority of an unconstitutional law he must be discharged, since his imprisonment "would be without any authority from the United States."[57] Doolittle admitted that when "a State court, upon constitutional questions as to the reserved powers, is coequal and coordinate with the Federal Supreme Court" there could be conflicts that might even lead to civil war. But, he believed, "still greater dangers" could result from allowing the federal court the absolute power to construe the Constitution for all the courts of the United States. This would lead "of necessity to absolutism and consolidation."[58] The proper remedy for federal usurpation had been pointed out long ago by Thomas Jefferson in a letter to Spencer Roane. It was not by revolution or by a dissolution of the Union; it was by the interposition of the "sovereign judiciary of the State." If a conflict resulted the ultimate arbiter should be the people who could resolve it by amending the Constitution.[59]

Toombs pointed out an essential difference, in his judgment, between the actions of Georgia and the Wisconsin judiciary. Georgia's theory was that "in whichever tribunal the jurisdiction first attached, it should remain." Wisconsin, on the other hand, interfered with the federal courts after they had obtained control of the case.[60] He admitted that the state courts had the right to judge, but what he refused to admit was that this meant they could disregard the Constitution and laws. And by a long line of judicial precedents the southern position on the question of fugitive slaves had been upheld. Toombs had no hope that the "Black Republi-

[54]*Ibid.*, March 7, 1860, Appendix, 155.
[55]*Ibid.*, Jan. 24, 1860, Appendix, 89.
[56]*Ibid.*, Appendix, 90.
[57]*Ibid.*, Feb. 24, 1860, Appendix, 122.
[58]*Ibid.*, Appendix, 125.
[59]*Ibid.*, Appendix, 126–27.
[60]*Ibid.*, Feb. 27, 1860, 892.

cans" would respect these judgments. What he intended to do then was to bring these men before the bar of public opinion.[61]

Toombs despaired of a peaceful settlement. In 1850 Georgia had declared that union depended upon the faithful execution of the Fugitive Slave Law and the enjoyment of equal rights in the territories. There had been, in his view, no faithful execution of the law. If the Republican Party was successful in the fall election, moreover, it would be a clear indication that slave owners would not be allowed to enjoy equal rights in the common territories of the United States. Well before South Carolina began the movement of the southern states out of the Union following Lincoln's election Toombs was prepared to throw down the gauntlet. "Defend yourselves," he passionately declared on January 24 in the Senate debate, "the enemy is at your door; wait not to meet him at the hearthstone—meet him at the doorsill, and drive him from the temple of liberty, or pull down the pillars and involve him in a common ruin."[62]

[61]*Ibid.*, 889.
[62]*Ibid.*, Jan. 24, 1860, Appendix, 93.

Denouement 12

In his annual message to Congress of December 3, 1860, James Buchanan warned that the South "would be justified in revolutionary resistance to the Government of the Union" if the northern states did not repeal their Personal Liberty Laws. The Constitution, "to which all the States are parties," would be "willfully violated" by them if this elementary act of justice and good faith was not proffered.[1] In such an event the South would have a moral right of revolution even though it had no constitutional right of secession. To avoid a violent sectional confrontation Buchanan wanted Congress to frame an "explanatory amendment" declaring, among other things,[2] that all state laws impairing the right to reclaim slaves "are violations of the Constitution, and are consequently null and void."

On the same day, December 3, the secessionists in South Carolina declared that to wait for a repeal of those laws would be nothing but submission, a dangerous submission to the revolution the North had effected in the government, changing it from a "confederated republic, to a national sectional despotism."[3] Five days before Christmas, 1860, South Carolina adopted its ordinance of secession creating the deepest crisis unionists had ever faced. Most of the remaining southern states were less precipitous, but for many the price for remaining in the Union was as high as it had been for the Palmetto state.[4] By the middle of January, 1861, it had become clear to Charles Francis Adams, one of the leading Republicans willing to make some concessions, that it was not compromise the southern leaders wanted, but domination: "no form of adjustment will be satisfactory to the recusant States which does not incorporate into the Constitution of the United States a recognition of the obligation to protect and extend slavery."[5]

[1] *Cong. Globe*, 36th Cong., 2d sess., Dec. 3, 1860, Appendix, 1 ff. Cf. Philip Shriver Klein, *President James Buchanan: A Biography* (University Park, Penn., 1962), 362.

[2] There was to be a recognition of the right of property in slaves where slavery then existed, and where it thereafter existed, an affirmation of the validity of the Fugitive Slave Law, and an acknowledgment of the duty to protect slavery in the common territories.

[3] *Charleston Mercury*, December 3, 1860 in Dwight L. Dumond, ed., *Southern Editorials on Secession* (Gloucester, Mass., 1964), 292.

[4] Cited in David M. Potter, *Lincoln and His Party in the Secession Crisis* (New Haven, 1962), 71.

[5] "Minority Report of the Committee of Thirty Three," *House Reports*, 36th Cong., 2d sess., no. 31, 3.

Undoubtedly the most volatile constitutional issue in 1860–61 was the problem of the status of slavery in the territories. Lincoln was "inflexible" on this matter: he stuck firmly to the policy of containment throughout the crisis. Slave owners stood equally as firm for "State Sovereignty" which was their "authority writ large."[6] On December 18, 1860, the conservative unionist John J. Crittenden introduced a set of compromise resolutions in the Senate, proposing to settle the territorial question by extending the Missouri compromise line. Debated in the special Senate Committee of Thirteen, in the House, and again in the Senate when reintroduced as a resolution from the Washington Peace Conference, the Crittenden proposals were defeated by the unwillingness of Republicans to compromise on this issue. The clash between the two irreconcilable constitutional theories of containment and of "State Sovereignty," the vehicles for all the tensions between the sections, finally resulted in disruption of the Union and civil war.[7]

Although the crisis of 1860–61 primarily revolved around the territorial problem, the conflict between different constitutional and legal ideas (whether the Constitution and laws were to secure human liberty or the needs of a particular class of men) was also laid bare in the fight over fugitive slaves and the Personal Liberty Laws. This story is worth more attention than is usually accorded to it, for it was an important part of the general confrontation between the sections after Lincoln's election.

For many years blacks had been sacrificed for the sake of union; for them, as Charles Francis Adams had noted earlier, our institutions were a "mockery." If Republicans, in the face of severe crisis, were willing to submit once again, the problem of fugitive slaves, and Personal Liberty Laws, might have been removed temporarily as a source of friction.

An overabundance of suggestions to this end were introduced in Congress after Buchanan's annual message. Several people sought explanatory amendments to settle longstanding interpretive conflicts, as the president had asked: others called for resolutions addressed to the free states expressing the sense of Congress, or for modifications in the federal law. On December 12 alone no fewer than twenty-three resolutions concerned with the sectional crisis were introduced in the House. Most of these touched on the matter of fugitive slaves, or on the Personal Liberty Laws.[8] The most extreme were those of William Smith of Virginia and Thomas Hindman of Arkansas. Smith suggested that the Committee of Thirty Three, the special House committee dealing with the crisis, be instructed to consider the policy of "declaring out of the Union every member thereof

[6]Bestor, "The American Civil War as a Constitutional Crisis," 333.

[7]Kenneth M. Stampp, *And the War Came: The North and the Secession Crisis 1860–1861* (Baton Rouge, 1950), 132 ff, 141; Bestor, "The American Civil War as a Constitutional Crisis," 351–52.

[8]*Cong. Globe*, 36th Cong., 2d sess., Dec. 12, 1860, 77–79.

which shall, by her legislation, aim to nullify an act of Congress." Hindman's idea was that any state having laws "defeating or impairing" the right of a master to reclaim his property "shall not be entitled to representation" in Congress as long as such laws remained on the books.

Republicans, throughout the debates, steadfastly opposed a constitutional amendment covering the Personal Liberty Laws, but many were willing to support a request from Congress to the states that they repeal all unconstitutional laws on their books. As early as December 17, 1860, a resolution introduced by Garnett Adrian of New Jersey in the House passed with only token opposition. This was a rather innocuous statement expressing the sense of Congress "that we deprecate the spirit of disobedience to that Constitution wherever manifested, and that we earnestly recommend the repeal of all statutes enacted by State Legislatures conflicting with, and in violation of that sacred instrument and the laws of Congress made in pursuance thereof."[9] A resolution to the same effect but more precisely aimed at the Personal Liberty Laws was introduced in the Committee of Thirty Three the following day by Henry Winter Davis of Maryland.[10] It was adopted by the committee, and on February 27, 1861, the House overwhelmingly endorsed it.[11]

Among the Republicans in Congress in 1860–61 just a few clung tenaciously to all the Personal Liberty Laws. Only Cadwalader C. Washburn of Wisconsin and Mason W. Tappan from New Hampshire dissented from the action of the Committee of Thirty Three in adopting the Davis resolution. If there were any unconstitutional statutes on the books, they argued, the federal judiciary would determine it.[12] They particularly objected to asking the free states to repeal laws that "delay" the operation of the federal law. The Supreme Court had declared such laws unconstitutional in *Prigg* v. *Pennsylvania*, but in their judgment this was an invasion of the reserved rights of the states. All the furor over these laws, they believed, was a charade, a "mere excuse for long meditated treason."[13]

At the same time, it is a mistake, often made, to infer that the Republicans who supported the position embodied in the Davis resolution were endorsing a movement to repeal all the Personal Liberty Laws. Their position was more elusive than that. Justin Morrill, for example, contended that many of the laws complained of were passed "to prevent the possibility of lawless seizure of free black men." He pointed out that the legislation of his home state, Vermont, was intended "to throw around all her

⁹*Ibid.*, Dec. 17, 1860, 107.
¹⁰"Journal of the Committee of Thirty Three," *House Reports*, 36th Cong., 2d sess., no. 31, 11–12.
¹¹*Cong. Globe*, 36th Cong., 2d sess., Feb. 27, 1860, 1262.
¹²A few Southerners, such as Jonathan S. Millson of Virginia, agreed with this contention. *Ibid.*, Jan. 21, 1861, Appendix, 77.
¹³"Minority Report of the Committee of Thirty Three," *House Reports*, 36th Cong., 2d sess., no. 31, 3–4.

inhabitants, however humble, the safeguards of the writ of habeas corpus and trial by jury, as well as to prevent the nefarious crime of kidnapping from being committed within her borders." All the states, he added, should have such laws. But he then concluded that if the state legislatures "have transcended the object aimed at" and passed laws in conflict with the Constitution they should be "repealed without debate."[14]

Lincoln's leadership in the crisis was, of course, crucial. On December 15, 1860, Lincoln explained his view in a letter to John A. Gilmer, marked "strictly confidential." He was still maintaining a public posture of "masterly inactivity." He said of the free state laws that, "I never have read one. If any of them are in conflict with the fugitive slave clause, or any other part of the constitution, I certainly should be glad of their repeal; but I could hardly be justified, as a citizen of Illinois, or as President of the United States, to recommend the repeal of a statute of Vermont, or South Carolina."[15] The same day South Carolina adopted its ordinance of secession Lincoln drew up three short resolutions expressing his response to the crisis. He gave these to Thurlow Weed who was to take them to Seward; he in turn would introduce them in the Senate. The second resolution declared that "all state laws, if there be such, really or apparently, in conflict with such law of Congress, [the Fugitive Slave Law], ought to be repealed; and no opposition to the execution of such law of Congress ought to be made."[16] The problem was that it was unclear which of the Personal Liberty Laws were in conflict with the Constitution, or the federal law. "So shifting," wrote the conservative *National Intelligencer* earlier in December, were these laws that it was difficult to determine "the number, nature, and animus." The only ones this paper found to be unconstitutional were those of Vermont, Massachusetts, Michigan, and Wisconsin, which interfered with the exercise of the powers of the fugitive slave commissioners.[17]

By the time Seward introduced Lincoln's proposals in the Committee of Thirteen on Christmas eve of 1860, Seward had changed the wording of the resolution to read: "The legislatures of the several States shall be respectfully requested to review all of their legislation affecting the right of persons recently resident in other States, and to repeal or modify all such acts as may contravene the provisions of the Constitution of the United States, or any laws made in pursuance thereof."[18] This resolution, which also covered the problem of free blacks going south, was defeated in the committee, with all of the southerners, except for Crittenden, opposed. It

[14]*Cong. Globe*, 36th Cong., 2d sess., Feb. 18, 1861, 1006.

[15]Lincoln to John A Gilmer, December 15, 1860 in Roy P. Basler, ed., *The Collected Works of Abraham Lincoln* (9 vols.; New Brunswick, N.J., 1953–55), 4: 152.

[16]Quoted in Potter, *Lincoln and His Party*, 168. Potter fully discusses the critical problems involved in ascertaining the text of Lincoln's proposed resolutions.

[17]*National Intelligencer*, December 11, 1860.

[18]"Journal of the Committee of Thirteen," *Senate Reports*, 36th Cong., 2d sess., no. 288, 10–11.

should be clear that the Republicans, under Lincoln's leadership, were not giving unequivocal support to the movement to repeal all the Personal Liberty Laws, even when they voted for the House resolution. The most they would concede was that unconstitutional laws should be repealed, leaving unsettled the question of which laws fell in this category and which did not.

Many Republicans, however, were willing to make one concession: they would accept congressional action on the subject of fugitive slaves. Despite the case of *Prigg* v. *Pennsylvania*, of course, there had been continued agitation over the question of congressional power to implement the fugitive slave clause. Lincoln for one was willing to endorse the power of Congress to act. Part of his first resolution of December 20 was "That the fugitive slave clause of the Constitution ought to be enforced by a law of Congress, with efficient provisions for that object." This concession was too much for some Republicans. Seward warned him that a portion of "our friends" would be "unwilling to give up their old opinion, that the duty of executing the constitutional provisions, concerning fugitives from service, belongs to the States, and not at all to Congress."[19] When he introduced Lincoln's proposals in the special Senate committee Seward deleted the explicit endorsement of congressional action.[20] With such a division within Republican ranks there virtually was no chance at all for Crittenden's proposed irrepealable constitutional amendment confirming the power of Congress over the subject of fugitive slaves.[21]

Even had Lincoln prevailed on this question the possibility was small to have worked out a viable compromise on the subject of runaways. The antagonisms between different conceptions of law and constitutional duty became very clear on this matter. The second half of Lincoln's first resolution read that the federal law should not oblige private persons to assist "in its execution, but punishing all who resist it, and with the usual safeguards to liberty, securing freemen against being surrendered as slaves." (In his inaugural on March 4 Lincoln asked: ". . . ought not all the safeguards of liberty known in civilized and human jurisprudence to be introduced, so that a free man be not, in any case, surrendered as a slave?")[22] Seward's resolutions narrowed Lincoln's "usual safeguards to liberty" to a trial by jury. There was no provision for habeas corpus. But even this was much too much for southern radicals.

Robert Toombs of Georgia proposed that the following be added as a "declaratory" clause to the Constitution: "fugitive slaves shall be surrendered under the provisions of the fugitive slave act of 1850, without

[19]Quoted in Potter, *Lincoln and His Party*, 168, n. 33.
[20]"Journal of the Committee of Thirteen," *Senate Reports*, 36th Cong., 2d sess., no. 288, 10–11.
[21]*Cong. Globe*, 36th Cong., 2d sess., Dec. 18, 1860, 114.
[22]Lincoln, *Collected Works*, 4: 264.

being entitled to either a writ of habeas corpus or trial by jury, or other similar obstructions of legislation by the States to which they may flee."[23] Toombs's proposed constitutional amendment showed clearly the irreconcilable nature of the dispute. As John A. Bingham said in January, 1861, in the House: "You say it is but the liberty of a slave that is involved. I say it is the liberty of a man that is involved."[24]

Only one measure came near resolving this problem, when it received the support of moderate Republicans like Morrill. This was a bill reported out of a subcommittee of five for the House Committee of Thirty Three. It provided for a jury trial in the federal court of the district from which the fugitive allegedly fled if he persisted in his claim to freedom after the judgment of the commissioner. It also provided that citizens of the free states would not have to assist in recapturing a runaway unless force was employed, or there was a reasonable expectation of force being used to prevent the recapture. These amendments would go part of the way toward meeting the objections of people in the free states. They were far less than what northern radicals would accept. In the Committee of Thirty Three C. C. Washburn made an unsuccessful effort to have these amendments modified to provide for a jury trial in the place where the seizure was made, and in all cases.[25]

Despite the fact that this bill was unsatisfactory to some it passed the House by a vote of ninety-two to eighty-three.[26] Opposition to the bill came from a variety of sources. The southern states still represented in Congress were almost solidly against the measure, as were Republicans like Thaddeus Stevens and John A. Bingham.

This House bill was not even debated in the Senate when Henry Wilson of Massachusetts, on March 2, objected to a second reading.[27] The House resolutions on the Personal Liberty Laws—they were in the form of joint resolutions—also received little attention in the Senate.[28] Congress then failed to do anything at all on the subject of fugitive slaves, and the Personal Liberty Laws. The "explanatory amendment" Buchanan sought had no chance, and the House bill modifying the federal law to meet northern objections, along with the House resolutions on the free-state laws, were buried in the Senate. Almost solid southern opposition, together with the opposition of radical Republicans, made it unlikely that the Senate would accept the modifications in the Fugitive Slave Law suggested by the House. If the Senate had endorsed the House resolutions, it would not have pla-

[23]"Journal of the Committee of Thirteen," *Senate Reports*, 36th Cong., 2d sess., no. 388, 3; cf. William Y. Thompson, *Robert Toombs of Georgia* (Baton Rouge, 1966), 150.

[24]*Cong. Globe*, 36th Cong., 2d sess., Jan. 22, 1861, Appendix, 83.

[25]"Journal of the Committee of Thirty Three," *House Reports*, 36th Cong., 2d sess., no. 31, 12, 29.

[26]*Cong. Globe*, 36th Cong., 2d sess., March 1, 1861, 1328.

[27]*Ibid.*, March 2, 1861, 1350.

[28]*Ibid.*, Feb. 28, 1861, 1266.

cated the southern leaders, for the free states still had to show their good faith, and acceptance of their constitutional duties, by repealing the Personal Liberty Laws.

I

According to the *National Intelligencer*, as noted before, only the laws of Massachusetts and Wisconsin, among those examined in this study, were unconstitutional beyond question because they directly interfered with federal processes, and it was there that the clash between conservatives and radicals reached a high point in January and February of 1861. This was appropriate since it was the laws of these two states that most clearly defined the constitutional and legal issues raised concerning fugitive slaves and the power of the state to protect free blacks.

On December 18, 1860, a group of influential Massachusetts conciliationists made public their address to the citizens of the state.[29] As his final public act former Chief Justice Shaw was the first to sign this appeal. He was joined by some of the most important jurists in the state such as Theophilus Parsons, Benjamin R. Curtis, Joel Parker, George Ticknor, and Jared Sparks. Desperately hoping to avert a breakup of the Union they recommended the unconditional repeal of the state's Personal Liberty Laws to demonstrate to the South the state's disposition to abide by the Constitution. Speaking in the spirit of Daniel Webster these men were all willing, as Leonard Levy has aptly said about Lemuel Shaw, to retreat for the moment from the cause of individual freedom out of concern for a higher value, the Union.[30] What they failed to see was what Charles Francis Adams perceived by January, 1861, that the secessionists were not seeking compromise, or even a few concessions, but domination.

Partially in response to the "Address" Charles G. Loring began to publish a series of papers in the *Boston Daily Advertiser*, in late December of 1860, in defense of the state laws. These were later collected and published under the title, *A Reading upon the Personal Liberty Laws*. Joel Parker countered with an elaborate examination of the whole sectional controversy entitled, *Personal Liberty Laws, (Statutes of Massachusetts,) and Slavery in the Territories, (Case of Dred Scott)*. This exchange between Loring and Parker was of real importance in the struggle over repeal.[31] Constitutional and legal arguments were broadly canvassed by both men, and their exchange served as a channel through which most of

[29]Curtis, *A Memoir of Benjamin Robbins Curtis*, 1: 329–35.
[30]Levy, *The Law of the Commonwealth*, 108.
[31]G. T. Anderson, "The Slavery Issue as a Factor in Massachusetts Politics from the Compromise of 1850 to the Outbreak of the Civil War," (Ph.D. dissertation, University of Chicago, 1944), 293 ff, is a good account of the political struggle over repeal, but does not include an examination of the constitutional-legal issues, or the Loring-Parker exchange.

the debate over the state laws flowed. They both dealt extensively with the "gist" of the question as phrased by the *New York Tribune*: "Are the Personal Liberty Laws unconstitutional?"[32]

"As now legally adjudged," Loring conceded, a claimant had the right to seize and remove a fugitive by his own efforts. He also had the right to seize and take him before a federal court or commissioner, or have him arrested and carried there, to obtain a certificate that would preclude "any further inquiry or examination into his right of possession by the local tribunals."

What then of the state habeas corpus? No one could deny, according to Loring, the right of the state courts to issue the writ to a federal officer or a private person in order to inquire into the legality of a restraint. To deny this much would be to destroy "all legal protection of personal liberty." A habeas corpus, issued in such cases, could not be construed to "impair, hinder or delay the exercise of any constitutional right, or the execution of any laws of the United States." Its sole purpose would be to ascertain whether there was such legal process as required by the federal law. This much, on the basis of Taney's judgment in *Ableman* v. *Booth*, was innocuous enough, but the statutes of Massachusetts went much further. Loring conceded that in the United States, where two separate judicial systems operate within the same territorial limits, it is understood that neither can intrude upon the legal processes of the other.[33] Any general language granting a power must be read with this limitation. When this principle of construction was understood the difficulties would disappear.

Loring, however, did propose certain modifications in the state's Personal Liberty Law. His proposals included relaxing the evidentiary requirements in cases where masters attempted to reclaim their property by their own efforts, and stipulating that nothing in the state habeas corpus statutes "shall be construed as conflicting, or intending to conflict, with the laws of the United States, or the lawful rights of any person claiming under any process thereof." He was also willing to see the portions of the state law closing the jails and imposing penalties on state officials repealed.[34]

In the face of a dangerous sectional clash that could easily break out into violence at any time Parker was temperamentally inclined to demand a good deal more. He was not disposed to accept Loring's subtle handling of the state's Personal Liberty Laws, particularly not that of habeas corpus. The jury trial provided in the act of 1855, Parker observed moreover, "was not designed merely to try the lawfulness of the detention, in a case where the master had made an arrest without process, but was expressly

[32]*New York Tribune*, January 18, 1861.
[33]Charles G. Loring, *A Reading upon the Personal Liberty Law* (Boston, 1861), 2–4.
[34]*Ibid.*, 4–8.

intended to try, in all cases, the question of his slavery or freedom," as the petitions to the legislature showed.

Others had argued—Loring did not develop this point—that the habeas corpus provisions were legitimate because the national and state governments had coordinate jurisdiction; where one had acquired a lawful custody the case was withdrawn from the other until the investigation was completed. But, Parker pointed out, "the jurisdiction of the United States is for the return of fugitives; the jurisdiction of the State courts is for setting free persons unlawfully restrained of their liberty; and so far from being co-ordinate, these . . . are . . . antagonistic." The state jurisdiction was, he wrote, subordinate, since it could not act "upon the subject matter until the former has acted, nor then, if the proceedings of the former are regular."[35] This was not, however, the way the Massachusetts laws functioned, and hence, they were unconstitutional.

Loring's interpretive defense of the Personal Liberty Laws, even though extremely refined at times, provided a focal point for some of the defenders of those laws. Parker's fulsome assault, on the other hand, pointed out very serious constitutional issues, issues which Loring had attempted to gloss over by construction. For Parker, and the other conciliationists who saw in the resolution of this struggle "the question of the final dissolution of the Union," Loring's gloss on what was "practical nullification" hardly was compelling. "The clause in the constitution, and the laws enacted under it," wrote Parker, "are not grievances which require to be redressed by revolution." The Personal Liberty Laws should be unconditionally repealed, he believed, to appease the unionists in the crucial border states.[36]

At the beginning of the year there seemed to be a strong possibility that repeal would be obtained in Massachusetts. Many of the state's most important jurists had signed the "Address," and in Congress Charles Francis Adams was still attempting to work out a compromise that would include a call for a repeal of unconstitutional laws. Several influential newspapers in the state also favored repeal.[37] On January 3, 1861, Governor Nathaniel P. Banks delivered his "Valedictory Address" to the legislature in which he added his weight to the cause of repeal: "Where the process, statute and jurisdiction is exclusively in either government, the other must surrender any claim to control the procedure, or qualify the final judgment."[38]

The incoming governor, John A. Andrew, however, was of a different mind. Before the end of the year 1860 he had gone to Washington where he

[35]Joel Parker, *Personal Liberty Laws*, (*Statutes of Massachusetts*,) *and Slavery in the Territories*, (*Case of Dred Scott*.) (Boston, 1861), 6, 18.

[36]*Ibid.*, 25, 48–49.

[37]Anderson, "The Slavery Issue as a Factor in Massachusetts Politics," 305–6.

[38]"Valedictory Address of His Excellency Governor Banks, to the Two Branches of the Legislature of Massachusetts, January 3, 1861." *Mass. Senate Document No. 1, 1861*, 25.

held a conference with Senators Sumner and Henry Wilson of Massachusetts, Doolittle of Wisconsin, and Lyman Trumbull of Illinois. These radicals resolved that the Union must be preserved, "though it cost a million lives."[39] Andrew considered Banks's "Address" an "execrable thing," and he was determined to follow another course.

In his inaugural Andrew came out solidly in favor of retaining the existing Personal Liberty Laws. He contended that the state had the right and duty to conduct an independent inquiry into any claim, even though a certificate had been issued.[40] The whole problem, he believed, "is a naked question of right between private persons, and of duty between the Commonwealth and its subjects." Conciliationists hardly could have expected anything else from a man who had been one of the commissioners appointed under the Personal Liberty Law of 1855.[41]

There were still some clear signs that Massachusetts was willing to follow a more conservative policy than demanded by antislavery zealots. On January 23, 1861, the Senate Committee on Federal Relations submitted a very brief report summarily rejecting the request for a law to end slave-hunting in the state. Senator William Northend merely cited the fugitive slave clause and added that the petitioners were seeking a law "for the accomplishment of a purpose clearly prohibited by the constitution."[42]

Throughout January, 1861, and into early February the subject of repeal of the Personal Liberty Laws was considered by a Joint Special Committee of the legislature.[43] Radicals poured in memorials like that signed by Samuel Sewall and Samuel Gridley Howe, among others, declaring that "this is a political and moral and not a legal or constitutional question . . . and it is, comparatively, unimportant what Judge A, or Professor B, or Governor C thinks of it in a legal point of view."[44] The Personal Liberty Laws, in their view, did nothing more than provide proceedings whereby an individual could test "the right which is claimed for the Fugitive Slave Act of 1850 to overthrow all the fundamental principles of free government." Another memorial declared that this was a peaceful method of "checking the encroachments of lawless power, and holding at bay the wild impatience of despotism roaring and gnashing for its prey."[45]

[39]William B. Hesseltine, *Lincoln and the War Governors* (New York, 1955), 110.

[40]"Address of His Excellency John A. Andrew, to the Two Branches of the Legislature of Massachusetts, January 5, 1861." *Mass. Senate Document No. 2, 1861,* 28, 34.

[41]Andrew's commission is filed with his papers in the Massachusetts Historical Society.

[42]"Report of the Committee on Federal Relations, on petitions to end slave-hunting." *Mass. Senate Document No. 17, 1861.*

[43]For the petitions in favor of repeal see *Mass., Senate Journal, 1861,* Mass. State Library, 82: 108, 111, 114, 123, 131, 140, 149, 159, 166, 174, 177, 186, 193, 201, 203, 213, 217, 229, 231, 236, 239, 245, 252, 257, 262, 277, 283, 292, 295, 306, 318, 339. For the remonstrances against repeal see *ibid.,* 82: 131, 198, 201, 203, 213, 215, 219, 239, 245, 252, 257, 309, 318, 404.

[44]"Remonstrance of Samuel Sewall and others," *Mass. Senate Document No. 34, 1861,* 6.

[45]"Memorial on the Personal Liberty Law," *Mass. House Document No. 121, 1861,* 35.

In the arguments before the Joint Special Committee Edward L. Pierce presented the ideas developed by Loring.[46] On January 29 Wendell Phillips appeared and gave a passionate exposition of the radical position. He was as candid as anyone could have wished when he admitted that he valued a Personal Liberty Law "not only for the protection that it gives to the free natives of Massachusetts, but for the measure of protection that it gives to fugitive slaves within the Commonwealth." The crux of the problem, as he saw it, was that the Fugitive Slave Law was "nothing less than making the slave law of the South the law of Massachusetts."[47] In this struggle between human freedom and slavery the Personal Liberty Laws provided a mechanism to test the validity of the federal law. He well knew that the courts had almost unanimously upheld that law, but those were judgments made in times of crisis, judgments which could be overturned.

On February 18, 1861, the Joint Special Committee submitted its report, along with a bill. This report must have been a severe disappointment to the conservatives, and particularly to Joel Parker, whose criticisms were branded as "to a certain extent, unjust, and founded on a misconception of the laws themselves." Those laws were not designed to defeat the federal law, but to protect the free citizens of the state. They encroached on the federal sphere no more than the laws regarding the manufacture and sale of liquor encroached on the exclusive federal control of foreign commerce. "The right to legislate for the recapture of fugitives," they noted, "does not extend the operation of such legislation to free persons who are not fugitives from service or labor."[48]

The doctrine in *Ableman* v. *Booth*, "not called for by the exigency of the case," had to be taken with some limitation, according to the committee. Surely there were cases in which the state habeas corpus could have its full force: "suppose one of her citizens is seized by an officer of the United States in the night time, to be spirited away as a witness beyond the jurisdiction of the State, . . . may not the State issue its *habeas corpus* to inquire into the cause and legality of such seizure?"

What the committee tried to do in framing a bill was to remove from the statute books provisions "fairly open to any constitutional doubt, and to retain every provision which can be safely and properly retained as a safeguard of freedom." This, of course, was the position advanced by Lincoln and adhered to in Congress by the Republicans. In the judgment of this committee it meant drawing a bill very much in accord with the suggestions of Charles Loring. Among its suggestions was a declaratory provision that would avoid "the imputation that our laws are intended to interfere with

---

[46] *Remarks of Edward L. Pierce, Before the Committee of the Legislature of Massachusetts, On the General Statutes Relating to Personal Liberty, At Their Hearing of Feb. 1, 1861* (Boston, 1861).

[47] *Argument of Wendell Phillips, Esq. Against the Repeal of the Personal Liberty Law, Before the Committee of Legislature, Tuesday, January 29, 1861* (Boston, 1861), 6.

[48] "Report of the Joint Special Committee," *Mass. Senate Document No. 53, 1861*, 5.

the laws of the United States," a provision that the rules of evidence would be those of the common law, and a stipulation that the volunteer militia could be used to quell riots.[49] The bill they introduced was designed to accomplish these objectives.[50]

In the last few days of February and into early March the bill was debated in the General Court. In the Senate debates even some conciliationists came around to support the measure. Speaking on February 27, for example, William Northend said that it "relieves the law from unconstitutional objections, and should be passed as reported." On the other hand, he would have preferred an unconditional repeal of all the Personal Liberty Laws, except those relating to the offence of kidnapping.[51] Objections to the bill came not so much from conservatives as from those who feared that it removed precious safeguards for personal freedom.[52] On March 20, 1861, nevertheless, the bill was passed by the General Court.[53] Despite the demands of several leading legal minds in Massachusetts the state's Personal Liberty Laws, although changed, were not repealed.

In Wisconsin a sharp battle was shaping up between conservatives and radicals by the end of 1860. At a Republican Fugitive Slave Law Convention it was resolved that the Personal Liberty Laws, securing habeas corpus and trial by jury to everyone within the state's ambit, were "essential to the security of civil liberty." Rather than support repeal these Republicans resolved to work to make the laws "more efficient in promoting the objects for which they were designed."[54] The conservative Democratic newspaper, the *Madison Argus and Democrat*, on the other hand, demanded that moderates in both sections should be the arbiters in the sectional dispute, and their principle should be "the Union and the equality of the States," not the "higher law."[55] A day later this paper asked its readers, "is it not better to stoop to some humiliations, and acquiesce in some compromise than to see all—credit, commerce, banks, trade, manufactures and the political Union of States, fall?"[56]

Republicans in Wisconsin were more inclined toward a vigorous antislavery stance than those in many other states, and among the most radical was the governor, Alexander W. Randall.[57] In his message to the legisla-

---

[49]*Ibid.*, 4, 6.

[50]"An Act Concerning Habeas Corpus and Personal Liberty," *Mass. Senate Document No. 53, 1861.*

[51]*Speech of Hon. William D. Northend, of Essex, In the Senate of Massachusetts, February 27, 1861, upon the Modification of the Personal Liberty Bill* (Boston, 1861), 4.

[52]*Boston Daily Advertiser*, March 6, 1861.

[53]*Mass. Session Laws, 1861*, 398–99. For the proceedings in the General Court see *Mass. House Journal, 1861*, Mass. State Library, 84: 363, 378, 388–90, 417; *Mass. Senate Journal, 1861*, Mass. State Library, 82: 307, 318–19, 333, 355, 362, 370, 375, 383, 392, 395, 407–9, 501.

[54]*Ripon Times*, quoted in *Daily Argus and Democrat*, December 18, 1860.

[55]*Argus and Democrat*, November 20, 1860.

[56]*Ibid.*, November 21, 1860.

[57]Hesseltine, *Lincoln and the War Governors*, 48–49, has an excellent sketch of Randall.

ture on January 10, 1861, he rejected the compromises being proposed,[58] and called instead for an increase in the state's militia. Randall gave a forceful defense of the Personal Liberty Laws. Such statutes, he said, should be found in every state: "The highest duty of the legislature of any civilized State, is to provide by every constitutional means for the protection of the rights of person of the citizens." If, however, after a "close examination and scrutiny," any provisions of the Personal Liberty Laws appeared to conflict with the Constitution it would be the duty of the legislature, "at your pleasure," to change the laws to bring them into harmony with the Constitution. He did not say that the state laws should not conflict with the Fugitive Slave Law (thus leaving that question open); rather, he concluded by saying that "while this government stands, and we consent to live under it, Liberty may pay to Slavery the price the Fathers agreed should be paid, but, with our consent, it shall pay no more."[59]

Despite the fact that there was very little hope for a complete repeal of the state's law, conservative Democrats introduced a measure to that effect. Republicans countered with instructions to the judiciary committee, which had the bill under consideration, that it should examine the laws "so as to make the same in all things conform to the Constitution of the United States, if in anything they are in conflict therewith." For the next several weeks this committee sat on the bill until the Democrats, on March 8, successfully forced it to report.[60]

On March 12, 1861, the judiciary committee released the bill with a report recommending a substitute. On the preceding Monday the Republicans in caucus had agreed to support a measure repealing large parts of the Personal Liberty Law,[61] although many were generally opposed to alterations of any kind.[62] Although the Republican-dominated judiciary committee reported in favor of repeal, it did so with very important qualifications. "It is certain," this committee noted, "that if the Fugitive Slave Law is unconstitutional the sovereign writ of habeas corpus is as available to thwart its operations without our Personal Liberty Law as with it. If it is constitutional, it follows that our statute is inoperative." The legitimacy of the federal law remained an open question, and on such matters the ultimate sovereign power was the people themselves. "By the quiet but omnipotent power of public opinion," they reported, "working revolutions more wonderful than the sword has ever known, laws destructive of the rights of the people or judicial decisions by which such laws are sustained, are rendered obsolete or their repeal enforced."

The Personal Liberty Laws, in their judgment, were largely symbolic expressions of the deep-seated sentiments of the people, who would continue to thwart the inhumane Fugitive Slave Law. The Personal Liberty

[58]*Ibid.*, 118.
[59]*Argus and Democrat*, January 11, 1861.
[60]*Wisc. Senate Journal, 1861*, 96, 354–55.
[61]*Argus and Democrat*, March 14, 1861.
[62]*Milwaukee Sentinel*, March 21, 1861.

Laws, as expressions of the doctrine of interposition, had a function to perform at one time, but the necessity had passed away, "and whatever just indignation devised it for protection against the most cruel and barbarous law known to civilized governments, no single instance has ever arisen for its application." Since these laws were of little practical use in 1861, and served as a "pretext" for secession, they could be repealed safely.

But they should not be repealed completely. The substitute offered by the judiciary committee retained that portion of the law of 1857 making it the duty of district attorneys to protect anyone seized from unlawful claims. The habeas corpus and jury-trial provisions of the Wisconsin law, patterned after those of Massachusetts, then were to be repealed. As a *quid pro quo*, however, the committee concluded with a request that the Fugitive Slave Law be modified.

On March 20, 1861, the senate accepted the substitute offered by the judiciary committee.[63] Eight days later the assembly voted to lay the bill on the table.[64] Repeal had come very close in Wisconsin, but it had failed.

Unlike the other states, however, where the subject was simply dropped after the outbreak of the Civil War, Wisconsin took the matter up again the following year. On January 10, 1862, a bill was introduced to repeal the objectionable sections of the state law. This bill went to a special committee.

On February 4 the "Majority Report" was submitted to the senate recommending repeal. For the sake of consistency of purpose, they argued, Wisconsin should modify its statutes. As long as "we are conducting this war, for the avowed purpose of putting down rebellion and upholding the Constitution, we should not ourselves disregard it." The doctrine that the Union was a compact, and the idea that the state had the power to nullify a federal law were incompatible, they contended, with the existence of a national government. "We are now in the midst of a terrible war," this report concluded, "for the restoration of the Union, and we would ask what right (with our Supreme Court decision, the resolutions of 1859, and the act under consideration, still in force,) we attempt to enforce obedience to the Constitution and laws of the United States."[65] The legislature agreed, and on June 17, 1862, the governor signed the bill repealing the "unconstitutional" features of the Wisconsin Personal Liberty Law.[66]

Farther to the east and south the effort to reverse the course of the preceeding decade met complete defeat in 1860–61, nor was it renewed after the outbreak of war. In New York conservatives, heavily supported by big merchants in the cities,[67] launched a vigorous campaign for repeal after Lincoln's election, but without causing more than a murmur in the state legislature. In January, 1861 the *New York Tribune*, speaking for more

[63] *Wisc. Senate Journal, 1861*, 376–78, 468.
[64] *Wisc. House Journal, 1861*, 783. For other proceedings see *ibid.*, 653–54, 675, 747–50.
[65] *Wisc. Senate Journal, 1862*, 6, 11, 162.
[66] *Wisc. House Journal, 1862*, 1001.
[67] Foner, *Business & Slavery*, 230.

New York Republicans than the more conciliatory *Albany Evening Journal* of Thurlow Weed, came out in support of the state's Personal Liberty Law. This law, said the *Tribune*, like the laws of the other free states, was not passed with the intention of nullifying an act of Congress. "The States that have passed them have merely exercised their unquestionable right to throw around their own citizens the ordinary legal and constitutional safeguards against kidnapping."[68] When the Republican caucus in New York voted sixty-seven to five against even discussing concessions to demands of slave owners, whatever slim chance there might have been for repeal died.[69]

In Ohio the repeal effort was a tepid affair at best, even though it had the support of the Republican governor, William Dennison.[70] A bill to repeal part of the 1857 law on kidnapping was referred to a select committee of one, Senator Jacob D. Cox, an antislavery Republican who later adopted a conservative position on black suffrage during the Reconstruction years.[71] Cox did not report back until the end of February, at which time the bill was buried.[72]

A more complete public scrutiny of the state law occurred in Pennsylvania in late 1860 when Lewis D. Vail of Philadelphia began an exchange with Governor John Letcher of Virginia, a southern moderate instrumental in the meeting of the Washington Peace Conference. Letcher had charged that the Pennsylvania laws were "designed to obstruct the execution of the fugitive slave law." It was Letcher's intention to bring to the attention of Pennsylvanians "a source of irritation that was doing as much to weaken the bonds of the Union, as any other one thing having a legal existence." Despite what the Court had said in *Prigg* v. *Pennsylvania* Letcher charged that the act of 1847 withdrawing state instrumentalities from use by claimants ran afoul of the law of 1793. "Is it not plainly and palpably their duty," he ended, "to aid in giving full effect to this requirement?"

Vail generally rested his case for the Pennsylvania laws upon Story's opinion in 1842. Section 5 of the act of 1847 was troublesome. Vail's defense of it rested in part upon the state constitutional provision that the privilege of the writ of habeas corpus could not be suspended unless the public safety required it in cases of rebellion or invasion. Since the law of 1847 prohibited state judges from taking jurisdiction of cases involving fugitive slaves, argued Vail, it might be contended that their habeas corpus jurisdiction also was removed. In order then to make the law constitutional Section 5 was added. Once informed of the fact that the party in custody

[68]*New York Tribune*, January 22, 1861.
[69]Stampp, *And the War Came*, 146. See *New York Senate Journal, 1861*, 395, 407, 502, 506, 567, 623; *New York House Journal, 1861*, 134, 141, 191, 273, 351, 597, 614, 655, 1016, 1050.
[70]Hesseltine, *Lincoln and the War Governors*, 117–18.
[71]*DAB*, 476–78.
[72]*Ohio Senate Journal, 1861*, 46, 111, 119.

was held by federal authority, of course, the state judge could proceed no further. There was, then, nothing unconstitutional about Section 5 after all, and the remaining sections of the law were based squarely on the opinion of the U.S. Supreme Court.[73]

Despite the fact that Vail described himself as a conservative, and was assailed in the North as a "proslavery dough-face" and in the South as an "abolitionist," he did not speak for all the conservatives in Pennsylvania. At a public meeting in Philadelphia, attended by some of the leading men of the city, a memorial was drawn up petitioning for repeal.[74] Another petition, presented in the senate on January 8, 1861, carried the signatures of 11,000 citizens of Philadelphia.[75] Repeal had also been urged by Governor Andrew Curtin.[76] Hurriedly the Pennsylvania Anti-Slavery Society prepared a counter petition asking "that instead of diminishing, the legislature would add to the safeguards."[77]

On January 16, 1861, Robert E. Randall of Philadelphia presented an elaborate argument in behalf of repeal in the state assembly. Except for the antikidnapping sections, he urged repeal on the grounds of either unconstitutionality or offensiveness. Prohibitions on the use of state instrumentalities directly conflicted with the Fugitive Slave Act of 1793, which provided for them, in Randall's judgment. The punishment of a violent recovery by self-help alone was invalid, moreover, because the state had no power "to prescribe the mode in which an act of Congress shall be executed."

Randall adopted completely the proslavery view on habeas corpus. "Our forefathers," he noted, "had no such fastidious ideas upon this subject of slavery, that a fugitive servant or slave could claim a trial by jury, or appeal to the writ of habeas corpus for relief." The habeas corpus never had been applicable in cases involving fugitive slaves, since slaves were property. The Fugitive Slave Law of 1850, moreover, prohibited the issuance of a habeas corpus to interfere with the proceedings of the "Federal tribunals."[78] The state law should be repealed.

Despite Randall's statement of the proslavery position, or perhaps because of it, Pennsylvania's legislature did not repeal any sections of the

[73] *Pennsylvania and the Fugitive Slave Law. The Statute of March 3d, 1847: Its Real Import Explained. Correspondence between the Hon. John Letcher, Governor of Virginia, and Lewis D. Vail, Esq. of Philadelphia. Views of the National Intelligencer upon the Subject* (Philadelphia, 1861), 2, 4, 5–7.

[74] Philadelphia Citizens: Petition to Pennsylvania Assembly to Repeal Sections of Penal Code Prohibiting Return of Fugitive Slaves, Pennsylvania Miscellaneous, 12. Library of Congress, Manuscript Division. See also *Penn. Senate Journal, 1861*, 53, 224, 271, 312; *Penn. House Journal, 1861*, 46, 49, 69, 120, 150, 246, 311, 467, 570.

[75] *Penn. Senate Journal, 1861*, 53.

[76] Hesseltine, *Lincoln and the War Governors*, 123.

[77] Pennsylvania Anti-Slavery Society, Executive Committee, Minutes (1856–70), Historical Society of Pennsylvania, Book no. 4, 52–54.

[78] *Speech of Robert E. Randall, of Philadelphia, on the Laws of the State Relative to Fugitive Slaves, Delivered in the House of Representatives of Pennsylvania, January 16, 1861* (Philadelphia, 1861), 4–6, 10–11.

personal liberty statutes of the state. In fact, no repeal bill was even discussed, merely the desirability of repeal.

II

Uniformly, then, the free states studied here refused to sacrifice the Personal Liberty Laws on the altar of union; they refused to bow before the southern quest for domination. Other than in Wisconsin, those laws passed through the secession crisis generally unscathed, only to be removed unheralded a few years later. In a 1910 digest of the laws of Pennsylvania, for example, a significant portion of the state's earlier law securing personal freedom was merely omitted with the notation that it was "rendered obsolete by the 13th amendment."[79] In a way they deserved better, for in the years before the Civil War these laws stand out as expressions of a continuous, and richly varied, commitment to the idea of liberty under law.

With the outbreak of the war, and the consequent end of slavery, this commitment was no longer bounded by the idea of "state sovereignty," or the idea that there could be a legitimate property interest in men acquired under state law. On June 28, 1864, Congress finally repealed the fugitive slave laws.[80] Prior to the war the antislavery commitment had been allowed free play only at the state level. The strategy had been to pit the law of the free states (resting upon the presumption of freedom for all men, and the view that all have standing to challenge any restraint upon their freedom) against the personalized justice condoned by the laws of the South which had been given an extraterritorial force in the fugitive slave clause of the Constitution. With the firing on Fort Sumter a new situation had been presented. As G. W. Hazelton said in his "Minority Report" to the special committee of the Wisconsin senate in 1862, "The Federal Government has passed from the grasp of the slave power, never, it is firmly believed to be restored to its possession. With this change new duties and new responsibilities are imposed upon, and must be assumed by that government." From this point on, he concluded, "the true interests of freedom are to be developed in our nation, not primarily by States acting in their individual spheres and according to their own peculiar and perhaps diverse inclinations, but by the whole body of the people operating through a national organization, in a common direction, and for a common purpose."[81] Among the first fruits of this new orientation were the Thirteenth and Fourteenth Amendments, which carried forward the commitment that had been embodied in the Personal Liberty Laws.

[79]Ardemus Stewart, ed., *A Digest of the Statutes of Law of the State of Pennsylvania* (4 vols.; Philadelphia, 1910), 4: 4404–5. See also *Mass. Session Laws, 1868,* 21; *Mass. Session Laws, 1881,* 1066 ff.; Clarence F. Birdseye, ed., *The Revised Statutes, Codes and General Laws of the State of New York* (3d ed.; New York, 1901), 2: 2084–85; *Ohio Session Laws, 1863,* 72; *ibid., 1866,* 16–17.
[80]McDougall, *Fugitive Slaves,* 75 ff.
[81]*Wisc. Senate Journal, 1862,* 224.

Appendix

Checklist of the Personal Liberty Laws

Vermont

1. 1806. An Act, to prevent kidnapping.
2. 1840. An Act, to extend the right of trial by jury.
3. 1843. An Act, for the protection of Personal Liberty.
4. 1850. An Act Relating to the Writ of Habeas Corpus to Persons Claimed as Fugitive Slaves, and the Right of Trial by Jury.
5. 1854. An Act for the Defence of Liberty and for the Punishment of Kidnapping.
6. 1858. An Act to Secure Freedom to All Persons within this State.

New Hampshire

1. 1846. An Act for the further protection of personal liberty.
2. 1857. An Act to secure freedom and the rights of citizenship to persons in this State.

Maine

1. 1821. An Act for the protection of the Personal Liberty of the Citizens, and for other Purposes.
2. 1821. An Act establishing the Rights to the Writ for replevying a person.
3. 1838. An Act against kidnapping or selling for a slave.
4. 1855. An Act further to protect personal liberty.
5. 1857. An Act additional to "an act further to protect personal liberty."
6. 1857. An Act declaring all slaves brought by their masters into this state free, and to punish any attempt to exercise authority over them.

Massachusetts

1. 1785. An Act directing the Process in Habeas Corpus.
2. 1788. An Act to prevent the Slave-Trade, and for granting Relief to the Families of such unhappy Persons as may be kidnapped or decoyed away from this Commonwealth.
3. 1787. An Act establishing the Right to, and the Form of the Writ De Homine Replegiando, or Writ for replevying a Man.
4. 1837. An Act to Restore the Trial by Jury, on Questions of Personal Freedom.
5. 1843. An Act further to Protect Personal Liberty.
6. 1855. An Act to protect the Rights and Liberties of the People of the Commonwealth of Massachusetts.
7. 1858. An Act to amend "An Act to Protect the Rights and Liberties of the People of the Commonwealth of Massachusetts."
8. 1859. Of Habeas Corpus, Personal Replevin, and Personal Liberty.
9. 1861. An Act concerning Habeas Corpus and Personal Liberty.

Connecticut

1. 1784. An Act concerning Indian, Mulatto, and Negro Servants and Slaves.
2. 1788. An Act to Prevent the Slave-Trade.
3. 1838. An Act for the fulfillment of the obligations of this State, imposed by the Constitution of the United States, in regard to persons held to service or labor in one State escaping into another, and to secure the right of Trial by Jury, in the cases herein mentioned.
4. 1844. An Act for the protection of Personal Liberty.
5. 1848. An Act to Prevent Slavery.
6. 1854. An Act for the Defense of Liberty in this State.

Rhode Island

1. 1848. An Act further to protect personal liberty.
2. 1854. An Act in amendment of an act entitled "An Act further to protect personal liberty."

New Jersey

1. 1798. An Act respecting slaves.
2. 1804. An Act for the gradual abolition of slavery.
3. 1818. An act to prohibit the exportation of Slaves or Servants of Colour out of this State.

4. 1820. An Act for the gradual abolition of slavery, and other purposes respecting slaves.

5. 1826. A Supplement to an act entitled "An act concerning slaves."

6. 1837. A Further Supplement to an act entitled, "An act concerning slaves."

7. 1846. An Act to abolish slavery.

8. 1846. An Act concerning fugitive slaves.

New York

1. 1799. An Act for the gradual abolition of slavery.

2. 1801. An Act concerning slaves and servants.

3. 1808. An Act to prevent the Kidnapping of free People of Colour.

4. 1813. An Act to prevent kidnapping of Free People of Colour.

5. 1817. An Act relative to slaves and servants.

6. 1819. An Act to amend an act entitled "an act relative to slaves and servants."

7. 1827. An Act to prevent Kidnapping.

8. *Revised Statutes*, 1828, Of the writ of habeas corpus, to bring up a Person to testify, or to answer in certain cases.

9. *Revised Statutes*, 1828, Of rape, maiming, kidnapping, and other offenses against the person, not herein before enumerated.

10. 1840. An Act more effectually to protect the free citizens of this state from being kidnapped or reduced to slavery.

11. 1840. An Act to extend the right of trial by jury.

Pennsylvania

1. 1780. An Act for the gradual Abolition of slavery.

2. 1785. An Act for the better securing personal liberty, and preventing wrongful imprisonments.

3. 1788. An Act to explain and amend an act, entituled [sic] "An Act for the gradual abolition of slavery."

4. 1820. An Act to prevent kidnapping.

5. 1826. An act to give effect to the provisions of the constitution of the United States, relative to fugitives from labor, for the protection of free people of color, and to prevent kidnapping.

6. 1847. An Act to prevent kidnapping, preserve the public peace, prohibit the exercise of certain powers heretofore exercised by judges, justices of the peace, aldermen and jailors in this commonwealth, and to repeal certain slave laws.

Indiana

    1. 1824. An Act relative to Fugitives from Labour.
    2. 1831. An Act relative to Crime and Punishment.

Illinois

    1. 1833. Offenses Against the Persons of Individuals. (Kidnapping section)

Ohio

    1. 1804. An Act, to regulate black and mulatto persons. (This law contained an antikidnapping section, although the act as a whole is scarcely a Personal Liberty Law).
    2. 1811. An Act Securing the benefits of the writ of habeas corpus.
    3. 1819. An Act to punish kidnapping.
    4. 1831. An Act to prevent kidnapping.
    5. 1839. An Act relating to fugitives from labor or service from other states. (Like the act of 1804 this one is not properly a Personal Liberty Law. It is listed because it contained an antikidnapping section.)
    6. 1847. An act further to amend the act securing the benefits of the writ of Habeas Corpus.
    7. 1857. An Act to prohibit the confinement of fugitives from slavery in the jails of Ohio.
    8. 1857. An Act to prevent Slaveholding and Kidnapping in Ohio.
    9. 1857. An Act to prevent kidnapping.

Michigan

    1. 1855. An Act to protect the rights and liberties of the inhabitants of this State.

Wisconsin

    1. 1857. Of the Writ of Habeas Corpus Relative to Fugitive Slaves.

Bibliography

PRIMARY WORKS

State Legislative Material

A. Massachusetts

Massachusetts presents a unique problem in that its legislative journals for most of the years of the nineteenth century (down to the Civil War) are not available in published form. The eighteenth century journals have been published, but they were of little use in this study, particularly because abolition in the state was a judicial process. Of the rare journals that were published in the nineteenth century only two were valuable: *The Journal of the House of Representatives of the Commonwealth of Massachusetts, 1857* (Boston, 1857); and *The Debates and Proceedings in the Massachusetts Legislature, At the Session which was begun at the State House in Boston, on Wednesday the second day of January, and was prorogued on Friday, the sixth day of June, 1856* (Boston, 1856). The others (which include all the journals for the years in which Personal Liberty Laws were passed) have been cited as: *Mass. House Journal,* or *Mass. Senate Journal,* with the year following. These manuscripts are in the Massachusetts State Library in Boston.

Published or unpublished, the journals are spare, generally giving little more than the proceedings on a bill. Personal papers were occasionally important as supplements: particularly valuable were the papers of Charles Francis Adams, and the letters of James W. Stone to Charles Sumner in the Sumner papers (see the listing under Unpublished Personal Papers). Also of considerable help were the speeches given by leading abolitionists before hearings of the General Court (see Other Contemporary Material).

Undoubtedly, however, the most significant legislative materials were the documents published by the senate and house, which included committee reports, petitions, and copies of bills introduced. These are bound together, in separate volumes, for each session of the legislature. All documents used in this study come from the period after 1837 when the legislature was frequently agitated over the Personal Liberty Laws. The most important are:

House Document No. 51 (1837). Report on the Trial by Jury in Questions of Personal Freedom.

House Document No. 41 (1843). Report of the Joint Special Committee of the Senate and House to whom was referred the petition of George Latimer and more than sixty-five thousand citizens of Massachusetts, also the message of his excellency the Governor, communicating a copy of all the correspondence between the governor or authorities of the State of Virginia and the Executive Department of this Commonwealth, touching the case of George Latimer.

Senate Document No. 51 (1851). Report of the Joint Special Committee, to which was referred so much of the Governor's Address as relates to the subject of Slavery, and to which was also referred numerous petitions from the inhabitants of the State, praying the Legislature to instruct their Senators and to request the Representatives in Congress to use their endeavors to procure a repeal of the "Fugitive Slave Law;" and also numerous other petitions praying the Legislature to provide further safeguards to protect the citizens in the enjoyment of their natural rights.

Senate Document No. 89 (1851). Report of the Special Senate Committee to inquire whether the freedom of any of the inhabitants of this Commonwealth is endangered through the remissness of any officers thereof, or if any officer has refused or neglected to serve any process for the arrest of any person charged as a criminal, and to inquire if any law for the security of personal liberty has recently been violated by officers of the city of Boston, or by officers of this Commonwealth, pretending to act under the orders of the officers of said city.

Senate Document No. 95 (1851). Senator Buckingham's proposed amendments to the bill he had introduced (see Doc. No. 51).

Senate Document No. 76 (1852). The report of the Joint Special Committee on the resolves of Delaware, New Hampshire, and New Jersey, to which was committed the petition of seventy-six legal voters of the town of West Boylston, for a law similar to the law of Vermont granting a trial by jury to fugitives, the petition of Josiah Trow and seventy-nine others, legal voters of the town of Buckland, for the enactment of a law granting the fugitive from slavery the right of trial by jury, and an order to consider the expediency of passing a law authorizing the executive to appoint commissioners to protect persons arrested as fugitive slaves.

Senate Document No. 3 (1855). Address of His Excellency Henry J. Gardner, to the Two Branches of the Legislature of Massachusetts, January 9, 1855.

Senate Document No. 162 (1855). Report of the Joint Standing Committee on Federal Relations.

Senate Document No. 86 (1858). Report of the Committee to whom was referred the Message of the Governor, dated March 19, recommending certain amendments to the 489th chapter of the Acts of 1855.

House Document No. 173 (1859). Report of the Committee on Federal Relations, to whom was referred the Petition of John M. Earle and sixteen thousand five hundred others, from the various towns in this Commonwealth, praying that the rendition of Fugitive Slaves may be by law prohibited in Massachusetts.

House Document No. 204 (1859). Substitute proposed by Mr. Davis of Bristol: "An Act Relating to the Writ of Habeas Corpus."

House Document No. 220 (1859). Substitute offered by Mr. Griffin, of Malden: "An Act Relating to Personal Liberty."

House Document No. 256 (1859). Substitute proposed by Mr. Wells of Greenfield: "An Act to secure Freedom to all Persons within this Commonwealth."

House Document No. 303 (1859). Bill reported by J. O. A. Griffin: "An Act Relating to the Writ of Habeas Corpus."

Senate Document No. 1 (1861). Valedictory Address of His Excellency Governor Banks, To the Two Branches of the Legislature of Massachusetts, January 3, 1861.

Senate Document No. 2 (1861). Address of His Excellency John A. Andrew, to the Two Branches of the Legislature of Massachusetts, January 5, 1861.

Senate Document No. 17 (1861). Report of the Committee on Federal Relations, on petitions to end slave-hunting.

Senate Document No. 34 (1861). Remonstrance of Samuel Sewall and others.

Senate Document No. 53 (1861). Report of the Joint Special Committee, to whom was referred so much of the Governor's Message as relates to that portion of the General Statutes regarding Personal Liberty, and also the Petitions and Remonstrances of divers persons for and against the repeal of the Personal Liberty laws, so called, and certain sections of the Act respecting the writ of Habeas Corpus.

House Document No. 121 (1861). Memorial on the Personal Liberty Law.

B. New York

The legislative journals for the senate and assembly of New York are all published and are readily available in a number of places, including the Library of Congress, the State Library of New York, and the New York and Wisconsin Historical Societies. Documents, including committee reports, governors' messages, and petitions, were published separately.

Assembly Document No. 359 (1838). Report of the Minority of the Committee on the Judiciary, on various petitions relating to slavery and the slave trade.

Assembly Document No. 185 (1842). Report of the Committee on the Judiciary on the correspondence between the Governor and the Executive officers of Virginia, South Carolina, and Georgia.

Senate Document No. 41 (1842). Report of the Committee on the Judiciary, on so much of the Governor's Message, and the accompanying documents, as relates to the controversy between New-York and Virginia, and the bill on that subject, which were referred to that committee.

Assembly Document No. 49 (1843). Report of the Committee on the Judiciary, on the matters of difference between the States of New-York and Virginia.

Assembly Document No. 60 (1843). Remonstrance of Numerous Citizens of the village of Salina, in the county of Onondaga, against the repeal of "The extension of the trial by jury law."

Assembly Document No. 141 (1843). Report of the Minority of the Committee on the Judiciary, on the subject of repealing the law extending the right of trial by jury, passed May 6, 1840, and also on the subject of repealing all laws relating to the writ *de homine replegiando*.

Senate Document No. 117 (1859). Report of the Majority of the Committee on the Judiciary, on the Senate Bill to protect Personal Rights and Liberties.

Senate Document No. 120 (1859). Report of the Minority of the Committee on the Judiciary, on the Senate Bill to protect Personal Rights and Liberties.

Senate Document No. 122 (1859). Report of Mr. Lamont in relation to the Personal Liberty Bill.

Assembly Document No. 100 (1860). Report of the Minority of the Select Committee, to which was referred the Personal Liberty Bill.

Available in a single copy is the following important report:

Report of the Select Committee on the Petitions to Prevent Slave Hunting in the State of New York, Feb. 11, 1860. Albany, 1860.
The only unpublished item that was valuable for this study was a copy of Assembly Bill no. 487, for the 1839 session. It is in the New York State Library, Albany. More often, copies of proposed laws were included in the committee reports.

C. Wisconsin

Wisconsin's legislative journals for these years are all published and may be found in the State Historical Society of Wisconsin. They are of considerable importance because resolutions and committee reports are incorporated in the body of the journals (or occasionally in an appendix) rather than being published separately. The following committee reports proved quite valuable:

"Report of the Select Committee to whom was referred so much of the Governor's Message as relates to the Fugitive Slave Act." *Senate Journal,* (1852), Appendix, 314–17.
"Report of the Select Committee to consider the request for state legislation." *Senate Journal,* (1853), 719–22.
"Report of the Judiciary Committee having under consideration a resolution instructing the committee to enquire into the expediency of passing a law to prohibit the use of jails and prisons in this state for the imprisonment of persons convicted under a law of the United States, known as 'the fugitive slave act.' " *Assembly Journal* (1855), 752–55.
"Minority Report of P. B. Simpson, concurred in by M. L. Martin." (On the bill to repeal the act of 1857.) *Senate Journal* (1858), 896–911.
"Report of the Judiciary Committee on No. 52, S." (This bill concerned repeal of the law of 1857.) *Senate Journal,* (1861), 376–78.
"Report of the Special Committee on No. 15, S." (Also a repeal bill.) *Senate Journal,* (1862), 159–62.
"Minority Report, on Repeal of (so-called) Personal Liberty Bill." *Senate Journal,* (1862), 216–25.

Unfortunately the committee reports do not include copies of bills being reported, as was usually the case in other states. It was possible to run down most of these bills in the Archives Division of the State Historical Society of Wisconsin, Madison. A copy of the bill introduced in 1855 (Assembly Bill no. 426) is there, along with copies of Senate Bill no. 118 (1857), one marked enrolled, and the other engrossed, which makes it possible to see the changes made in the course of the debate. On the other hand, the bill introduced in 1853 is simply missing from the archives.

D. Ohio

All journals of the Ohio legislature are published, but it is difficult to find a complete collection. One is in the Legislative Reference Service Library at the state capital building in Columbus. Like the Wisconsin journals these are of particular importance because they contain the reports of committees and proposed resolutions.

Unfortunately, as in Wisconsin, exact copies of the bills proposed were not included in the committee reports. Moreover, at the time research was being done on this study the materials in the state archives were not readily available because they were in storage while the depository was being overhauled. The terms of the bills, however, can be gathered from comments made in the committee reports, by amendments proposed, by occasional remarks made in the legislature, in newspapers, and in antislavery society reports. The personal papers of leading legislators were either unavailable or unrevealing. Except for the committee reports, the Ohio legislative materials available for this study were more disappointing than for any other state.

The committee reports are as follows:

"Report of the Standing Committee on the Judiciary." *House Journal* (1838), 153. This report concerns the request for trial by jury.

"Report of the Standing Committee on the Judiciary, to which was referred sundry petitions of citizens of Ohio, praying that the right of trial by jury may be extended to every human being in the state." *Senate Journal* (1838), 305–10.

"Report of the Select Committee to which was referred the numerous petitions of the citizens of this State, asking the repeal of certain laws, imposing restrictions and disabilities upon persons of color, not found in the constitution, and which the petitioners aver to be contrary to its principles, and also praying that the right of trial by jury, may be secured to all persons within its jurisdiction." *Senate Journal* (1838), 572–86.

"Report of the Standing Committee on the Judiciary, to which was referred sundry petitions praying for an amendment of the act entitled 'an act relating to fugitives from labor or service from other States,' Passed February 26, 1839." *House Journal* (1841), 212–33.

"Report of the Select Committee, to which was referred petitions and memorials relating to the disabilities of Persons of Color." *House Journal* (1842), Appendix, 2–7.

"Report of the Majority of the Standing Committee on the Judiciary, on House Bill No. 54." *House Journal* (1845), Appendix, 45–55.

"Report of the Minority of the Standing Committee on the Judiciary, on House Bill No. 54, for the protection of personal liberty, &c." *House Journal* (1845), Appendix, 56–64.

E. Pennsylvania

Pennsylvania's lean legislative journals are valuable chiefly in following the progress of a bill. One notable exception to the relative spareness of the journals is: *Proceedings and Debates of the General Assembly of Pennsylvania.* 4 vols. Philadelphia, 1788 (as taken in shorthand by Thomas Lloyd).

As in Ohio and Wisconsin committee reports are occasionally included, but for Pennsylvania they are of less value. Copies of bills are not included, although the content of the important ones can be gleaned from newspapers, proposed amendments, personal papers of members of the legislature, and antislavery society reports. Of particular moment were the papers of William M. Meredith (see the listing under Unpublished Personal Papers), the unpublished materials of the Pennsylvania Abolition Society, and an unpublished petition: Philadelphia Citizens.

Petition to Pennsylvania Assembly to Repeal Sections of Penal Code Prohibiting Return of Fugitive Slaves, 1860–61, Manuscript Division, Library of Congress, Pennsylvania Miscellaneous, 12.

The reports of committees valuable for this state were:

"Report relative to the abolition of slavery in the District of Columbia, and in relation to the colored population of the country." *House Journal* (1838), 2: 991–1003.

"Report of the Committee on the Judiciary System." *House Journal* (1850), 495–500.

Published separately from the journals was the following:

Reports of the Majority and Minority of the Select Committee of the House, in Relation to the Existing Federal Relations of the State, as a member of the Union. Harrisburg, 1850. Copy in the Free Library of Philadelphia.

Laws

Copies of the laws passed were found in one of two places: either in the session laws or in the revised statutes (which are often little more than compilations of existing laws). Sometimes the only copy available was in the revised statutes; otherwise, the session laws are cited. Complete collections of the session laws are not readily available everywhere; for this study the excellent collection of materials in the University of Washington Law Library was used. In addition to the session laws the following special collections were used:

A. Massachusetts

The Perpetual Laws of the Commonwealth of Massachusetts, From the Commencement of the Constitution, in October, 1780, to the Last Wednesday in May, 1789. Boston, 1789.

The Laws of the Commonwealth of Massachusetts, From November 28, 1780 . . . to February 28, 1807. With the Constitutions of the United States of America, and of the Commonwealth, Prefixed. 3 vols. Boston, 1807.

Mann, Horace, and Metcalf, Theron. *The Revised Statutes of the Commonwealth of Massachusetts, passed November 4, 1835; to which are subjoined, An Act in Amendment thereof, and an Act Expressly to Repeal the Acts which are Consolidated therein, Both Passed in February 1836; and to which are Prefixed the Constitutions of the United States and of the Commonwealth of Massachusetts.* Boston, 1836.

Cushing, Luther S., and Metcalf, Theron. *Supplements to the Revised Statutes. General Laws of the Commonwealth of Massachusetts, Passed Subsequently to the Revised Statutes. Volume I. Containing the Statutes from 1836 to 1853 Inclusive . . .* Boston, 1854.

The General Statutes of the Commonwealth of Massachusetts: Revised by Commissioners Appointed under a Resolve of February 16, 1855, Amended by the Legislature, and Passed December 28, 1859. Boston, 1860.

B. Ohio

Swan, Joseph R. *Statutes of the State of Ohio, of a General Nature, in Force, December 7, 1840.* Columbus, 1841.

————. *Statutes of the State of Ohio, of a General Nature, in Force January 1st, 1854; With References to Prior Repealed Laws.* Cincinnati, 1854.

C. Pennsylvania

Dallas, Alexander James. *Laws of the Commonwealth of Pennsylvania.* 2 vols. Philadelphia, 1793.
————. *Laws of the Commonwealth of Pennsylvania.* 2 vols. Philadelphia, 1797.
Laws of the Commonwealth of Pennsylvania. 4 vols. Philadelphia, 1810. (1700–1810).
Brightly, Frederick C. *A Digest of the Laws of Pennsylvania, Originally compiled by John Purdon.* 9th ed. Philadelphia, 1862.
Stewart, Ardemus. *A Digest of the Statute Law of the State of Pennsylvania from the Year 1700 to 1903, Originally compiled in 1811 by John Purdon, Esq.* 4 vols. 13th ed. Philadelphia, 1910.

D. Wisconsin

The Revised Statutes of the State of Wisconsin, Passed at the Second Session of the Legislature, Commencing January 10, 1849. Southport, 1849.
The Revised Statutes of the State of Wisconsin: Passed at the Annual Session of the Legislature Commencing January 13, 1858, and Approved May 17, 1858. Chicago, 1858.

E. New York

Laws of the State of New York Passed at the Sessions of the Legislature Held in the Years 1777 (to 1801) Inclusive. 5 vols. Albany, 1886–87.
Van Ness, William P., and Woodworth, John. *Laws of the State of New-York and Passed at the Thirty-Sixth Session of the Legislature, with Marginal Notes and References, Furnished by the Revisors.* 2 vols. Albany, 1813.
The Revised Statutes of the State of New-York. 3 vols. Albany, 1829.
The Revised Statutes of the State of New-York. 3 vols. 2d ed. Albany, 1836.
Blatchford, Samuel. *Statutes of the State of New-York, of a Public and General Character, Passed from 1829 to 1851, Both Inclusive, with Notes, and References to Judicial Decisions, and the Constitution of 1846.* Auburn, 1852.
Edmonds, John W. *Statutes at Large of the State of New York, Revised Statutes as They Existed on the 1st Day of July, 1862.* 5 vols. Albany, 1863.
Birdseye, Clarence. *The Revised Statutes, Codes and General Laws of the State of New York.* 3 vols. 3d ed. New York, 1901.

F. Federal

Peters, Richard, ed. *The Public Statutes at Large of the United States of America.* 11 vols. Boston, 1845.

Antislavery Society Proceedings

Of the proceedings that have been published, the best holdings are found in the Library of Congress, the State Historical Society of Wisconsin, and the Boston Public Library. The unpublished material includes the following:

Manuscript Collection Belonging to the Pennsylvania Society for Promoting the Abolition of Slavery, for the Relief of Free Negroes Unlawfully Held in

Bondage, and for Improving the Condition of the African Race. 11 vols. Historical Society of Pennsylvania.

Minutes of the Pennsylvania Society for promoting the Abolition of Slavery and the relief of Free Negroes unlawfully held in Bondage. 4 vols. Historical Society of Pennsylvania.

Pennsylvania Abolition Society. Acting Committee. Minutes. 3 vols. Historical Society of Pennsylvania.

Pennsylvania Abolition Society Papers. Legal Section and Miscellany–Runaway Slaves. Historical Society of Pennsylvania.

Pennsylvania Abolition Society Papers. 10 boxes. Historical Society of Pennsylvania.

Pennsylvania Friends Association for Advocating the Cause of the Slave, and improving the condition of the free People of Color. Minute Book, 1837–41. Manuscript Division, Library of Congress.

Pennsylvania Anti-Slavery Society. Executive Committee Minutes, 1856–70, Book 4. Historical Society of Pennsylvania.

Minutes of the Proceedings of the New York Society for promoting the Manumission of Slaves; and for protecting such of them as have been, and may be, liberated. Commenced January 1798. Jan. 16, 1798–Dec. 1814. New-York Historical Society.

Manumission Society. New York City. Standing Committee. Minutes. July 15, 1817–Jan. 11, 1842. New-York Historical Society.

Manumission Society. New York City. Minutes. Mar. 11, 1807–July 8, 1817; Jan. 13, 1829–Apr. 11, 1849. New-York Historical Society.

The published materials used were:

A. New York

First Annual Report of the Proceedings of the New York State Anti-Slavery Society, Held at Peterboro' October 22, 1835. Utica, New York, 1835.

Proceedings of the First Annual Meeting of the New-York State Anti-Slavery Society, Convened at Utica, October 19, 1836. Utica, New York, 1836.

The First Annual Report of the New York Committee of Vigilance, for the Year 1837, Together with Important Facts Relative to their Proceedings. New York, 1837.

The Annual Report of the New York Committee of Vigilance, for the Year 1842, with Interesting Facts relative to their Proceedings. New York, 1842.

First Annual Report Presented to the New York Anti-Slavery Society, May 12th, 1854, By its Executive Committee. New York, 1854.

B. Pennsylvania

Proceedings of the Anti-Slavery Convention, Assembled at Philadelphia, December 4, 5, and 6, 1833. New York, 1833.

First Annual Report of the Board of Managers of the Philadelphia Anti-Slavery Society. Philadelphia, 1835.

Minutes of the Fifth Annual Convention for the Improvement of the Free People of Colour. Philadelphia, 1835.

Proceedings of the Pennsylvania Convention, Assembled to organize a State Anti-Slavery Society, at Harrisburg, on the 31st of January and 1st, 2d and 3d of February 1837. Philadelphia, 1837.

Thirteenth Annual Report, Presented to the Pennsylvania Anti-Slavery Society, By its Executive Committee, October 15, 1850. Philadelphia, 1850.

Fourteenth Annual Report, Presented to the Pennsylvania Anti-Slavery Society. By Its Executive Committee, October 7, 1851. With the Proceedings of the Annual Meeting. Philadelphia, 1851.

Fifteenth Annual Report, Presented to the Pennsylvania Anti-Slavery Society, By its Executive Committee, October 25, 1852. With the Proceedings of the Annual Meeting. Philadelphia, 1852.

Twenty-First Annual Report Presented to the Pennsylvania Anti-Slavery Society, By its Executive Committee, October 6th, 1858, with the Resolutions of the Annual Meeting, Constitution of the Society and Declaration of Sentiments. Philadelphia, 1858.

C. Ohio

Proceedings of the Ohio Anti-Slavery Convention, Held at Putnam, on the Twenty-Second, Twenty-Third, and Twenty-Fourth of April, 1835. n.p., n.d. Ohio Historical Society.

Report on the Condition of the People of Color in the State of Ohio. From the Proceedings of the Ohio Anti-Slavery Convention, held at Putnam, on the 22d, 23d, and 24th of April, 1835. n.p., n.d., in Bailey Pamphlets, vol. 39, Rare Book Room, Library of Congress.

Report of the Second Anniversary of the Ohio Anti-Slavery Society, Held in Mount Pleasant, Jefferson County, Ohio, on the Twenty-Seventh of April, 1837. Cincinnati, 1837.

D. Massachusetts

The Second Annual Report of the Massachusetts Abolition Society: Together with the Proceedings of the Second Annual Meeting, Held at Tremont Chapel, May 25, 1841. Boston, 1841.

Eleventh Annual Report, Presented to the Massachusetts Anti-Slavery Society, By Its Board of Managers, January 25, 1843. Boston, 1843.

Twelfth Annual Report, Presented to the Massachusetts Anti-Slavery Society, By Its Board of Managers, January 24, 1844. Boston, 1844.

Nineteenth Annual Report, Presented to the Massachusetts Anti-Slavery Society, By Its Board of Managers, January 22, 1851. Boston, 1851.

Twenty-First Annual Report Presented to the Massachusetts Anti-Slavery Society By Its Board of Managers, January 26, 1853. Boston, 1853.

National Organizations

Minutes of the Proceedings of a Convention of Delegates from the Abolition Societies Established in different Parts of the United States, Assembled at Philadelphia. Philadelphia, 1794–1837. (Under slightly different titles these minutes of the American Convention were published rather consistently down through the 1820s, but there were virtually none in the 1830s until the final meeting in 1837.)

The Annual Report of the American and Foreign Anti-Slavery Society, Presented at the General Meeting, Held in Broadway Tabernacle, May 11, 1847. New York, 1847.

The Annual Report of the American and Foreign Anti-Slavery Society, Presented at New York, May 8, 1849. New York, 1849.

The Annual Report of the American and Foreign Anti-Slavery Society, Presented at New York, May 7, 1850. New York, 1850.

The Annual Report of the American and Foreign Anti-Slavery Society, Presented at New York, May 11, 1852. New York, 1852.

First Annual Report of the American Anti-Slavery Society. New York, 1834.

Fourth Annual Report of the American Anti-Slavery Society, with the Speeches Delivered at the Anniversary Meeting Held in the City of New York, on the 9th May, 1837. New York, 1837.

Fifth Annual Report of the Executive Committee of the American Anti-Slavery Society. New York, 1838.

Sixth Annual Report of the Executive Committee of the American Anti-Slavery Society, with the Speeches Delivered at the Anniversary Meeting Held in the City of New York, on the 7th of May, 1839. New York, 1839.

Annual Report Presented to the American Anti-Slavery Society, By the Executive Committee, at the Annual Meeting, Held in New York, May 9, 1855. New York, 1855.

Annual Report, Presented to the American Anti-Slavery Society, By the Executive Committee, at the Annual Meeting, Held in New York, May 7, 1856. New York, 1856.

Annual Reports of the American Anti-Slavery Society, By the Executive Committee, for the Years ending May 1, 1857, and May 1, 1858. New York, 1859.

Annual Report of the American Anti-Slavery Society; By the Executive Committee, For the Year Ending May 1, 1859. New York, 1860.

Annual Report of the American Anti-Slavery Society, By the Executive Committee, For the Year Ending May 1, 1860. New York, 1861.

Twenty-Eighth Annual Report of the American Anti-Slavery Society, By the Executive Committee, for the Year Ending May 1, 1861. New York, 1861.

Congressional Materials

The published records of Congress, of course, were essential in this study. The following were of primary importance:

Annals of Congress
    2d Cong., 2d sess., 1792–93.
    4th Cong., 1st sess., 1795–96.
    6th Cong., 1st sess., 1799–1800.
    15th Cong., 1st sess., 1817–18.
    15th Cong., 2d sess., 1819–20.
    17th Cong., 1st sess., 1821–22.
Congressional Globe
    25th Cong., 2d sess., 1837–38.
    30th Cong., 1st sess., 1847–48.

31st Cong., 1st sess., 1849–50.
32d Cong., 1st sess., 1851–52.
36th Cong., 1st sess., 1859–60.
36th Cong., 2d sess., 1860–61.
38th Cong., 1st sess., 1863–64.

House Journal
2d Cong., 2d sess., 1792–93.
4th Cong., 1st sess., 1795–96.
6th Cong., 1st sess., 1799–1800.
15th Cong., 1st sess., 1817–18.
15th Cong., 2d sess., 1819–20.
17th Cong., 1st sess., 1821–22.

Senate Journal
2d Cong., 2d sess., 1792–93.
4th Cong., 1st sess., 1795–96.
6th Cong., 1st sess., 1799–1800.
15th Cong., 1st sess., 1817–18.
15th Cong., 2d sess., 1819–20.
17th Cong., 1st sess., 1821–22.

Senate Reports
30th Cong., 1st sess., 1847–48, no. 143. Senator Butler's report from the judiciary committee on the petition of Kentucky for a more effective fugitive law.
36th Cong., 1st sess., 1860–61, no. 288. Journal of the Committee of Thirteen.

House Reports
36th Cong., 2d sess., 1860–61, no. 31. Journal of the Committee of Thirty Three.
36th Cong., 2d sess., 1860–61, no. 31. Report of the Majority of the Committee of Thirty Three.
36th Cong., 2d sess., 1860–61, no. 31. Minority Report of the Committee of Thirty Three.

In addition to this material various unpublished congressional documents in the National Archives proved invaluable. Of particular importance were copies of bills introduced down to 1821. There are copies of the Senate fugitive slave bill of 1792, with the proposed amendments, in the Senate File, 2A-B1, 2d Cong., 2d sess., as well as copies of the following: H. R. 18, 15th Cong., 1st sess.; H. R. 280, 15th Cong., 2d sess.; H. R. 35, 17th Cong., 1st sess. Also important were the petitions in the Legislative Records Branch, National Archives. Of particular value were those filed under the following numbers: 6A-G1.1. (House); 14A-G1.1 (House); 14A-G13.3 (Senate); 15A.-G12.2 (Senate); and 33A-H21 (Senate).

Cases

An indispensable source for cases involving runaway slaves and free blacks is Helen Tunnicliff Catterall, ed. *Judicial Cases Concerning American Slavery and the Negro* (5 vols.; Washington, D.C., 1937). In addition to the excerpts contained in Catterall the following full reports, listed chronologically, have been used in preparing this study. They do not, of course, exhaust the cases on the topic.

Margaret v. *Muzzy* (Mass., 1763) in L. Kinvin Wroth and Hiller B. Zobel, eds. *Legal Papers of John Adams.* 3 vols. Cambridge, 1965. Case No. 40.

Oliver v. *Sale* (Mass., 1771) in Josiah Quincy, Jr. *Reports of Cases Argued and Adjudged in the Superior Court of Judicature of the Province of Massachusetts Bay, Between 1761 and 1772.* Boston, 1865.

The Case of James Sommersett, a Negro, on a Habeas Corpus. State Trials, 20 (June, 1772). (English).

Pirate, alias Belt v. *Dalby.* 1 Dallas 167. (Pa., 1786).

Respublica v. *Negro Betsey, et al.* 1 Dallas 469. (Pa., 1789).

Respublica v. *Richards.* 2 Dallas 225. (Pa., 1795).

Hudgins v. *Wrights.* 1 Hening & Munford 133. (Va., 1806).

Skinner v. *Fleet.* 14 Johnson 263. (N.Y., 1817).

Wright, alias Hall v. *Deacon.* 5 Sergeant & Rawle 62. (Pa., 1819).

Rankin v. *Lydia.* 2 A. K. Marshall 468. (Kentucky, 1820).

Lewis v. *Fullerton.* 1 Randolph's Reports 15. (Va., 1821).

Commonwealth v. *Camillus Griffith.* 2 Pickering 11. (Mass., 1823).

Commonwealth v Case. Niles' Register, 3d series, no. 5, vol. 3, (October 2, 1824). (Pa.)

Worthington v. *Preston,* 30 Fed. Cas. 645. (Oct., 1824).

Saul v. *His Creditors.* 5 Martin (N.S.) 569. (La., 1827).

The Slave Grace. States Trials, new series, 2 (1823–1831), (Nov. 1827). (English).

Jack v. *Martin.* 12 Wendell 311. (N.Y., 1834).

Jack v. *Martin.* 14 Wendell 507. (N.Y., 1835).

In re Martin. Fed. Cas. No. 9, 154. (1835).

Commonwealth v. *Thomas Aves.* 18 Pickering 193. (Mass. 1836).

De Lacy v. *Antoine.* 7 Leigh 438. (Va., 1836).

Report of the Holden Slave Case, Tried at the January Term of the Court of Common Pleas, for the County of Worcester, A. D., 1839. Worcester, 1839. (Mass.)

Prigg v. *Pennsylvania.* 41 U.S. 1060. (1842). On this case see also the National Archives Microfilm No. M-215, roll 3, U.S. Supreme Court, Minutes, 1: 4479, 4482, 4488, 4522–24, and film No. M-216, roll 2, U.S. Supreme Court Dockets, vol. E, p. 2330.

Thornton v. *Demoss.* 13 Mississippi 609. (1846).

Field v. *Walker.* 17 Alabama 80. (1849).

"Fugitive Slave Law. U.S. Circuit Court. Before the Hon. Samuel Nelson, Associate Justice of the Supreme Court of the United States." *The New-York Legal Observer,* 9 (June, 1851): 161–73.

In re Sims. 61 Cushing 285. (Mass., 1851).

Trial of Thomas Sims, on an Issue of Personal Liberty, on the claim of James Potter, of Georgia, against Him, as an alleged Fugitive from service. Arguments of Robert Rantoul, Jr. and Charles G. Loring, with the Decision of George T. Curtis. Boston, April 7–11, 1851. Boston, 1851.

United States vs. Charles G. Davis. Report of the Proceedings at the Examination of Charles G. Davis, Esq., on a Charge of Aiding and Abetting in the Rescue of a Fugitive Slave. Boston, 1851.

In re Sherman M. Booth. 3 Wisconsin 1. (1854).

In re Booth and Rycraft. 3 Wisconsin 144. (1855).

Dred Scott v. *Sandford* 60 U.S. 701. (1857).

Ableman v. *Booth*. 62 U.S. 506. (1859).
Ex parte Bushnell. 9 Ohio State 77. (1859).
Arnold v. *Booth*. 14 Wisconsin 180. (1861).

Newspapers and Journals

A. Newspapers

African Observer, 1824.
Boston Atlas, 1855.
Boston Daily Advertiser, 1855.
Boston Evening Transcipt, 1837, 1842.
Daily Argus and Democrat, 1857. (Madison, Wis.)
Daily Wisconsin, 1857. (Milwaukee)
Emancipator and Free American, 1842. (Boston)
Friend of Man, 1836–37. (Utica, N.Y.)
Genius of Universal Emancipation, 1822–23. (Greenville, Tenn.)
Human Rights, 1835–39. (New York)
Latimer Journal, and North Star, 1842–43. (Boston)
Liberator, 1831–61. (Boston)
Milwaukee Daily Sentinel, 1857.
National Anti-Slavery Standard, 1860–61. (New York)
National Intelligencer, 1860–61. (Washington, D.C.)
New York Evening Post, 1850.
New York Times, 1857–61.
New York Tribune, 1842–61.
Niles' Weekly Register, 1817–37.
Pennsylvania Freeman, 1838–52. (Philadelphia)
Pennsylvanian, 1847. (Philadelphia)
Philanthropist, 1837–43. (Cincinnati)
Poulson's American Daily Advertiser, 1820, 1826. (Philadelphia)
Public Ledger, 1847, 1850, 1859. (Philadelphia)

B. Journals

American Jurist and Law Magazine, 1837–43. (Boston)
American Whig Review, 1850, 1851. (New York)
Monthly Law Reporter, 1838–1845. (Boston)
United States Magazine and Democratic Review, 1850–51. (New York)

Unpublished Personal Papers

Adams Family Papers. Massachusetts Historical Society.
John A. Andrew Papers. Massachusetts Historical Society.
William Bigler Papers. Historical Society of Pennsylvania.
Sherman M. Booth (Miscellaneous Manuscripts). State Historical Society of Wisconsin.
Salmon P. Chase Papers. Manuscript Division, Library of Congress.
Richard H. Dana, Jr. Papers. Massachusetts Historical Society.
William Lloyd Garrison Papers. Boston Public Library.
Joshua R. Giddings Papers. Ohio Historical Society.

Samuel May Papers. Boston Public Library.
William M. Meredith Papers. Historical Society of Pennsylvania, and Pennsylvania (Box)-Legislature. New York Public Library.
Byron Paine Papers. State Historical Society of Wisconsin.
John Fox Potter Papers. State Historical Society of Wisconsin.
Slavery. Miscellaneous Manuscripts. Box 1 (Edwin Clarke Letters). New-York Historical Society.
Lysander Spooner Papers. New-York Historical Society.
Charles Sumner Papers. Houghton Library.
Vaux Papers. Historical Society of Pennsylvania.
Gideon Welles Papers. Manuscript Division, Library of Congress.
Weston Papers. Boston Public Library.
Elizur Wright Papers. Manuscript Division, Library of Congress.

Published Personal Papers

Adams, John Quincy. *Memoirs of John Quincy Adams, comprising portions of His Diary from 1795 to 1848.* Edited by Charles Francis Adams. 12 vols. Philadelphia, 1876.
Bowditch, Vincent Y. *Life and Correspondence of Henry Ingersoll Bowditch.* 2 vols. Boston and New York, 1902.
Calhoun, John C. *The Works of John C. Calhoun.* Edited by Richard K. Cralle. 6 vols. New York, 1870.
Channing, William E. *The Works of William E. Channing, D.D.* 8th ed. 6 vols. Boston, 1848.
Curtis, Benjamin Robbins. *A Memoir of Benjamin Robbins Curtis, LL.D. with some of His Professional and Miscellaneous Writings.* Edited by his son, Benjamin R. Curtis, Jr. 2 vols. Boston, 1879.
Dana, Richard Henry, Jr. *The Journal of Richard Henry Dana, Jr.* Edited by Robert F. Lucid. 3 vols. Cambridge, 1968.
Douglass, Frederick. *The Life and Writings of Frederick Douglass.* Edited by Philip Foner. 4 vols. New York, 1950.
Evarts, William M. *Arguments and Speeches of William Maxwell Evarts.* Edited by Sherman Evarts. New York, 1919.
Garrison, Wendell Phillips, and Jackson, Francis. *William Lloyd Garrison 1805–1879: The Story of His Life Told by His Children.* 4 vols. Boston and New York, 1894.
Jay, William. *Miscellaneous Writings on Slavery.* Boston, 1853.
Lincoln, Abraham. *The Collected Works of Abraham Lincoln.* Edited by Roy P. Basler. 9 vols. New Brunswick, N.J., 1953–1955.
Mann, Horace. *Slavery; Letters and Speeches.* Boston, 1851.
Rantoul, Robert, Jr. *Memoirs, Speeches, and Writings of Robert Rantoul, Jr.* Edited by Luther Hamilton. Boston, 1854.
Seward, William H. *An Autobiography from 1801 to 1834. With a Memoir of His Life, and Selections from His Letters, 1831–1846.* Edited by Frederick W. Seward. New York, 1891.
Stewart, Alvan. *Writings and Speeches of Alvan Stewart, on Slavery.* Edited by Luther Rawson Marsh. New York, 1860.

Story, Joseph. *Life and Letters of Joseph Story*. Edited by William Wetmore Story. 2 vols. Boston, 1851.

Sumner, Charles. *The Works of Charles Sumner*. 15 vols. Boston, 1870–83.

Webster, Daniel. *The Writings and Speeches of Daniel Webster*. 18 vols. Boston, 1903.

Weld, Theodore Dwight. *Letters of Theodore Dwight Weld, Angelina Grimke Weld and Sarah Grimke 1822–1844*. Edited by Gilbert H. Barnes and Dwight L. Dumond. 2 vols. New York, 1934.

Other Contemporary Material

Address of the Committee Appointed by a Public Meeting, Held at Faneuil Hall, September 24, 1846, for the Purpose of Considering the Recent Case of Kidnapping From our Soil, and of taking Measures to Prevent the Recurrence of Similar Outrages. Boston, 1846.

Agg, John, reporter. *Proceedings and Debates of the Convention of the Commonwealth of Pennsylvania, to Propose Amendments to the Constitution, Commenced at Harrisburg, May 2, 1837*. 13 vols. Harrisburg 1838.

Aiken, S. C. Rev. *The Laws of Ohio, In Respect to Colored People, Shown to be Unequal, Unjust, and Unconstitutional*. Cleveland, 1845.

Aptheker, Herbert, ed. *A Documentary History of the Negro People in the United States*. 2 vols. New York, 1951.

Bourne, George. *The Book and Slavery Irreconcilable. With Animadversions upon Dr. Smith's Philosophy*. Philadelphia, 1816.

Bowditch, Henry I., compiler. *The Latimer Case and Its Results for Liberty in the Free States*. Boston, 1843. This collection of materials is in the Massachusetts Historical Society.

Bowditch, William I. *The Rendition of Anthony Burns*. Boston, 1854.

———. *Slavery and the Constitution*. Boston, 1849.

Callicot, T. C. *Speech of Hon. Theophilus C. Callicot of Kings, against the Personal Liberty Bill. In Assembly, March 14, 1860*. Albany, 1860.

Carter, Nathaniel, and Stone, William L., reporters. *Reports of the Proceedings and Debates of the Convention of 1821*. Albany, 1821.

Chase, Salmon P. *Speech of Salmon P. Chase, In the Case of the Colored Woman, Matilda, who was Brought Before the Court of Common Pleas of Hamilton County, Ohio, By Writ of Habeas Corpus, March 11, 1837*. Cincinnati, 1837.

"Chronicles of Kidnapping in New-York," *American Anti-Slavery Reporter*. (June, 1834).

Clarke, James Freeman. *The Rendition of Anthony Burns. Its Causes and Consequences. A Discourse on Christian Politics, Delivered in Williams Hall, Boston, on Whitsunday, June 4, 1854*. Boston, 1854.

Commager, Henry Steele. *Documents of American History*. 6th ed. 2 vols. New York, 1958.

Curtis, George T. *Two Letters to the Editor of the New Bedford Mercury*. Boston, 1854.

Dawson, Henry ("H.D." ?) "Reclamation of Fugitive Slaves," *The New-York Legal Observer*, 7 (May, 1849): 129–36.

_____ . "Extradition of Fugitive Slaves," *The New-York Legal Observer*, 9 (Jan., 1851): 1–11.

Dorr, James A. *Objections to the Act of Congress, Commonly called the Fugitive Slave Law Answered, In a Letter to Hon. Washington Hunt, Governor Elect of the State of New York.* New York, 1850.

Dumond, Dwight Lowell, ed. *Southern Editorials on Secession.* Gloucester, Mass., 1964.

The Duty of Pennsylvania Concerning Slavery. Philadelphia, n.d., Copy in the Historical Society of Pennsylvania.

Elliott, Jonathan. *The Debates in the Several State Conventions on the Adoption of the Federal Constitution.* Philadelphia, 1836–45.

An Examination of Mr. Bradish's Answer to the Interrogatories Presented to Him by a Committee of the State Anti-Slavery Society, October 1, 1838. Albany, 1838.

Farrand, Max, ed. *The Records of the Federal Convention of 1787.* rev. ed. 4 vols. New Haven, 1966.

The Fugitive Slave Bill: Its History and Unconstitutionality: With an Account of the Seizure and Enslavement of James Hamlet, and his Subsequent Restoration to Liberty. New York, 1850.

Furness, William Henry. *A Discourse Occasioned by the Boston Fugitive Slave Case, Delivered in the First Congregational Unitarian Church, Philadelphia, April 13, 1851.* Philadelphia, 1851.

_____ . *Christian Duty. Three Discourses Delivered in the First Congregational Unitarian Church of Philadelphia May 28th, June 4th and June 11th, 1854; With Reference to the Recent Execution of the Fugitive Slave Law in Boston and New York.* Philadelphia, 1854.

Goodell, William. *Our National Charters: For the Millions. I. The Federal Constitution of 1788-9. II. The Articles of Confederation, 1778. III. The Declaration of Independence, 1776. IV. The Articles of Association, 1774. With Notes, Showing their Bearing on Slavery, and the Relative Powers of the State and National Governments.* New York, 1860.

_____ . *Views of American Constitutional Law. In its Bearing upon American Slavery.* Utica, 1844.

Great Union Meeting. Philadelphia. December 7, 1859. Philadelphia, 1859.

Holmes, Arthur. *Speech of Hon. Arthur Holmes, of Cortland. In Assembly, March 9, 1859.* Albany, 1859.

Johnson, B. R. *Speech of Hon. B. R. Johnson, on the Personal Liberty Bill. In Assembly, March 14, 1860.* Albany, 1860.

Letcher, John, and Vail, Lewis D. *Pennsylvania and the Fugitive Slave Law. The Statute of March 3d, 1847; Its Real Import Explained. Correspondence between the Hon. John Letcher, Governor of Virginia, and Lewis D. Vail, Esq., of Philadelphia. Views of the National Intelligencer upon the Subject.* Philadelphia, 1860.

A Letter to the Hon. Samuel A. Eliot, Representative in Congress from the City of Boston, in Reply to His Apology for voting for the Fugitive Slave Bill. Boston, 1851.

"Letters and Documents Relating to Slavery in Massachusetts." *Massachusetts Historical Society Collections*, 3, 5th series. Boston, 1877.

Lincoln, Charles Z., ed. *State of New York. Messages from the Governors.* 11 vols. Albany, 1909.

Lord, John C., D.D. *"The Higher Law" in its application to the Fugitive Slave Bill. A Sermon on the Duties Men Owe to God and to Governments.* Buffalo, 1851.

Loring, Charles G. *A Reading upon the Personal Liberty Laws of Massachusetts.* Boston, 1861.

McKitrick, Eric L., ed., *Slavery Defended: The Views of the old South.* Englewood Cliffs, N.J., 1963.

May, Samuel J. *The Fugitive Slave Law and Its Victims.* rev. and enlarged ed. New York, 1861.

Mayo, A. D., *The Personal Liberty Bill. An Address to the Legislature and People of New York.* Albany, 1859.

Mellen, G. W. F. *Argument on the Unconstitutionality of Slavery, Embracing an Abstract of the Proceedings of the National and State Conventions on this Subject.* Boston, 1841.

Memorial to the Senate and House of Representatives of the Commonwealth of Pennsylvania from the people of colour of the city of Philadelphia and its vicinity. Philadelphia, 1832.

Needles, Edward. *An Historical Memoir of the Pennsylvania Society, for Promoting the Abolition of Slavery; the Relief of Free Negroes Unlawfully Held in Bondage, and for Improving the Condition of the African Race. Compiled from the Minutes of the Society and other official Documents.* Philadelphia, 1848.

Northend, William. *Speech of Hon. William D. Northend, of Essex, In the Senate of Massachusetts, February 27, 1861, upon the Modification of the Personal Liberty Bill.* Boston, 1861.

Observations on the Rev. Dr. Gannett's Sermon, entitled "Relation of the North to Slavery." Boston, 1854.

Official Report of the Debates and Proceedings in the State Convention, Assembled May 4th, 1853, to Revise and Amend the Constitution of the Commonwealth of Massachusetts. 3 vols. Boston, 1853.

Olin, Chauncey C. "A History of the early Anti-Slavery excitement in the state of Wisconsin from 1842 to 1860." (Unpublished manuscript, State Historical Society of Wisconsin, approximate date, 1861.)

Paine, Byron, and Smith, A. D. *Unconstitutionality of the Fugitive Act: Argument of Byron Paine, Esq. and Opinion of Hon. A. D. Smith, Associate Justice of the Supreme Court of the State of Wisconsin.* n.p., n.d., approximately 1855. State Historical Society of Wisconsin.

Palfrey, John G. *Papers on the Slave Power, First Published in the "Boston Whig," In July, August, and September, 1846.* Boston, 1846.

Parker, Joel. *Personal Liberty Laws, (Statutes of Massachusetts,) and Slavery in the Territories, (Case of Dred Scott.)* Boston, 1861.

Parker, Theodore. *The New Crime Against Humanity. A Sermon Preached at the Music Hall, in Boston, on Sunday, June 4, 1854.* Boston, 1854.

Parrish, John. *Remarks on the Slavery on the Black People; Addressed to the Citizens of the United States, Particularly to those who are in Legislative or Executive Stations in the General or State Governments; and also to such Individuals as Hold them in Bondage.* Philadelphia, 1806.

Peabody, Andrew P. *Position and Duties of the North with Regard to Slavery.* Newburyport, Mass., 1847.

Pennock, Abraham L.; Rhoads, Samuel; and Taylor, George W. *The Non-Slaveholder.* vols. 1–3. Philadelphia, 1846–47.

Phillips, Wendell. *Argument of Wendell Phillips, Esq. Against the Repeal of the Personal Liberty Law, Before the Committee of the Legislature, Tuesday, January 29, 1861.* Boston, 1861.

————. "Constitutionality of Slavery." *The Massachusetts Quarterly Review,* 4 (Sept., 1848): 463–509.

————. "James C. Alvord." *The Liberty Bell.* Boston, 1841.

————. *No Slave-Hunting in the Old Bay State. Speech of Wendell Phillips, Esq., before the Committee on Federal Relations, In Support of the Petitions asking for a Law to prevent the Recapture of Fugitive Slaves, in the Hall of the House of Representatives, Thursday, February 17, 1859.* Boston, 1859.

Phillips, Wendell, ed. *The Constitution a Pro-Slavery Compact; or Selections from The Madison Papers, ec.* New York, 1844.

Pierce, Edward L. *Remarks of Edward L. Pierce, Before the Committee of the Legislature of Massachusetts, on the General Statutes Relating to Personal Liberty, at their Hearing of Feb. 1, 1861.* Boston, 1861.

Poore, Benjamin Perley. *The Federal and State Constitutions, Colonial Charters, and other Organic Laws of the United States.* 2d ed. Washington, D.C., 1878.

Porter, Kirk H., and Johnson, Donald Bruce, compilers. *National Party Platforms, 1840–1960.* Urbana, Ill., 1961.

Randall, Robert E. *Speech of Robert E. Randall, of Philadelphia, on the Laws of the State Relative to Fugitive Slaves, Delivered in the House of Representatives of Pennsylvania, January 16, 1861.* n.p., n.d., Copy in the Boston Public Library.

Rantoul, Robert, Jr. *THE FUGITIVE SLAVE LAW. Speech of Hon. Robert Rantoul, Jr., of Beverly, Mass., Delivered Before the Grand Mass Convention of the Democratic Voters of the Second Congressional District of Massachusetts, Holden at Lynn, Thursday, April 3, 1851.* Boston, 1851.

Report of the Commissioners appointed to Revise the General Statutes of the Commonwealth. Part 3. Boston, 1834.

Report of the Commissioners on the Revision of the Statutes. In Five Numbers, 1858. Boston, 1858.

A Review of the Trial, Conviction and Sentence, of George F. Alberti, for Kidnapping. n.p., n.d. Copy in the Historical Society of Pennsylvania.

Richardson, J. D., ed. *Compilation of the Messages and Papers of the Presidents, 1789–1897.* 10 vols. Washington, D.C., 1907.

"The Right of Trial by Jury." *The Anti-Slavery Record* 3 (August, 1837).

Sharp, Granville. *Letter from Granville Sharp of London to the Maryland Society for Promoting the Abolition of Slavery, and the Relief of Free Negroes and Others, Unlawfully Held in Bondage.* Baltimore, 1793.

Shiperd, J. R. *History of the Oberlin-Wellington Rescue.* Boston, 1859.

Spencer, Charles S. *An Appeal for Freedom Made in the Assembly of the State of New York, March 7th, 1859.* Albany, 1859.

Spooner, Lysander. *A Defence for Fugitive Slaves, Against the Acts of Congress of February 12, 1793, and September 18, 1850.* Boston, 1850.

————. *The Unconstitutionality of Slavery.* Boston, 1860.

Stearns, Charles. *The "Fugitive Slave Law" of the United States, Shown to be Un-constitutional, Impolitic, Inhuman, and Diabolical.* Boston, 1851.

Sunderland, Rev. La Roy. *Antislavery Manual, Containing a Collection of Facts and Arguments on American Slavery.* New York, 1837.

Sutliff, Milton. *Speech of Mr. Sutliff of Trumbull, on the Resolutions Introduced by Him Relative to the Constitutional Powers of Congress, and the Fugitive Slave Bill. In Senate . . . January 14, & 15, 1851.* Columbus, 1851.

Talbot, Thomas H. *The Constitutional Provision Respecting Fugitives from Serv-ice of Labor, and the Act of Congress, of September 18, 1850.* Boston, 1852.

Thomas, Benjamin F. *A Few Suggestions upon the Personal Liberty Law and "Secession" (so called). In a Letter to a Friend.* Boston, 1861.

Torrey, Jesse. *American Slave Trade; or, An Account of the Manner in which the Slave Dealers take Free People from some of the United States of America, and carry them away, and sell them as Slaves in other of the States; and of the hor-rible Cruelties practised in the carrying on of this most infamous traffic.* London, 1822.

Willard, Samuel. *The Grand Issue: An Ethico-Political Tract.* Boston, 1851.

Yates, William. *Rights of Colored Men to Suffrage, Citizenship and Trial by Jury: Being a Book of Facts, Arguments and Authorities, Historical Notices and Sketches of Debates—With Notes.* Philadelphia, 1838.

Legal Treatises

Bacon, Matthew. *A New Abridgement of the Law.* 7 vols. Philadelphia, 1811.

Blackstone, Sir William. *Commentaries on the Laws of England.* 4 vols. London, 1765-69.

Brooks, Jehiel. *Fugitive Slave Laws: A Compilation of the Laws of the United States and of States in Relation to Fugitives from Labor.* Washington, D.C., 1860.

Butler, William Allen. *The Revision of the Statutes of the State of New York, and the Revisers.* New York and Albany, 1889.

Cobb, Thomas R. R. *An Inquiry into the Law of Negro Slavery in the United States of America. To which is prefixed, An Historical Sketch of Slavery.* Philadelphia, Savannah, 1858.

Dane, Nathan. *A General Abridgement and Digest of American Law, With Occa-sional Notes and Comments.* 8 vols. Boston, 1824.

Hurd, John Codman. *The Law of Freedom and Bondage in the United States.* 2 vols. Boston, 1858-62.

Hurd, Rollin C. *A Treatise on the Right of Personal Liberty, and on the Writ of Habeas Corpus and the Practice Connected with it: With a View of the Law of Extradition of Fugitives.* Albany, 1858.

Kent, James. *Commentaries on American Law.* 10th ed.; 4 vols. Boston, 1860.

Morris, Phineas Pemberton. *A Practical Treatise on the Law of Replevin in the United States.* Philadelphia, 1869. Second edition.

Notes on the Revised Statutes of New York. Albany, 1830.

Sergeant, Thomas. *Constitutional Law. Being a Collection of Points Arising upon the Constitution and Jurisprudence of the United States which have been settled By Judicial Decisions and Practice.* Philadelphia, 1822.

Story, Joseph. *Commentaries on the Conflict of Laws.* Boston, 1846.

———. *Commentaries on the Constitution of the United States.* 2d ed.; 2 vols. Boston, 1851.

Stroud, George M. *A Sketch of the Laws Relating to Slavery in the Several States of the United States of America.* Philadelphia, 1827.

———. *A Sketch of the Laws Relating to Slavery in the Several States of the United States of America.* Philadelphia, 1856. Second edition, considerably enlarged.

Wheeler, Jacob D. *A Practical Treatise on the Law of Slavery. Being a Compilation of all the Decisions made on that Subject, in the Several Courts of the United States, and State Courts.* New Orleans, 1837.

SECONDARY WORKS

Articles

Bestor, Arthur. "State Sovereignty and Slavery: A Reinterpretation of Proslavery Constitutional Doctrine, 1846–1860." *Journal of the Illinois State Historical Society*, 54 (Summer, 1961): 117–80.

———. "The American Civil War as a Constitutional Crisis." *American Historical Review*, 69 (Jan., 1964): 325–52.

Boucher, Chauncey W. "In Re That Aggressive Slavocracy," *Mississippi Valley Historical Review*, 8 (June–Sept., 1921).

Burke, Joseph C. "What Did the Prigg Decision Really Decide?" *The Pennsylvania Magazine of History and Biography*, 93 (Jan., 1969): 73–85.

Cantor, Milton. "The Writ of Habeas Corpus: Early American Origins and Development," in Harold M. Hyman and Leonard W. Levy, *Freedom and Reform: Essays in Honor of Henry Steele Commager.* New York, 1967.

Chafee, Zechariah. "The Most Important Human Right in the Constitution." *Boston University Law Review*, 32 (1952).

Cohen, Maxwell. "Habeas Corpus Cum Causa—The Emergence of the Modern Writ." *Canadian Bar Review*, 18 (1940): 10, 172.

Corwin, Edward S. "The 'Higher Law' Background of American Constitutional Law." *Harvard Law Review*, 42, no. 2 (Dec., 1928), 149–85; no. 3 (Jan., 1929), 365–409.

Cushing, John D. "The Cushing Court and the Abolition of Slavery in Massachusetts: More Notes on the 'Quok Walker Case.'" *American Journal of Legal History*, 5 (1961): 118–44.

David, C. W. A. "The Fugitive Slave Law of 1793 and its Antecedents." *Journal of Negro History*, 9 (Jan., 1924): 18–25.

Davis, David Brion. "The Emergence of Immediatism in British and American Antislavery Thought." *Mississippi Valley Historical Review*, 49 (Sept., 1962): 209–30.

Eaton, Clement. "A Dangerous Pamphlet in the Old South." *Journal of Southern History*, 2 (1936): 1–12.

Gara, Larry. "The Fugitive Slave Law: A Double Paradox." *Civil War History*, 10 (Sept., 1964): 229–40.

Hagan, Horace H. "Ableman vs. Booth." *American Bar Association Journal*, 17 (Jan., 1931): 1–20.

Johnson, Allen. "The Constitutionality of the Fugitive Slave Acts." *Yale Law Journal*, 31 (1921): 161–82.

Leslie, William R. "The Pennsylvania Fugitive Slave Act of 1826." *Journal of Southern History*, 18 (Nov., 1952): 429–45.

———. "A Study in the Origins of Interstate Rendition: The Big Beaver Creek Murders." *American Historical Review*, 57 (Oct., 1951): 63–76.

Levy, Leonard. "Sims' Case: The Fugitive Slave Law in Boston in 1851." *Journal of Negro History*, 35 (Jan., 1950): 39–75.

McManus, Edgar J. "Antislavery Legislation in New York." *Journal of Negro History*, 46 (Oct., 1961): 208–16.

Mason, Vroman. "The Fugitive Slave Law in Wisconsin, With Reference to Nullification Sentiment." *State Historical Society Proceedings* (Wis.), (1895), 117–44.

Morrow, Ralph E. "The Proslavery Argument Revisited." *Mississippi Valley Historical Review*, 47 (June, 1961): 79–93.

Nadelhaft, Jerome. "The Somerset Case and Slavery: Myth, Reality, and Repercussions." *Journal of Negro History*, 51 (July, 1966): 198–209.

Nogee, Joseph L. "The Prigg Case and Fugitive Slavery, 1842–1850." *Journal of Negro History*, 39 (April, 1954): 185–205.

Oaks, Dallin H. "Habeas Corpus in the States: 1776–1865." *University of Chicago Law Review*, 32 (1961–65): 243–88.

O'Brien, William, S. J., "Did the Jennison Case Outlaw Slavery in Massachusetts?" *William and Mary Quarterly*, 3d series, 17 (1960): 219–41.

Roper, Donald M. "In Quest of Judicial Objectivity: The Marshall Court and the Legitimation of Slavery." *Stanford Law Review*, 21 (Feb., 1969): 532–40.

Rosenberg, Norman L. "Personal Liberty Laws and Sectional Crisis: 1850–1861." *Civil War History*, 17 (March, 1971): 25–45.

Schafer, Joseph. "Stormy Days in Court—The Booth Case." *Wisconsin Magazine of History*, 20 (1936): 89–110.

Schnell, Kempes Y. "Anti-Slavery Influence on the Status of Slaves in a Free State." *Journal of Negro History*, 50 (Oct., 1965): 257–73.

Schwartz, Harold. "Fugitive Slave Days in Boston." *New England Quarterly*, 27 (June, 1954): 191–212.

Shapiro, Samuel. "The Rendition of Anthony Burns." *Journal of Negro History*, 44 (Jan., 1959): 34–51.

Way, R. B. "Was the Fugitive Slave Clause of the Constitution Necessary?" *The Iowa Journal of History and Politics*, 5 (July, 1907): 326–36.

Books

Adams, Alice Dana. *The Neglected Period of Anti-Slavery in America (1808–1831)*. Boston, 1908.

Aptheker, Herbert. *Nat Turner's Slave rebellion*. New York, 1966.

Barnes, Gilbert H. *The Antislavery Impulse 1830–1844*. New York, 1933.

Brauer, Kinley J. *Cotton versus Conscience: Massachusetts Whig Politics and Southwestern Expansion, 1843–1848*. Lexington, 1967.

Campbell, Stanley W. *The Slave Catchers: Enforcement of the Fugitive Slave Law, 1850–1860*. Chapel Hill, N.C., 1970.

Cochran, William C. "The Western Reserve and the Fugitive Slave Law: A Prelude to the Civil War." Publication no. 101, The Western Reserve Historical Society *Collections*. Cleveland, 1920.

Congress, U.S. *Biographical Directory of the American Congress, 1774–1961.* Washington, D.C., 1961.

Craven, Avery. *The Coming of the Civil War.* Chicago, 1966.

———. *The Growth of Southern Nationalism, 1848–1861.* New Orleans, 1953.

Current, Richard N. *Daniel Webster and the Rise of National Conservatism.* Boston, 1955.

Curtis, George Ticknor. *Life of Daniel Webster.* 2 vols. New York, 1870.

Davis, David Brion. *The Problem of Slavery in Western Culture.* Ithaca, N.Y., 1966.

Donald, David. *Charles Sumner and the Coming of the Civil War.* New York, 1960.

Drake, Thomas E. *Quakers and Slavery in America.* New Haven, 1950.

Duberman, Martin. *Charles Francis Adams: 1807–1886.* Boston, 1961.

Duberman, Martin, ed. *The Antislavery Vanguard: New Essays on the Abolitionists.* Princeton, 1965.

Dumond, Dwight. *Antislavery: The Crusade for Freedom in America.* New York, 1966.

Eaton, Clement. *The Freedom-of-Thought Struggle in the Old South.* New York, 1964.

Elkins, Stanley M. *Slavery: A Problem in American Institutional and Intellectual Life.* Chicago, 1959.

Filler, Louis. *The Crusade Against Slavery, 1830–1860.* New York, 1960.

Foner, Philip S. *Business & Slavery: The New York Merchants & the Irrepressible Conflict.* Chapel Hill, N.C., 1941.

Frank, John P. *Justice Daniel Dissenting: A Biography of Peter V. Daniel, 1784–1860.* Cambridge, Mass., 1964.

Freehling, William W. *Prelude to Civil War: The Nullification Controversy in South Carolina, 1816–1836.* New York, 1965.

Fuess, Claude M. *Daniel Webster.* 2 vols. Hamden, Conn. 1963.

———. *The Life of Caleb Cushing.* 2 vols. New York, 1923.

Gara, Larry. *The Liberty Line: The Legend of the Underground Railroad.* Lexington, Ky., 1961.

Genovese, Eugene D. *The Political Economy of Slavery: Studies in the Economy and Society of the Slave South.* New York, 1967.

Greene, Lorenzo J. *The Negro in Colonial New England.* New York, 1942.

Haines, Charles Grove, and Sherwood, Foster N. *The Role of the Supreme Court in American Government and Politics, 1835–1864.* Berkeley and Los Angeles, 1957.

Hamilton, Holman. *Prologue to Conflict: The Crisis and Compromise of 1850.* Lexington, Ky., 1964.

Jaffa, Harry. *Crisis of the House Divided: An Interpretation of the Issues in the Lincoln-Douglas Debates.* New York, 1959.

Jenkins, William S. *Pro-Slavery Thought in the Old South.* Chapel Hill, N.C., 1935.

Johnson, Allen, and Malone, Dumas, eds. *Dictionary of American Biography.* 22 vols. New York, 1928–44.

Klein, Philip Shriver. *President James Buchanan: A Biography.* University Park, Pa., 1962.

Kraditor, Aileen S. *Means and Ends in American abolitionism; Garrison and his critics on strategy and tactics, 1834–1850.* New York, 1969.

Lader, Lawrence. *The Bold Brahmins, New England's War Against Slavery; 1831–1863.* New York, 1961.

Levy, Leonard W. *The Law of the Commonwealth and Chief Justice Shaw.* New York, 1967.

Lewis, Walker. *Without Fear or Favor: A Biography of Chief Justice Roger Taney.* Boston, 1965.

Litwack, Leon F. *North of Slavery: The Negro in the Free States, 1790–1860.* Chicago, 1961.

Locke, Mary Stoughton. *Anti-Slavery in America from the Introduction of African Slaves to the Prohibition of the Slave Trade (1619–1808).* Gloucester, Mass., 1964.

Lofton, John. *Insurrection in South Carolina: The Turbulent World of Denmark Vesey.* Yellow Springs, Ohio, 1964.

Lynd, Staughton. *Class Conflict, Slavery, and the United States Constitution.* Indianapolis, New York, 1967.

McDougall, Marion Gleason. *Fugitive Slaves: 1619–1865.* Boston, 1891.

McManus, Edgar J. *A History of Negro Slavery in New York.* Syracuse, 1966.

Milton, George Fort. *The Eve of Conflict: Stephen A. Douglas and the Needless War.* Boston and New York, 1934.

Moore, George H. *Notes on the History of Slavery in Massachusetts.* New York, 1866.

Morgan, Donald G. *Justice William Johnson: The First Dissenter.* Columbia, 1954.

Nevins, Allan. *The Emergence of Lincoln,* 2 vols. New York, 1951.

―――――. *Ordeal of the Union.* 2 vols. New York, 1947.

Nichols, Roy Franklin. *The Disruption of American Democracy.* New York, 1967.

Phillips, Ulrich B. *The Course of the South to Secession.* Edited by E. Merton Coulter, New York, 1939.

Potter, David M. *Lincoln and His Party in the Secession Crisis.* New Haven, 1962.

Ratner, Lorman. *Powder Keg: Northern Opposition to the Antislavery Movement, 1831–1840.* New York, 1968.

Richards, Leonard L. *"Gentlemen of Property and Standing": Anti-Abolition Mobs in Jacksonian America.* New York, 1970.

Riddle, A. G. *The Life of Benjamin F. Wade.* Cleveland, 1886.

Rogers, George C., Jr. *Evolution of a Federalist: William Loughton Smith of Charleston (1758–1812).* Columbia, S.C., 1962.

Sellers, Charles Grier, ed. *The Southerner as American.* Chapel Hill, N.C., 1960.

Siebert, Wilbur H. *The Underground Railroad from Slavery to Freedom.* New York, 1898.

Smith, Charles W., Jr. *Roger B. Taney: Jacksonian Jurist.* Chapel Hill, N.C., 1936.

Smith, William Henry. *A Political History of Slavery.* New York, 1903.

Stampp, Kenneth. *And the War Came: The North and the Secession Crisis, 1860–1861.* Baton Rouge, 1950.

——— . *The Peculiar Institution.* New York, 1956.

Swisher, Carl Brent. *Roger B. Taney.* Hamden, Conn., 1961.

Sydnor, Charles S. *The Development of Southern Sectionalism, 1819–1848.* Baton Rouge, 1948.

Ten Broek, Jacobus. *Equal under Law.* New York, 1965.

Thomas, John L. *The Liberator: William Lloyd Garrison.* Boston and Toronto, 1963.

Trefousse, H. L. *Benjamin Franklin Wade: Radical Republican from Ohio.* New York, 1963.

Turner, Edward Raymond. *The Negro in Pennsylvania: Slavery—Servitude—Freedom, 1639–1861.* Washington, 1911.

Tyler, Alice Felt. *Freedom's Ferment: Phases of American Social History from the Colonial Period to the Outbreak of the Civil War.* New York, 1962.

Van Deusen, Glyndon G. *William Henry Seward.* New York, 1967.

Warden, Robert B. *An Account of the Private Life and Public Services of Salmon Portland Chase.* Cincinnati, 1874.

Warren, Charles. *The Supreme Court in United States History.* 2 vols. Boston, 1926.

Wilson, Henry. *History of the Rise and Fall of the Slave Power in America.* 3 vols. Boston and New York, 1872.

Wiltse, Charles M. *John C. Calhoun: Nullifier, 1829–1839.* Indianapolis, 1949.

——— . *John C. Calhoun: Sectionalist, 1840–1850.* Indianapolis, 1951.

Zilversmit, Arthur. *The First Emancipation: The Abolition of Slavery in the North.* Chicago, 1967.

Ph.D. Dissertations

Anderson, G. T. "The Slavery Issue as a Factor in Massachusetts Politics from the Compromise of 1850 to the Outbreak of the Civil War." University of Chicago, 1944.

Leslie, William Raymond, "The Fugitive Slave Clause, 1787–1842: A Study in American Constitutional History and in the History of the Conflict of Laws." University of Michigan, 1945.

Schnell, Kempes Y. "Court Cases Involving Slavery: A Study of the Application of Anti-Slavery Thought to Judicial Argument." University of Michigan, 1955.

Shaw, Warren Choate. "The Fugitive Slave Issue in Massachusetts Politics, 1780–1837." University of Illinois, 1938.

Thornbrough, Emma Lou. "Negro Slavery in the North: Its Legal and Constitutional Aspects." University of Michigan, 1946.

Yanuck, Julius. "The Fugitive Slave Law and the Constitution." Columbia University, 1953.

Index

THE JOHNS HOPKINS UNIVERSITY PRESS

This book was composed in Times Roman text and Helvetica Light Condensed
display type by Jones Composition Company, Inc. from a design by Alan Tyson.
It was printed on 60-lb. Sebago, MF, regular, stock and bound in Holliston Roxite
by Universal Lithographers, Inc.

Library of Congress Cataloging in Publication Data

Morris, Thomas D   1938-
   Free men all.

   Bibliography: p.
   1. Personal liberty laws.   I. Title.
KF4545.S5M67   342'.73'085   73-8126
ISBN 0-8018-1505-3